Contested Democracy and the Left in the Philippines after Marcos

Contested Democracy and the Left in the Philippines after Marcos

NATHAN GILBERT QUIMPO

Monograph 58 / Yale Southeast Asia Studies

Library of Congress Catalog Card Number: 2007-937873
International Standard Book Number: *paper* 978-0-938692-91-1
cloth 978-0-938692-90-4

Second impression

Distributor:
Yale University Southeast Asia Studies
P.O. Box 208206
New Haven, Connecticut 06520-8206
U.S.A.

Printed in U.S.A.

Contents

Illustrations

FIGURES

MAPS

ABBREVIATIONS AND ACRONYMS

ABA	Alyansang Bayanihan ng mga Magsasaka, Manggagawang-Bukid at Mangingisda (Cooperative Alliance of Peasants, Farm Workers and Fishers)
ACF	Active Citizenship Foundation
Akbayan	Kaakbay ng Sambayanan (Ally of the People)
AKO	Adhikain at Kilusan ng Ordinaryong Tao (Aspirations and Movement of the Common People)
AMIN	Anak-Mindanao (Scions of Mindanao)
Aniad	Antique Integrated Area Development
ANP	Alliance for New Politics
ANU	Australian National University
APL	Alliance of Progressive Labor
ARC	agrarian reform community
ARMM	Autonomous Region of Muslim Mindanao
Bandila	Bansang Nagkaisa sa Diwa at Layunin (Nation United in Spirit and Purpose)
BAP	Bankers' Association of the Philippines
Barrios	Building Alternative Rural Resource Institutions and Organizing Services
Batman	Barangay Administration Training Manual
Batman Consortium	see BBGC
Bayan	Bagong Alyansang Makabayan (New Patriotic Alliance)
BBGC	Barangay-Bayan Governance Consortium (also called the Batman Consortium)
BDP-PRA	Barangay Development Planning through Participatory Resource Appraisal
BIADP	Barangay Integrated Area Development Program
Biglead	Bicol Grassroots Leaders for Empowerment and Development

Bisig	Bukluran para sa Ikauunlad ng Sosyalistang Isip at Gawa (Federation for the Advancement of Socialist Theory and Praxis)
BMP	Bukluran ng Manggagawang Pilipino (Solidarity of Filipino Workers)
BOBG	Basic Orientation for Barangay Governance
CARHRIHL	Comprehensive Agreement on Respect for Human Rights and International Humanitarian Law
Caret	Center for Agrarian Reform, Empowerment, and Transformation
CARP	Comprehensive Agrarian Reform Programme
CBCP	Catholic Bishops' Conference of the Philippines
CCR	Consortium on Constitutional Reform
CER	Consortium on Electoral Reforms
CFC 04	Citizens for Con-Con 2004
CIU	Confederation of Independent Unions
CMR	Central Mindanao Region (of the Communist Party of the Philippines)
CODE-NGO	Caucus of Development NGO Networks
Comelec	Commission on Elections
Compel	Citizens for Meaningful and Peaceful Elections
Con-Ass	constituent assembly
Con-Con	constitutional convention
ConCom	constitutional commission
Concord	Constitutional Correction for Development
Confreedem	Confederation for Freedom and Democracy
CPAR	Congress for a People's Agrarian Reform
CPGD	Center for Politics, Governance and Development
CPP	Communist Party of the Philippines
CPT	Communist Party of Thailand
CSO	civil society organization
DA	Democratic Alliance
DG	discussion group
Dialogs	Direct Action for Local Governance Seminar
DILG	Department of Interior and Local Government

DPA	deep-penetration agent
DSK	Demokratiko-Sosyalistang Koalisyon (Democratic-Socialist Coalition)
ECOP	Employers Confederation of the Philippines
ECPG	Empowering Civic Participation in Governance
EDSA	Epifanio de los Santos Avenue
ELF	Education for Life Foundation
Empower	Global Coalition for the Political Empowerment of Overseas Filipinos
FDC	Freedom from Debt Coalition
FOPA	Forum for Philippine Alternatives
GDP	gross domestic product
GNP	gross national product
GO	governmental organization
HMB	Hukbong Mapagpalaya ng Bayan (People's Liberation Army)
Hukbalahap	Hukbo ng Bayan laban sa mga Hapon (People's Anti-Japanese Army)
IAD	integrated area development
IBP	Interim Batasang Pambansa (Interim National Parliament)
ID	identification
IDC	Iranun Development Council
IDPG	Institute for Democratic Participation in Governance
IMF	International Monetary Fund
IPD	Institute for Popular Democracy
IPER	Institute for Political and Electoral Reform
IPG	Institute of Politics and Governance
ISI	Institute for Strategic Initiatives

Kaiba	Kababaihan para sa Inang Bayan (Women for the Mother Country)
Kaisahan	Kaisahan Tungo sa Kaunlaran ng Kanayunan at Repormang Pansakahan (Unity for Rural Progress and Agricultural Reform)
KAKAMMPI	Kapisanan ng mga Kamag-anak ng Migranteng Manggagawang Pilipino, Inc. (Association of Families of Overseas Filipino Workers and Migrant Returnees)
Kalahi	Kapit-Bisig Laban sa Kahirapan (Linking Arms against Poverty)
Kampi	Kabalikat ng Malayang Pilipino (Partner of the Free Filipino)
Kasapi	Kapulungan ng mga Sandigan ng Pilipinas (Assembly of Pillars of the Philippines)
KBL	Kilusan ng Bagong Lipunan (New Society Movement)
KFR	kidnapping for ransom
KMU	Kilusang Mayo Uno (May First Movement)
Kompil	Kongreso ng Mamamayang Pilipino (Congress of Filipino Citizens)
KPD	Kilusan para sa Pambansang Demokrasya (Movement for Nationalism and Democracy)
KPML	Kongreso ng Pagkakaisa ng Maralitang Lungsod (Congress of Unity of the Urban Poor)
Kumare-Kumpare	Kilusang Mamamayan para sa Repormang Elektoral (People's Movement for Electoral Reform)
Laban	Lakas ng Bayan (Strength of the People)
LACC	Labor Advisory and Consultative Council
LAMMP	Laban ng Makabayang Masang Pilipino (Struggle of the Nationalist Filipino Masses)
Lakas	Lakas ng Sambayanan (Strength of the People)
LDP	Laban ng Demokratikong Pilipino (Struggle of Democratic Filipinos)
Learn	Labor Education and Research Network
LGC	Local Government Code

LGCNet	Local Governance Citizens' Network
LGU	local government unit
LP	Liberal Party
MILF	Moro Islamic Liberation Front
MLG	Marxist-Leninist Group
MLPP	Marxista-Leninistang Partido ng Pilipinas (Marxist-Leninist Party of the Philippines)
MNLF	Moro National Liberation Front
NaFFAA	National Federation of Filipino-American Associations
Namfrel	National Citizens Movement for Free Elections
NAPC	National Anti-poverty Commission
ND	national democratic, national democrat
NDF	National Democratic Front
NGO	nongovernmental organization
NP	Nacionalista Party (Nationalist Party)
NPA	New People's Army
NPC	Nationalist People's Coalition
NSC	National Security Council
NUCD	National Union of Christian Democrats
OF	overseas Filipino
PADC	People's Alternative Development Center
Pakisama	Pambansang Kilusan ng mga Samahang Magsasaka (National Movement of Farmers' Organizations)
Pandayan	Pandayan para sa Sosyalistang Pilipinas (Forging a Socialist Philippines)
PARRDS	Partnership for Agrarian Reform and Rural Development Services
PDAN	Philippine Drug Action Network
PDP	Partido ng Demokratikong Pilipino (Filipino Democratic Party)

PDSP	Partido Demokratiko-Sosyalista ng Pilipinas (Democratic-Socialist Party of the Philippines)
PEPE	Popular Education for Popular Empowerment
Philnet-RDI	Philippine Network of Rural Development Institutes
Pilar	People's Institute for Local Governance Advocacy and Research
Pinatubo	Pinag-isang Lakas sa Pagbabago (Consolidated Power for Change)
Pirma	People's Initiative for Reform, Modernization and Action
PKI	Partai Komunis Indonesia (Indonesian Communist Party)
PKP	Partido Komunista ng Pilipinas (Communist Party of the Philippines)
PM	Partido ng Manggagawa (Workers' Party)
PMP (1)	Partido ng Manggagawa ng Pilipinas (Filipino Workers' Party)
PMP (2)	Partido ng Masang Pilipino (Party of the Filipino Masses)
PnB	Partido ng Bayan (People's Party)
PO	people's organization
Popdem	popular democratic, popular democrat
Pop-ed	popular (political) education
PPC	People Power Coalition
PPD	Partido Proletaryo Demokratiko (Democratic Proletarian Party)
PRA	participatory rural appraisal
Prodem	Promoting Local Initiatives for Democracy and Justice
PRP	People's Reform Party
PRRM	Philippine Rural Reconstruction Movement
PT	Partido dos Trabalhadores (Workers' Party [of Brazil])
PTC	permit to campaign

RHB	Rebolusyonaryong Hukbong Bayan (Revolutionary People's Army)
RPA-ABB	Revolutionary People's Army-Alex Boncayao Brigade
RPM-M	Rebolusyonaryong Partido ng Manggagawa-Mindanao (Revolutionary Workers Party-Mindanao)
RPM-P	Rebolusyonaryong Partido ng Manggagawa-Pilipinas (Revolutionary Workers Party-Philippines)
Saligan	Sentro ng Alternatibong Lingap Panligal (Center for Alternative Legal Assistance)
SD	social democratic, social democrat
SEED	Small Economic Enterprises Development
SEW	socioeconomic work
SIAD	sustainable integrated area development
Siglaya	Siglo ng Paglaya (Century of Freedom)
SIM-CARRD	SIAD Initiatives in Mindanao-Convergence for Agrarian Reform and Regional Development
SK	Sangguniang Kabataan (Youth Council)
SKDOP	Sultan Kudarat Descendants Organization of the Philippines
Speed	Solidarity for Peace, Empowerment and Equity-Led Development
SPP (1)	Socialist Party of the Philippines
SPP (2)	Sosyalistang Partido ng Paggawa (Socialist Workers' Party)
SRA	Social Reform Agenda
SULAT	Sustainable Local Alternative Technologies
TI	Transparency International
Trapo	traditional politician

UG	underground
Ugnayan-Victoria	Ugnayan ng mga Mamamayan Tungo sa Kaunlaran ng Victoria (People's Coordinating Council for the Development of Victoria)
Ugnayan-LB	Ugnayan ng mga Samahang Pamayanan ng Los Baños (Coordinating Council of Community Organizations of Los Baños)
ULR-TF	Urban Land Reform Task Force
UNDP	United Nations Development Programme
USAID	U.S. Agency for International Development
WB	World Bank

Acknowledgments

WHEN THE PHILIPPINE REVOLUTIONARY MOVEMENT split in 1992–93, I found myself wondering what I would be doing for the rest of my life. After having been deeply involved in the movement for twenty-three years (twenty years in the Philippines and three years in the Netherlands), I was no longer sure if I should continue being a full-time political activist, as I had been through most of that time. What had gotten me involved in activism in the first place—identification with the poor and oppressed and their struggles for social justice—remained very strong in me. But my personal circumstances had greatly changed. For one, I was in the Netherlands, waiting for my application for political asylum to be approved. More important, I felt very theoretically inadequate. I believed that the long years of following—or sometimes working around—the party line had somehow straitjacketed my thinking and that I was out of touch with what was being discussed in theoretical debates within the modern Left and intellectual circles in general.

After a long absence of eighteen years, I returned to academe, pursuing a master's degree in international relations at the University of Amsterdam. At that time, I was not yet thinking of shifting to an academic profession. I just felt that I would need a university degree to find a good job. (Like many of my activist contemporaries, I had not been able to finish my undergraduate degree, having gone on to working full time in the anti-Marcos movement.) I also felt that continuing my studies would perhaps help me get rid of intellectual fixations and rigidities.

I remained undecided about career options even after obtaining refugee status and finishing my M.A. in 1994 and acquiring Dutch nationality in 1996. Finally, in 1998, I decided to explore the option of a scholarly career. I returned to the Philippines and taught political science and sociology at the University of the Philippines. While teaching, I tried to build (or rebuild) and maintain close links with various progressive political and social movements and groups, people's organizations, and nongovernmental organizations. I also became involved in a research project on the armed conflict and peace process in Mindanao. It was in the course of my teaching stint at the university that I finally resolved to shift to an academic career. I realized that by conducting studies on important political and social issues and developments with scholarly rigor, taking into account critical new concepts and theories, I would directly or indirectly be helping those seeking to bring about progressive political and social change. I believed that an academic career would serve as a good complement to my past activist life and perhaps the consummation of it: the activist-scholar.

Turning oneself from a revolutionary activist into an academic is not particularly difficult. But the going gets rough when one is already well above forty. I am indebted to many friends, a good number of whom were former *kasamas* (comrades) in the movement, who gave advice and/or agreed to serve as references and thus helped me land my first teaching job and/or obtain a doctoral scholarship. In particular, I give my thanks to Joel Rocamora, Dodong Nemenzo, Jenny Franco, Jun Borras, Walden Bello, Len Abesamis, Kit Collier, Cynch Bautista, Jojo Abinales, Temy Rivera, Raul Pertierra, Randy David, Henk Overbeek, Kees Biekart, Ed Tadem, Tesa Encarnacion-Tadem, Maris Diokno, Jean Miralao, Lester Ruiz, Men Sta. Ana, and Wingie Villamil. I also thank John Sidel, whose advice and MPhil seminars at the School of Oriental and African Studies in London helped provide me with a good theoretical preparation for my doctoral research.

I am grateful to the Australian National University (ANU) and the Australian government for awarding me a doctoral scholarship, which allowed me the luxury of working full time on my dissertation. I owe a lot to the members of my supervising panel—Ben Kerkvliet, Harold Crouch, Ron May, and for a time, Kit Collier (again)—for all the advice and support they gave as supervisors and as personal friends, in the course of doing my research. My deep gratitude goes to Ben and Harold, who were very thorough in their critiques of my research proposal and draft chapters, urging me to dig and read more and challenging me to think deeper, while always respecting my ideas and views. Among the many friendships I established with fellow doctoral scholars, I am particularly happy to have had the company and support of Neilson Mersat, Lorraine Salazar, Hwang In-won, Shun Ono, Marzuki Mohamad, Yuko Kitada, Taufiq Tanasaldy, Kikue Hamayotsu, Michael Karadjis, and Thu Thuy Pham, and among the research fellows Nicki Saroca and Jennifer Amyx. For their warmhearted assistance and good cheer, I thank Bev Fraser, Lynne Payne, Allison Ley, Jill Wolf, and other members of the staff of the Department of Political and Social Change.

My sisters Emilie and Lillian, and their husbands Phil Wickett and the late John Walsh, even while based in the other side of the Australian continent (Perth), helped me feel that I was not too far away from family. In the Filipino Australian community of Canberra, I am very grateful for the warm reception and encouragement of Melinda Tria-Kerkvliet, my cousin Tess and her husband Neil Trudinger, Lulu and Mark Turner, the Doronilas (Amando, Lulu, and Noonee) and the rest of the ANU Philippine Studies Group, and the Club of ANU Filipino Students.

In conducting my fieldwork in the Philippines, I incurred debts to many former *kasamas* in the movement and to the staffs of various nongovernmental organizations who facilitated my field visits and interviews. I am especially grateful to Joel Rocamora (again) and the staff of the Institute for Popular Democracy, who took me in as a research fellow and provided me with a most welcoming, collegial, and stimulating place to work; to Rey "Enteng" Gueco, who always kept me abreast of ideological, political, and organizational controversies and debates within the Left and always and promptly gave good critiques of my drafts; and to Roy and Tina Delima, who greatly facilitated my field visits to various areas in Mindanao and, by drawing me farther into a participant-observer role, helped me gain much deeper insights into the Left's engagement in various political processes. I also express my thanks to Ric Reyes, Ronald Llamas,

Melay Abao, Etta Rosales, Risa Hontiveros-Baraquel, Marie Labajo, and Teng Ambolodto of Akbayan; Councilor Pete Laviña and his wife Evelyn; the staffs of People's Alternative Development Center, SIAD Initiatives in Mindanao—Convergence for Agrarian Reform and Regional Development and the Alternate Forum for Research in Mindanao in Davao City; Mayor Eksam Lloren and his staff in Jagna, Bohol; the staffs of the People's Institute for Local Governance Advocacy and Research and the Center for Agrarian Reform Empowerment and Transformation in Laguna; the staff of Solidarity for Peace, Empowerment and Equity-Led Development in Cotabato City; Rodel Mercado and the staff of Pneuma in Eastern Samar; Mayor Jay Zacate of Sulat, Eastern Samar; Mayor Jerry dela Cerna of Governor Generoso, Davao Oriental; Councilor Len Magayanes and the staff of the Center for Advocacy and Participatory Governance; Tom Villarin and the staff of the Institute of Politics and Governance; Vimvim Santos and the staff of People's Global Exchange; Mon Casiple and the staff of the Institute for Political and Electoral Reform; Gerry Bulatao, Orlando Balean, and the staff of Empowering Civic Participation in Governance; and Lecie Arce and Helen Bonga of Sanlakas. I also appreciate the help of those who provided me with materials or comments on my drafts—Thea Soriano, Nina Iszatt, Marisol Estrella, Denden Alicias, Djorina Velasco, Jay Carizo, Teresa Melgar, Kiko Isaac, Sol Santos and August Espiritu. In the Netherlands, I am indebted to the Filippijnengroep Nederland and the Philippine-European Solidarity Centre—Komite ng Sambayanang Pilipino for letting me use their resources.

I profusely thank Joji Trabajo and Kees Ruigrok, who let me stay with them practically the whole time I was based in the Philippines, and my sister Susan and her husband, George Chiu, who also accommodated me at their place many times. My thanks also go to the Political Science Department of the University of the Philippines for granting me a research fellowship.

Some other friends to whom I am also indebted cannot be mentioned. The nature of their work demands that they continue to maintain good relations with groups identified with the extreme Left.

In revising my dissertation for publication, I am grateful to the members of the board of examiners for my Ph.D.—Garry Rodan,

Rosanne Rutten, and Mark Thompson—and to James Scott and an anonymous reviewer. They came up with perceptive, thought-provoking, and very encouraging comments and suggestions.

Some of the chapters of the book have been adapted from my articles "Oligarchic patrimonialism, bossism, electoral clientelism and contested democracy in the Philippines," *Comparative Politics* 37 (January 2005):229–50 (revised for chap. 1); and "The left, elections and the political party system in the Philippines," *Critical Asian Studies* 37 (March 2005):3–28 (revised for chap. 4). I thank the City University of New York, publisher of *Comparative Politics* (http://web.gc.cuny.edu/jcp) and BCAS, Inc., publisher of *Critical Asian Studies* (http://www.bcasnet.org), for their kind permission to reproduce the adapted texts. I also thank the staff of Cartographic Services, Research School of Pacific and Asian Studies, Australian National University for producing all the maps in the book, and Jimmy A. Domingo for making the cover photo.

In loving memory, I am deeply thankful to my parents, who so valued a good education for their children that they worked and sacrificed a lot to be able to send all of us to the best of schools and endured much tension, disappointment, and anguish during the turbulent 1970s. My brothers Jan and Jun, who lost their lives fighting for democracy and social justice, have always inspired me to continue working for the ideals they fought for. I am also thankful to my other brothers, sisters, and close relatives for all the moral support and encouragement they gave from afar.

My utmost gratitude goes to my beloved partner and companion, Anja, who helped me much, much more than anybody else over the past twelve years in my endeavors to turn myself into a worthy scholar.

The Philippines with regions and provinces

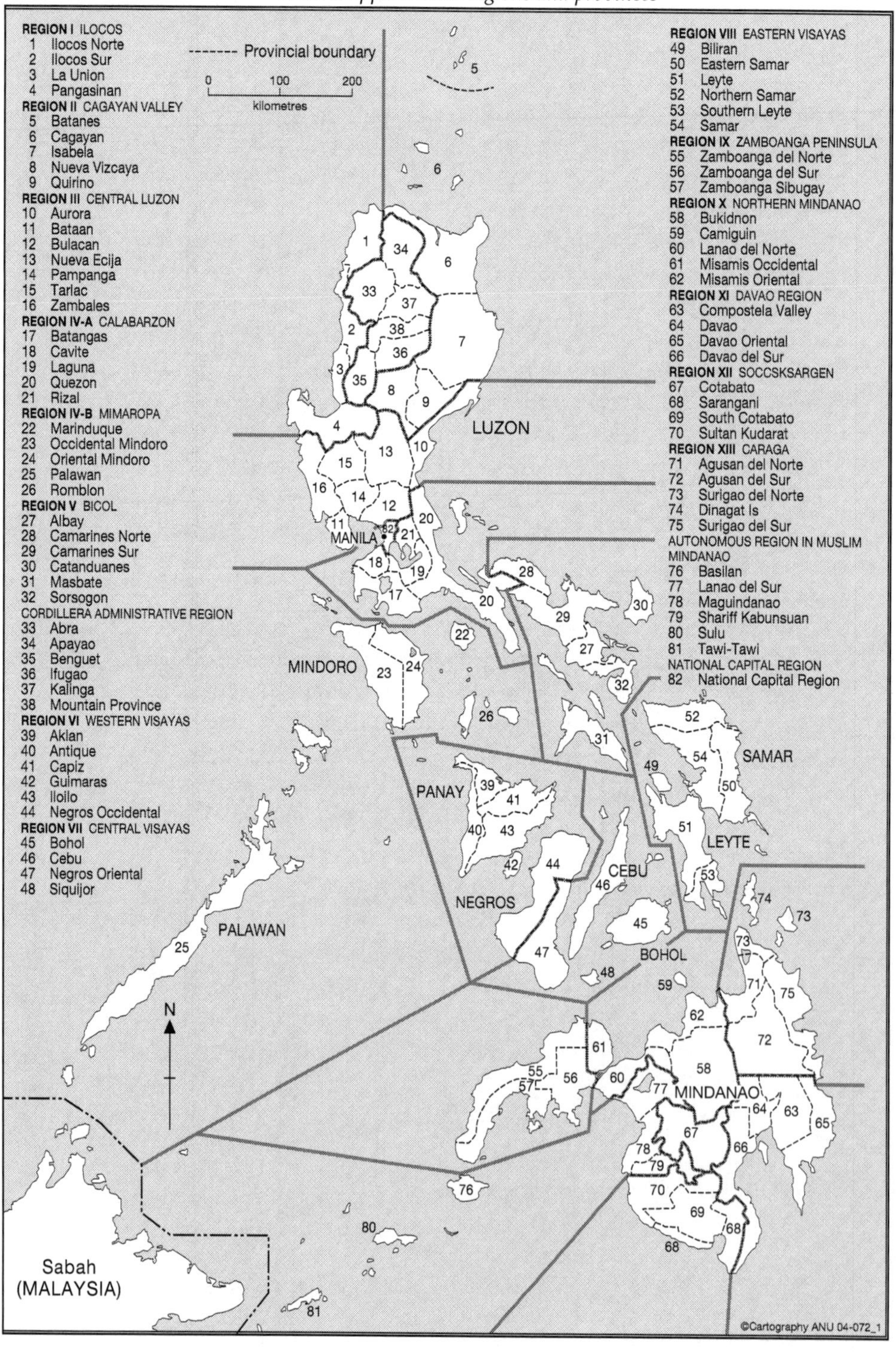
REGION I ILOCOS
1 Ilocos Norte
2 Ilocos Sur
3 La Union
4 Pangasinan
REGION II CAGAYAN VALLEY
5 Batanes
6 Cagayan
7 Isabela
8 Nueva Vizcaya
9 Quirino
REGION III CENTRAL LUZON
10 Aurora
11 Bataan
12 Bulacan
13 Nueva Ecija
14 Pampanga
15 Tarlac
16 Zambales
REGION IV-A CALABARZON
17 Batangas
18 Cavite
19 Laguna
20 Quezon
21 Rizal
REGION IV-B MIMAROPA
22 Marinduque
23 Occidental Mindoro
24 Oriental Mindoro
25 Palawan
26 Romblon
REGION V BICOL
27 Albay
28 Camarines Norte
29 Camarines Sur
30 Catanduanes
31 Masbate
32 Sorsogon
CORDILLERA ADMINISTRATIVE REGION
33 Abra
34 Apayao
35 Benguet
36 Ifugao
37 Kalinga
38 Mountain Province
REGION VI WESTERN VISAYAS
39 Aklan
40 Antique
41 Capiz
42 Guimaras
43 Iloilo
44 Negros Occidental
REGION VII CENTRAL VISAYAS
45 Bohol
46 Cebu
47 Negros Oriental
48 Siquijor
Provincial boundary
0 100 200
kilometres
REGION VIII EASTERN VISAYAS
49 Biliran
50 Eastern Samar
51 Leyte
52 Northern Samar
53 Southern Leyte
54 Samar
REGION IX ZAMBOANGA PENINSULA
55 Zamboanga del Norte
56 Zamboanga del Sur
57 Zamboanga Sibugay
REGION X NORTHERN MINDANAO
58 Bukidnon
59 Camiguin
60 Lanao del Norte
61 Misamis Occidental
62 Misamis Oriental
REGION XI DAVAO REGION
63 Compostela Valley
64 Davao
65 Davao Oriental
66 Davao del Sur
REGION XII SOCCSKSARGEN
67 Cotabato
68 Sarangani
69 South Cotabato
70 Sultan Kudarat
REGION XIII CARAGA
71 Agusan del Norte
72 Agusan del Sur
73 Surigao del Norte
74 Dinagat Is
75 Surigao del Sur
AUTONOMOUS REGION IN MUSLIM MINDANAO
76 Basilan
77 Lanao del Sur
78 Maguindanao
79 Shariff Kabunsuan
80 Sulu
81 Tawi-Tawi
NATIONAL CAPITAL REGION
82 National Capital Region
LUZON
MANILA
MINDORO
PANAY
NEGROS
CEBU
BOHOL
SAMAR
LEYTE
PALAWAN
MINDANAO
N
Sabah
(MALAYSIA)
©Cartography ANU 04-072_1

Introduction

IN FEBRUARY 1986, an awesome groundswell of popular opposition to authoritarian rule—known as "people power"—toppled the Philippines' corrupt dictator, Ferdinand Marcos. The popular uprising was the culmination of a long series of mass protest actions and mobilizations staged by a broad array of antidictatorship forces coming from various sectors of Philippine society. Through more than thirteen years of authoritarian rule, Marcos also had to contend with armed resistance from Maoist insurgents and Muslim secessionists—very bloody conflicts that claimed tens of thousands of lives. With Marcos's fall and the restoration of democracy under President Corazon Aquino, the Philippines became part of the so-called third wave of democratization in the late twentieth century (Huntington 1991).

Even with Marcos gone, however, the Philippines has not really experienced much of a respite from political and social turmoil. The first few years of the newly restored democracy proved most difficult. The Aquino government conducted peace negotiations with communist insurgents and Muslim secessionists, but the talks failed to produce comprehensive peace agreements. The armed conflict between government troops and these rebel forces continued. Posing a much more immediate threat, rebel factions in the Philippine military launched a series of coup attempts and military revolts in 1986–90, of which seven were major coup attempts (M. Thompson 1995:168–69, 221). Fortunately for the fragile democracy, none succeeded. The 1990s saw a reduction—though not a cessation—in armed hostilities between government and rebel forces. The turn of the century witnessed new convulsions. In January 2001, another people power uprising ousted another corrupt ruler, President Joseph Estrada. Less than four months later, Estrada's supporters countered with their own show of force, which culminated in an attack on the presidential palace by a throng of armed pro-Estrada followers. Their turbulent protest was quickly quelled. In July 2003, rebel elements in the military, demanding the resignation of President Gloria Macapagal Arroyo and top military officials, staged another failed military mutiny.

Political and social turbulence has not just been a phenomenon of the authoritarian and postauthoritarian periods in the postcolonial Philippines. A few years after the country became an independent republic in 1946, tensions between the rich landed elite and poor landless peasants that had been building since the 1930s came to a head in the Huk rebellion, in which the communists played a prominent role.[1] Since the early postcolonial years, Philippine elections have often been marred—or even marked—by corruption, fraud, and terrorism, or what Filipinos have dubbed "the three Gs": "guns, goons, and gold." Amid growing poverty and social disparities, a new communist insurgency and an armed Muslim secessionist movement emerged in the late 1960s and early 1970s. In Manila, radical student demonstrators chanting "Down with imperialism, feudalism, and bureaucrat capitalism!" and armed with pillboxes and Molotov cocktails clashed with policemen, who wielded truncheons and at times opened fire with their high-powered rifles.

The Philippines' apparent proneness to political and social ruptures has to be viewed within the context of the country's grave social disparities, especially those based on class and ethnic cleavages. An elite few control much of the country's wealth, while millions wallow in poverty. In 2000, the top 20 percent of Philippine society earned 54.4 percent of the country's family income (National Statistical Coordination Board 2003), even as 39.4 percent of the population (33.7 percent of Filipino families) lived below the poverty line (NSO 2002).[2] Despite decades of agrarian reform, the majority of Filipino peasants continue to be landless or nearly landless, as large tracts of land remain in the hands of a small number of landowners (Borras 2004:10). Workers receive wages that are far below what their families need for a decent living.[3] In the big cities, the high-walled plush villages of the affluent stand in stark contrast to large shanty communities nearby.[4] The Muslims of Mindanao and other minority ethnic communities, many of whom have already been displaced from large parts of their ancestral lands, continue to experience various forms of discrimination (Quimpo 2000:19–36).

Despite certain changes in its composition over the decades, the Philippine elite, on the whole, is a fairly entrenched lot. Once largely based on a landed aristocracy, the oligarchy is now much more diverse, with many of its old members moving more into business and commerce and some noveaux riches replacing some of the old clans.[5] The members of the elite—old and new—dominate the country's main political parties, which are indistinguishable from one another in ideology and program. Knowing that access to the government apparatus and its resources is all important in maintaining their hold on wealth and power, they often resort to patronage or the proverbial three Gs at election time. Factions of the oligarchic elite, when in government, endeavor to extract as much as they can from or through their positions.[6]

Infamous quotes showing the shameless rapacity of members of the elite abound. In response to criticisms that some of her relatives had suddenly become rich after the imposition of martial law in 1972, Imelda Marcos, the dictator's wife, declared: "Sometimes you have smart relatives who can make it. ... My dear, there are always people who are just a little faster, more brilliant, more aggressive."[7] Such thinking was by no means restricted to the period of Marcos's patrimonial dictatorship. As early as 1949, Senate president Avelino Cruz, then being investigated for certain questionable financial dealings, took President Elpidio Quirino to task.

> Why did you have to order an investigation, honorable Mr. President? If you cannot permit abuses, you must at least tolerate them. What are we in power for? We are not hypocrites. Why should we pretend to be saints when in reality we are not? We are not angels. And besides, when we die we will all go to hell. Anyway, it is preferable to go to hell where there are no investigations, no Secretary of Justice, no Secretary of the Interior to go after us!
>
> (Gleeck 1993:88)

In 1998, when President Estrada was criticized for appointing cronies to highly paid directorships in government-owned corporations, appointee Rolando Meyer commented on television: *"Weather-weather lang yan"* (To each his own time). With Estrada in power, it was the turn of his coterie of friends and supporters to enjoy the spoils (Coronel 1998).

The Philippines is the only country that had two leaders included on the list of the world's ten most corrupt leaders in the 2004 Global Corruption Report of the Berlin-based Transparency International (TI). Marcos placed second; Estrada ranked tenth. After being in power for twenty years, Marcos amassed $5 to $10 billion. Estrada's loot was $78 to $80 million in less than three years as president (Doronila 2004).

Politics in the Philippines, with all the patronage and corruption, has been regarded as so murky that ordinary Filipinos have come to derogatorily refer to most politicians as *trapos*. A Filipino term of Spanish origin, *trapo* is an old rag that is used to wipe dirt from any surface and ends up collecting all kinds of grime (L. Constantino 1991:6). *Trapo* began to be used early in the Aquino period to mean "traditional politician," that is, a politician engaging in patronage, corruption, fraud, or terrorism, especially those closely linked with powerful political families. Since the early 1990s, the term has become so widely used that many politicians have made great efforts to avoid getting tagged as such and to project themselves as being non-*trapo* or even anti-*trapo*.

The resilience of traditional politics cannot be underestimated. Representatives of the elite, many from the political clans of the pre-martial-law years, dominated the Aquino government and brought back the old politics. In time, more and more politicians identified with the Marcos regime returned—as part of the opposition or the administration party or coalition. With the ouster of the corrupt "boss" president, Estrada, through another dramatic display of people power in January 2001, it would have seemed that anti-*trapo* forces had scored a spectacular victory. In her inaugural speech, President Arroyo (2001) stressed the need to outgrow "our traditional brand of politics based on patronage and personality" and to promote a politics of reform. Quickly enough, however, it was back to *trapo* politics. Arroyo, the daughter of a former president, picked a Cabinet with many familiar faces from the Aquino and Ramos administrations, most of them from powerful political families.

The Importance of the Study

This book is about postauthoritarian politics in the Philippines, focusing on the problems and difficulties in the deepening of the country's "newly restored" democracy and on the Left's role in this process.

Why is a study on contemporary Philippine politics important? As the object of close scrutiny by Filipino and Western (especially American) scholars for over a century, the Philippines has been the site of some seminal studies on democracy and politics in developing countries. The studies, which dwell on such themes as colonial democracy, patron-client relations, machine politics, bossism, everyday politics, patrimonial rule, democratic revolution, and elite democracy, cannot but lend particular significance to a present-day study.

A second, and perhaps much more significant, reason for studying current Philippine politics is that the country has been experiencing continuing political and social unrest and encountering tremendous obstacles to the consolidation and deepening of democracy. After people power ousted Marcos in 1986, there were great expectations that the Philippines would soon be able to achieve rapid economic growth and a stable democracy. With the failure of the government's "structural adjustment" schemes and with the continued depredation of government resources by members of the oligarchic elite, the country has failed to attain these objectives (Bello et al. 2004:chaps. 1 and 7). It has instead been plunged into worsening turmoil, which has already been marked by several dramatic ruptures. Apart from having to deal with strong and highly critical social movements, the elite-controlled government now has to contend with a revived communist insurgency, an indomitable Muslim secessionist movement and restive factions within the military. In a list drawn up by Samuel Huntington (1991:253–54) of "third-wave democracies" with "severe contextual problems," the Philippines and Peru came out on top, each with five such problems. For the Philippines, the thorny problems were major insurgency, extreme poverty, severe socioeconomic inequality, substantial external debt, and extensive state involvement in the economy.

Hardly any new or newly restored democracy could now rival the Philippines in the wide array of its grave contextual entanglements. If Huntington were to produce an updated list, ethnic conflict and terrorism would jack up the country's major woes to seven. The Philippines commands attention, both on its own terms and for what it can teach about political dynamics and the consolidation and deepening of democracy in postauthoritarian countries, especially those with deep social fissures.

In studies of Philippine politics, unequal relations or elite domination has been a constant theme. Reviewing analyses of the country's politics since it gained independence, Benedict Kerkvliet (1995, 1996) notes that there are basically three prominent theoretical frameworks or interpretations of Philippine politics: the patron-client, factional framework; the elite democracy or patrimonial view; and the neocolonial or dependency analysis. The *patron-client interpretation*, which has long been regarded as being the most influential, holds that Philippine politics is "about personal relations and networks linked by kinship, friendship, exchange of favors, influence, and money" (Kerkvliet 1996:136). The relationship between patron (politician) and client (voter) is mutually beneficial but unequal. Elite domination is somewhat camouflaged by personalistic ties. The *elite democracy* or *patrimonial view* argues that the Philippine political system, despite having formal democratic institutions, is essentially run by an elite few who use their wealth and power to control the country's resources. Public office serves as a means for members of the elite to enrich themselves. While acknowledging the persistence of patron-client ties, the patrimonial/elite democracy analysis regards intimidation, coercion, and violence as also widespread. The *neocolonial* or *dependency* framework shares much of the elite democracy view but sees the Filipino elite's power as limited and foreign interests as actually dominating the country.

As will be shown in chapter 1, the elite democracy view has emerged as the dominant framework of Philippine politics since the fall of the Marcos dictatorship. Variations of the elite democracy interpretation include "cacique democracy" (Anderson 1988), "oligarchic democracy" (Kingsbury 2001), and a "weak state" captured by the elite (McCoy 1993b). Over the past twelve years or so, political and social scientists have come up with variants of the elite democracy view that are even more damning characterizations of Philippine politics, showing how corruption and violence have become embedded in the political system. Paul Hutchcroft (1998a), for instance, describes the Philippines as having a "patrimonial oligarchic state," a weak state preyed on by a powerful oligarchy. John T. Sidel (1999) depicts "bossism"—the mafia-style rule of local strongmen—as a common phenomenon in the country.

Elite democracy and its variants sound grim—perhaps too grim. From these characterizations, it would seem that what goes on in the political scene simply revolves around, and depends on, the actions and machinations of the country's oligarchic elite, that Philippine politics is nothing more than *trapo* politics and elections demonstrate the rule of patronage and guns, goons and gold. Outside of the return to the ways of formal democracy, there is no further resonance from the people power so awesomely manifested in February 1986 and again in January 2001. There is little prospect for real political and social change, for the deepening of democracy.

Something is amiss here, however. Philippine politics cannot simply be reduced to elite domination. There has long been popular resistance to the rule of the entrenched politico-economic elite. Widespread poverty, grave social inequalities, and continuing elite domination of the country's politics have provided fertile ground for political dissent. Past explosions of popular discontent—the Huk and Maoist rebellions, three EDSA uprisings,[8] and the armed Muslim secessionist movement—did not merely arise from cold war animosities, from opposition to authoritarian rule or corrupt rulers, or from ethnic conflict. They were all manifestations of popular opposition to elite politics too. Furthermore, the continuing turmoil since the dramatic events of 2001, apart from the long-standing armed challenges of Maoist insurgents and Muslim secessionists, indicates that the resistance has not died down at all. The Philippines may, in fact, now be entering a potentially significant phase as popular forces, challenging the rule of the oligarchic elite, strive to deepen the democratization process and institutionalize people power.

The success or failure of the democratic deepening process will have a great bearing on whether Philippine democracy becomes (or remains) consolidated. In the 1990s, some political scientists (M. Thompson 1996:197; Case 1999:469, 485) assessed Philippine democracy as already consolidated. The series of astonishing events in the first half of 2001 and the failed military mutiny of July 2003, however, have raised doubts as to whether this is indeed so or remains so.[9] Whatever the case may be, ultra-rightist (militarists), ultra-leftist (CPP), and other extremist forces have time and again tried to exploit the tensions and discord between the economic and political elite, on one hand, and the subordinate classes and marginalized sectors and communities, on the other, to try to topple the government through violent means.

Thus far, I have explained the importance of a study on postauthoritarian politics and the deepening of democracy in the Philippines. But why a particular focus on the Left?

The Philippine Left, which consists of various communist, socialist, and social democratic movements, parties, groups, and currents, is virtually the only organized political force that has long challenged elite domination of the country's political system. The Left's challenge has come in various forms: armed struggle, open mass movements, electoral and parliamentary struggle, and so on. Since the fall of Marcos, many organizations, groups, and personages of the church or religious sector, business and the middle class have come forward to denounce patronage politics and corruption and push for political reform. However, they have largely restricted their political involvement to the civil society sphere and have seldom set up political parties to compete with the traditional parties of the elite.[10] Nonleftist party-list groups in Congress have mainly attended to the immediate concerns of their sectoral constituents and have not undertaken any significant initiatives against *trapo* domination. Like many middle-class reformists, some leaders or sections of the Left have ended up in *trapo* parties or coalitions, but a major part of the Left has always persisted in the fight against elite politics.

What has long been open to question, however, is whether the Left has ever had, or now has, a role to play in the democratization process. Since the late 1960s, the Philippine Left has been dominated by the Maoist Communist Party of the Philippines (CPP), its armed wing, the New People's Army (NPA), and the CPP-aligned "national democratic" (ND) movement (Nemenzo 1996b:146; Weekley 2001:1), which have been engaged in a "protracted people's war" to overthrow the "reactionary" Philippine state. The CPP's proffered alternative—"people's democracy" or "national democracy"—has been dismissed as being no different from the fallen one-party dictatorships of Eastern Europe and the Soviet Union. With the CPP casting a long shadow, the Philippine Left has often been regarded more as a threat to democracy than as a positive force for democratization.

Over the past decade or so, new, leftist parties and groups have emerged and they are now coming to the fore. Rejecting Stalinism, they have embraced political pluralism and are moving toward an integral view of democracy. Working closely with allied people's organizations (POs) and nongovernmental organizations (NGOs), the emergent leftist parties have identified with the subordinate or marginalized classes, sectors, and communities, and taken up their issues and concerns. The new, leftist parties and groups advocate a "new politics" to replace *trapo* politics, and they endeavor to provide form and leadership to popular struggles against elite hegemony and to deepen democracy.

Argument and Overview of the Study

How exactly is democracy—and politics in general—in the Philippines to be characterized or interpreted? What is being done to deepen Philippine democracy and rid it of the various deprecatory adjectives being appended to it? What role is the Left playing in this process? Is the Philippine Left a democratizing force or a threat to democracy?

In this study, I put forward a three-part argument. The first part consists of an alternative interpretative framework of Philippine politics. In my view, the three main interpretations of Philippine politics—the patron-client, factional framework, the elite democracy or patrimonial view, and the neocolonial or dependency analysis—tend to be somewhat static, one-sided, and top-down. The elite democracy framework, which has now emerged as the dominant interpretation (with variations such as cacique democracy, the patrimonial oligarchic state, and bossism), tends to focus only on elite action and intraelite competition and to ignore the efforts and struggles for popular empowerment and social justice of major sections of the subordinate classes and marginalized sectors—for "democracy from below." As the first part of my argument, I contend that far from being simply an elite democracy the Philippines is a *contested democracy* in which the elite and the *trapos* strive to maintain a formal democracy with "free and fair" elections that they can easily manipulate and dominate and in which large sections of the poor and marginalized classes, sectors, and communities, and some sections of the middle and upper classes as well, work and fight for a participatory and egalitarian democracy.

Flowing from the first, the second part of my argument is that the deepening of democracy in the Philippines mainly involves the transformation of an elite-dominated formal democracy into a participatory and egalitarian one, a process that cannot but consist of intense social contestation. In the sense that the elite strives to maintain the formal democracy of a truncated type and the poor and marginalized fight for a more substantive democracy, the process of the deepening of democracy takes on the character of a struggle of democracy from below versus elite democracy.

The third part of my argument has to do with the Philippine Left. I contend that while the CPP and the ND movement remain the single biggest sector of the Left and still pose a threat to Philippine democracy, new, leftist parties and groups are proving themselves to be a positive force for the deepening of democracy. Getting into the thick of the struggle for democracy from below, the emergent leftist groups have been striving to break the hegemony of the oligarchic elite in both civil society and the state arena and have made small but important breakthroughs and gains. In working for democratic deepening, however, the emergent leftist forces are encountering great difficulties not only in fighting against the *trapos'* patronage politics and avoiding getting ensnared in *trapo* traps but also in defending themselves from harassment and violence from the Stalinist Left.

This study covers the *broad* Philippine Left. During my fieldwork, I interviewed leaders and representatives, as well as local activists, of the major Left parties and the POs/NGOs aligned with them.[11] The party leaders and members I interviewed were mostly operating "above ground"—the open, legal sphere—but there were also some working in the revolutionary underground (UG). In this study, I discuss developments about the two older and more established leftist parties in the Philippines—the CPP (and the open legal parties and groups aligned with it) and the social democratic Partido Demokratiko-Sosyalista ng Pilipinas (PDSP) or Democratic Socialist Party of the Philippines. I devote more attention, however, to emergent leftist parties such as the multitendency Akbayan and the labor-based Partido ng Manggagawang Pilipino (PMP) or Filipino Workers' Party and organizations and groups linked with them.[12] For a more in-depth analysis of leftist engagement in both civil society and the state arena, especially at the local level, I focus on Akbayan, which appears to have made significant gains in working, and combining its efforts, in both spheres. In my examination of the Philippine Left, I sometimes draw from my own experience of having been a very active participant of it—having spent twenty-three years in the ND movement (1970–92), the last twenty as a member of the CPP.

The first two chapters of this book are devoted to general analyses of Philippine politics and of the Philippine Left. Chapter 1 reviews the various interpretations of Philippine politics, traces their historical development and their periods of relative hegemony, and analyzes why one framework gained ascendancy over the others over a given period. It then argues the case for an alternative interpretative framework: contested democracy.[13] Chapter 2 presents the spectrum of leftist parties and groups, their historical development, and the changing views within the left regarding democracy. It then appraises the Philippine Left's record vis-à-vis democratization, both in the transition to democracy and in the postauthoritarian period.

Succeeding chapters elaborate on how the leftist parties (especially the emergent ones), in coordination with allied POs and NGOs, have been doing battle with elite rule and *trapo* politics in various spheres. Chapter 3 focuses on the engagement of new, leftist parties and groups in civil society, an arena in which the Philippine Left has traditionally been strong. It examines the emergent leftist parties' involvement in contentious politics, as well as in development work, and scrutinizes how they have grappled with different versions of the "civil society argument" with regard to democratization. Delving into the Left's engagement in the electoral arena, chapter 4 analyzes the Left's changing views and behavior as regards elections, how leftist parties and groups have shifted from boycotting elections to participating in them, and how they have moved from an instrumental to an integral view of democracy. It also appraises the Left's electoral gains and losses. Chapter 5 discusses the Left's engagement in public office and governance, the response of the emergent leftist parties to coalition politics and government decentralization, and their efforts in promoting participatory local governance. It also discusses how the Left has dealt with contending strategic perspectives in governance.

Chapter 6 tackles two special areas of concern for the emergent leftist parties and groups: (1) popular political education aimed at countering the pervasive influence of *trapo* culture; and (2) working for political reforms, particularly those geared toward promoting popular participation and empowerment and weakening the *trapos'* hold on Philippine politics. Chapter 7 dissects the political work of one of the new, leftist parties, Akbayan, at the local level, studying how it builds a politico-electoral base in a municipality or city. It examines Akbayan's ways of opening new areas for expansion, the engagement of local party units in civil society and the state arena, and the establishment and strengthening of local party units.

The conclusion reviews the major points discussed, puts the Philippines' contested democracy and the emergent Left's role in democratization in comparative perspective, and looks into the prospects for the transformation of the Philippines' elite-dominated democracy into a participatory and egalitarian democracy.

Concepts of Democracy

Democracy, in its classical meaning, is "rule by the people." In an effort to explain how it is technically possible for the people to rule,

Joseph Schumpeter (1943:269) came up with his pathbreaking empirical and procedural definition of *democracy,* or more precisely the *democratic method,* as "that institutional arrangement for arriving at political decisions in which individuals acquire the power to decide by means of a competitive struggle for the people's vote." Today Schumpeter's minimalist, empirical concept continues to have prominent adherents, such as the third-wave theorists. Huntington (1991:6–9) asserts that free and fair elections are "the central procedure of democracy" and, in fact, "the essence of democracy, the inescapable sine qua non." He defines a political system as democratic "to the extent that its most powerful collective decision makers are selected through fair, honest, and periodic elections in which candidates freely compete for votes and in which virtually all the adult population is eligible to vote."

Since the 1970s, other procedural concepts have emerged that define *democracy* more broadly. According to Robert Dahl (1971:2), the minimal conditions under which "polyarchy," or political democracy, can exist are that "all full citizens must have unimpaired opportunities: (1) to formulate their preferences; (2) to signify their preferences to their fellow citizens and the government by individual and collective action; (3) to have their preferences weighed equally in the conduct of the government, that is, weighed with no discrimination because of the content or source of the preference." These three opportunities, he adds, are dependent on certain institutional guarantees: freedom to form and join organizations, freedom of expression, the right to vote, eligibility for public office, the right of political leaders to compete for support, alternative sources of information, free and fair elections, and institutions for making government policies depend on votes and other expressions of preference.

Proceeding from Dahl's conditions and institutional guarantees for democracy, Larry Diamond, Juan J. Linz, and Seymour Martin Lipset (1989:xvi) define *democracy* as a political system that meets the following conditions: (1) meaningful and extensive competition among individuals and groups (especially political parties) for government positions at regular intervals and excluding the use of force; (2) a highly inclusive level of political participation in the selection of leaders and policies; and (3) a level of civil and political liberties—freedoms of expression, association, the press, and so on—sufficient to ensure the integrity of political competition and participation. On the basis of this, Georg Sørensen (1993:12) summarizes the basic elements of *political* democracy as "competition, participation and civil and political liberties."

The concepts of Dahl and Diamond et al. are said to be "middle-range" concepts of democracy. David Held (1996) puts forward a much broader and more comprehensive model of democracy that goes beyond procedural concerns to substantive and normative ones as well and beyond the political realm to the social and economic realms. Held, who combines insights from classical democracy, republicanism, liberal democracy, and Marxism, sees the "principle of autonomy" as an essential premise of modern democracy. He defines the principle as follows.

> [P]ersons should enjoy equal rights and, accordingly, equal obligations in the specification of the political framework which generates and limits the opportunities available to them; that is, they should be free and equal in the determination of the conditions of their own lives, so long as they do not deploy this framework to negate the rights of others.

The institutionalization of the principle of autonomy requires a process of "double democratization"—"the interdependent transformation of both state and civil society." Held envisages a model of state and society called "democratic autonomy" or "liberal socialism," whose features include, among others, the constitutional enshrinement of the principle of autonomy; a competitive party system (with active control of elected politicians); a broad bundle of social and economic rights apart from "state" (political) rights; direct participation in local community institutions; and a combination of self-managed, socially owned or socially regulated enterprises and diverse forms of private enterprise.

As Philip Green (1993:2) succinctly puts it, democracy is a contested idea. This can already be gleaned from the differing concepts of democracy presented. Perhaps the sharpest clash has been between Schumpeter's minimalist model and the "long-range" models. Taking Schumpeter's side, Huntington (1991:6, 9) argues that defining democracy in terms of the source of authority or purposes, or of such ideals as *liberté*, *egalité*, and *fraternité* gives rise to serious problems of ambiguity and imprecision and that only Schumpeter's procedural definition provides analytical precision and empirical referents. "Fuzzy norms," he quips, "do not yield useful analysis." Held (1996:177–98) criticizes Schumpeter for reducing democracy to being merely an institutional arrangement for generating and legitimating leadership, with only a tenuous relation to "rule by the people." In Held's view, Schumpeter's democratic system is a competitive elitist model in which political elites in parties and public offices are the only full participants. Political participation of the masses is largely restricted to voting, since they are regarded as being unable to form reasonable judgments about pressing political questions.

In this study on democratization and the Left in the Philippines, I make extensive use of two conceptualizations of democracy that emphasize a key theme of the left—equality—and attempt to bridge the short-, middle- and long-range models of democracy. The first comes from the Marxist tradition and the second, from the non-Marxist.

Ernesto Laclau and Chantal Mouffe (1985:chap. 4, 1987:79), avowed post-Marxists—"without apologies"—advance the concept of *radical and plural democracy*, which they view as the deepening of the democratic revolution, the extension of "the two great themes of the democratic imaginary—equality and liberty" to more and more social spheres. Laclau and Mouffe do not reject liberal democracy but advocate a type of "radical liberal democracy," one that seeks "to use the symbolic resources of the liberal democratic tradition to struggle against relations of subordination not only in the economy but also those linked to gender, race, or sexual orientation, for example" (Mouffe 1996:20). Balancing the demand for equality, the demand for liberty finds expression in *pluralism*, which Mouffe (1996:20) defines as "the principle that individuals should have the possibility to organize their lives as they wish, to choose their own ends, and to realize them as they think best." Laclau and Mouffe (1985:178) are for socialism, as they still see the need to eradicate oppressive capitalist relations of production. Mouffe (1993:90) declares: "Understood as a process of democratization of the economy, socialism is a necessary component of the project of radical and plural democracy." Unlike the traditional Left, however, they view socialism not as the main goal but only as one of the components of the radical democratic project.

I also make use of some ideas on democracy of Evelyne Huber, Dietrich Rueschemeyer, and John D. Stephens (1997; Rueschemeyer et al. 1992), whose writings on capitalist development and democracy in advanced capitalist countries, Latin America, and the Caribbean are in the fine tradition of Max Weber and Barrington Moore. Huber et al. present three types of democracy: formal, participatory, and social. By *formal democracy*, they mean a political system that combines four features: regular free and fair elections, universal suffrage, accountability of the state's administrative organs to the elected representatives, and effective guarantees for freedom of expression and association as well as protection from arbitrary state action. Huber et al. hold that formal democracy is valuable not only in its own right but also, and more important, in that it tends to be more than merely formal—it makes deepening toward more fully participatory democracy and progress toward increasing social and economic equality possible. *Participatory democracy* is a political system that meets the four criteria of formal democracy plus a fifth: high levels of participation without systematic differences across social categories (such as class, ethnicity, and gender). *Social democracy* includes a sixth criterion: increasing equality in social and economic outcomes.[14]

The models of democracy advanced by Laclau and Mouffe and Huber et al. are similar in that they both accept liberal democracy, view the deepening of democracy in terms of moving from liberal democracy to a more egalitarian order (not just on the basis of class), and integrate socialism in, and subsume it to, the new democratic system. The two models differ in that Laclau and Mouffe's model devotes special attention to pluralism while Huber et al.'s stresses popular participation.

While Laclau and Mouffe and Huber et al. put particular emphasis on the deepening aspect of the democratization process in postauthoritarian countries, other scholars of democratization stress the consolidation aspect. It is useful, writes Guillermo O'Donnell (1992:18), to conceptualize the processes of democratization as actually implying two transitions: first, the transition from an authoritarian regime to a democratic government; and, second, the transition from this government to the consolidation of democracy. An influential concept of democratic consolidation is that of Juan Linz (1990:158), who describes a consolidated democracy as "one in which none of the major political actors, parties, or organized interests, forces, or institutions consider that there is any alternative to democratic processes to gain power, and that no political institution or group has a claim to veto the action of democratically elected decision-makers." To put it simply, democracy must be seen as the "only game in town."

Viewed in Linz's terms, democratic consolidation, although certainly a worthy objective, is perhaps a much too limited one. Even a country where democracy is already generally perceived as the only game in town could still very well be, as Huber et al. put it, a "deficient" or "truncated" formal democracy.[15] In a country such as the Philippines, a protracted period of widespread poverty, grave disparities, and social discontent is apt to provide opportunities for antidemocratic elements to mount a significant challenge to the government. A process of *deepening* democracy is essential, even if only to prevent a consolidated democracy, particularly a deficient formal one, from turning or lurching back into an unstable condition —or from being overthrown.

Social Contestation and the Deepening of Democracy

Democratization involves great social contestation. In a comparative study of the democratization processes in Switzerland and Mexico over a period of two centuries, Doug McAdam, Sidney Tarrow, and Charles Tilly (2001:chap. 9) observe that democratization unfolds through mechanisms similar to those found in social movements, cycles of contention, revolutions, and nationalism. Their study bears out the observation that democratization is not the result of elites simply determining for a polity when and how democratic changes are to be undertaken. McAdam et al. emphasize the role of intense popular contention, citing in particular the armed conflicts over forms and powers of government that swept Switzerland in 1830–48, and the revolutionary decade starting in 1910 that saw the explosion of peasants' and workers' struggles, as well as coups and countercoups, in Mexico. They conclude: "[D]emocratic polities form through contentious politics and reshape contentious politics as they form."

As in the transition to democracy, the deepening of democracy involves contestation. Rueschemeyer et al. (1992:46, 269–71) and Huber et al. (1997:323), in their studies of capitalist development and democracy, put conflict among different classes and class coalitions at the very core of the democratization dynamics—in the processes of both achieving formal democracy and moving toward greater social and economic equality. In advanced capitalist countries, Latin America and the Caribbean, democratization was both pushed forward and opposed by class interest—on the whole, subordinate classes fought for democracy and classes benefiting from the status quo (especially the landlord class) resisted democracy. Rueschemeyer et al. and Huber et al. dispute the orthodox Marxist and liberal social science notion that the bourgeoisie are the primary agent of democracy, showing how capitalists often supported competitive elections and parliamentary government but rarely pushed for full democracy.

Strongly influenced by Antonio Gramsci's ideas on hegemony, Laclau and Mouffe (1985:72, 171–76) and Mouffe (1988:103–4) see the deepening of democracy and the attainment of radical and plural democracy as basically consisting of a struggle for hegemony of popular forces against conservative reaction, particularly the "New Right." They envisage the formation of a new historic bloc that brings together a broad range of groups fighting for liberty and equality in different social categories. Within such a bloc, Laclau and Mouffe see the emergence of a new collective will articulating the democratic demands of the different groups. The "expansive hegemony" respects the autonomy and specificity of the different democratic struggles, with no single struggle being privileged over others.[16] On the means for achieving radical and plural democracy, Laclau and Mouffe (1985:152, 177–78) reject the classic Jacobin—and traditional Marxist—concept of revolution, which they believe privileges "*one* foundational moment of rupture" and "the confluence of struggles into a unified political space" and is thus incompatible with the plurality that the new political imaginary recognizes. They emphasize instead "the *process* character of every radical transformation—the revolutionary act is, simply, an internal moment of the process" (emphasis Laclau and Mouffe's).

Spelling out the role of the Left in the deepening of democracy, Laclau and Mouffe (1985:176) advise: "In the face of the project [of the New Right] for the reconstruction of a hierarchic society, the alternative of the Left should consist of locating itself fully in the field of the democratic revolution and expanding the chains of equivalents between the different struggles against oppression." The hegemonic strategy of the Left, they add, resides "not in the abandonment of the democratic terrain but, on the contrary, in the extension of the field of democratic struggles to the whole of civil society and the state."

The ideas of Huber et al. and Laclau and Mouffe on social contestation in the democratization process, especially in the deepening aspect, are highly relevant to the Philippines. As will be shown in the coming chapters, Huber et al.'s thesis on class conflict—subordinate classes fighting for, and dominant classes resisting, full democracy (i.e., democracy that is participatory and egalitarian, not just formal)—holds true for the Philippines as well. Laclau and Mouffe's post-Gramscian ideas on the hegemonic struggle seem to find expression in the efforts of organizations and groups with different democratic demands (not just based on class but also on gender, ethnicity, social sector, etc.) to join forces in a struggle against the rule of the oligarchic elite. No longer dismissing liberal democratic processes and institutions as fake or "bourgeois," some emergent leftist parties and groups have located themselves fully in the democratic struggles and are working toward the creation of a new popular hegemonic bloc. Rejecting the Jacobin and traditional Marxist concept of revolution, they look at radical transformation not—or no longer—as a single foundational moment of rupture but as a process with both slow changes and ruptures.

That democracy is contested in both meaning and substance is at the heart of the concept of contested democracy that I put forward. I look at the contest over democracy, however, not so much in terms of either one or the other concept (e.g., either the minimalist or the broad-range model). Informed by the "bridging" concepts of democracy of Laclau and Mouffe and Huber et al., I view the contest more as a struggle between those who want a new (or newly restored) democracy to remain a formal—and deficient—liberal democracy and those who seek to transform this truncated formal democracy into a participatory and egalitarian one. With the Philippine elite mainly representing one side, and subordinate classes and communities the other, the contest over the deepening of democracy has taken the form of elite democracy versus democracy from below.

1

Contested Democracy: An Alternative Interpretation of Philippine Politics

SINCE THE TOPPLING OF THE MARCOS DICTATORSHIP by a popular uprising in February 1986, the Philippines has been held up as a shining example of the restoration of democracy. The Philippines' people power uprising, one of the most dramatic and distinctive events of the "third wave" of democratization, is credited with having had a "demonstration effect" on other popular uprisings in Asia. The term *people power* itself has been added to the lexicon of "democratic revolutions" and has even become something of an international buzzword signifying "a peaceful, spontaneous popular revolt that topples an unbending dictatorship" (M. Thompson 1995:1, 2004:18).

Despite the regular holding of elections since Marcos's fall, however, many of the studies of Philippine politics since 1986 have tended to paint a not too democratic picture of the country or to qualify the Philippines' democracy with a variety of deprecatory adjectives. Early on, the post-dictatorship Philippines was already characterized as essentially being the return to a predictatorship "elite democracy" (Hawes 1987; Nemenzo 1988; Bello and Gershman 1990; Stauffer 1990; Timberman 1991; Caoili 1991) or "cacique democracy" (Anderson 1988).[1] Since then, the Philippine political system has been described as one dominated by powerful political clans or families (Gutierrez et al. 1992; McCoy 1993b), a "weak state" captured or manipulated by strong social forces (Miranda 1991; Rivera 1994; Villacorta 1994; May 1998), an "oligarchic democracy" (Hewison, Robison, and Rodan 1993; Kingsbury 2001), a "low-intensity democracy" (Gills et al. 1993), a "patrimonial oligarchic state" (Hutchcroft 1998a), a democracy in which "bossism" is a common phenomenon (Sidel 1999), and a "clientelist electoral regime" (Franco 2001). The characterizations cast doubt as to whether rule by the people truly prevails in the Philippines. Even those who assess Philippine democracy as already being consolidated, question its quality, acknowledging such serious and persistent problems as human rights violations, an unreformed social structure, and political corruption (M. Thompson 1996:197; Case 1999:469, 485).[2] In many of the studies, such features of the premartial-law political system as patron-client relations (Landé 1965), elite politics (Simbulan 1965), and the political machine (Scott 1969; Machado 1972) are acknowledged to have persisted or re-emerged.

Instead of simply focusing on the post-Marcos period, Kerkvliet (1995, 1996) has examined the various characterizations and interpretations of *postcolonial* Philippine politics. As mentioned earlier, he has concluded that there are basically three prominent theoretical frameworks or interpretations of Philippine politics: the patron-client, factional framework; the elite democracy or patrimonial view; and the neocolonial or dependency analysis. Kerkvliet does not delve into the historical development of the three frameworks. While admitting that he found the three interpretative frameworks useful, he expresses a certain amount of dissatisfaction, saying that a great deal of the country's politics tends to be left out of one or all three. He presents several domains of Philippine political life—elections, politicians, political movements, and everyday politics—in which values, motivations, aspirations, and relationships could not be adequately explained by the three interpretations.

This chapter examines the various interpretations of Philippine politics and presents an alternative interpretation. I first trace the historical development of the patron-client, neocolonial, and elite democracy frameworks, presenting the variations in each. In my view, the three frameworks are historically embedded. Each of the three had a period of relative hegemony, the periods roughly corresponding with three important phases in Philippine postcolonial history: the preauthoritarian, authoritarian, and postauthoritarian periods. I explain why one framework gained ascendancy over the others and how the frameworks accounted—or failed to account—for regime change, for instance, from a democratic to an authoritarian regime or vice versa. Not all the frameworks and their variants make a clear distinction between *political system, state* and *regime,* but I point out the distinctions when these have been made. I show the main weakness of the three frameworks: their static, one-sided, and top-down view of Philippine politics. I then present an alternative interpretation of Philippine politics, which I am denoting as the contested democracy framework.

Contested democracy is the combination of the elite democracy interpretation, now the dominant interpretation, with a popular empowerment or democracy from below element. In the Philippines, the very meaning of democracy is contested. For the country's ruling elite, democracy involves mainly elections, a formal democratic exercise that they can easily manipulate for selfish ends. Major sections of the country's subordinate classes and marginalized communities and groups and even part of the upper classes, however, want democracy to mean greater popular participation in decision making and social and economic equality. In the past, efforts toward democracy from below have been somewhat adulterated or deformed by influences of Stalinism and Maoism and also, to some extent, clientelism and populism. Elite democracy and democracy from below are currently the two major competing strands in Philippine politics. They are, in a sense, opposites, but the outcome of the contest need not mean a complete disempowerment of one side by the other nor a regression to authoritarianism. Formal democracy, previously deficient due to its "elite" features, can be deepened into a participatory and egalitarian democracy.

The Patron-Client, Factional Framework

The seminal work on the patron-client, factional framework is Carl Landé's now classic *Leaders, Factions, and Parties: The Structure of Philippine Politics*. It came out in 1965, at a time when social scientists of various disciplines and from various parts of the globe devoted considerable attention to patron-client structures, with case studies of clientelist forms and dynamics in different world regions but especially in Latin America, Southeast Asia, and southern Europe (see Schmidt et al. 1977). Landé (1965, 1967, 1968) observed that the

Philippines' two major political parties then (the Nacionalista and Liberal parties) were identical in their policies, ideological positions and sources of support; that intraparty solidarity was weak and that interparty switching was endemic. He found that the Philippine polity, unlike Western democracies, was structured less by organized interest groups than by networks of personal ties, to a great extent, dyadic ties involving exchanges of favors between prosperous patrons and their poor and dependent clients. In each province, the two main parties were structured by vertical chains of patron-client relationships extending from wealthy, landed political leaders at the provincial level, to lesser gentry politicians in the towns, to village leaders, and finally to ordinary peasants. The parties took on "the role of general benefactor, offering to every sort of individual some limited but tangible reward . . . and rewarding each town which supported them with some visible public works project." In Landé's view, Philippine parties could not be dismissed simply as parties of the upper class. The pyramids of patron-client relationships cut across classes, as well as ethnolinguistic communities and religious affiliations, satisfying most of the needs of those in all social strata.

Landé's study on the patron-client framework actually drew from, and belonged to, a series of studies primarily employing the anthropological approach, which emphasized the element of personalism in Philippine politics. Landé gained insights on the nature of patron-client relationships and on the multifunctional character of local factions from Frank Lynch and Mary Hollnsteiner, respectively. Lynch (1959) had described the relationship between the upper and lower classes—how the former were expected to sponsor community activities, to lend money during times of scarcity, and to intercede in dealings with government officials (i.e., to play the role of "big people" to the "little people") and how the latter, in turn, were expected to reciprocate in terms of services and loyalty. Hollnsteiner (1963) had developed Lynch's concept of the "alliance system," depicting a more extensive network of reciprocal relationships. Four basic social relationships result from or culminate in the structuring of an alliance system: kinship, *compadrazgo* (ritual kinship), reciprocal obligations or services, and associational ties. Hollnsteiner drew special attention to the concepts of *utang na loob* and *hiya* as moral forces in the regulation of behavior.[3] According to Jean Grossholtz (1964), Filipinos are integrated into the Philippine political system as individuals, not groups, and through highly personal bargaining mechanisms. Philippine political parties build a coalition of personalities on the basis of highly particular and personal considerations. Because they are based on personalities, the parties are in a constant state of flux. Thus, little in the way of a stable, distinctive program of government policies is possible.

Landé's patron-client model was groundbreaking. Patron-client relations, as a reality of Philippine everyday life, date as far back as the Spanish colonial period. No less a figure than the Philippine national hero Jose Rizal somewhat described it in his second novel, *El Filibusterismo* (1889): "In the Philippines it is a well-known fact that patrons are needed for everything, from the time one is christened until one dies, in order to get justice, to secure a passport, or to develop an industry" (translated in Derbyshire 1963:290)." It was Landé, however, who first came up with an analysis of the major role patron-client relations play in Philippine politics.

Many scholars, journalists, diplomats, and other observers were strongly influenced by Landé's patron-client model. Largely on the basis of his work on patron-client relations, Landé has been cited as being "[p]erhaps the most influential student of Philippine politics in the last four decades" (Rocamora 1998:2). As late as 2001, it was still being said that Landé's patron-client framework enjoyed hegemonic status in Philippine political studies (Ileto 2001:13). The period over which it held hegemonic status in the Philippines, however, is actually much shorter than commonly believed. As Amando Doronila (1985:99) rightly puts it, the patron-client model built by Landé was the rather widely accepted model of *pre-martial-law* Philippines politics.

By the end of the 1960s, the inadequacies of the patron-client framework began to become apparent. In his study of Philippine elections in 1946–69, Hirofumi Ando (1971) found that, while the electoral process basically conformed to the patron-client model, material resources and rewards had become "too diffusedly distributed" and many members of the elite could no longer meet the voters' demands through remunerative means alone. He noted a serious mutation in the compliance system: the threat or use of physical violence—a feature supposed to be alien to the patron-client model.[4] With increasing intraelite competition, politicians hired more and more "private security guards." Political warlords emerged with their private armies. Ando also observed the use of fraud such as the falsification of election returns.

Studies by other scholars tended to show that Landé's model itself was becoming outdated. James Scott (1969, 1972b) and Kit Machado (1971, 1972) argued that traditional clientelist relationships were eroding and the traditional faction based on patron-client bonds was being transformed into the *political machine,* a form of political organization common in the United States at the turn of the twentieth century.[5] According to Scott, the machine, instead of relying on traditional patterns of deference, resorted to widespread use of concrete, short-run, material inducements to secure cooperation. Occasionally, the machine "boss" also used charisma, coercion, or ideology. To generate broad support on a continuing basis, machine parties wielded patronage on a distinctive scale. Graft for party funds, help with the law, and selective nonenforcement became, like patronage, part of the bundle of short-run inducements. Machado (1972:15) perceived the rise of the political machine as "a common political response to change in societies that are in early stages of modernization and that are following the democratic pattern of political development." He linked the emergence of the political machine in the country to two other important changes: the replacement of notables from old leading families in positions of leadership with upwardly mobile "new men" from humble backgrounds, and the adoption of more professional criteria for recruitment to such positions. For Machado, the changes offered great potential for the democratization of Philippine towns and the eventual stabilization of party organization in the country.

As the inadequacies of the original patron-client framework became more apparent, the concept of clientelism began to change. Defending the patron-client model, Thomas Nowak and Kay Snyder (1970) maintained that the organization of Philippine politics had not changed in basic structural characteristics and that it remained strongly clientelist oriented even in the cities. They defined *clientelist politics*, however, as "a system of exchange which is particularistic, non-programmatic, and non-ideological" (Nowak and Snyder 1970: 261). The political machine was merely a more specialized form of clientelist politics that had evolved in response to the increased differentiation and growth of urban areas.[6]

In a study of the 1969 presidential elections, Arthur Alan Shantz (1972) traced the roots of Philippine political parties not to patron-client bonds but to "kinship and fictive kinship systems of allegiance" and such Filipino traits as *pakikisama* and *utang na loob*.[7] Philippine parties were two vast national coalitions of local political organizations bound together by the vertical hierarchy of public offices and their rewards and the social hierarchy of wealth. Shantz noted that election excesses had risen, and he attributed this to increased individuals' demands relative to the normative capacity of the political system to fulfill them. He appended a long list of cases of violence, coercion, and other irregularities committed during the 1969 elections.

The cogency of the patron-client model continued to decline. Even its principal author could no longer deny its inadequacies. In a study of networks and groups in Southeast Asia, Landé (1973) drew up a number of consequences resulting from heavy reliance on patron-client and other dyadic methods of goal attainment. Some of these chipped away at the benign and integrative picture of the patron-client model he had earlier drawn. He acknowledged, for instance, that reliance on dyadic methods produced dissatisfaction among those not receiving rewards, that by permitting favoritism it contributed to near anarchy in many areas and eroded public confidence in the system of government, and that it made the mobilization of political support immensely costly. Landé virtually conceded the demise of the patron-client model: "While traditional patron-client relationships appear to be breaking down in many peasant societies, other types of dyadic structures and techniques will continue to play a part in politics as long as political actors seek and are able to advance their interests particularistically" (Landé 1973:127).

Landé's attempt to expand the patron-client model to encompass other personal ties and dyadic structures did not help much. In a study of politics, patronage, and class conflict in Central Luzon, Willem Wolters (1983) found that by the late 1960s and early 1970s patron-client relations and other forms of personal intermediation did not have a stable and permanent character and did not provide structural linkages between the local community and the central state. Landownership had become less important as a basis for power and prestige. Moreover, landlord-tenant relations were no longer on a patron-client basis. They "had become much less persistent, the scope of the exchange had narrowed, the tie binding the parties had become weaker and less comprehensive, and was more instrumental in character" (Wolters 1983:218). Meanwhile, the state apparatus had become increasingly important as a provider of capital. Huge amounts of government money were being distributed along particularistic lines—pork barrel funds during elections, for instance—but such patronage could be dispensed without recourse to patron-client ties.[8]

In 1974, in contrast to their 1970 findings, Nowak and Snyder (1974a, 1974b; Nowak 1974) saw a decline in the integrative capacity of clientelist machines. Such factors as greater social mobilization, ethnic diversity, and urbanization had made patronage resources scarcer, thus heightening intraelite competition and eventually rendering clientelist machines less effective in mobilizing broad groups of people. The reduced strength of these machines intensified the potential for more violent forms of mass activity, which in turn provoked such responses from the elite as the declaration of martial law. Thus, Nowak and Snyder linked the shift to authoritarian rule with a decline in the integrative capacity of clientelist structures.

Martial law rendered the political machine model moot. As was pointed out by Scott (1969:1143), the political machine form can occur only in a setting where, among other factors, the selection of political leaders is through elections. Under martial law, Marcos put an end to elections, at least for a time. He did the same for the political machines. Two years after the imposition of martial law, Machado (1974a, 1974b) revised his erstwhile optimistic view of the "new men" of the now virtually defunct political machines. He predicted that the new professionals, lacking independent resources, would likely be absorbed by Marcos's authoritarian system.

By the mid-1970s, the patron-client model, even with its "clientelist machine" variant, had outlived its usefulness as an interpretative framework of Philippine politics. While patron-client bonds could still account for a great deal of the political behavior in both rural and urban areas, they could not explain, in Kerkvliet's words, "the role of violence, coercion, intimidation, monetary inducements, and the considerable autonomy elites have to manipulate formal democratic procedures to their liking" and "the influence, even control of foreign interests over Philippine politics" (Kerkvliet 1995:405). The exchange of favors in a patron-client relationship was apt to lead to a bit of corruption, but the large-scale corruption and, most especially, the violence and coercion, went far beyond the placid clientelist order originally painted. In the decade prior to martial law, elections had become so marred by corruption, fraud, and the threat or use of force that "guns, goons, and gold" had become a byword in Philippine politics. After the 1969 elections, the losing presidential candidate candidly protested that Marcos had "out-gunned, out-gooned and out-gold" him (Abueva 1970:62). The 1971 elections were marked by a record 534 violent incidents and 905 deaths (Linantud 1998:301). The patron-client model also could not convincingly explain martial law. To state that the breakdown of clientelist machines brought about martial law was to admit that there were factors well outside of patron-client bonds that had to be considered.

The Neocolonial or Dependency Framework

Philippine left-wing nationalists have long articulated the neocolonial or dependency interpretation of Philippine politics. According to Renato Constantino (1970, 1978), the United States exercised "indirect colonial rule" over the Philippines even after granting it independence in 1946 by continuing to dominate the Philippine economy, retaining it as a market for American goods, a source of raw materials, and an open field for American investments. To guarantee such economic control, the United States maintained military bases and tied the country to various military pacts. The Filipino economic and political elite was merely "a sub-elite within an essentially colonial framework" (R. Constantino 1970:123). Alejandro Lichauco (1973) traced the country's ills—massive and deepening poverty, rising unemployment, runaway inflation, the infantile state of military and productive capacities, the disoriented educational system, and social anarchy—directly or indirectly to the country's neocolonial status. Philippine communists, who had propagated the neocolonial interpretation of Philippine politics since the late 1940s, were much more strident in their critiques of neocolonialism.[9] During the period of the stormy protest rallies of 1970–72, the writings of nationalist authors gained wide readership. The resurgence of the nationalist movement was no doubt influenced by the worldwide "rediscovery of imperialism" (Magdoff 1969) and the rise of the dependency school in Latin America, both of which occurred in the late 1960s and early 1970s.

With the advent of martial law, the neocolonial or dependency interpretation gradually replaced the patron-client model as the predominant interpretation of Philippine politics. The increased dependence of the Marcos regime on economic and military assistance from the United States and multilateral aid agencies such as the International Monetary Fund (IMF) and the World Bank (WB) was an added factor for its rise. Some scholars of elite politics, an early version of the elite democracy framework, moved over to the neocolonial framework.[10]

Under martial law, Marcos clamped down on all dissent and threw thousands of dissenters, including many nationalist writers, into detention. For a while, there was a lull in nationalist and anti-imperialist literature in Philippine academia. In the vacuum, political scientists supportive of martial law echoed Marcos's pitch that martial law was an effort to "reform society"—or a "democratic revolution" against communists on the one hand and "oligarchs" on the other—that would ultimately build a "New Society" in which class and interest conflicts would be replaced by an organic harmony of interests and social discipline (Agpalo 1973; Dubsky 1974; Muego 1975).

Non-Filipino academics and foreign-based Filipino scholars critical of martial law, however, could not be covered by Marcos's clampdown. Characterizing Marcos's imposition of martial law as a coup, Robert Stauffer (1973) asserted that foreign control over the

Philippine economy had held back economic development to such an extent that conditions had made a resort to authoritarian rule extremely likely. According to Jonathan Fast (1973), the Philippines had long served as a politically tranquil base for U.S. imperialism, but martial law—an attack by Marcos on his bourgeois rivals—and the establishment of a "bourgeois dictatorship" had plunged the Philippines into an unprecedented political crisis. Walden Bello and Severina Rivera (1977) argued that the Marcos dictatorship remained in power primarily because of the vast quantities of military and economic assistance—the "logistics of repression"—it received from the United States. Later Stauffer (1979) showed how authoritarian support, ideological and material, from a metropolitan nation (the United States) had been used by antinationalist groups in the Philippines to overthrow the existing political system and institute a "dependent-authoritarian regime."

In the late 1970s, the nationalist movement resurged in the Philippines. Old and new writings of nationalist scholars again circulated widely. A lively, multisided debate over the "mode of production" took place.[11] Leftists aligned with the CPP defended the thesis that the Philippines was a "semicolonial and semifeudal" country in which emerging bourgeois leaders had been co-opted by imperialism and turned into "big comprador-bourgeois" (Ferrer 1984). Those identified with the pro-Moscow Partido Komunista ng Pilipas (PKP), argued that it was a backward neocolony being groomed under the "new international division of labor" to become an industrial one, albeit only engaged in the production of labor-intensive commodities for export (Magallona 1982). The dependency perspective, wrote Randolf S. David (1980:83), essentially "stresses the importance of examining the relationship of domination and dependency between the advanced capitalist countries (metropolitan countries) and the underdeveloped countries (also known as satellites or peripheral economies) as a way of accounting for the poor countries' continuing underdevelopment." A good number of the dependency or world-systems scholars used the historical approach in explaining how the Philippines became a dependent-capitalist state or was integrated into the capitalist world-system. The "articulation" school claimed that capitalism in the neocolonies "articulated" or intermeshed with precapitalist modes and that the transition to capitalism thus remained incomplete (Rivera 1982a, 1982b; Bautista 1984).

Due to continuing restrictions on free expression, the mode of production debate tended to avoid deep, open discussion of Philippine politics. But a number of scholars did venture. Rigoberto Tiglao (1979), for instance, argued that the Philippines' "backward capitalism" had generated an unstable state machinery and prevented the smooth operation of elections. Moreover, limited capital sources and the existence of large power groupings arising from landownership and the bureaucracy resulted in "explosive intra-elite struggles to capture a prime source of capital accumulation—the state" (Tiglao: 1979:45). Complete centralization of political authority was needed to manage these contradictions.

Going over the mode of production debate in the Philippines in retrospect in 2001, Kathleen Weekley (2001:51) concluded that the debate, as in other countries, did not really get anywhere. In her assessment, it was highly theoretical and empirically weak. Moreover, it was based on questionable assumptions, restricted by narrow terms of reference, and "dogged by a tendency to pit detailed textual exegeses of Marx against each other."

Meanwhile, foreign-based scholars further expounded on the neocolonial/dependency theme. Presenting a conventional neocolonial picture, Stephen Shalom (1981) traced how the United States had restored the Philippines' prewar elite to power, defined the terms of Philippine independence to preserve U.S. economic and strategic interests, intervened in the political crisis of the early 1950s, maintained military and economic aid to further its own interests and those of local allies, and backed the imposition of martial law. Bello, David Kinley, and Elaine Elinson (1982) exposed the "development debacle" of the World Bank's policies in the Philippines. In the analysis of Bello et al., Marcos's authoritarian rule reflected the shift in U.S. policy in the third world from the traditional line of promoting elite-dominated democracies (or "elite democracies") as the means of U.S. control to supporting repressive allied regimes. In its "colonization [of the Philippines] without an occupation force" (Bello et al. 1982:13), the United States used the world's largest development aid institution. Extending massive aid to the Philippines, the WB aimed "to stabilize the deteriorating political situation and to more thoroughly integrate the Philippine economy into the international capitalist order" (Bello et al. 1982:38). The WB's failed development effort in the Philippines was particularly significant in that it "was the first coordinated, broad front experiment in technocratic, authoritarian modernization" and "was not just a country program but a larger model for Third World development" (Bello et al. 1982:200).

In a study of the political economy of transnational corporate investment in Philippine agriculture, Gary Hawes (1984) conceptualized the Philippine state "not as a sovereign actor representing in a democratic manner the interest of pluralist groups, but rather as a penetrated and class-dominated state." Like other third world countries, the Philippines had been integrated into the world economy in a dependent role. Hawes depicted the Philippine state as an instrument for class domination, the defender of the general interests of capital. Institutions and practices such as patron-client ties, building political organizations, and government subsidization of food prices were merely attempts to mask the state's partiality.

The neocolonial or dependency theories dominated scholarly studies and debates on Philippine politics during the Marcos authoritarian period. Little was heard from the adherents of the patron-client model. The picture of neat dyads of benign patron-client ties simply could not gibe with the stark reality of flagrant Marcosian plunder and repression. Not long after the fall of Marcos, however, the influence of the neocolonial view, in turn, waned. Many scholars had never believed or no longer believed that Marcos had merely been a U.S. puppet. "[I]t is perhaps part of the colonial legacy," commented Landé (1981:1164), "that there remains an exaggerated view of what the American government can accomplish in the Philippines."

The Elite Democracy or Patrimonial Framework

Dante Simbulan's 1965 study on the Philippine socioeconomic elite and "elite politics" appears to be the pioneering study on the patrimonial/elite democracy framework. Simbulan had the same observations as Landé on the indistinguishability of the country's two main parties, loose party identification, and frequent defections, but, utilizing Laswell's theory on the elite, he came up with a different explanation. The parties were similar because they were essentially alliances of leaders coming from the same socioeconomic stratum, the elite. Simbulan showed that the Philippine elite had a long history marked by a remarkable continuity. He traced how Spanish colonizers turned the precolonial *datus* (chiefs) and *maharlikas* (nobles), together with mestizos, into the privileged local class, the *principalía*; how this privileged class accumulated land, wealth, and power under Spanish and American colonial rule; and how the *principalía* evolved into the modern-day elite. The Philippines' two major parties had formal rules on party organization patterned after the American model, but the power relations in the social structure impinged on the formal organization. In the provinces, factions composed of elite families, especially "political dynasties," served as the nuclei of party organization, and provincial politics revolved around the interests of these elite family groupings. To win an election, elite politicians made effective use of money (including public funds), "gifts," violence and fraud, and cultural norms. While in office, they utilized political power to enrich themselves and their backers. Philippine political parties were elite, not multiclass, parties. Far from satisfying the needs of the occupants of various social strata, they served only the interests of the modern *principalía*.

Early in the post-dictatorship period, the possible return to predominance of the patron-client model was precluded. In a study of "Philippine colonial democracy" (Paredes 1988b), Ruby Paredes, Michael Cullinane, Glenn May, and Alfred McCoy make a much more carefully documented and nuanced presentation on the remarkable continuity of the Philippine elite and the practice of elite politics from the waning years of Spanish colonialism till the end of the American era. When formal elections were first introduced in the Philippines in the 1880s, the Spanish colonial authorities allowed municipal elites to contend for local dominance. Fierce factional rivalries for local power and its perks ensued. An "electoral style of dexterous manipulation" emerged, and "leaders were schooled in the art of using government, not in the ethos of public service" (Paredes 1988a:7). Under American colonial rule, electoral politics started out as a contest of the elite and it remained such throughout. The American authorities disparaged the municipal politicians as "*caciques,* or corrupt local autocrats" (Paredes 1988a:7), yet they relied on them moving up through elections from the municipal to the provincial and finally to the national level. Filipino leaders saw themselves as the "directing class," "an entity that knows how to govern," as distinguished from the popular masses, "an entity that knows how to obey" (Cullinane 1988:104). Filipino politicians entered into a complex web of clientelist relations involving their local supporters, as well as American officials. The dyads stretched from the villages, towns, and provinces not just to the national capital, as Landé had put it, but all the way to Washington (McCoy 1988:155–56). "Denied equality with Americans under law," writes Paredes (1988a:6), "Filipino leaders adopted tactics of guile and manipulation to win from American patrons political concessions they needed to maintain the loyalty of their Filipino clients." In time, guile and manipulation graduated to coercion and force. By the 1930s, provincial politics already displayed "a marked predilection for institutionalized violence" (Paredes 1988a:11). Apart from deforming Landé's patron-client pyramid, the account by Paredes and her colleagues of Philippine colonial politics belies his assertion that "Filipinos have under American tutelage been imbued with the belief that nepotism and corruption are bad for the country and not to be tolerated" (Landé 1965:54).

The term *elite democracy* appears to have caught on fast in the post-Marcos era, drawing many former adherents of the neocolonial/dependency framework. Hawes (1987), Francisco Nemenzo, Jr., (1988), Bello and Gershman (1990), Stauffer (1990), Timberman (1991), and Caoili (1991) all use the term, characterizing the coming to power of Corazon Aquino as the restoration of elite democracy. Bello and Gershman point out that elite politicians won the vast majority of the posts in the 1987 and 1988 polls thanks to "the combination of money, high media visibility, leftist ambivalence, and the continuing strong influence of patron-client relationships" (1990:42–43). Elite democracy is more complicated than authoritarian rule.

Borrowing from Gramsci, they characterize elite democracy as being "based on the creation of cultural or ideological hegemony, obtaining the consent of the ruled through the use of institutions, symbols, and processes that enjoy a strong degree of legitimacy among the ruled" (Bello and Gershman 1990:51). Elections serve as the means for the relatively peaceful alternation in power among rival elite factions. Through mass socialization and the enormous advantage conferred by wealth and resources on elite politicians, elite democracy screens out fundamental challenges to the social status quo.

Most of the other postauthoritarian interpretations of Philippine politics—cacique democracy, domination by political clans or families, oligarchic democracy, low-intensity democracy, strong society and weak state, oligarchic patrimonialism, bossism, and clientelist electoralism—are variations on the theme of elite rule. Like Simbulan, Benedict Anderson (1988) seeks to underscore the continuity of the lineage of the Philippines' present-day elite from the caciques of the Spanish colonial era. Thus, Anderson coins the term *cacique democracy,* the marriage of American electoralism with Spanish caciquism. He sees the beginnings of Philippine political dynasties in the "palmy days" of the American colonial period, when provincial and local elective offices proliferated and caciques stacked these offices with their relatives and friends. Private armies and warlords emerged in the early postcolonial years when the landed elite sought to subdue restive peasants and restore uncontested cacique rule. The oligarchy faced no serious domestic challenges from 1954 to 1972, "the full heyday of cacique democracy in the Philippines." In resorting to authoritarian rule, Marcos was either the "Master Cacique" who pushed the destructive logic of the old order to its natural conclusion, or "Manila's Louis Napoleon," who understood that "wealth serves power" and that "the key card is the state." Cacique democracy returned after Marcos, and members of the traditional political families again dominated electoral politics.[12]

In a study of the 1987 congressional and 1988 local elections, Eric Gutierrez, Ildefonso Torrente, and Noli Narca (1992) observed that "old horses" (candidates belonging to political clans or families) crowded the electoral battlefield and the elections marked the "return of the oligarchs." Through such a showing, the political clans had reasserted themselves as the real source of power in Philippine electoral politics. Gutierrez et al. conclude that the clan rather than the party is the more dominant form of political organization in the country and that clan affiliation is a more decisive factor in electoral outcomes. Analyzing the 1992 elections, James Putzel (1995a) concurs that the essential character of machine politics in the Philippines continues to be determined by clan identities.

Felipe Miranda (1991) and Temario Rivera (1994), paraphrasing Migdal, characterize the Philippines as having a weak state and strong, well-organized, social forces taking advantage of state resources for vested-interest use. Miranda draws particular attention to the aggressiveness of oligarchic interests (political-economic clans). Religious groups, business groups, NGOs and armed challengers also compete with the state for preeminence, and the transnational influence of the United States and multilateral lending institutions remains strong. Rivera argues that the Philippine state was dominated by an entrenched elite based on land and merchant capital and by foreign capitalists. Lacking the "embedded autonomy" found in other "developmental states" in Asia, the Philippine state had been captured by competing social interests and had not been able to build the effective social coalition necessary for sustainable industrial development.

To find an explanation for the Philippines' laggard economic growth, Paul Hutchcroft (1991, 1993, 1998a) examines the relationship between the state and dominant economic interests, focusing on the banking sector, and finds that the obstacles to the country's sustained development lie in the very nature of the political system. Commenting on Belinda Aquino's (1987) and David Wurfel's (1988) characterizations of the Marcos dictatorship as "the politics of plunder" and "patrimonial" or "neopatrimonial" authoritarianism, respectively, Hutchcroft argues that patrimonialism runs much deeper and has not been limited to the Marcos regime. The Philippine state is itself a *patrimonial oligarchic state*, a weak state preyed on by "a powerful oligarchic class that enjoys an independent economic base outside the state, yet depends upon particularistic access to the political machinery as the major avenue to private accumulation" (Hutchcroft 1998:12). He characterizes the capitalist system prevailing in the Philippines as *rent capitalism*[13] (as opposed to production-oriented capitalism), in particular, *booty capitalism*, where "a powerful oligarchic business class extracts privilege from a largely incoherent bureaucracy" (Hutchcroft 1998:19–20). The Philippines' patrimonial oligarchic state and booty capitalism constitute a "development bog" in which the postwar Philippine economy has repeatedly become mired. Hutchcroft argues that unless there is greater development of the state apparatus the Philippines will be unable to achieve sustained economic success.

There are still other references to "oligarchy" and "oligarchic" rule. Richard Robison, Kevin Hewison, and Garry Rodan (1993) and Damien Kingsbury (2001:chap. 12) refer to the Philippines as an "oligarchic democracy"—basically the same as an elite democracy. In several case studies of Philippine "political families," a group of social scientists headed by Alfred McCoy (1993b) further explores the relationship between a "weak state" and "powerful political oligarchies." According to McCoy (1993a:10), two key elements appear to have contributed to the emergence of these powerful elite families: "the rise of 'rents' as a significant share of the nation's economy and a simultaneous attenuation of central government control over the provinces."[14] Elite families are organized on the basis of the *kinship network*—a working coalition consisting of people related by blood, marriage, and ritual kinship. A "fissiparous, even volatile factionalism" has resulted from such flexible kinship ties being brought into the political arena. To maintain themselves in power, the political families resort to various tactics and methods but most especially to political violence and "rent seeking," with the former being prevalent in the provinces and the latter concentrated in the capital. The interaction between the state and the rent-seeking political families has been synergistic. "Simply put," writes McCoy (1993a:10), "the privatization of public resources strengthens a few fortunate families while weakening the state's resources and its bureaucratic apparatus."

The Philippines is one of four case studies of "low intensity democracies" in a study conducted by a group headed by Barry Gills, Joel Rocamora, and Richard Wilson (1993).[15] Gills et al. invoke the American counterinsurgency catchphrase "low intensity conflict" to show that the struggle to define *democracy* has become a major ideological battle. Low intensity democracies are newly restored third world democracies that have formally instituted such features of Western liberal democracies as periodic elections but have preserved ossified political and economic structures from an authoritarian past and failed to broaden popular political participation in a meaningful way. In the four countries studied, the society is characterized by a big gap between the rich and the poor, and the new democracy is "compromised by, if not subservient to, the established power structure," with the civilian conservative government, the military, and business elite forming a "hegemonic bloc." A "dictatorship" over the working class and other popular sectors persists, usually in the form of a strengthened presidential office.

John T. Sidel (1995, 1999) draws attention to the phenomenon of "bossism" in the Philippines. He uses the term *bossism,* instead of *caciquism* or *clientelism,* to underscore the institutional structures inherited by the Philippine state from the American colonial era and the role of violence and coercion in shaping the country's economic accumulation, political competition, and social relations. Sidel (1999:19) defines *bosses* as "predatory power brokers who achieve monopolistic control over both coercive and economic resources within given territorial jusrisdictions or bailiwicks." He examines patterns of bossism at the municipal, district, provincial, and national levels, ending up with a brief account of the Marcos martial law era—"a protracted period of national-level boss rule" (Sidel 1999:144). While concurring with Hutchcroft's thesis on the Philippine state's being an object of oligarchical plunder, he also portrays the Philippine state as itself predatory—"a complex set of predatory mechanisms for the private exploitation and accumulation of the archipelago's human, natural, and monetary resources" (Sidel 1999:146). Comparing the Philippine experience with those of other countries in Southeast Asia and Latin America, Sidel avers that bossism is common in democracies that have underdeveloped and weakly insulated state apparatuses and are in an early stage of capital accumulation. Influenced by Sidel, Olle Törnquist (1999:128, 165) propounds that "populist bossism" has prevailed in the Philippines since the fall of Marcos and describes the country as an "elitist boss-democracy."

To Jennifer Franco (2001:71), the postdictatorship regime in the Philippines, just like its preauthoritarian counterpart, is a *clientelist electoral regime*—"an electorally competitive national regime which falls short of the minimum democratic threshold because of the persistence of local authoritarian enclaves." Like Sidel, Franco pays particular attention to the role of coercion at the local level of the political system. Instead of bossism, however, Franco (2001:16) opts to use "authoritarian clientelism," described by Jonathan Fox as a situation in which "imbalanced bargaining relations require the enduring political subordination of clients and are reinforced by the threat of coercion."[16] Franco's concept of electoral clientelism clearly departs from Landé's concept of benign patron-client relationships and is more akin to the elite democracy model.

A Critique of the Prominent Interpretations of Philippine Politics

Historian Reynaldo Ileto (2001) has launched a stinging broadside against a number of American scholars for their "colonial" and "orientalist" construction of Philippine politics. Among them are some scholars identified with the patron-client and patrimonial/elite democracy frameworks. Ileto (2001:16) inveighs against Landé for portraying the Philippine political system as consisting of "pale imitations, distortions, or outright contradictions of the ideal [i.e., the Western liberal model]." While I certainly agree with Ileto that Landé's postulation on "American tutelage" does belong to colonial discourse, I do not think that the same can be said of Landé's patron-client paradigm. Ileto dismisses it as being an old paradigm that merely had a "rebirth" in the 1960s. As I mentioned earlier, patron-client relationships actually date back to the Spanish colonial period. By pointing out how such ties influence Filipinos' political behavior, Landé has made a significant contribution to Philippine political science. Patron-client ties, while overdrawn in Landé's model, have been and remain an important feature of the country's political dynamics. Ileto criticizes Landé for noting such "peculiarities" of Philippine political parties as indistinguishability, constant affiliation switching and fluidity. However, other political and social scientists—Filipino and non-Filipino—have observed the same features and rightly referred to them not just as peculiarities but as the faults of a weak party system.

Instead of castigating the likes of Cullinane, May, McCoy, Anderson, and Sidel for colonial or orientalist discourse, as Ileto does, I applaud their efforts in trying to reverse colonial historiography. In the main, they dispel the myth of the U.S. colonial period being a golden age, and they show how the institutional legacies of U.S.-imposed "colonial democracy" facilitated the emergence and entrenchment of oligarchs and warlords. Most creditable is *Philippine Colonial Democracy*, which Cullinane, May, and McCoy cowrote with Paredes and which Ileto unfortunately did not include in the works reviewed.[17] Ileto rightly chastises some American scholars for depicting Filipino elite leaders only as self-serving "big men," practically devoid of a patriotic or civic ethos. Nonetheless, I tend to agree with patrimonial/elite democracy model adherents that as far as the contemporary oligarchic elite is concerned private gain far outweighs public benefit. Ileto further excoriates McCoy, Cullinane, and Sidel for depicting the reality of Philippine politics as consisting of "the familism, localism, corruption, and violence that essentially underlie Filipino political behavior" (Ileto 2001:21). I could in large part concur with Ileto on this charge. Such a charge, however, can also be leveled against most of the other adherents of the patrimonial/elite democracy model, Filipino and non-Filipino. Patronage and guns, goons and gold may well be reflective of Filipino *elite* political behavior but not the entirety of Filipino political behavior.

This brings me to my main criticism of the prominent paradigms of politics in the Philippines. I contend that the three prominent frameworks or interpretations of Philippine politics—the patron-client, neocolonial/dependency and patrimonial/elite democracy models (including such variants of the last model as the patrimonial oligarchic state and bossism)—suffer from a major weakness: their static, one-sided, and top-down view of Philippine politics.[18]

For the patron-client framework, its inability to account for intra-elite violence was bad enough. Perhaps most egregious, it was blind to the serious class and ethnic tensions that threatened to tear Philippine society apart. Once before, in the early 1950s, landlord-peasant tensions had resulted in a mighty explosion—the Huk rebellion. The rebellion was crushed by the mid-1950s, perhaps explaining why the patron-client model saw only tranquil patron-client relationships.[19] As high levels of landlessness and social inequality persisted, however, the class tensions built up again. A new communist insurgency, headed by the CPP, began in the late 1960s. In 1970–72, tens of thousands of students, workers, urban poor, and peasants marched into the streets of Manila and other urban centers. Strongly influenced by the revolutionary Left, they railed against "imperialism, feudalism, and bureaucrat capitalism." A number of rallies turned into pitched battles between policemen using truncheons and high-powered rifles and demonstrators hurling stones, Molotov cocktails, and pillboxes. By the time Marcos imposed martial law, the revolutionary movement had spread nationwide and established guerrilla zones in many areas. Meanwhile, in Mindanao, disputes over land between Christian settlers and increasingly displaced Muslims heated up. Paramilitary groups formed by Christian and Muslim warlords terrorized Muslim and Christian communities, respectively. After Marcos declared martial law, all hell broke loose in Mindanao. Muslim rebels called for independence from "Philippine colonialism." The communist insurgency, the Muslim secessionist movement, and the stormy protest rallies shattered the patron-client model's tranquil landscape of an integrative multiclass, multiethnic society.

With its pyramid of vertical dyads, the patron-client framework presents a rigid, top-down picture of Philippine politics. Since a patron-client relationship involves two parties unequal in status, wealth, and influence, Philippine politics is thus a pyramid of these lopsided relationships. The picture cannot show those who resist or try to break out of these unequal relationships. At best, they are aberrations. The problem is that in times of social tension the aberrations become too numerous.

The neocolonial/dependency model also depicted power, domination, and control as flowing from top to bottom, from the United States to its puppet Marcos and his cabal, to their local cohorts, and finally down to the masses. The revolutionary forces basically saw themselves as working outside of this political system, and they sought to overthrow the reactionary state. Before the

February 1986 uprising, it seemed to many who adhered to the neocolonial perspective that the U.S. would decide Marcos's political fate. In the case of the CPP, such thinking proved disastrous. The revolutionary Left boycotted the fateful 1986 presidential elections and was left out of the revolution it claimed to lead.

The patrimonial/elite democracy model, also a pyramidical model, follows a logical continuum of hierarchical politics dating back to the colonial era. Colonialism nurtured the domestic elite; "colonial democracy" reared it in the ways of patronage, manipulation and coercion (see Paredes 1988). Hence, it can be said that colonial rule and postcolonial elite rule form one continuous thread. At times, democratic structures and processes or their trappings partly or wholly masked their hierarchical nature. Both colonial rule and postcolonial elite rule, in fact, had authoritarian and democratic phases in them. The long colonial era included a long period of authoritarian Spanish rule, a brief experience with Spanish colonial democracy, a short but extremely bloody American authoritarian period, a "golden era" of American colonial democracy, and an authoritarian Japanese occupation. The postcolonial era has had two democratic periods with an authoritarian one sandwiched in between.

The patrimonial/elite democracy interpretation of Philippine politics appears to be superior to the two other prominent interpretations, however. Unlike the patron-client model, it takes corruption, fraud, coercion, and violence into account. And while the elite democracy model may regard foreign interests as at times or often infringing on Philippine sovereignty, it does not have an exaggerated view, as the neocolonial model tends to have, of the power of these external forces to determine the course of political events in the country.

Although the patrimonial/elite democracy framework has now gained ascendancy, it nonetheless has critical weaknesses. As another static, top-down model, the elite democracy model tends to see what happens in the Philippines as mainly resulting from the actions and machinations of the elite—the corrupt caciques, predatory oligarchs, and bosses—or factions of the elite. But elite action and intraelite competition have not always been the decisive factor in shaping events. While actions of the opposition elite and the "Cory magic" certainly contributed to the downfall of Marcos in 1986, people power, not elite power or persona, was the decisive factor in the toppling of the corrupt dictator. Then again, in 2001, people power proved to be the most crucial element in ousting Estrada, another corrupt president.

The very terms *elite democracy, cacique democracy, oligarchic democracy, patrimonial oligarchic state, weak state, strong oligarchy* and *boss rule* (or *boss-democracy*) do not portray or capture fully the real dynamics of Philippine politics. A number of adherents of the patrimonial/elite democracy framework, in fact, tend to minimize or virtually ignore the efforts of popular forces fighting against elite hegemony. "Nonoligarchic social forces," writes Hutchcroft (1998a:54), somewhat dismissively, "never seem to achieve the 'critical mass' necessary to force major overhaul of the system." Only in the very last paragraph of his book on bossism does Sidel (1999:154) acknowledge the hard work of NGO activists, investigative journalists, and labor, peasant and urban poor organizers in resisting the predations of local bosses, adding that "[s]uch efforts are amply deserving of both attention and support."

Not all of those who pursue the elite politics theme, however, present a one-sided or lopsided view. Franco provides a more balanced picture and an integrated analysis of both elite rule and the popular opposition to it. To make sure that the "clientelist electoral regime" does not appear to be capturing the essence of political dynamics in the pre- and postauthoritarian Philippines, she also presents social-movement-based efforts at democratization. Franco's account departs from the overly elite centered depictions of Philippine politics in the general run of the patrimonial/elite democracy model.

An Alternative Interpretation of Philippine Politics

The alternative paradigm of contested democracy is more appropriate for explaining Philippine politics today. It takes into account not just the workings of elite politics but also the actions of forces from below, thus building on previous work by scholars such as

Kerkvliet, Franco, and David Wurfel, who have tried to encompass a fuller range of ideas, organizational bases and cleavages beyond the patron-client, neocolonial, and elite democracy approaches.

A contested democracy approach acknowledges that colonial rule and postcolonial elite rule constitute a single continuous seam in Philippine politics yet contends that they are not the only important thread. The fight against hierarchical structures—the struggle for independence and popular empowerment or democracy from below—is the other major thread. The Filipinos' yearning for independence was manifested in the many wars and battles fought by the native inhabitants against Spanish colonization, the numerous revolts waged against Spain, the revolution of 1896, the Filipino-American War and Moro-American War, the campaign for Philippine independence, and the resistance against Japanese occupation. With the granting of independence in 1946, the efforts to assert Philippine sovereignty against foreign intervention or domination continued, but the focal point of the fight against hierarchy swung to social justice and popular empowerment against elite rule.

The two main strands in present-day Philippine politics—elite democracy and democracy from below—represent two competing concepts of democracy. Elite democracy, that is, a truncated or deficient form of formal democracy in which the oligarchic elite dominates, is basically what the elite seeks to maintain. During the colonial period, the Philippine elite fought for independence and democracy, as did the lower classes. After the United States granted independence, members of the elite were all for elections and parliamentary government . . . but not much more. The capitalists and landlords resisted demands for popular empowerment and social justice. When Marcos imposed martial law, large sections of the elite supported him, at least initially. "[T]hough alienated business elites helped to oust Marcos," notes Case (2002:263), "they afterward filled the presidency with one of their own, re-entered the Congress, and recaptured state agencies. They then thwarted the land reforms that had been mooted, as well as new deregulatory measures that threatened the Marcos-era monopolies they had inherited." The behavior of the Philippine elite basically confirms the thesis of Rueschemeyer et al. that classes benefiting from the status quo go as far as pushing for the installation (or restoration) of formal democracy—with deficiencies at that—but resist moves for a more substantive one.

The oligarchs and bosses of the post-Marcos era basically ride on the minimalist concept of democracy that equates democracy with elections. Such a concept is most useful and convenient for members of the elite for it allows them the greatest leeway to manipulate political structures and processes in their favor. Elections could well be regular and relatively free and fair—in general, candidates would be able to speak out, organize, and assemble freely. To win an election, the elite politician could bank on his or her economic and political clout and take advantage of deferential patron-client ties or, when he or she tires of the *compadrazgo* bit, simply resort to less personalistic forms of patronage. When this approach does not suffice, then perhaps vote buying or a bit of pressure would do the trick. In extreme situations, the boss-politician could resort to the full regalia of guns, goons, and gold. Once in power, *trapos* make the most of their positions to further enrich themselves and the oligarchs behind them through rents and plunder and to entrench themselves.

Philippine postcolonial history has been marked by powerful movements with nascent elements of democracy from below. Peasant struggles for land reform were at the core of the Huk rebellion and are at the core of the Maoist insurgency. The CPP's armed struggle is now one of the world's longest-running insurgencies. Fighting between the government and the insurgents has already claimed over 43,000 lives (Cabreza 2003). While many may abhor the CPP's ends and means, the intensity and longevity of its armed struggle indicate the depth of popular opposition not just to Marcos's authoritarian rule but also to elite rule in general. The struggles of the Muslims against oppression and discrimination lie at the core of the armed Muslim secessionist movement, which has been even more intense than the communist insurgency. About 120,000 people have been killed in the armed conflict between the government and Muslim rebels, and over 200,000 have been forced to flee to Sabah in Malaysia (Muslim and Cagoco-Guiam 1999:16).

In the toppling of Marcos, too much credit has often been given to intraelite conflict and too little to popular movements. Commendably, Franco (2001:chaps. 4–5) shows the prominent role played by the grassroots movements in the broad resistance to the Marcos dictatorship. In the mid-1970s, long before the assassination of Benigno Aquino, mass movements of workers, urban poor, and students had already reawakened in Metro Manila. In 1980–81, tens of thousands of both rural and urban masses took to the streets all over the country, especially at the time of the March 1981 plebiscite and the May 1981 presidential election. The Aquino assassination in August 1983 sparked what Franco calls a "civic uprising" involving not just the popular forces but also large sections of the middle class and the opposition elite. The people power revolt of 1986, albeit elite led, was primarily the culmination of the long struggle of popular forces against dictatorship, certainly not just the product of intraelite competition.

The long history of the struggle of subordinate classes and marginalized communities for popular empowerment and social justice indicates that for many Filipinos the minimalist concept of democracy does not suffice. Before and during Marcos's authoritarian rule, however, democracy from below remained nascent and somewhat adulterated, as the popular movements were influenced by Stalinist or Maoist parties that espoused "people's democracy" or "national democracy," a fig leaf for one-party dictatorship. Since the fall of Marcos, the influence of doctrinaire Marxism has declined, and democracy from below has taken a less adulterated form. Democracy from below stresses greater popular participation in decision making as well as social and economic equality, moving toward Huber et al.'s concept of participatory and social democracy and Laclau and Mouffe's concept of radical and plural democracy. It has found organized expression in many people's and nongovernmental organizations and social movements, as well as in new political parties and groups that oppose elite and *trapo* politics and espouse a "new politics." The advocates of democracy from below aim to bring Philippine democracy much closer to the classical meaning of *democracy*—"rule by the people." Democracy, in other words, is people power.

Nemenzo (1996a:56) explains the clash between the two concepts of democracy as follows.

> "Democracy" is the most abused word in the political vocabulary. It has been used to justify repression and elite rule. Lately, however,

> the narrow bourgeois definition that limits democracy to formal procedures for electing officials is being broadened in the usage of the popular movement. In the years to come, the ideological struggle will revolve around the conflict between two notions of democracy: elite rule and people's power.

In the sense that the very meaning and content of democracy are contested, contested democracy would be a more accurate interpretative framework of Philippine politics. The contested democracy framework remedies the rigid and elite-focused view of the elite democracy framework by integrating the democracy from below element. The oligarchs, caciques, bosses, and *trapos* are still very dominant in Philippine politics, but their predatory rule has been challenged and continues to be challenged by the poor and marginalized.

The Philippines would easily fall under the category that Huber et al. (1997:330, 337–39) describe as a "truncated" or "deficient" formal democracy, enjoying competitive elections and universal suffrage but suffering from weak accountability, uneven protection of civil and political rights, and patrimonial practices. Like the Latin American democracies, the Philippines is encountering mounting obstacles to the deepening of democracy: political and economic power concentrated in a few, weak state autonomy from dominant class interests, and international pressure for market-oriented but socially inequitable policies. In the Philippine democratic-deepening process, the contestation between the entrenched economic-political elite and the subordinate classes and marginalized communities is becoming a drawn-out struggle on the "missing" features or attributes of formal democracy and, more important, on more substantive democracy. As an alternative interpretation of Philippine politics, contested democracy graphically captures the dynamics and tensions within a deficient formal democracy that is seemingly unable to move forward.

Democracy from Below and the Deepening of Philippine Democracy in the Post-Marcos Era

The question of democracy from below—the efforts of forces identified with subordinate classes, communities, and groups in Philippine society to bring about popular empowerment and social justice—has grown in urgency. The Philippines is now perhaps one of the world's worst class-divided societies. As mentioned earlier, a small percentage of the population controls the country's economic resources, while the great majority live in poverty. Despite land reform, landholding became more concentrated between 1960 and 1990 (Gerson 1998:49). The gap between the rich and the poor, instead of narrowing, has turned into a gaping chasm. In 1957, the country's richest 20 percent received 7.5 times the share of the poorest 20 percent of the population; in 2000, this grew to 12.4 times.[20] Worse, the members of the elite flaunt their wealth and power—their huge, high-walled mansions with manicured lawns, their flashy cars and ostentatious parties, their bodyguards and security men with high-powered rifles—even as some of the urban poor scavenge and live in garbage dump sites, amid filth, stench, and fumes.[21] To help their families to live more decently or to provide a good education for their siblings or children, hundreds of thousands of Filipinos have had to seek jobs abroad, many becoming victims of abuses and human trafficking. The Philippines has become the world's "largest migrant nation" (Avendaño 2000).

Inexpedient economic policies adopted by the government, together with corruption and plunder by members of the oligarchic elite, have wrought great damage on the economy. Under pressure from the IMF and WB, the government has pursued various "structural adjustment programs" since the Marcos era, stressing first trade liberalization, then debt repayment, and finally free-market transformation marked by rapid deregulation, privatization, and trade and investment liberalization. Instead of spurring development, the programs have produced low and volatile growth and widening poverty and inequalities (Bello, Docena et al. 2004). Corruption has sapped the government's coffers. According to a study of the Economist Intelligence Unit, 20 to 30 percent of the national budget was being lost to graft every year (Cordingley 2001). In 1997, the Office of the Ombudsman of the Philippines estimated that the government lost $48 billion to corruption over the previous twenty years, exceeding the country's $40.6 billion foreign debt (World Bank 2000:3).[22] Over the past decade, the budget deficit and debt of the national government have reached such high levels that the Standard Chartered Bank of London has warned of a possible Argentina-type economic collapse (Bello, Nacpil and Nemenzo 2004).[23] Eleven economists of the University of the Philippines lay the blame for the huge budget deficit on large tax evaders, and also on the three main branches of the government, for their inaction or for abetting these tax evaders (De Dios et al. 2004:6). Bello, Lidy Nacpil, and Ana Marie Nemenzo (2004) cite the unilateral trade liberalization program pursued by neoliberal technocrats and the never-ending and rising payments to foreign creditors as among the key culprits. Thanks to neoliberalism and booty capitalism, the Philippines has degenerated from being Asia's second most developed postwar economy to the region's "sick man." Over the past thirty years, the Philippines' annual gross domestic product (GDP) growth has averaged a mere 3.1 percent, about half the rate of other Asian countries (Wallace 2004).[24]

Certain sections of the country's elite with strong connections in government have contributed greatly to environmental destruction and degradation. Large logging and mining firms have been identified as being among the chief culprits for what one environmental group has declared "the world's most rapid and massive deforestation."[25] Only 18 percent of the country remains forested, compared to 49 percent in 1950, and 70 percent in 1903 (Center for Environmental Concerns 1996; H. Thompson 2001). Deforestation has greatly magnified the disaster potential of natural calamities. Thousands have died in flash floods and landslides during typhoons in areas of rapid deforestation—more than six thousand in southern Leyte in November 1991 and more than one thousand in Quezon Province in December 2004 (H. Thompson 2001; Calumpita 2005). Tailings and heavy metals from corporate mines have also caused the destruction of many rivers and water bodies. Eleven out of fifty major saltwater fishing areas are overfished due mainly to the encroachment of commercial fishing vessels into shallow waters (Center for Environmental Concerns 1996). Among all the countries in Southeast Asia, the Philippines scored the lowest in environmental protection and conservation efforts according to a survey conducted by Yale University, Columbia University, and the World Economic Forum (Nazareno 2002).

The Muslims of Mindanao and other minority ethnic communities, who were considered inferior to Christianized Filipinos during the colonial period, continue to be treated like second-class citizens. The development disparity between "Christian" and "Muslim" areas has been particularly marked. The Muslim provinces are among the most economically backward in the entire country. In 2000, poverty incidence among families in the Autonomous Region of Muslim Mindanao (ARMM) stood at 66 per cent, far above the national average of 33.7 percent.[26]

For those whose attention had been glued, since the 1986 people power uprising, to the actions and manipulations of the oligarchs and *trapos,* the ouster of President Estrada through People Power II (or EDSA II) served as a reminder that democracy from below is still very much the other running thread in Philippine politics. Some Western observers waxed critical of people power, with one even commenting that "ousting presidents by revolution has become a bad national habit" and that people power was nothing more than "mob rule" (Spaeth 2001). What these observers did not seem to fathom is that a lot of democratic processes and structures, from the political party system to mechanisms for horizontal accountability and even the rule of law, have not yet been institutionalized, that they have remained such because *trapos* want to leave them that way for easy manipulation and that sometimes the only recourse the people have to check the abuses of the predatory elite is direct action.

Even EDSA III was to a significant extent a protest against elite politics. Most of the "great unwashed"[27] who gathered at EDSA in support of the deposed Estrada and later attacked Malacañang Palace came from the poorest of the poor. Among the masses, Estrada, a former "action" movie star, had many political supporters as well as fans. They harbored deep resentments against the rich and felt alienated from all the dirt and hypocrisy of elite politics. While people power did oust two corrupt presidents, one should nonetheless avoid taking a romanticized view of the Filipino masses. Not all explosions of protest involving large numbers of people can be regarded as genuine manifestations of people power. Given the longstanding role of patron-client ties in Philippine politics, large numbers of them remain vulnerable to clientelism and populism.

Throughout his long reel and political life, Estrada had shrewdly cultivated the image of a man fighting for the downtrodden. He victimized the poor he was supposed to be championing not just through patronage and corruption, but also through the socially inequitable policies he pursued as president.[28] Sadly, clientelist-populist appeals still worked at the time of EDSA III.

Since People Power I, the term *people* [or popular] *empowerment* has become very common, and it has been associated with POs, NGOs, and social movements. Societal organizations have mushroomed all over the country and ventured into a wide array of concerns. The Philippines is now reputed to have the third-largest NGO community in the developing world, behind Brazil and India, and probably the world's highest NGO density (Clarke 1998a:193; Hilhorst 2003:11). Many of the POs and NGOs are at the core of various social movements that have waged campaigns on land reform, labor relations, women's rights, peace, the U.S. military presence, globalization, and overseas Filipinos. Some have employed "programmatic demand making" to influence the crafting of national policies (Magadia 2003:19). A growing number have ventured into development work and promoted people's participation in governance, challenging traditional, top-down approaches.

Not to be discounted in such a class-divided country as the Philippines are forms of everyday resistance by ordinary people in rural villages and urban poor communities against the elite, capitalists, and the government (Kerkvliet 1990:16–17, 244–47 and 1995:418). Through forms that are often nonconfrontational, indirect, and somewhat hidden, the poor resist the claims on them by the rich and the powers that be and assert their own claims on what, they believe, rightfully belongs to them. Examples of everyday resistance against the rich include making jokes or uttering insulting remarks out of earshot, secretly taking rice or tools, footdragging, or taking flight. As noted by Kerkvliet, such nonconfrontational, indirect forms have sometimes served as the basis, in combination with other circumstances, for organized confrontational resistance. In a study of the rise and decline of the ND revolutionary movement in Davao in the 1980s, Christopher Collier (1997:283, 292) found that an indigenous idiom of exploitation and oppression with deep cultural and spiritual roots—a "little tradition" of everyday resistance—resonated quite well with the language of the ND movement. He contends, however, that the privileging of the "great tradition" of "Marxism-Leninism-Mao Zedong Thought" over vernacular expressions of resistance eventually prevented their organic articulation into what Gramsci has called a "collective national-popular will."

Of late, the adherents of democracy from below have ventured into the main playing field of the elite, an arena whose ins and outs, modus and tricks, the oligarchs have mastered in over a century of experience—elections. Doing battle with *trapos* in the electoral arena follows a simple logic. Explosions of people power and a strong and vibrant civil society are not enough if oligarchs and *trapos* still call the shots and make a mess of people's lives. Since the approval of the party-list system in 1995, PO/NGO-based forces have built new political parties representing marginalized sectors. Fledgling "new politics" parties such as Akbayan, Partido ng Manggagawa (PM), Alyansang Bayanihan ng mga Magsasaka, Manggagawang-Bukid at Mangingisda (ABA), Adhikain at Kilusan ng Ordinaryong Tao (AKO), Anak-Mindanao (AMIN) and Sanlakas have managed to win congressional seats and/or a number of local government posts.

Contested democracy, as an alternative paradigm of Philippine politics, highlights the element of agency apart from contestation. Formal liberal democracy, despite its deficiencies, provides the opportunity for subordinate classes and communities to push for popular empowerment, and, further, for a more equitable distribution of the country's wealth, and ultimately bring about a stable, more participatory and egalitarian democracy. Toward that end, one can expect in the years to come more expressions and explosions of that bad national habit—people power.

2

Threat to Democracy or Democratizing Force?

THE LEFT IN SOUTHEAST ASIA has declined and lost its "accustomed position as a strategic leader in the struggle for civil society." Thus conclude Kevin Hewison and Garry Rodan (1996:66) in a historical survey of the Southeast Asian Left. According to the two scholars, the Left played a pivotal role in the development of civil society ("non-state political space") from the 1920s to the 1970s through their efforts to build organizations of peasants, workers, and other under-privileged persons. Communist and socialist movements became most influential during the anticolonial and nationalist struggles and immediately after World War II. In the late 1940s, communists in some Southeast Asian countries launched or relaunched armed struggles. The outbreak of the cold war brought hard times for the Left. "[B]y the mid- to late-1950s, throughout Southeast Asia," Hewison and Rodan write (1996:54), "the Left, including anti-Communist socialists who had supported constitutional opposition, was being repressed or forced underground. In many places, repression resulted in an intensification of armed struggles." Over the next few decades, leftist movements in Southeast Asia suffered major reverses and even crushing defeats.[1]

By highlighting the role of the Southeast Asian Left in developing civil society, Hewison and Rodan tend to cast it in a positive light. This appears to run contrary to a widespread negative view of the Left as being a threat to democracy, a view engendered by the intense counterinsurgency campaigns waged by governments all over Southeast Asia against armed communist or "leftist" (read communist) movements.

As elsewhere in the region, the Left in the Philippines has been regarded in many quarters as constituting a threat to democracy or during Marcos's authoritarian rule as an impediment to the restoration of democracy. The "threat to democracy" view is premised on the facts that Filipino communists have been involved in two major insurgencies aimed at overthrowing the Philippine republican state and that their proffered alternative has been patterned after the one-party dictatorships of the Soviet bloc countries or China. The PKP figured prominently in the Huk rebellion of the late 1940s and early 1950s. In the late 1960s, the Maoist CPP launched a revolutionary armed struggle, which is ongoing and now one of the world's longest-running insurgencies. Some scholars, however, have countered or at least modulated the threat to democracy view, portraying Philippine communists as having been in the forefront of the anti-dictatorship movement for a long period (Rocamora 1994a:34) or as having contributed to peaceful democratic transition, albeit in an ironic or curious way (Anderson 1998b:277; Wurfel 1990:130).

In their assessment of the Left's decline in Southeast Asia, Hewison and Rodan make no exception for the Philippine Left. In this regard, they appear to concur with a number of scholars who take a much more critical view of the communists. Muthiah Alagappa (1995:31) has dismissed the Left as a declining threat, whereas Mark Thompson (1996:195) has relegated it to being a mere military nuisance.[2] The assessment that the Philippine Left has declined is largely based on the fact that the CPP and the CPP-aligned ND movements have gone through a long and deep crisis triggered by their being left out of the people power uprising in 1986 and culminating in a highly acrimonious internal party struggle and split in 1992–93.

Has the Philippine Left been a democratizing force or has it been a threat to democracy? Whichever it is, does it continue to be so? Has the Left truly been a strategic leader in the struggle for civil society? And is it indeed in decline and a marginalized force?

In this chapter, I put forward three points regarding the Left and democratization in the Philippines. First, the Philippine Left, far from being a spent force, is very much alive and has made a certain degree of recovery in recent years. Second, the traditional Left—the communist movement—has exhibited both democratic and undemocratic features but has been more of an undemocratic than a democratic or democratizing force. Its instrumentalization of POs/NGOs and the social movements negates its supposed leading role in the struggle for civil society. And, last, while the CPP remains a threat to Philippine democracy, new Left parties and groups that are more democratically oriented have emerged and are now making an earnest bid to challenge the hegemony of the oligarchic elite not just in civil society but also in the state arena—elections and governance. In the Philippines' contested democracy, the emergent leftist parties are endeavoring to become true representatives of democracy from below.

The Philippine Left

The term *left* has generally been used to refer to those who want change, favor more equality and resort to nontraditional, even radical or revolutionary means. For Hewison and Rodan (1996:42), the common denominator of the Left is "an emphasis on alternatives to the individualism of market relationships and a commitment to values which advance public and collective interests." In the Philippines, the term *left* has been associated with communist, socialist, and social democratic (SD) movements, parties, groups, and currents. In the light of the country's colonial history, Philippine leftists have strongly opposed colonial, "neocolonial," and "imperialist" rule or "foreign interference" in the country's political, economic, and cultural life. Although Philippine leftists generally refer to themselves as the Left and are regarded by other political forces as such, there appears to be no general consensus on who comprises the Right and the Center. The Left has tended to view all the major electoral parties as rightist, but none of these parties bills itself as such, and all have tended to avoid using the rightist, centrist or leftist labels to describe themselves.

The oldest leftist party in the Philippines is the PKP, which was founded in November 1930 amid growing peasant and labor unrest. The party, headed by labor leader Crisanto Evangelista, set as its objectives the "immediate, complete and absolute independence of the Philippines from the U.S., overthrow of American imperialism and domestic capital, betterment of living and working conditions of the working class, and establishment of a Soviet government in the country" (Saulo 1990:174). Less than a year after the PKP's founding, the American colonial regime declared it an illegal organization. A thaw in U.S.-Soviet relations in the face of the threat of fascism led to a lifting of the ban in the late 1930s. In March 1938, the PKP merged with the peasant-based Sosyalistang Partido ng Pilipinas (SPP) or Socialist Party of the Philippines, which was strong in Central Luzon, a hotbed of agrarian unrest. During the Japanese occupation (1942–45), the PKP and its allies formed the Hukbo ng Bayan laban sa mga Hapon (Hukbalahap) or People's Anti-Japanese Army—Huks, for short—which waged guerrilla war against the Japanese. After the war, the PKP, together with other progressive groups,[3] established the Democratic Alliance (DA), which fielded some candidates in the first postwar elections. Machinations of the Roxas administration barred six DA congressmen-elect, all from Central Luzon, from assuming their posts. Agrarian tensions in Central Luzon heated up once again, finally exploding into the Huk rebellion, with veterans of the Hukbalahap serving as the core of the Hukbong Mapagpalaya ng Bayan (HMB) or People's Liberation Army. After the defeat of the Huk rebellion, the PKP shifted to a parliamentary struggle.[4] In the 1960s, the PKP revived to some extent, successfully building new mass organizations. The party soon suffered splits, however. Maoist elements broke away in 1967 and eventually formed a new communist party. When the PKP decided to collaborate with Marcos shortly after the imposition of martial law, more dissidents left and formed the Marxist-Leninist Group (MLG). In 1974, the PKP entered into a "national unity" pact with Marcos, in which it agreed to disarm and disband the HMB. The decision proved politically costly. Marcos did release PKP political prisoners, grant amnesty to party members and allow PKP-aligned mass organizations to operate freely, but he did not substantially implement promised reforms, especially land reform.[5] The PKP lost much of its base to the CPP. Toward the end of authoritarian rule, the PKP became more critical of Marcos and again revived briefly.[6] Since the fall of the socialist regimes in Eastern Europe, the PKP and the PKP-aligned alliance, the Confederation for

Freedom and Democracy (Confreedem), have experienced great difficulty in expanding their ranks and they have not fielded candidates in elections.

Still widely considered to be the biggest single bloc within the Philippine Left are the CPP and the CPP-aligned ND movement. Established in December 1968, the CPP originated from the group of mostly young communists who had broken away from the PKP. Jose Maria Sison, the leader of the breakaway group, became its chairman. Denouncing "U.S. imperialism, feudalism and bureaucrat capitalism," the new party called for the revolutionary overthrow of the "reactionary" Philippine state. As an alternative to the "semicolonial and semifeudal" order, the CPP vowed to establish a "national democracy" or "people's democracy," an intermediate stage on the road to socialism. Shortly after the party's founding, some ex-Huks, led by Bernabe Buscayno, who were looking for alliances with workers, students, and progressive liberals, managed to link up with Sison. Thus, in March 1969, the new communist party came to have a guerrilla army, the New People's Army or NPA (Törnquist 1991:1684).[7] The CPP-NPA immediately launched a Mao-style protracted people's war. The ND network includes the "revolutionary united front"—National Democratic Front (NDF)—and thousands of open, legal ND organizations grouped under a coalition, the Bagong Alyansang Makabayan (Bayan) or New Patriotic Alliance.

The NDs first burst into the limelight in the early 1970s, when ND activists seized the initiative during the upsurge of the youth and student movement, which soon turned into more generalized protests among the country's lower classes and marginalized sectors. Through their militance, zeal, and organizational skill, the NDs spread throughout the archipelago. When Marcos imposed martial law in September 1972, the CPP-NPA immediately called for intensifying the armed struggle. In the early years, the Marcos dictatorship arrested, tortured, detained, or killed thousands of ND cadres and activists. In time, however, the movement adjusted to the repressive conditions and began a multipronged advance. Guerrilla zones were set up in almost all strategic mountainous areas. The urban mass movement revived and developed. The ND movement peaked during the first half of the 1980s. The NDs, operating both underground and above ground, proved to be the biggest, best organized, and most militant force within the broad anti-Marcos movement. The NDs, however, committed a grave error in the homestretch. Failing to see that a decisive showdown with the dictatorship loomed, the ND forces campaigned for a boycott of the 1986 "snap" presidential elections. Thus they boxed themselves out of the people power uprising that toppled Marcos and swept Corazon Aquino into the presidency. In the wake of the boycott fiasco, a furious debate ensued within the CPP and ND ranks. The NDs' image, sullied by the boycott error, was further tarnished by revelations of excesses committed in several "anti-infiltration campaigns," in which hundreds of cadres, activists, and guerrillas suspected of being government spies were arrested, tortured, and executed.[8]

In 1987, the NDs participated in elections for the first time, fielding candidates in the first post-Marcos congressional elections. Taking on the *trapos*, the ND electoral party, the Partido ng Bayan (PnB) or People's Party, campaigned on a platform of "new politics" (Vizmanos 1987). It was badly thrashed—all its senatorial candidates lost, and only two congressional candidates won.

The ND movement declined. Membership dipped, guerrilla zones contracted, and disagreements within the CPP deepened. By the late 1980s, revolutionary strategy became the main bone of contention within the party. There were those who adhered to the Maoist version of protracted people's war, which stressed the primacy of armed struggle over the mass movement. Others favored the Vietnamese version, which put "political struggle"—ranging from open legal struggle to insurrection—on the same footing as armed or military struggle. And still others pushed for a Nicaragua-style "insurrectional strategy," in which guerrilla warfare played a secondary role to the "insurrectional mass movement."[9] Unresolved differences over strategy and tactics and internal democracy were compounded, following the collapse of socialist states in Eastern Europe, by disagreements over the causes of the crisis of socialism and the vision of an alternative society. The main divide regarding the roots of socialism's crisis was between those who saw "revisionism" (departure from the "fundamental principles of Marxism-Leninism-Mao Zedong Thought") as being the main culprit, and those who put the blame on "Stalinism." The anti-revisionists visualized an alternative Philippine society that would adhere to the basic Maoist model featuring central planning, state ownership of the main means of production, and a "people's democratic government" with the CPP as the vanguard party (Liwanag 1992b). Viewing

Figure 2.1 *The debate within the CPP on the fall of socialism in Eastern Europe and the alternative Philippine society*

	Reaffirmists	Rejectionists
Cause of the downfall of socialism in Eastern Europe and the Soviet Union	Eastern European countries were no longer socialist; they had turned capitalist. Ruling communist parties in Eastern Europe had fallen into 'revisionism' (i.e., turned against the basic principles of Marx, Lenin, Stalin, and Mao).	Eastern European countries had developed a distorted form of socialism: Stalinism.
	The basic principles of Marxism-Leninism-Mao	The Stalinist distortions of Marxism were:
	1. central planning, state ownership of factories, and so on; and	1. command economy and
	2. people's democracy (with democratic centralism and the CPP as the vanguard party)	2. one-party dictatorship.
Rectification	Reaffirm basic principles of Marx, et al., combat revisionism	Reject Stalinism
Vision of an alternative society in the Philippines	Features:	Features:
	1. central planning; state ownership of factories, and so on;	1. mixed economy and
	2. people's democracy (with democratic centralism and the CPP as the vanguard party)	2. pluralist democracy

the "command economy" and the "one-party dictatorship" as "Stalinist distortions," the anti-Stalinists envisaged a "mixed economy" and a "pluralist democracy" (Editorial Staff, *Ang Bayan* 1991).[10]

The debates came to a head in early 1992, when Sison, who was living in exile in Utrecht, the Netherlands, and whose resumption of the party chairmanship was being disputed, put out a controversial document entitled "Reaffirm Our Basic Principles and Rectify the Errors," in which he lashed out at critics of protracted people's war and the antirevisionist line. Sison asserted that the party's longstanding strategy should be credited for the gains achieved through the years. He claimed that setbacks suffered by the party in recent years were due to the influences of a wrong line—a line of "urban insurrectionism" and "military adventurism," as well as "modern revisionism," allegedly propagated by "detractors" of protracted people's war. The CPP chairman came to the defense of Stalin and attacked "Gorbachovites" within the party. To eradicate "erroneous" influences, Sison called for a return to the fundamental principles of the Maoist line and the launching of a "rectification campaign," including the removal of those "incorrigibles" persisting in promoting "deviations" (Liwanag 1992a).[11] Sison succeeded in having "Reaffirm" approved by the tenth plenum of the Central Committee in mid-1992, which characterized the internal ideological struggle as a "two-line struggle" between revolution and counterrevolution (Party Organizations in the Visayas 1993; Rocamora 1994a:120).

All hell broke loose. Critics of "Reaffirm" vehemently objected to both its content and the process through which it had been made. The tenth plenum itself was questioned by a large number of party members for the lack of a quorum and adequate democratic discussions within the party organization prior to approval of major draft papers. Both reaffirmists and rejectionists came out with thick, highly polemical position papers.[12] The debates spilled out into the public arena in December 1992 when Sison, from his home in Utrecht, faxed press statements to Manila, accusing three former members of the CPP Executive Committee of being "renegades" and part of the government's intelligence and psychological warfare scheme to destroy the CPP (*Philippine Daily Inquirer* 1992). In the months that followed, Sison and his followers stepped up their verbal attacks against "military agents," "terrorists," and "counter-revolutionaries." In response, the rejectionists denounced Sison for being a "dictator" and "degenerate communist" and for his "Stalinist style of leadership" and "dogmatism" (Branigin 1993, Timonera 1993a).

In less than a year after the tenth plenum, Sison won over the majority of the party's national and regional committee leaders to his side. Sison and his followers removed large numbers of CPP members from the party roster through such means as "preventive suspension," "disenfranchisement," "reorganization," "streamlining" and outright expulsion. In reaction, dissenting units declared their autonomy from, or rejection of, Sison's "Stalinist faction" in the latter half of 1993, in effect formalizing the split within the revolutionary movement.[13] Many more members left or became passive. The NPA, NDF, and the open ND mass organizations and alliances also split, mainly along the same regional and sectoral lines, with the reaffirmists and their allies also having the upper hand numerically on a nationwide scale.[14]

For two years, the reaffirmists and the rejectionists engaged in highly acrimonious open polemics. A major factor in the acrimony was the reaffirmists' adoption of the "revolution versus counterrevolution" framework. By CPP practice, a "counterrevolutionary" or "enemy agent" is a legitimate target for physical elimination. The outbreak of violence became very possible in the light of pronouncements made by a CPP spokesman in December 1993 and again in April 1994 that four leading members of the opposition—Romulo Kintanar, Filemon Lagman, Ricardo Reyes, and Arturo Tabara—would be tried by "people's courts" and that they were likely to receive the death penalty (Estella 1993; *Philippine Daily Inquirer* 1994). Outside observers, including left-leaning political personalities, academics, and newspaper columnists, as well as members of international NGOs and solidarity groups, urged the two sides to exercise restraint and sobriety.[15]

Several communist or workers' parties have emerged from the ranks of the rejectionists, all of which now claim to reject Stalinism and Maoism.[16] The rejectionist parties have put more stress on the political or mass struggle rather than on armed or military struggle or have suspended or abandoned the latter altogether. The most prominent rejectionist parties are as follows.

- Rebolusyonaryong Partido ng Manggagawa—Pilipinas (RPM-P) or Revolutionary Workers Party, which was formally established in May 1998 and originally consisted of former units of the CPP's Visayas Commission and some cadres from the former Manila-Rizal Regional Committee;
- Partido ng Manggagawang Pilipino (PMP) or Filipino Workers' Party, set up in January 1999, which now has the main chunk of the CPP's former Manila-Rizal Committee and National United Front Commission;[17]
- Rebolusyonaryong Partido ng Manggagawa—Mindanao (RPM-M), the CPP's former Central Mindanao Regional Committee and now a section of the Fourth International, whose attempted fusion with RPM-P forces fell through.

Somewhat allied with the rejectionists is the Marxista-Leninistang Partido ng Pilipinas (MLPP), which was originally with the reaffirmists—part of the CPP's Central Luzon regional organization—but bolted out of the CPP in late 1997. The RPM-P, RPM-M, and MLPP have guerrilla groups, but only MLPP is still actively engaged in armed struggle. The RPM-P has signed an initial peace agreement with the government, and the RPM-M is engaged in peace talks. The electoral party Partido ng Manggagawa (PM) or Workers' Party and the multi-sectoral alliance Sanlakas are aligned with PMP; Alab Katipunan, with RPM-P; Anak-Mindanao (AMIN) with RPM-M; and Kilusan para sa Pambansang Demokrasya (KPD) or the Movement for Nationalism and Democracy with MLPP.[18]

The Partido Demokratiko-Sosyalista ng Pilipinas (PDSP) is the main SD party in the Philippines. It is headed by Norberto Gonzales, Jr., who currently sits in the Arroyo Cabinet as national security adviser. The SD movement emerged in the Philippines in the late 1960s when young activists and progressive churchpeople belonging to reformist organizations saw the need not just to address the country's social ills but also to check the spread of communism. In the early 1970s, the SDs competed with the NDs for the leadership of the social movements. After Marcos imposed martial law, the SDs,

Figure 2.2 *Major leftist parties in the Philippines*

Communist/National Democratic (ND) Tradition	
Marxist-Leninist-Maoist	**Marxist-Leninist**
Underground party: CPP (Communist Party of the Philippines) Guerrilla army: NPA (New People's Army) Allied legal parties: Bayan Muna, Anakpawis, Gabriela	Legal Party: PKP (Partido Komunista ng Pilipinas)
Underground party: MLPP (Marxist-Leninist Party of the Philippines) Guerrilla army: RHB (Rebolusyonaryong Hukbong Bayan) Allied legal party: None	Underground party: PMP (Partido ng Manggagawang Pilipino) Guerrilla army: None Allied legal parties: PM (Partido ng Manggagawa), Sanlakas
	Underground party: RPM-P (Rebolusyonaryong Partido ng Manggagawa—Pilipinas)* Guerrilla army: RPA-ABB (Revolutionary People's Army—Alex Boncayao Brigade) Allied legal party: Alab Katipunan
	Underground party: RPM-M (Rebolusyonaryong Partido ng Manggagawa—Mindanao)* Guerrilla army: RPA-M (Revolutionary People's Army—Mindanao) Allied legal party: AMIN (Anak-Mindanao)

*Peace negotiations with the Philippine government are ongoing. The RPM-P has signed preliminary agreements with the government on "confidence-building" measures.

Figure 2.2 *(continued)*

Mixed (ND/SD/Independent Socialist) Tradition	Social Democratic (SD) Tradition	
Socialist	**Progressive**	**Social Democratic**
Legal party: Akbayan Formed by four political blocs: • Popular democrats (ND trad.) • Bisig (Independent socialist) • Pandayan (SD trad.) • Siglaya (ND trad.)	Legal party: ABA/AKO (Alyansang Bayanihan ng mga Magsasaka, Manggagawang-Bukid at Mangingisda/Adhikain at Kilusan ng Ordinaryong Tao), merger of a peasants' party with an urban poor party.	Legal party: PDSP (Partido Demokratiko-Sosyalista ng Pilipinas)
	Legal party: Abanse Pinay, a women's party	

(Data from interviews and discussions with leaders of leftist parties) alarmed that all channels for legitimate dissent were being closed, contemplated armed resistance. The PDSP was established in May 1973 with Gonzales and a Jesuit priest, Romeo Intengan, as its top leaders (Hofileña 2002a:10). The new party described itself as "nationalist, democratic, socialist, revolutionary." Its basic ideological foundation was "authentic humanism," which emphasized the essential equality among human beings, the social nature of man and the universal purpose of property. In 1976, PDSP set up an armed group, Sandigan, which engaged in a few guerrilla actions in Southern Tagalog and southeastern Mindanao. In the 1978 elections for the Interim Batasang Pambansa (IBP), Marcos's Interim National Parliament, the SDs managed to wrest control of the campaign machinery of the broad opposition alliance, Lakas ng Bayan (Laban) or Strength of the People from the NDs (Partido Demokratiko-Sosyalista ng Pilipinas 1982:6–8, 19–20). After forging ties with the MNLF, PDSP managed to have a small contingent of its guerrilla "army" train under MNLF auspices in Sabah, Malaysia.[19]

Independent of PDSP, members of another SD group, Kapulungan ng mga Sandigan ng Pilipinas (Kasapi) or Assembly of Pillars of the Philippines linked up with certain leaders of the traditional opposition. Together, they hatched up and carried out symbolic acts of terror, hoping to ignite an insurrection. The military, however, busted both the first urban guerrilla group, dubbed by the Marcos media as the "Light-a-Fire-Movement," which had engaged in arson, and the second insurrectionary group, the April 6 Liberation Movement, which had moved up to bombings (M. Thompson 1995:chap. 5).

In 1982, some SDs, mostly from Mindanao, together with their allies established the Partido ng Demokratikong Pilipino (PDP) or Filipino Democratic Party, a legal, grassroots-based, and reform-oriented party that espoused a "democratic socialist" ideology. Lacking national projection, PDP merged the following year with Laban, which was dominated by better known and more seasoned politicians. It soon lost its character as a nontraditional party (Gutierrez 1994b:99–100; Abao 1997:277).

The SDs expanded rapidly once again with the groundswell of the antidictatorship movement following the assassination of opposition leader Benigno Aquino in 1983. When many allies of the NDs withdrew from Bayan in 1985, the SDs organized a rival coalition, Bansang Nagkaisa sa Diwa at Layunin (Bandila) or Nation United in Spirit and Purpose. The SDs campaigned for Corazon Aquino in the 1986 polls and took an active part in the people power uprising. For their role at EDSA, some SD leaders were appointed to government positions.

With the restoration of democracy, SD formations such as Kasapi and Pandayan para sa Sosyalistang Pilipinas (Pandayan) or Forging a Socialist Philippines intensified their organizing efforts at the grassroots level and among students and professionals. In November 1988, PDSP, Kasapi, Pandayan, and other SD groups forged the Demokratikong-Sosyalistang Koalisyon (DSK) or Democratic-Socialist Coalition. This quickly fell apart, however, as Kasapi and Pandayan increasingly resented PDSP's attempts at "domination" and its "cooptation" by the government. Although the PDSP regards itself as a leftist party, other leftist parties and groups no longer consider it to be such and in fact see it as being just another *trapo* party.[20]

Two new parties come from the SD tradition: the ABA-AKO coalition and Abanse Pinay (Advance Filipina). The ABA-AKO is the coalition of a peasant party-list organization—Alyansang Bayanihan ng mga Magsasaka, Manggagawang-Bukid at Mangingisda (ABA) or the Cooperative Alliance of Peasants, Farm Workers and Fishers—and an urban poor organization—Adhikain at Kilusan ng Ordinaryong Tao (AKO) or Aspirations and Movement of the Common People. It seeks "to liberate the peasantry and the urban poor from the shackles of domination, exploitation and oppression through enactment of appropriate legislative measures" (Commission on Elections 2004:6). The ABA's leaders are identified with the Federation of Free Farmers, the biggest confederation of peasant organizations in the pre-martial-law era. Abanse Pinay is a party-list organization that aims to advance women's rights and welfare to "mainstream" women in politics and to fight for legislation that addresses gender and women's concerns (Jimenez-David 2003:5; Sarenas 1999:7).

Akbayan is a mix of various progressive groups and political tendencies. Four political blocs were involved in its formal establishment in January 1998: Bukluran para sa Ikauunlad ng Sosyalistang

Isip at Gawa (Bisig) or the Federation for the Advancement of Socialist Theory and Praxis, which consisted of ex-PKP members, ex-NDs, ex-SDs, Christian socialists, and "nonaligned" activists who wanted to develop a socialist program distinct from that of the NDs and SDs; the SD group Pandayan; the "popular democrats" or "popdems," a tendency within the ND movement that sought to put emphasis on "popular empowerment" after EDSA I; and Siglo ng Paglaya (Siglaya) or Century of Freedom, a rejectionist group that characterized itself as the "democratic bloc" of the ND movement.[21] Siglaya has since broken up; a section of it, now called Padayon, has taken its place in Akbayan. The popdems dissolved themselves as a political bloc in 1999.

The Revival of the Left

In arguing that the Left in modern Southeast Asia has lost its leading position in the struggle for civil society,[22] Hewison and Rodan (1996:42–43, 58–62, 66) attribute its decline to the "economic triumph of capitalism" in the region, which stands in contrast to "the negative example of state-led socialist experiments around the world." Another factor cited is the delinking of nationalism from socialism and the successful appropriation of nationalist ideology for capitalist development in the region. A range of liberals and social reformers coming from new social forces belonging to different classes—the bourgeois, middle and working classes—is said to have taken the place of communists and socialists in leading the development of civil society. Hewison and Rodan cite NGOs, whose personnel are often drawn from the middle classes, as being among the "new political oppositions" and as being critical avenues for expanding nonstate political space. To a significant extent, Hewison and Rodan echo the view of scholars who regard the middle class as the main bearer of democratization, and who, in the case of the Philippines, even characterize People Power I and II as middle-class revolts (Huntington 1991:97–98; Adriano 2003a:4; Landé 2001:101).

Hewison and Rodan may have spoken a bit too soon about the Philippine Left. Through the late 1980s and most of the 1990s, the Left in the Philippines was indeed at an ebb. Not anymore. The Philippine Left has revived. In 2001, activists of Bayan, Akbayan, PM, Sanlakas, and other left-wing organizations were among those in the forefront of the huge rallies and mass actions that culminated in People Power II and the ouster of the boss-president Estrada. In recent years, CPP-NPA guerrilla actions have picked up again, although they seem not to have yet reached the peak levels of the 1980s. The United States and other Western states, as well as of the Arroyo government, have tried to isolate the CPP-NPA internationally by labeling it a "terrorist" organization. They have also tried to cut off its funding sources by freezing its bank assets. These "counterterrorist" measures have proven largely ineffective. The Philippine government, despite tagging the CPP-NPA as terrorist, has been forced to resume peace negotiations with its "united front" arm, the NDF. The holding of talks in Oslo, with the Norwegian government playing a virtual mediating role, constitutes a major diplomatic gain for the NDF. In the 2001 and 2004 elections, the CPP-NPA, asserting its de facto control of guerrilla zones, intensified its collection of "permit to campaign" (PTC) fees from candidates wishing to campaign in these zones. The government could not do much to prevent the CPP-NPA from extorting millions of pesos through PTC. Meanwhile, the ND electoral party Bayan Muna topped the 2001 and 2004 party-list ballot, both times getting the maximum three congressional seats allowed in the party-list system. Two other ND groups, Anakpawis and Gabriela, also won party-list seats in 2004. Other leftist groups made it to the winning column in the party-list vote in 1998, 2001, and / or 2004: Akbayan, PM, Sanlakas, AMIN, ABA-AKO, and Abanse Pinay. Apart from their party-list victories, Akbayan, Bayan Muna, and Sanlakas have won some government posts at the *barangay* (village), municipal, city, and provincial levels. The PDSP has garnered a congressional seat through the district system. In the pursuit of the "people's agenda," leftist parties and groups, as well as POs and NGOs identified with different strands of the Left, have kept up the pressure on the government through the "parliament of the streets."

A major factor in the resilience of the Philippine Left is that capitalism in the Philippines has not been as successful as in the other modern countries of Southeast Asia. Over the past few decades, in fact, the Philippines has lagged behind its neighbors in economic growth. Moreover, most Filipinos have not enjoyed the economic benefits of capitalist development. As mentioned earlier, great numbers of Filipinos live in poverty: 39.4 percent of the population according to official government statistics but as much as 74 percent according to "self-rated poverty" surveys.[23] Because of the Philippines' laggard economic growth, the state and the capitalist class have not had as much success as in neighboring countries in appropriating nationalist ideology for capitalist development. Conversely, Philippine leftist parties and groups, which have placed a good part of the blame for the country's ills on global capitalism, imperialism, or neoliberal globalization, have had some success in projecting themselves as the genuine nationalists.

Another factor is the more sophisticated character of the CPP/NDS, long a powerful force in the Philippine Left. From the 1950s until the 1970s, Maoism was a major force in the Left in Southeast Asia. At one time or another within this period, in fact, communist parties that adhered to Maoism or were strongly influenced by it became a major or even dominant force in the Left in Burma, Cambodia, Indonesia, Malaya / Malaysia, the Philippines, Singapore, and Thailand. Adhering to Mao's doctrine of "encircling the cities from the countryside," the communist parties in Burma, Malaya, North Kalimantan (in Borneo), and Thailand built guerrilla zones and waged guerrilla warfare in the countryside and maintained only a skeletal support network in the cities. They remained largely rural insurgencies and were eventually crushed or terribly debilitated by massive government counterinsurgency campaigns (Hobday 1986:229–70). A major factor in the implosion of the Communist Party of Thailand (CPT), aside from its ill-considered attacks on the monarchy and the Sino-Vietnamese split, was its refusal to modify strategy by adopting the more mixed urban-rural approach successfully used by the Vietnamese (Marks 1991:374–75). In multiethnic Malaya and Burma, the pro-Beijing communist parties were further hamstrung by their inability to expand beyond a single ethnic community (Hobday 1986:230, 256). The Partai Komunis Indonesia (PKI) or Indonesian Communist Party followed Mao's party and united front principles, but, in contrast to its Burmese, Malay and Thai counterparts, engaged in purely parliamentary struggle. When the Suharto regime resorted to extreme repression, the PKI cadres and activists had no rural guerrilla areas to escape to and were massacred and wiped out. The CPP has not restricted itself to waging a rural insurgency nor to engaging in a purely parliamentary struggle. The party has constantly avowed the primacy of armed struggle over legal, political struggle and of the rural over the urban arena. In actual practice, however, the political struggle and the urban arena have often taken equal or higher priority. Apart from waging armed struggle in the countryside, the NDs have engaged in open, legal, mass movements mainly in major urban centers and have ventured into open coalitions, as well as revolutionary alliances; women's, indigenous peoples', and environmental issues; liberation theology; urban guerrilla warfare; international work (including "diplomatic struggle" and organizing overseas Filipinos); peace negotiations; and, since 1986, electoral struggle and work in government.

Revulsion against elite and *trapo* politics is another factor in the Left's revival. In 1987, the slogan of a new politics (as opposed to *trapo* politics) did not really catch on. Since then, the call for a new politics seems to have brought some support to the Left, not just in mass campaigns and mobilizations but also, to an appreciable extent, in the electoral sphere.

The assertion that the middle class has assumed the leading role in the struggle for democratization in the Philippines is highly disputable. The middle class did have a sizable and very visible presence in People Power I and may have even comprised the majority at EDSA in People Power II. But most of those at People Power I and in the mass protests all over the country leading up to both People Power I and II came from the lower classes.[24] In both events, it was not the middle class but the elite that exercised effective leadership. This was clearly borne out by the results: the establishment (in EDSA I) and perpetuation (in EDSA II) of an elite-dominated democracy. The leading figures in both events, Corazon Aquino and Gloria Macapagal Arroyo, were not from the middle class. They were members of the elite—of powerful political families in fact. As Case (2002:14) correctly points out, after the Philippine middle class had helped to end authoritarian rule, it then acquiesced to what some analysts have called "oligarchic" democracy.

"Flight" rather than "fight" perhaps better characterizes the mood of a good number of middle-class Filipinos. The Philippine middle class remains small—a mere 10 to 12 percent of the country's working population (Bautista 2000:1).[25] The main reason for this is that many middle-class Filipinos, appalled with the country's downward drift, have opted to seek better lives abroad. It is estimated that half of the Philippine middle class lives in the Philippines and the other half abroad (Carandang 2004). The *International Herald Tribune* (Perlez 2002) reports that educated Filipinos, disillusioned with the country's poor economy, rampant corruption and crime, and terrible pollution, have indeed been leaving the Philippines in droves. "For those who have lost faith, the answer is going overseas," says Sheila Coronel of the Philippine Center for Investigative Journalism. "You don't join a political organization, you line up at an embassy."

While NGOs with personnel coming mainly from the middle class have indeed mushroomed, independent organizations of the working masses—POs—have likewise proliferated, and through them the masses have directly fought for the their rights and welfare. Hewison and Rodan (1996:61) themselves admit that a vigorous independent labor movement continues to exist in the Philippines. Furthermore, many leaders and members of POs and NGOs, including organizations of mainly middle-class professionals, maintain close links with leftist parties and groups and look to them for political direction or leadership. Unlike the situation in Thailand where many former CPT and leftist cadres turned their energies to NGOs and shunned further involvement in radical politics (Ungpakorn 2003:chap. 10; Chutima 1994:146–47; Maisrikrod 1997:155), leftists in the PO/NGO network in the Philippines have remained active in, or supportive of, leftist parties.

Democratic and Undemocratic Features

Historically, the Philippines' two main communist parties—the PKP and the CPP—have always regarded the country's democracy as not being a genuine one. They have described the Philippines, in fact, as a "fascist" or "reactionary" dictatorship of feudal landlords and comprador capitalists still very much under the thumb of U.S.

imperialism. Both the PKP and the CPP have asserted that genuine democracy cannot be achieved as long as the country remains under neocolonial rule and continues to have grave disparities in the distribution of its wealth and resources between the elite few and the toiling masses. Armed revolution, leaders of these parties have argued, is the only way to defeat the imperialists, landlords, and compradors, and bring about economic and political democracy (Saulo 1990:163; Guerrero 1979a:chap. 3).

In place of "farcical" democracy, the PKP envisaged a New Democracy, a state that would be in the hands of the "democratic classes" (peasants, workers, intellectuals, and the national bourgeoisie) and would pave the way for socialism and the "dictatorship of the proletariat" (Santayana 1950:60–62; Kerkvliet 1977:224). The CPP has advocated a people's democracy—the People's Democratic Republic of the Philippines—like Mao's People's Republic of China and Kim Il Sung's Democratic People's Republic of Korea. The existing "joint reactionary dictatorship" of the exploiting classes would be replaced with a "united front dictatorship" (patterned after Mao's "people's democratic dictatorship")—"a joint dictatorship of all revolutionary classes and strata under the leadership of the proletariat" (Guerrero 1979a:162). Both the PKP and the CPP saw themselves as the leading detachment of the working masses and believed that this vanguard role would continue after revolutionary victory (Santayana 1950:62; Partido Komunista ng Pilipinas 1996:chap. 4; Guerrero 1979a:chap. 3). The "socialist" and "people's" democracies of the Soviet Union, China and other communist states have, of course, now been discredited as having been or being one-party dictatorships. In 1989–92, the "socialist democracies" of Eastern Europe fell one after another in quick succession, as the masses rose up against their "vanguards."

When the PKP was founded in 1930, it was not actually engaged in armed struggle against the state. It can be said that the Philippine communist movement could have evolved differently, that is, taken the parliamentary road, eschewed armed struggle, and accepted political pluralism, as the Eurocommunists did. But then it could very well be argued that repression by state forces and the private armies and goons of powerful political families left the communist forces with no other choice but to take up arms. Such repression reached extreme levels during periods of authoritarian rule—the Japanese occupation and the Marcos dictatorship. Even during the periods of "colonial" or postcolonial democracy, the communists and their supporters suffered repression and unwarranted exclusion from the democratic process: the banning of the PKP and the incarceration of its leaders in 1931; the harassment of Huks in 1945 and the nonproclamation of winning DA candidates in 1946; and, at a time when the PKP had already given up the armed struggle, the enactment of the Anti-subversion Law in 1957, outlawing the PKP and similar organizations.[26]

As the agents for the establishment of a one-party dictatorship, the PKP and the CPP could be dismissed as having been nothing more than undemocratic forces and threats to democracy (or the restoration of democracy). Such an assessment, however, needs to be qualified. The struggles the PKP and CPP waged toward the attainment of power exhibited an intriguing combination of democratic and undemocratic elements, and the two parties actually played both positive and negative roles vis-à-vis the democratization process in the Philippines.

The contribution of the PKP and the CPP, together with their supporters and allies, in furthering democracy and democratization is far from inconsequential. In 1946–86, the PKP and the CPP, together with their supporters and allies, steadfastly and consistently struggled against economic and political domination by the country's oligarchic elite and espoused a more egalitarian society. They promoted popular participation and empowerment, organizing and mobilizing the masses, especially at the grassroots level, for various economic, political, and social endeavors—from local self-help projects all the way to nationwide mass protest actions. In the dark years of Marcos's martial law, the NDs built open, legal mass organizations, legal programs and legal institutions despite the dictatorship's moves to restrict the right of free association and to muzzle dissent. After the Aquino assassination, the NDs, together with the SDs and other leftist groups, built a myriad of "cause-oriented groups" and coalitions that served as the backbone of the mass movement in the waning years of the dictatorship.[27] The legal mass organizations, legal programs and cause-oriented groups were among the precursors of what are now known as POs and NGOs, which have proliferated all over the country and are involved in a wide range of concerns—development work, sectoral issues, health, human rights, environment, etc. Although many of today's POs and NGOs are not aligned with the left, a good part of the credit for their flourishing belongs to the left.

The NDs played a crucial role in the restoration of democracy in 1986. In their efforts to topple the Marcos dictatorship and replace it with a CPP-dominated "united front dictatorship," the NDs waged guerrilla warfare, organized countless mass protest actions all over the country, and were indeed at the forefront of the antidictatorship struggle. Such fierce resistance weakened the dictatorship and greatly helped erode its domestic and international support. The NDs' political and military struggles helped set the stage for the Marcos regime's eventual ouster through people power. The country's oligarchic elite and Washington had no choice but to agree to a return to democratic rule. Wurfel (1988:130) observes: "The [communist] insurgency in a curious way contributed to a peaceful democratic transition. It catalyzed unity in the opposition elite and motivated American support for liberalization because Marcos seemed to be feeding the fires of revolution, not controlling them." Anderson (1998b:277) credits the revolutionary Left with being "the first and foremost factor" in the downfall of the Marcos dictatorship. "The rapid growth of the CPP-NPA," he explains, "so alarmed the United States that it finally turned against Marcos and eventually hauled him into golden imprisonment in Hawaii." Thus, in an ironic twist, the NDs' bid to set up a one-party dictatorship ultimately and significantly contributed to an unintended outcome: the restoration of democracy, albeit a deficient one.

Outweighing the democratic or democratizing features of the PKP and the CPP, however, are their undemocratic features. Besides the undemocratic character of their alternative to the current Philippine state and society, the PKP and the CPP have been undemocratic in their internal workings and their relations with POs, NGOs, and other political forces.[28] Structures within have tended to be top-down, hierarchical, even patriarchal.[29] Party leaders have made important decisions, such as implementing the 1986 boycott, without the benefit of free and thorough discussion and debate involving the entire party organization. Through the party's "political officer" system, representatives of a higher organ "give general and particular guidance" to lower organs. As the party newspaper itself admits, some political officers tend to merely transmit the higher organ's policies and plans and others do not sufficiently explain the general calls (Editorial Staff, *Ang Bayan* 1985:6). Party-aligned mass organizations, POs, and NGOs, especially those established on the initiative of the party, have tended to lack or lose organizational integrity. The CPP strategy has been said to be "totalizing" in the sense that "it viewed all other significant struggles, such as those for women's rights, minority rights, and environmental well-being, as aspects of the broader struggle against fascism and imperialism, which was 'central' and thus claimed strategic priority" (Bello 1993:13).

When the CPP-aligned NDs became the single biggest force in the antidictatorship movement in the early and mid-1980s, they tried to impose their views on other progressive parties and groups, particularly the much smaller formations, and developed vanguardist airs and illusions.[30] In their grim determination to seize power and win total victory, the PKP and CPP at times resorted to maneuver and manipulation, and even to intimidation and terror, in relating not only with their enemies and tactical allies but with their mass base and supporters as well.[31] Such undemocratic practices were partly conditioned or reinforced by the conspiratorial style of work of a revolutionary party forced to go underground and by the military style of a guerrilla army.[32]

One sees in these undemocratic practices the portents of things to come if and when orthodox communists do get to power (see Slovo 1989). The communist party, having failed to acquire the democratic habit in its internal workings while out of power, would experience great difficulty imbibing it in the course of running the country. As the experiences of socialist states ruled by Stalinist parties have shown, soon after achieving victory, the communist party enshrines its vanguard role in the country's constitution and relegates all other parties, if they are allowed to exist at all, to permanent subordinate status. Democratic features such as the active political involvement of popular organizations do not simply vanish. In fact, soon after revolutionary victory, the communist party can very well promulgate radical changes for popular participation at the grassroots level. Over the years, however, as the party wins election after election and entrenches itself in power, the undemocratic features overwhelm and virtually obliterate the democratic elements. Once vibrant popular organizations become mere appendages and mouthpieces of the party and the state. In China, as pointed out by Georg Sørensen (1993:22–23), the communist government pushed structural reforms and systems of local participation and succeeded in bringing about democratic changes at the microlevel in its early years. As time passed, however, the state's centralizing tendencies negated them and authoritarianism increasingly became the order of the day.

In the case of the CPP, probably the most damning proof of its undemocratic ways are its gross violations of international humanitarian law. Foremost among these have been the horrendous purges conducted by the party in the 1980s against suspected enemy spies within its ranks. Between 1982 and 1989, various leading committees of the CPP launched massive campaigns to rid the party of "deep-penetration agents" (DPAs). Hundreds—possibly even thousands—of innocent cadres and activists were brought to makeshift prison camps, tortured and summarily killed by their own comrades.[33] Despite strong criticism from international human rights groups, the CPP has persisted in such practices as summary executions and kangaroo "people's courts."[34] In imposing and collecting "revolutionary taxes" on landlords, business enterprises, and small farmers, the CPP-NPA has often resorted to coercion or violence. Businesses refusing to pay risk having their property destroyed, their operations disrupted, or even their owners killed (Lawyers Committee for Human Rights 1990:7; Damazo 2003:16–18). According to the party newspaper, the NPA conducts economic sabotage actions "to mete punishment to those who defy payment of revolutionary taxes, maltreat their workers and employees and whose business adversely affects the ecology and people's livelihood" (Editorial Staff, *Ang Bayan* 1987a:14). The CPP-NPA has also engaged in kidnapping for ransom and common criminal acts. In January 2003, in an attempt to justify its assassination of former NPA chief Kintanar, the CPP blamed him for kidnappings-for-ransom, armed bank robberies and hold-ups, thereby inadvertently admitting that the CPP-NPA had been involved in these criminal activities (Quimpo 2003). As growing evidence shows, the Plaza Miranda bombing of 1971 may well be included in the CPP's record of heinous acts.[35] Not yet in power, the CPP already has its hidden crimes, official truths, and official lies. What can one expect of it when it reaches the pinnacle of power?

An Instrumental View of Democracy

Kenneth Roberts (1998:18–19) notes that in Latin American countries the Left's view of democracy changed in the course of the countries' shift from dictatorship to democracy in the late 1970s and early 1980s. Prior to that time, he says, two responses to formal democratic institutions and procedures predominated in the Latin American Left. The first was the boycott on the grounds that electoral democracy was a tool and a facade for bourgeois class rule. The second was participation in these institutions, though only as a way to "accumulate forces" for an eventual revolutionary confrontation. Latin American leftists did not regard electoral democracy as integral to the revolutionary project. With the end of military or authoritarian regimes beginning in the late 1970s, many leftist groups shifted from armed to parliamentary struggle and became integrated into the new electoral democracies. In a good number of Latin American countries, the Left reentered the political center stage no longer via the bullet but via the ballot. Leftist parties became the main opposition parties in Brazil, Uruguay, and El Salvador, apart from Nicaragua (the Sandinistas, who lost power in 1990); junior partners in centrist governments, as in Chile and Venezuela; and major forces in Mexico and the Dominican Republic. Despite the many flaws and limitations of the new regimes, the Left gradually learned to recognize and accept the intrinsic value of formal democratic institutions. The left learned to care about formal democracy because, to borrow from Huber et al. (1997:323), it tended to be more than merely formal—it made free and open debate over competing projects for society, as well as deepening to more participatory and egalitarian democracy, possible. Democracy became a central element of the socialist project, as essential as its anticapitalist economic and social components. Thus, the outright rejection and instrumental view of democracy were replaced by an integral conception of democracy (Roberts 1998:19).

Latin American leftist parties started to democratize their own internal processes and their relations with organizations in civil society, abandoning the verticalism characteristic of vanguardist politics. Brazil's Partido dos Trabalhadores (PT) or Workers' Party, for instance, institutionalized mechanisms of rank-and-file participation and established a characteristic "bottom-up" style (Alves 1993:235). The leftist parties also began to appreciate the importance of the autonomy of popular organizations and social movements. The rejection of a monolithic model paved the way for broader intraleftist unity—the convergence of a larger number of parties and ideological currents (Ellner 1993:11, 16).

Unlike the case in Latin America, the instrumental view of democracy still has a very strong influence within the Left in the Philippines. The CPP, in particular, still seeks to overthrow the "reactionary" Philippine state through armed means even though its warfare has been stuck at the guerrilla level for over thirty-eight years with no signs of its ever graduating to the regular warfare it aims to reach. And notwithstanding the fall of the one-party dictatorships in the Soviet Union and Eastern Europe in 1989–92, the CPP still dreams of setting up a "national democratic" variant in the Philippines with itself as the vanguard (Liwanag 2001).

The CPP continues to view the Philippines' current democratic order as reactionary and attaches no intrinsic value to the country's formal democratic institutions and procedures. For some time, the parameters of the debate within the CPP regarding these institutions remained similar to those of the pre-1980 Latin American leftist debate: outright rejection or instrumental use. In the wake of the boycott fiasco of 1986, the NDs established PnB, which fielded candidates in the 1987 elections. Just before the elections, the CPP denounced elections and the legislature as "bourgeois" and "props for counterrevolution" (Editorial Staff, *Ang Bayan* 1987a). After

PnB's crushing defeat in its electoral debut, the CPP emphasized that the electoral struggle was inferior and subordinate to the armed struggle and the mass movement (Editorial Staff, *Ang Bayan* 1988:25). The NDs gradually lost interest in PnB, and it faded away. Only much later, after other leftist groups had scored modest victories in the 1998 party-list vote, did the NDs again toss their hats into the ring. However, they did not go beyond the instrumental framework. Those NDs who viewed the electoral struggle as a useful tool for the eventual armed seizure of state power prevailed over more hard-line Maoists, who stood for rejecting any meaningful participation. The NDs set up Bayan Muna and fielded candidates in the party-list and local elections. During the electoral campaign itself, the NPA harassed the rivals of Bayan Muna, especially other leftist parties, even barring them from entering and campaigning in areas where NPA guerrillas operated. Showing just how cynical it was of the entire electoral process, the CPP-NPA, as in previous elections, extorted large sums from candidates of different parties for "permits to campaign" (PTCs) in guerrilla zones (Mogato 2003). In the May 2004 elections, the NDs fielded six party-list groups, but only three made it to the winning column (Bayan Muna, Anakpawis, and Gabriela).[36] Nonetheless, the NDs doubled the number of their seats in Congress from three to six. As before, the NPA collected PTC fees and harassed other leftist groups (Rosales 2004).

The CPP's instrumental view of democracy is not limited merely to elections and the legislature. It holds for the question of human rights as well. The CPP's former secretary-general, who views human rights as "bourgeois-liberal" rights, has declared:

> The struggle for "human rights" is a legitimate and necessary part of the overall national democratic struggle. In my opinion, however, it should be confined to the sphere of tactical struggle or the struggle for reforms, used as only one of the means or forms of organization in working or forging alliances with those in the upper sections of the petty bourgeoisie and the national bourgeoisie and with their bourgeois-reformist organizations; in working within the state bureaucracy and the military, and other reactionary institutions like the Church, in order to divide the reactionary classes; and in drawing sympathy and support for our struggle from bourgeois-liberal political forces and institutions of other countries. It is also an important instrument in principled political negotiations of revolutionary and progressive forces with the reactionary government or any part of this. Also in

> dealing with important international organizations dominated by imperialism and reaction like the United Nations.
>
> (Baylosis 1994:6, translated from Filipino)

Even those in the CPP who claim to accept the universality of human rights assert that the only genuine human rights movement is one that pursues the ND line (J. Sison 1995). For the NDs, human rights have become a political tool, a weapon to be appropriated for the ND movement. From the Marcos authoritarian period to the post-Marcos "elite democracy" era, NDs have time and again denounced the Philippine state for violations of human rights and international humanitarian law in order to "expose and oppose" its "reactionary" character. Yet the CPP has rarely acknowledged responsibility for its own violations, often putting the blame on "left opportunists," "gangsters," "putschists," and other miscreants, who have purportedly managed to worm themselves into the party (Casiple 1996:16–17).

In the course of peace negotiations, the NDF has signed the Comprehensive Agreement on Respect for Human Rights and International Humanitarian Law (CARHRIHL) with the Philippine government, but neither side has really conducted serious investigations into human rights violations of which it is accused of perpetrating. On the part of the NDF, it would seem that the agreement and, for that matter, the entire process of peace talks are intended more for scoring points in its "diplomatic struggle." According to a former NDF cadre in Europe, the NDF wants to use the talks as a means to attain "belligerency status," to expand and consolidate its forces, and to provide legitimacy to Sison's continued stay as a political exile in the Netherlands.[37]

The instrumental view is reflected even further in the CPP's approach to POs and NGOs, alliances and coalitions, social movements, and indeed civil society as a whole. As mentioned earlier, the party took the lead in building and nurturing "legal mass organizations" and "legal institutions and programs" in the dark days of repression under Marcos. Party and ND elements provided much needed assistance or guidance in the formative period. Gradually, however, the party increased its influence or control over these organizations—through clandestine party or ND cells within or through political officers from without (oftentimes persons from the underground).[38] Many organizations came to be regarded as being "party-led" or "party-influenced" (as they were referred to in internal party communications). Thus, from being instruments of popular empowerment, they were transformed into mere "transmission belts" of party policies and directives.[39]

R. Constantino (1996:37) criticizes the CPP's vanguardist relations with its united front formation, the NDF, and with legal ND organizations. The NDF

> was merely an artificial creation because most of the organizations under its umbrella were of the same ideological persuasion and recognized the vanguardist role of the CPP. Even the legal fronts of the underground hardly concealed their connection with the vanguard party and vice versa. Such a set-up bred a centralized uniformity instead of a genuine respect for difference, which a more broad-based front would have naturally generated. The result was a zealous adherence to the "one correct line" brought down by the party. Technically, therefore, there seemed to be no real ideological difference between members of other organizations within the NDF and those of the CPP who took key leadership roles in the front.
>
> The same set of conditions prevailed in other legal organizations where CPP influence was present. Non-party elements felt the pressures of CPP cadres and this led to their alienation from CPP-led or CPP-influenced coalitions or organizations. Pluralism and democratic dialogue were stifled by sectarian proselytization.

The tension between those for and those against party "guidance" within many "party-led or influenced" organizations persisted for long periods and sometimes resulted in open clashes. In the 1986 boycott, many legal mass organizations took a boycott stance only after party and ND elements within (and also from without), following "democratic centralism," campaigned hard and sometimes even resorted to maneuvering and arm-twisting, to get the boycott position carried. Many members of mass organizations resisted. Nonetheless, almost all of the major open ND organizations and alliances went for the boycott (Editorial Board, *Praktika* 1986; National Youth and Student Department, CPP 1986). A similar situation arose in the party's campaign for a rejection of the new constitution in 1987. Another ruckus flared up in June 1989 when the ND trade union center, Kilusang Mayo Uno (KMU) or the May First Movement, issued a statement after the Tiananmen massacre without first consulting affiliate federations, virtually condoning the violence of the Chinese state against protesting students and workers. The statement, it turned out, had actually been formulated by the CPP's National Trade Union Bureau. Four years later, in the midst of the ideological conflict within the CPP/ND ranks, three major federations disaffiliated from KMU, decrying "external dictation on KMU policy and programs" and the violation of "the integrity of trade union structures" (National Federation of Labor Unions, National Federation of Labor and United Workers of the Philippines 1993). In a study of the CPP and the peasant movement, Putzel (1995b:645–46) traces the roots of the party's "instrumentalist approach" to the peasantry to the very foundations of Marxist-Leninist theory and historical practice. It was in the traditional communist mold, he writes, to treat all people's struggles and organizations in an instrumental fashion, always subordinating these to the party and its goal of seizing state power.

The CPP's instrumentalist approach to POs, NGOs, alliances, social movements, and civil society contradicts the notion that the traditional Left in the Philippines has been a strategic leader in the struggle for civil society. The party's efforts in building POs and NGOs and promoting social movements, especially during the period of dictatorship, when there were hardly any, may well have contributed to popular empowerment. But subsequent efforts at "managing" (to borrow from Putzel) POs, NGOs, and social movements had the reverse effect—popular disempowerment.

Since its founding, the CPP has maintained its leading role in the revolutionary struggle for the establishment and consolidation of the "people's democratic state" (Congress of Re-establishment, CPP 1968b:61–63; Guerrero 1979a:162–66). After the fall of the socialist regimes in Eastern Europe, the CPP (Communist Party of the Philippines 1991:52) reemphasized its vanguard role: "As a matter of principle and practice, the Party is the comprehensive leader and center of the Philippine revolution in both national democratic and socialist stages. It leads the armed struggle, the united front, mass movement, the organs of political power and eventually the People's Democratic Republic of the Philippines." This implies that in the event of revolutionary victory POs, NGOs, and the social movements would all be made to toe the CPP's line.

An Emerging Democratic Left

Dictatorships in many parts of the globe have fallen. Democratization has become an international buzzword. Among the authoritarian regimes that have been toppled are the one-party dictatorships of Eastern Europe and the former Soviet bloc. China, which only a few decades ago stridently proclaimed that "Revolution is the main trend in the world today," is now too busy building "market socialism" (read capitalism). In the Philippines itself, authoritarian rule has long been over. The oligarchic elite still controls the country's politics, but the political space in which forces working for popular empowerment can move and operate has expanded. The very necessity and wisdom of armed struggle, especially of a protracted nature, have been put into question. Over thirty years of armed conflict—not just the communist insurgency but also the Moro rebellion—have exacted a terrible toll in human lives and economic and social costs and have helped perpetuate and aggravate a culture of violence. Moreover, it is now widely perceived that faxes, e-mails, and text messaging, when used to mobilize people power, are more effective tools in felling undemocratic regimes and corrupt rulers than the barrel of a gun.

The Philippine Left—or at least part of it—has been moving on too. Since the fall of the Marcos dictatorship, and especially since the CPP split, the general trend among the emergent political parties of the Left has been to move away from armed or military struggle and adopt a nonarmed political strategy characterized by engagement in both the mass movements and electoral struggles. Some of the new Left parties and groups have changed not only their strategies and tactics but also, in significant part, their goals. The long-term goal of socialism remains basically unchanged, although the emergent leftist groups find it difficult to explain in concrete terms what this would look like and how it would be achieved. The change in goals has more to do with attitudes toward democracy. In this regard, the development of the Philippine Left parallels that of the Latin American Left, though apparently some years behind and only to a certain extent.

For SD groups, socialism *and* democracy had always been their avowed strategic goals. In the late 1980s, however, SD groups such as

Pandayan and Kasapi were much more open and willing to open lines of communication with other leftist groups, such as the popdems and Bisig, conduct joint endeavors with them, and engage them in discussion and debate. In the popdems' publication *Conjuncture,* Pandayan vice chairman Benjamin T. Tolosa, Jr. (1990:8–9) explained that, although democratic socialists viewed political democracy as a genuine popular achievement, they believed that the fullness of democracy could only be achieved through the establishment of socialism. "The socialist project," he wrote, "is thus one of 'democratization': the extension and deepening of democracy from the political to the economic and socio-cultural realms. It aims at the 'equalization of power' in all spheres." He outlined a strategy for democratic socialists based on a post-Marxist analysis of the state as still dominated by a ruling elite but capable of being penetrated by initiatives of popular forces.

> The strategy seeks to construct democracy and socialism 'from below': a democracy and socialism founded on a conscienticized and organized citizenry based in strong, independent people's organizations. The strategy calls for democratic socialist intervention at various points of struggle—both within and outside the formal structures of government. The objective is the consolidation of democratic socialist centers of power (including victories on the level of popular consciousness) towards the conquest and transformation of the state. A central goal is the establishment of a form of representative democracy which is dynamically linked with organs of direct democracy in the workplace and the community.

It took a bit of time for significant sections within the ND ranks to come round to Pandayan's position. Rejecting the post-Marcos state as a "fake" or "bourgeois" democracy, most NDs still regarded a "proletarian" or "people's democracy" ruled by a vanguard party as the only true democracy. As long they still held on to such a notion, they could not make the shift from an instrumental to an integral view of democracy. The issue of political pluralism proved pivotal. In the late 1970s and early 1980s, the issue had already figured in internal debates in the CPP, particularly in relation to the NDF program.[40] After EDSA I, the NDs discussed it more openly. When the NDs formed their first electoral party, PnB, they billed it as the party of new politics. In its platform, PnB (Partido ng Bayan 1986:1–2) carried the standard ND line of being for a nationalist and democratic government. Through the initiative of more forward-looking elements within, however, it also advocated for such nonstandard fare as "popular democracy" and a "pluralistic political system." After its poor showing in the 1987 elections, PnB faded away. Pluralism, however, gained more adherents within the ND ranks. According to Jones, all the CPP leaders with whom he spoke, including reputed hard-liner Rodolfo Salas, the CPP chairman in 1977–86, expressed a preference for at least a nominally pluralist political system over a one-party state (Jones 1989:278). Together with Bisig, Pandayan, Kasapi, and other leftist groups, the popdems held discussions on the problems and prospects of political pluralism in the Philippines (Coronel Ferrer 1989:5–6). In 1991, however, opponents of pluralism began with an oblique counterattack, striking out at the Sandinistas for practicing pluralism instead of "people's democratic dictatorship" in Nicaragua (Editorial Board, *Rebolusyon* 1991:6). With the publication of "Reaffirm," political pluralism became one of the main points of divergence between the reaffirmists and rejectionists. The reaffirmists considered pluralism—and correctly so—a negation of the CPP's permanent vanguard role. After upholding political pluralism and rejecting vanguardism, many rejectionists began to accept multiparty democracy and pluralism (Tubongbanwa 1992; Rocamora 1992; Concerned Communist Party of the Philippines Members 1993:166–67) and move from an instrumental to an integral view of democracy.

Shortly after the CPP split, some rejectionists, together with other non-ND-tradition leftists and members of Philippine solidarity groups, held a conference in San Francisco, California, in April 1993, for the purpose of "reexamining and renewing the Philippine progressive vision." The participants of the "Forum for Philippine Alternatives" (FOPA) resolved to carry on with the new politics, but this time highlighting its pluralistic and popular democratic features and further developing the concept. No longer just anti-*trapo*, the new politics took on features that departed from the not too democratic orthodox CPP approach. New politics, as redefined by the FOPA participants, saw its strength as emanating from the confluence of plural initiatives rather than from unity around one central strategy and program. It distrusted "totalizing ideologies" and resisted a centralized direction. It regarded political struggle not as a process that would lead to a climactic seizure of state power but as a gradual process of transformation of the power relationships in society—the transformation of elite democracy to mass, popular democracy. Popular empowerment was viewed as a process of building up a "parallel power" in civil society that would eventually alter the exercise of state power (Bello 1993:11, 17–18).

A movement built along new politics lines would contend in different political arenas, "but especially under a regime of elite democracy, in the electoral struggle, which is, whether we like it or not, the current source of legitimacy on who governs." The movement would continue to engage in mass mobilizations or "the parliament of the streets," and its strategy would also include a program of governmental reform—"transforming the formal structure of the state to make it less resistant to the attainment of the people's interests." The main elements of the vision and program of the movement would be democracy, equity and redistribution, growth, and national sovereignty. Thus, FOPA clarified that democracy would have to be released from its identification with elite-dominated elections and that equity and distribution would have to be divorced from the failed Soviet and Chinese models of socialism (Bello 1993:21–22).

To signify a complete break with the instrumentalist approach of the CPP to POs, NGOs, and civil society, the emergent leftist forces have taken an unequivocal stand on the integrity and autonomy of POs/NGOs vis-à-vis political parties, as well as the state. Taking off from Held's "principle of autonomy," the participants of the FOPA conference expressed a firm belief in "the capacity of the people to reason and deliberate, to be self-reflective, and to exercise self-determination" (Gershman 1993:170). At a PO-NGO conference held in March 1994, leading rejectionists emphasized that POs/NGOs were not mere transmission belts of the party or the state but entities that had lives of their own. Deriding the CPP penchant for setting up and then dissolving POs/NGOs at will, the participants asserted that POs/NGOs were not mere tactical formations serving the party's political agenda but strategic formations that would keep on working for popular empowerment even after the socialist victory (PO-NGO Conference 1994:5, 20, 35).

In 1997, Ricardo Reyes (1998:106), a rejectionist leader and former CPP Politburo member, expounded on a model for the relationship of the political movements with POs/NGOs.

> We stand for the autonomous development of social movements and civil society vis-à-vis the political movements. We respect the integrity and independent dynamism of the NGOs, trade unions, mass organizations and other formations of civil society. Vanguardist attitudes toward these organizations and employing organizational control over them must be shunned from our practice. Instead, we engage them in a dialogue of praxis. Socialists joining these organizations must respect their integrity and must behave as such.
>
> On the other hand, socialists must exercise the right to criticize regressive tendencies in the NGO-PO community, particularly the rise of bureaucratism and privilege, and campaign to further democratize organizations of civil society.

By and large, the emergent leftist parties appear to be doing fairly well in putting into practice their avowed aim to respect the integrity and autonomy of the POs/NGOs. They have done away with the ND practices of political officers giving "guidance" to POs/NGOs and of party or underground (UG) cells holding secret meetings ahead of PO/NGO meetings to formulate "proposals" on the latter's course of action. For the ex-ND parties and groups that are still UG or have UG components, observing the autonomy of POs/NGOs and open electoral parties aligned with them has proven to be quite a challenge. At times, their cadres and activists, accustomed to the tight, highly centralized, and hierarchical organizational system of the CPP-NPA days, fall into old habits.[41] Being an open political party, Akbayan does not encounter the problem of relations between UG and open formations. The multitendency party, however, has encountered certain intraparty problems perceived, at least by some, as having to do with the relations between the "political blocs" (tendencies) and between members and nonmembers of the blocs. In the January 2001 congress, several leading personages and their allies withdrew from the party, claiming bloc manipulation in the election of party-list candidates, a charge the party leadership has denied.[42]

Since the CPP split and the FOPA conference, however, an important question regarding democracy appears to be not quite resolved. Recognizing the intrinsic value of democratic institutions and processes, Akbayan and the new groups from the SD tradition have taken an integral view of democracy. The rejectionist Marxist-Leninist parties (PMP, RPM-P, and RPM-M) and MLPP, however, appear not to have shifted fully to such a view. While rejecting the CPP's protracted people's war, the ex-ND parties still entertain the possibility of a Jacobin-style seizure of state power.[43] A fine line actually distinguishes the positions of the two flanks of the emergent Left, and this has to do with the question of popular insurrection. In the light of EDSA I, II, and III, none of the new, leftist parties and groups has ruled out popular insurrection or uprising as a possible recourse of the mass movement. The ex-NDs view popular insurrection as the possible culmination of the revolutionary struggle for seizing power—what Laclau and Mouffe (1985) refer to as the "foundational moment of rupture." Akbayan and the SD-tradition groups, however, see it as but a part of a protracted process of social and political change. In 1997, Reyes (1998:98), now one of the leaders of the Akbayan, wrote: "To prepare for 'the moment' remains a socialist responsibility. It still is an essential ingredient of the socialist élan. This 'moment' however need not always be the 'grand moment' of cataclysmic revolutions of the past. It may be 'moments,' junctures where radical changes can also be realized if revolutionary socialists live up to the challenge." Criticizing leftist groups that continued to define their revolutionary objective in terms of "smashing the existing state machine," Nemenzo (1996a:54) declares: "This all or nothing attitude is a debilitating form of dogmatism." The new, leftist groups are still in a flux. Some of the ex-ND groups may yet turn fully to an integral view of democracy as they go deeper into the state arena (elections and governance).

Democracy from Below and the Emergent Left

In the Philippines' contested democracy, the Left has always identified itself with, and built its base among, the peasants, workers, and other marginalized groups and communities struggling against elite rule. The single biggest bloc of the Left, however, cannot really be considered as truly representing democracy from below. The CPP and the CPP-aligned ND movement have proven to be antidemocratic in their behavior and practice in both the Philippine polity and their internal workings. Moreover, what they proffer as an alternative to elite democracy—national democracy or people's democracy—redounds to nothing more than a one-party dictatorship. The Left in the Philippines has acquired an undemocratic or antidemocratic taint largely because of the CPP's and the NDs' undemocratic ways. The CPP and the ND movement, however, no longer hold a hegemonic position in the Left. Long before the CPP split, other forces of the Left had already emerged or revived and expanded. Since the split, the Left has become even more "plural," as more positive-looking leftists put it. Emergent leftist parties and groups such as Akbayan, PMP, ABA-AKO, and RPM-M show promise of becoming viable leftist projects as well as true representatives of democracy from below.[44] Some of the new formations, particularly Akbayan and PMP, have been growing rapidly, building chapters all over the country.

The emergent leftist forces have continued the leftist tradition of forging close links with the poor and marginalized. Unlike the traditional parties of the elite, which have nebulous party organizations, the new, leftist parties and groups have been striving to build party chapters and a political-electoral base at the grassroots level. In contrast to the elite character of the traditional parties, the new left parties seek to have a truly "mass" character. Apart from promoting the popular movements engaged in "pressure" or contentious politics, the new, leftist groups and allied POs/NGOs have also become much more involved in more "constructive" and not-too-contentious politics—development work. Unlike the CPP, the new, leftist parties and groups are for untrammeled and noninstrumentalizing popular empowerment, recognizing and respecting the integrity and autonomy of POs, NGOs and the social movements. Like the postauthoritarian Latin American Left, the new Philippine Left has come to appreciate the positive aspects of the country's democracy, despite all its deficiencies and fragility, and the opportunities it has opened for the deepening of democracy. The emergent leftist parties are learning to recognize the intrinsic value of formal democratic institutions and procedures and have adopted or are moving toward an integral view of democracy. Precisely because of their growing appreciation of democratic processes and institutions, the new leftist forces have expanded beyond their involvement with POs, NGOs, and social movements, a sphere where the Left as a whole has already proven its mettle and clout, and ventured into the state arena—elections and governance—long the turf of the oligarchic elite and one of the Left's weakest spots. There is, however, a much more straightforward reason: explosions of people power and a strong and vibrant civil society are fine, but they are far from enough as long as oligarchs and *trapos* still call the shots. "Autonomous popular strength," declared Akbayan founding and current president Ronaldo Llamas (1996:69), "has to be translated into political strength capable of determining state policies and programs that bring about social change."

Most of the new, leftist parties burst onto the public scene during the first party-list elections in 1998. Groups such as ABA, AKO, Abanse Pinay, Akbayan, and Sanlakas all espoused the new politics, presenting it as the antithesis of *trapo* politics, and this helped them in winning congressional seats in their first election bids. The emergent Left hammered on the theme of new versus *trapo* politics. In April 2000, the representatives of Akbayan and Sanlakas in the Lower House captured the headlines when they courageously exposed large-scale corruption in government—a payola scandal that involved their very colleagues in Congress (Marfil and Esplanada 2000).[45] The anti-*trapo* movement surged when President Estrada himself was implicated in a multimillion-peso illegal gambling racket. All the leftist parties and groups mobilized their forces for the ouster of Estrada, who, as the impeachment proceedings soon showed, was the near quintessence of *trapo* politics. When Estrada, utilizing various legal maneuvers and mobilizing his *trapo* allies in the Senate, seemingly managed to bring the corruption investigation against him to a dead end, hundreds of thousands of people poured into the streets in indignation and forced him to flee Malacañang Palace. Unlike in People Power I, when the Left was largely left out, in People Power II the Left was among those in the forefront.

Since EDSA II, virtually every group working for political and electoral reform has talked about the new politics. When the NDs reentered the electoral arena in 2001, they readopted the term. President Arroyo, who herself rose to power through patronage politics and now heads a *trapo*-dominated ruling coalition, hitched herself to the bandwagon, promising new politics to the sea of people at EDSA during her inauguration in January 2001. This constituted a moral victory for the emergent Left. But it also meant that the new, leftist parties would have to go beyond "exposing and opposing" *trapo* politics and get into the nitty-gritty of putting new politics into practice in their engagement in both civil society and the state.

Due to continuing ideological and political differences among the new, leftist parties and sometimes even personal differences among their leaders, the emergent Left has remained divided and has not witnessed a grand merger or coalition. The bickering and splintering that beset the rejectionist ranks, and to a lesser extent the SD ranks, through most of the 1990s have greatly subsided. The trend now, in fact, seems to be toward unity. The most significant unions have been the formal coalition of four political blocs (Bisig, Pandayan, the popdems, and Siglaya) into Akbayan in 1998; the merger of PMP, PPD and the Sosyalistang Partido ng Paggawa (SPP) or Socialist Workers' Party into a bigger PMP in 2002;[46] and the ABA-AKO merger in 2003. The new, leftist parties and allied POs/NGOs have also formed tactical alliances on a variety of issues and concerns, which will be discussed in forthcoming chapters.

Since the CPP split, the emergent leftist parties and groups have had to endure harassment from the NPA, especially during election campaigns. A most troubling development in recent years, however, has been the NPA executions of leading rejectionists, whom the CPP-NPA regards as "renegades" and "counterrevolutionaries," as well as members of the new leftist parties (Rousset 2003:7–9). The CPP-NPA acknowledged assassinating two rejectionist leaders, former NPA chief Kintanar in January 2003 and RPM-P founding chairman Tabara in September 2004, and is one of the prime suspects in the killing of PMP founding chairman Lagman in February 2001. Kintanar, Tabara, and Lagman were three of the four whom the CPP had marked for "people's court" in December 1993. The NPA has also been hitting at other leftist targets. From August 1999 to August 2002, the NPA conducted nineteen armed operations against members of the MLPP in Central Luzon, killing twelve and wounding fifteen. (In the 2002 encounters, some NPA guerrillas were also killed as the MLPP fought back.) The NPA also killed two RPM-M cadres in Central Mindanao in 2001. Unarmed leftist groups have also been targeted. In 2003, the NPA executed a peasant leader in the Bondoc peninsula (Quezon Province) and a *barangay* captain in Agusan del Norte, both local leaders of Akbayan. Apart from all the killings, the CPP-NPA has resorted to threats and other forms of intimidation. The new, leftist parties and groups have publicly denounced the CPP-NPA's killings and intimidation, but the CPP-NPA has continued with impunity.

All the new, leftist parties that I have listed above are convinced of the necessity of political engagement in both civil society (the mass movements) and the state arena. The parties listed vary greatly in the levels of their engagement in the two spheres. Still concentrating on building its mass base, the MLPP still has not made an entry into the electoral arena. The electoral parties aligned with RPM-P have not yet been successful in winning a party-list seat. The RPM-M-aligned AMIN has twice made it to the party-list winning column, but the political work of both RPM-M and AMIN still remains largely confined to Mindanao. The ABA-AKO and Abanse Pinay have restricted their electoral engagement only to the party-list vote. Akbayan and PMP are the new, leftist parties whose engagement in both civil society and the state arena appears to be more extensive than that of the others.[47] Hence, in the following chapters I will go into more detail in discussing the political work of Akbayan and PMP, as well as the POs/NGOs and the political blocs and groups aligned with them.

3

The Emergent Left's Engagement in Civil Society

AFTER THE EDSA UPRISING OF 1986, there was a much greater recognition within the Philippine Left of the importance of the "political struggle"—the mass movements (including people-power-type uprisings) and the electoral struggle. Within the ND ranks, some viewed the political struggle as being as fundamental and decisive as armed or military struggle. Others, however, began to regard open, legal, political struggle as the main form of struggle or even questioned the necessity or judiciousness of continuing the armed struggle in the postauthoritarian era (Rocamora 1994a:74–79, 96, 105; Weekley 2001:chap. 6). Some popdems and mainstream NDs began to discuss Gramsci's concepts of hegemony, civil society and the "war of position" (Francisco 1994:4).[1] After the CPP split, most of the rejectionists gradually moved away from armed struggle and concentrated on the mass movements and the electoral struggle. Nonetheless, they continued to adhere to the orthodox Marxist-Leninist position of eventually seizing state power through armed revolution.[2] Meanwhile, the popdems who had initially explored Gramsci's ideas, together with some rejectionists, endeavored to develop civil society as an analytical tool.

While the NDs (including the popdems) were still grappling with the revised or new thinking on the political struggle and civil society, the term *civil society* itself, vigorously promoted by donor agencies, the government, the churches, business, media and the PO/NGO community, shot to prominence in the Philippines, as elsewhere, and figured prominently in the literature on democracy and democratization. Soon, *civil society* became a buzzword even within the left, including the ND ranks. In the course of their engagement in civil society, the various leftist groups were exposed not only to different notions of civil society but also to different versions of the civil society argument vis-à-vis democracy and democratization.

According to Michael Foley and Bob Edwards (Foley and Edwards 1996:39; Edwards and Foley 2001:5–8), there are two broad versions of the "civil society argument." Civil Society I, which harks back to Alexis de Tocqueville and is today forcefully put forward by scholars such as Robert Putnam, stresses the importance of associational life and a strong and vigorous civil society in producing "social capital" and promoting, maintaining, and consolidating democracy.[3] Civil Society II, which figures prominently in the literature on democratic transition in Eastern Europe and Latin America, views civil society as a sphere of social and political life that is independent of the state and capable of mobilizing opposition to a tyrannical regime. I shall refer to Civil Society I as *associational civil society* and Civil Society II as *counterweight civil society*. Since the fall of many authoritarian regimes during the third wave of democratization, associational civil society appears to have become the more influential version. In the Philippines, it has propagated a "harmony" model of politics, one that has tended to downplay the very real conflict between the country's oligarchic elite and the poor and marginalized classes, sectors, and communities.

Critics have raised all sorts of objections to associational and counterweight civil society and put forward their own definitions, concepts, or reconfigurations of civil society, which I shall later show. Unfortunately, however, they have not come up with an alternative civil society argument, particularly in relation to democracy and democratization.

The experiences of emergent leftist groups in the Philippines in their engagement in civil society seem to point to a plausible alternative. Although they were influenced to a certain extent by both associational and counterweight civil society, some of them have also developed an alternative civil society argument, one that appears to hew closely to the radical democratic perspective developed by Ernesto Laclau and Chantal Mouffe. The argument, which I shall dub *hegemonic* (or *counterhegemonic*) *civil society*, draws mainly from Antonio Gramsci's concept of civil society but rejects certain traditional Marxist views on the state and revolution. Hegemonic civil society views the consolidation and deepening of democracy not so much in terms of building a dense and vibrant civil society or developing it as a powerful counterpoise to the state but more in terms of internal contestation—the struggle of subordinate classes and marginalized groups against the hegemonic elite *within* civil society.

Philippine civil society, with "probably the highest NGO density in the world" (Hilhorst 2003:11), has been a battleground of contending versions of the civil society argument. In their efforts in the sphere of civil society to transform the Philippines' elite-dominated democracy into a more participatory and egalitarian one, the emergent leftist groups in the Philippines have had to wade through the Babel of civil society concepts and arguments. The development of their work in civil society has followed the twists and turns of their engagement with the contending versions of the civil society argument.

From "Mass Organizations" and "Mass Movement" to "Civil Society"

Before the 1990s, most of the leftists in the Philippines had never heard of "civil society." The term appears often enough in the writings of Marx, Engels, and Gramsci, but the CPP had always put a higher premium on the study of Mao's works, not those of Marx and Engels, and considered Gramsci a "revisionist." In the late 1960s and the early 1970s, leftist activists helped build "mass organizations" of peasants, workers, and the urban poor and launch "mass movements." For the NDs, the armed struggle and the mass movements were the component forms of their revolutionary struggle. Under Marcos's martial law, the NDs managed to set up "legal mass organizations," "legal institutions," and "legal programs," despite repressive conditions. Working closely with anti-Marcos groups and personages in church institutions and religious-run schools, the SDs set up their own mass organizations and grassroots-oriented programs. The waning years of the dictatorship saw the proliferation of "cause-oriented groups" involved in the anti-Marcos struggle.

With the restoration of democracy, there was a further burgeoning of these organizations, this time called "people's organizations" (POs) and "nongovernmental organizations" (NGOs). *Social movement* was used interchangeably with *mass movement*.[4] Inspired by EDSA I, the framers of the 1987 Constitution recognized the positive role of POs/NGOs in advancing the people's welfare and interests by enshrining this in the charter itself.[5] While many of today's POs/NGOs are not leftist in orientation, part of the credit for the proliferation of these vehicles of popular participation belongs to the left.

Within the Philippine left, initial usage of the term *civil society* can be traced to "nonparty political formations" of the left (now more often referred to as political blocs), especially the popdems.[6] To these political blocs, two major events provoked interest in the concept of civil society: the people power uprising of 1986 (EDSA I) and the collapse of the socialist regimes of Eastern Europe in 1989–92.

According to popdem Oscar Francisco (1994:2), the post-EDSA I discussions on civil society emanated from four intersecting sources —academe, the churches, leftist political blocs, and governmental and quasi-governmental institutions. Within the Left, the discourse was related to the opportunities opened up by EDSA I, as well as to the crisis of the Left that followed the NDs' disastrous boycott of the 1986 elections. "The failure of the communist party-led political formations to intervene in the 1985–87 conjuncture," wrote Francisco, "led many popular organizations to search for non-orthodox analytical means to understand what had happened and, equally important, to guide their next course of action." The popdems presented "popular democracy" as the "democratic component of national democracy" (De la Torre 1987:1–10). In elaborating on popular empowerment and the role of POs/NGOs, some popdems drew from Gramsci's ideas on hegemony, civil society, and the war of position.

Gramsci (1971:12, 56n, 239) accepted the orthodox Marxist-Leninist position that the state (or "political society") is the coercive instrument of the ruling class. However, he also put forward the notion that the state, in the broader—and *integral*—sense, consists of political and civil society, each corresponding to a particular function exercised by the ruling class throughout society—political society the function of "direct domination" or command and civil society the function of "hegemony." Civil society was "the hegemony of a social group over the entire national society exercised through the so-called private organizations, like the Church, the trade unions, the schools, etc." Social hegemony meant that the great masses of the population gave their "'spontaneous' consent" to the general direction imposed on social life by the dominant class. Gramsci (1971:133, 231–39) contended that in countries, such as czarist Russia, where civil society was "primordial and gelatinous," the capture of state power through a frontal attack—or a "war of movement" (or "maneuver")—was feasible. However, in advanced capitalist countries, where civil society was more developed, a different strategy had to be employed: a war of position—a struggle for hegemony in which the working class would seek to wrest political, intellectual, and moral leadership from the bourgeoisie and to build a multiclass bloc with a new "national-popular collective will." In the long term, the counterhegemony in civil society would come to encompass political society.

"Gramsci," explained Francisco (1994:4), "had likened the state to a fort and the trenches it represents to civil society. The popdems argued that to seize the fort, revolutionaries must first overrun the trenches. They also pointed out that it is in civil society where many of the exploitative power relations operate and thus 'hegemony' too must be contested here." The popdems, however, failed to make much headway. Worse, their comrades looked at them askance. Steeped in orthodox Marxist-Leninist thinking, mainstream NDs regarded the seizure of state power as the central task of the revolution. To them, Gramsci's war of position was a diversion that could even make people abandon the revolution. To CPP leaders, the popdems exhibited strong tendencies toward "reformism" or "right opportunism."

The collapse of the socialist regimes in Eastern Europe added another element to the discussions on civil society within the Philippine Left: a critique of Stalinism. "Civil society died with socialism's coming to power [in Eastern Europe and the Soviet Union]," noted Isagani Serrano (1992a:28). "Socialists minded it only, and in their own peculiar way, while still on the road to power. Then they chose to suppress it when they got there." In a conference of PO/NGO leaders, Joel Rocamora advocated for a "state and civil society" framework (counterweight civil society) to fight state encroachments on civil society and to distinguish the societal alternative of the democratic Left from that of the Stalinists (PO-NGO Conference 1994:5).

The experience of the Polish workers (Solidarity) in the 1980s has been held up as a prime example of the clash between civil society and a repressive state. Although Gramsci had been mainly concerned with the bourgeois state and civil society, his ideas on hegemony and civil society influenced the Polish workers, who were up against a totalitarian state. Gramsci (1971:170) had associated the state with coercion and force and civil society with consent (hegemony) and freedom. Solidarity moved toward the contraction of the realm of coercion (state) and the expansion of the realm of freedom (civil society). Instead of directly challenging the state, the workers ignored it and built a democratic, pluralist, "parallel society." By following a strategy of constructing (or resurrecting) civil society, Solidarity as a social movement eventually achieved hegemony in Polish society. The delegitimized and weakened party-state crumbled (Kumar 1993:386–88).[7]

For the emergent groups in the Philippine left, EDSA I and the collapse of socialism in Eastern Europe brought the Gramscian concept of civil society to the fore—but along two quite dissimilar threads. Initially, EDSA I triggered a conceptualization of civil society as an arena of struggle for hegemony between the oligarchic elite and the working masses and their allies (hegemonic civil society). The collapse of the socialist regimes thrust the notion of civil society as a countervailing force to the state (counterweight civil society). Hegemonic civil society emphasized the struggle for hegemony within civil society; counterweight civil society focused on the conflict between civil society and the state.

Gramsci's ideas on hegemony, civil society, and the war of position did not figure as one the main issues of the 1992–93 CPP debate, which centered on the strategy for seizing state power. "Nowhere in the 'Reaffirm-Reject' debate," bewailed Francisco (1994:4), "does 'civil society' appear as a conceptual tool." The emergent leftist groups, however, continued to grapple with Gramsci's ideas. By

1993, the new, leftist groups had moved to a post-Marxist perspective on democracy and the democratization process akin to Laclau and Mouffe's strongly Gramsci-influenced "radical democracy."

At the FOPA conference held in San Francisco, California, in April 1993, some rejectionists, together with other non-ND leftists and members of Philippine solidarity groups, arrived at the consensus that political struggle should be viewed "not as a process that led to a climactic seizure of power in the Leninist style but as a gradual process of transformation of the power relationships enveloping society." They saw popular empowerment as "a process of building up a 'parallel power' in 'civil society' that would reduce class power and ultimately transform the exercise of state power" (Bello 1993:18). Drawing from Gramsci and some post-Marxist theorists, FOPA defined civil society as "an arena of social and political life autonomous from state domination where progressive values and political parties can be articulated, counter-hegemonic institutions can be created, which can nurture and nourish the creation of autonomous political actors who are able to articulate and defend their interests, propose alternative projects for structuring the state and society, and transform the relations of state and society" (Gershman 1993:170).The FOPA participants viewed the counterhegemonic struggle not just as a class conflict but as a challenge to all relations of inequality and domination.[8] Regarding democracy, Walden Bello (1992:5), one of FOPA's main organizers and at one time Akbayan's honorary chairman, stated: "[R]ather than conceive of an unbridgeable gulf between formal democracy and substantive democracy, we would like to see how substantive democracy can be pushed within the tradition of formal and elite democracy so that there is a continuation in some way, as well as having some elements of a break."

The Rise of Associational Civil Society

The popdems achieved normative unity on civil society (1) as a terrain of struggle and (2) as a laboratory to "demonstrate a viable alternative at the local level" (Francisco 1994:5), but they also continued to hold on to the view of civil society as a counterweight to the state. Making civil society a laboratory for a viable alternative was actually part of the counterhegemonic struggle, but the popdems wanted to emphasize that they would engage not just in contentious politics but also in development work.[9] When the popdems, Bisig, Pandayan, and Siglaya coalesced and formed a new party, eventually named Akbayan, it essentially adopted the same framework.

Just as the popdems and company were still refining their conceptualization of hegemonic and counterweight civil society, however, the associational version came to the fore in the Philippines, as elsewhere. Foreign funding agencies, the government, church institutions, and business groups, among others, began to promote "people's participation" or "civil society participation" in development, governance, election monitoring, voter education, and advocacy for human rights, women's rights, and environmental protection, and to emphasize the importance of a strong and vigorous civil society for the country's democracy. Soon, due in large part to all the promotion for a "strong civil society" by proponents of associational civil society, the term *civil society* became most fashionable.

As in many other countries, foreign funding agencies have been the biggest factor in the rise of associational civil society in the Philippines. According to Thomas Carothers (1999a:44, 207), the 1990s witnessed an upsurge in "democracy assistance" from the United States and other international donors to developing countries, Eastern Europe, and the former Soviet Union—an upsurge brought about by a confluence of "the global trend toward democracy, the end of the cold war and new thinking about development." Aid explicitly for "strengthening civil society" became a common feature of the assistance package. The Philippines has received democracy assistance from many donor countries and agencies, mostly Western. A good part of the aid has gone to POs/NGOs. The U.S. Agency for International Development (USAID), for instance, has extended "civil society grants" to various "civil society organizations" (CSOs) aiming to broaden people's participation in public policy formulation and implementation. The Philippine government has time and again endorsed a "strong civil society," as well as attempted to harness the support of civil society for its initiatives. The Aquino administration launched the Kabisig movement to promote closer coordination among government agencies, local governments, and POs/NGOs (Goertzen 1991).[10] Later, President Ramos endeavored to mobilize civil society support for his social reform agenda (Republic of the Philippines 1995).

While viewing the increased attention of funding agencies to the strengthening of civil society as a positive development, Carothers (1999a:221–22, 248) has observed that many of these funders subscribe to a romantic or stereotyped notion of civil society. They have overstressed, he says, a particular sector: policy-related NGOs carrying out advocacy work and civic education on what the funders consider to be "core democracy issues," and they have come up with a "denatured, benevolent view of civil society's role in political life." By referring to these advocacy NGOs as "civil society organizations," the funding agencies give the false impression that these few represent the core or the majority of those in civil society. Furthermore, the funders expect advocacy NGOs to be nonpartisan, even in places where neutrality is difficult to achieve, for example, where political parties are built mainly on personal loyalties, clan networks and ethnic delineations.

Whether as wholesome bowling leagues and bird-watching societies (associational) or a plucky counterforce to a repressive state (counterweight), civil society has been made to seem "warm and fuzzy" when it is actually "a bewildering array of the good, the bad, and the outright bizarre" (Carothers 1999b:20). For over a decade now, many critics have showed the flaws and weaknesses in the two main versions of the civil society argument.

Contrary to the assertions of advocates of associational civil society, a strong and vibrant civil society can have negative effects on democracy or democratization. Where political institutions and structures are weak, for instance, this may pave the way for fascist dictatorship, as in Weimar Germany (Berman 1997) and Mussolini's Italy (Putzel 1997:939–49), and foster further divisiveness in societies already fractured along ethno-regional and sectarian lines, as in Africa (Encarnacion 2000:12). A dense civil society may very well consist of both democratic and antidemocratic associations, liberal and illiberal organizations, and civic and uncivic groups (Foley 1996;

Tamir 1998). Hence, there is civil and uncivil society, or good civil society and bad civil society (Kopstein and Hanson 1998; Chambers and Kopstein 2001). Civil society may have a negligible impact on interpersonal trust (Booth and Richard 2001:50), and associational life may breed both social and unsocial capital (Levi 1996).

Counterweight civil society tends at times to emphasize civil society as the dichotomous opposite of the state. Such a dichotomy brings about such problems as "the idealisation of civil society; the fostering of a zero-sum conception of the relationship between state and civil society; the obscuring of attempts to gain state power to shape relationships in civil society; and the conceptual concealment of those ambiguous but significant relationships between state and society" (Rodan 1996a:22).

Both associational civil society (in its neo-Tocquevillean form) and counterweight civil society tend to marginalize political organizations, especially parties (Foley and Edwards 1996:42). Perhaps the biggest problem with both associational and counterweight civil society, however, is that they tend to downplay the importance of gross inequalities of power and resources within civil society (Rodan 1996a:4) and to gloss over "the real, and often sharp, conflicts among groups in civil society."[11] (For many developing countries, a question more basic than bowling alone or in a league is whether the masses can afford such a pastime of the rich and the middle class.)

Associational civil society appears to be the version of civil society that "revisionist neoliberalism" promotes. According to Giles Mohan and Kristian Stokke, the neoliberal development strategy, while continuing to stress market deregulation, now gives attention to institutional reforms and social development too. Under revised neoliberalism, civil society has become an arena for attaining development objectives. Its role, however, is merely to "exert organised pressure on autocratic and unresponsive states and thereby support democratic stability and good governance." Revisionist neoliberals base their notion of participation and empowerment on a "harmony model of power," which holds that "the empowerment of the powerless could be achieved within the existing social order without any significant negative effects upon the power of the powerful" (Mohan and Stokke 2000:248–49).[12]

In the early 1990s, leftist groups in the Philippines outside of the popdems, Bisig, and Pandayan were reluctant to use the term *civil society*. With all the hoopla—and funding—revolving around associational civil-society-type of projects, however, many left-aligned POs/NGOs, as well as leftist political blocs, including those identified with the NDs, soon clambered onto the civil society bandwagon. The legal left substituted or alternated such old terms as *mass organizations* and *mass movements* with *civil society* or portrayed allied POs/NGOs as being the most active or even the leading sector of civil society. In communicating with the masses, leftist activists simply used *civil society* and did not bother to find or coin a vernacular term for the English one. The rejectionist Marxist-Leninist parties, despite the enthusiastic use of *civil society* by the legal political blocs aligned with them, remained suspicious, partly in reaction to the aggressive propagation of associational civil society by powerful entities. One waxed critical of the moves of the World Bank, the Catholic Church, and President Ramos, among others, to use the civil society concept for their own ends (Rebolusyonaryong Partido ng Manggagawa—Pilipinas 2000:22–23).

Since the 1990s, Philippine civil society has been a battleground for contending views of the civil society argument: associational, counterweight and hegemonic. Leftist parties and groups—even those that basically remained in the mass movement framework and merely wanted to ride on the warm and fuzzy civil society one—had to deal with associational civil society. The pitch of the big institutional players for "strengthening civil society" was almost overwhelming. Both POs and NGOs aligned with these leftist groups could not but be affected by all "strong civil society" hype, because they, too, were recipients of foreign funding. As is well known, Philippine NGOs, like their counterparts in other developing countries, are heavily dependent on foreign funding, and many international donor agencies impose their views on how their work should proceed (Mendoza 1995). Ben Reid (2004:29–40) argues that the Philippine government has succeeded in co-opting SD "CSOs" by drawing key SD figures into government and getting the CSOs involved in the planning and implementation of its "poverty alleviation" programs.

NGO Movement versus Political Party

According to Foley and Edwards (1996:42), both Civil Society I (associational) and Civil Society II (counterweight) tend to undervalue specifically political associations, especially parties. Associational civil society stresses "the political benefits of an apolitical civil society," while counterweight civil society centers on "politically mobilized social actors outside customary political associations." The downplaying of political parties showed up in the Philippines, too, and affected the Left. A book that surprisingly had considerable influence in some leftist circles, *Getting to the 21st Century: Voluntary Action and the Global Agenda*, stresses the role of civil society as a primary agent of development, expounds on four generations or stages of strategies of development-oriented POs/NGOs (including national and global networks for the fourth stage), and ignores political movements, organizations, and parties completely—as if POs/NGOs have no links with them whatsoever (Korten 1990).

After the CPP split and failed attempts to unite SD groups, many leftists who had quit, been expelled, or cut themselves off from the CPP and the PDSP continued to be actively involved in small political groups and/or POs/NGOs. Among themselves, however, the rejectionists found it difficult to overcome ideological, political, and even personal differences. Meanwhile, people who had left or broken off with the PDSP were likewise unable to form a new party. With the new, leftist forces in disarray, many former ND cadres and activists began to distance themselves from the political groups, limit their political activities, and focus on PO/NGO work. A good number even dropped all involvement in political activities. Non-ND POs/NGOs, on the other hand, had "a strong anti-statist bias partly in reaction to ND conceptions of alternative political and economic organization." PO/NGO activists, in general, had come to "abhor traditional politicians with a passion approaching moral revulsion" (Morales 1993: viii). Often heard were comments such as "NGOs and politics should never mix," which suggested that NGOs should restrict themselves to development and leave politics to the politicians (Serrano 1992b:13). Many POs/NGOs aligned with leftist groups simply drifted away from them.

On the other hand, as POs/NGOs became increasingly assertive, many observers perceived them as playing a more important political role. They were reputedly taking the lead not only in development efforts (Goertzen 1991; Brillantes 1994:584) but also in the democratization process, in fact taking the place of conventional actors—political parties and interest groups—in the latter (Tigno 1993:60). In championing the interests of the underprivileged and advancing the "struggle for civil society," NGOs had become a new "political opposition" (Hewison and Rodan 1996:63). They filled a vacuum left by the political party system by articulating the political demands of subordinate classes and sectors and middle-class sections alienated from the traditional political parties.[13] Some prominent leftists, as well as some scholars, wrote about the "NGO movement" and "NGOs as a social movement" (Morales 1993:vii; Lopa 1995:37–71; Alegre 1996:2–48). When the Communist Party of Thailand collapsed in the 1980s, many former cadres and activists eventually found their way into NGOs, which began to resemble a social movement, and into pro-capitalist parties (Ungpakorn 2003:chap. 10; Chutima 1994:146–47; Maisrikrod 1997:155). After the CPP split, a similar possibility for former CPP/ND cadres and activists loomed.

Many within the emergent leftist groups, however, still believed in the necessity of a political party—not one to replace POs/NGOs but one with deep roots in and close ties with, the progressive PO/NGO community. Of what use is a strong and vibrant civil society if at the end of the day the oligarchic elite and the *trapo* parties still call the shots? Engagement in elections proved decisive in resolving the political party question.

A few years before the CPP split, there were already some leftist groups and individuals within as well as outside the ND and SD ranks who wanted to take the electoral struggle more seriously. They refused to toe the official lines and adopt the electoral strategies of the CPP and PDSP. The popdems had become increasingly frustrated with the CPP's doctrinairism, and Pandayan was frustrated with the PDSP's growing tendency to "compromise" with the government and the *trapos* in the ruling coalition.

The popdems, Bisig, and Pandayan worked together to rejuvenate the Left's electoral challenge. In 1990, they launched Project 1992 in an effort to build a national "Center-Left" coalition for the 1992 national elections. After months of "shuttle diplomacy" among various leftist groups, however, the project fell through, as the "three little pigs"—as some NDs disparagingly called them—failed to draw in the mainstream NDs and the other SD formations. Unfazed, the threesome poured its energy into Project 2001, billed as "an electoral movement of the NGO community." Involved in the project were various PO and NGO alliances from all over the country, including the Caucus of Development NGO Networks (CODE-NGO), the largest coalition of NGOs (Gutierrez 1994b:107–10). Former congressman Florencio Abad (1991), one of Project 2001's main initiators, called on the PO/NGO community to intervene in the electoral process in four ways: raising political consciousness,[14] lobbying for electoral reforms, developing a people's platform, and giving actual support to specific candidates. Through 1991, the POs and NGOs worked closely together on the first three. But CODE-NGO balked on the fourth point. To avoid a split, Project 2001 refrained from endorsing candidates. Frustrated once again, the popdems, Bisig, and Pandayan formed themselves into a loose nonparty formation, Kaakbay ng Sambayanan (Akbayan)[15] or Ally of the People. Akbayan adopted the development agenda of the POs/NGOs in Project 2001 and endorsed the slate of the Liberal party (LP) and PDP, headed by Senators Jovito Salonga and Aquilino Pimentel, Jr., becoming the third member of the national coalition (Rood 1991: 110–1). By then, however, the election campaign was about to begin.

The Salonga-Pimentel slate lost badly. Out of seven presidential aspirants, Salonga came in sixth, getting even fewer votes than Imelda Marcos. The Salonga-Pimentel defeat was a particularly bitter pill to swallow for the members of Akbayan. It was clear to them that the grassroots strength of the political blocs and POs/NGOs had not proven sufficient enough to be translated into an electoral force (Valte 1992:5). Moreover, the "three little pigs" of Akbayan fell far short of their objectives. They had hoped not just to help progressive candidates win but also to inject as much new politics in the campaign as they could and to expand their own ranks in the course of the campaign. Untried and untested in the electoral game, Akbayan did not have much influence in the running of the Salonga-

Pimentel campaign, which had relied mainly on the traditional networks of the LP and PDP.

Many of the activists in the political blocs, especially those involved in the Salonga-Pimentel campaign, had had enough of being a NGO movement without a party and playing second fiddle to the traditional parties. The 1993 FOPA conference emphatically rejected the idea of a NGO movement without a party.

> A loose coalition or aggregation of PO's and NGO's does not a political movement make. NGO's and PO's serve to articulate the diverse community and sectoral demands of civil society, not to serve as 1001 substitutes for a political movement. ... The role of a political movement is to comprehensively articulate different issues into a vision and political program, draw support from a variety of issue-based civil society-based coalitions without absorbing them or being absorbed by them, and organize this support from organized civil society and unorganized citizenry into a bid for state power.
>
> Bello 1993:20

The FOPA conference specified a political party as the appropriate agent for articulating a comprehensive vision of change. The political movement would contend in different political arenas—in mass movements and, "especially under a regime of elite democracy, in the electoral struggle, which is, whether we like it or not, the current source of legitimacy on who governs" (Bello 1993:21).

The idea of a political party prevailed over an NGO movement—but perhaps to a fault. Due to continuing ideological and political differences, the emergent leftist groups formed several parties instead of just one.

Civil Society as a Terrain of Struggle

For the Philippine Left, mass or social movements have been the most common manifestation of popular participation in politics. In fact, they are an arena in which the Left has achieved a certain level of expertise. This comes not from studying "academic" social movement theory but from years and years of practical experience and a little "guidance" from the writings of Marxist and non-Marxist leftist thinkers. Through regular assessments of the national and international situations, CPP/ND cadres and activists have often managed to gauge what has now been dubbed in social movement theory as the "political opportunity structure." They have "aroused, organized and mobilized" peasants, workers, women, youth and students to mount "contentious" collective challenges against the state and the powers that be. In the course of setting the "tactical political line" and conducting "propaganda work," they have done "framing work"—turning grievances into broader and more resonant claims and rousing "hot cognitions" around them, as Sidney Tarrow (1998:21) defines it. By forging coalitions, expanding organizations and networks, and launching campaign after campaign, they have been able many times to sustain collective action and a few times to help bring about "cycles of contention" or, as in January 2001, even popular uprisings.[16]

As early as the Aquino period, POs/NGOs participating in policy-making, including many aligned with emergent leftist groups, had learned how to employ "programmatic demand making." Magadia (2003:19) defines this as "the presentation and communication to government of an articulated position regarding a policy issue, wherein societal concerns are expressed comprehensively, as to include general principles, particular provisions, and even some implementing guidelines." Apart from staging rallies and demonstrations and airing their views in the mass media, coalitions such as the Congress for a People's Agrarian Reform (CPAR), Labor Advisory and Consultative Council (LACC), Urban Land Reform Task Force (ULR-TF), and Philippine Drug Action Network (PDAN) participated at varying levels in public hearings, congressional committee hearings, discussions with legislators, and so on, in pushing for agrarian reform, labor relations reform, urban land reform, and the passage of the generic drug policy, respectively. In the case of CPAR and LACC, programmatic demand making reached the most advanced form—"a proposal in actual legislative format." Agrarian reform generated tremendous public support: "almost all major sectoral organizations and many respected and well-known individuals issued position statements or solidarity statements on agrarian reform in general, or on particular aspects of the proposed alternatives." Of the four policy areas mentioned, agrarian reform had the highest intensity of "political catalysis." In the end, however, the landlord-honeycombed

Congress considerably watered down key provisions of the main agrarian reform bill, and CPAR regarded the Comprehensive Agrarian Reform Law of 1988 as a victory of the landed elite. Congress likewise passed Republic Act 6715, a labor relations law, which the LACC denounced as antilabor. However, despite a medium level of PO/NGO participation and mobilization and of political catalysis, the urban land reform movement succeeded in getting the pro-urban poor Urban Development and Housing Act enacted and signed into law. The PDAN likewise succeeded with the Generic Drugs Act (Magadia 2003).

Leftist groups and allied POs/NGOs scored their biggest victory in policy-making participation during Aquino's time, when the Philippine Senate rejected the extension of the U.S. military bases agreement after huge demonstrations and strong lobbying by the broad anti-bases movement. The U.S. bases policy area probably exceeded even agrarian reform in the intensity of political catalysis.

During the Ramos period, two cases of overseas Filipino (OF) workers sentenced to death triggered massive protests in the Philippines, as well as in the overseas Filipino community. In the case of Flor Contemplacion, a Filipino maid who was hanged for the murder of another Filipino maid and the latter's four-year-old ward in Singapore, the protests were not only directed against the Singaporean government but also against the Philippine government, which was reported to have done little to help her. Several months later, when Sarah Balabagan was sentenced to death in Saudi Arabia for killing her employer, who had raped her, the outpouring of protest prompted the Philippine government to intervene. She was eventually released. The POs/NGOs linked with the left participated actively in the protests (Melencio 1995; Tesoro and Lopez 1996).

For the emergent leftist groups, many of which have come from the ND and SD ranks, civil society has been more than just a familiar terrain of struggle. Over the past decade, they seem to have made their mark in social movements and to be holding their own vis-à-vis the NDs, doing even better than the NDs in certain sectors and areas.

With substantial bases in the rural areas, Akbayan, ABA-AKO, and the Marxist-Leninist rejectionist parties have been actively involved in the struggles of peasants on such issues as agrarian reform, land-grabbing, recognition of land titles, land conversion and the coconut levy. Three of the country's biggest peasant federations are affiliated with Akbayan, and these federations are part of two of the biggest PO-NGO coalitions pushing for agrarian reform, the Partnership for Agrarian Reform and Rural Development Services (PARRDS) and the People's Campaign for Agrarian Reform Network. The ABA-AKO is backed by the half-century-old Federation of Free Farmers, still one of the country's largest peasant federations. In actual membership, the peasant federations affiliated with Akbayan and ABA-AKO now probably far outstrip the NDs' open peasant organizations, but the latter can rely on the rural mass base of the CPP-NPA for its peasant mobilizations.[17] The RPM-P, MLPP, and RPM-M are particularly strong in former CPP-NPA guerrilla zones in Western Visayas, Central Luzon, and Central Mindanao, respectively.

The POs/NGOs currently aligned with Akbayan and ABA-AKO have been in the forefront of the struggle for agrarian reform, striving to make the most out of the 1988 agrarian reform law while continuing to explore possibilities for more progressive legislation. During the Ramos and Estrada periods, PARRDS adopted a "*bibingka* strategy" of forging coalitions between proagrarian reform forces "from below" (social movement actors) and "from above" ("state reformists" such as agrarian reform secretaries Ernesto Garilao and Horacio Morales, Jr.).[18] Other peasant and agrarian reform groups, however, became increasingly critical of the slow pace of reform implementation under Estrada-Morales and Morales's alleged partiality toward certain peasant groups. Frictions arose within both the agrarian reform PO-NGO community and Akbayan. After Estrada's fall, the dissonance subsided somewhat.[19]

Both the PMP and Akbayan are strong in the labor sector. Two large labor centers are aligned or affiliated with them: Bukluran ng Manggagawang Pilipino (BMP) or Solidarity of Filipino Workers, with PMP; and the Alliance of Progressive Labor (APL) with Akbayan. The BMP broke away from the CPP-aligned labor center in 1993, at the time of the CPP split. To distinguish itself from the ND labor movement, BMP describes itself as being "militant, socialist and democratic."[20] The APL, established in 1996 after ten years of labor organizing by Bisig, Pandayan, and independents, espouses "social movement unionism."[21] Each has a few hundred local affiliates—labor unions and associations—with tens of thousands of members. Apart from fighting for workers' rights and welfare at the factory or plantation level, BMP and APL have also been active in struggles for wage increases, tax cuts, rollbacks of oil prices and water and electricity rates, and the repeal of antilabor laws, as well as on national political and social issues.[22] Among the organizations of government employees, the Akbayan-affiliated Confederation of Independent Unions (CIU) is now the largest.[23] Also aligned with PMP is the Kongreso ng Pagkakaisa ng Maralitang Lungsod (KPML) or Unity Congress of the Urban Poor, the biggest coalition of organizations of urban poor communities, which is particularly strong in Metro Manila.[24] The ABA-AKO and Akbayan also have strong affiliate organizations in urban poor areas.

Abanse Pinay has its main base in the women's movement, but other groups, such as Akbayan and PMP, have many members and allies in women's groups too. They have all worked for women's empowerment, for ending unequal power relations between the sexes, and for the passage of laws related to women trafficking, domestic violence, and so on. (Sarenas 1999; Center for Legislative Development 2003). The emergent leftist parties and groups also have POs/NGOs aligned with them in other sectors (youth and students, other professionals, overseas Filipinos, etc.) and communities (the Moro and other indigenous peoples). In line with its "tri-people approach," the Mindanao-based RPM-M has helped organize and maintained close links with POs/NGOs of Christians, Moros, and *lumad* (non-Moro indigenous peoples) in war-torn Mindanao, opposed military escalation time and again, and undertaken peace-building initiatives.[25]

The Freedom from Debt Coalition (FDC), an alliance of POs, NGOs, and political blocs of the emergent Left, has long been in the forefront of campaigns asserting economic nationalism. It has often inveighed against the WB and the IMF for "meddling" in the country's economic affairs, imposing disadvantageous conditions in extending loans, and thus driving the country deeper in debt. In the FDC's view, IMF-WB conditions to ensure debt repayment force developing countries, such as the Philippines, to reduce education and health spending, eliminate food subsidies, devalue national currencies, and freeze wages—"belt tightening measures that exacerbate poverty, reduce our country's ability to develop a strong domestic economy, and allow multinational corporations to exploit workers and the environment." Among the more recent projects heavily promoted by the IMF-WB in the Philippines, the FDC has vigorously opposed the privatization of water and power services. "[I]nstead of better services and lower rates," it charges, "services continue to deteriorate and rates continue to skyrocket." [26]

In recent years, the emergent leftist parties and groups and allied POs/NGOs have been able to stage bigger rallies and demonstrations and wage wider mass campaigns over various issues. On such red-letter occasions as the president's state of the nation address, Labor Day and Human Rights Day, the new, leftist groups have aired their denunciations or criticisms of government policies as well as their advocacies. They have also been quick to react to important developments and have had a share in some big successes. Foremost among the victories of the popular movement was, of course, People Power II, which will be discussed later. In 2002, the new, leftist parties, among others, energetically campaigned against the "purchased power adjustment," an electricity surcharge imposed by the country's main electricity firm, Meralco. The Supreme Court eventually declared the surcharge illegal and found Meralco, owned by the powerful Lopez clan, guilty of overcharging (Nuguid and Quezon 2003). In 2003, some new, leftist groups participated actively in the movement that successfully stopped the impeachment of the chief justice of the Supreme Court, Hilario Davide. The impeachment, apparently based on flimsy charges, had been initiated by politicians identified with Eduardo Cojuangco, a former Marcos crony, whose business interests had been adversely affected by recent Supreme Court rulings (Dacanay 2003; Doronila 2003). In 2004, after a Filipino driver, Angelo de la Cruz, was taken hostage by an extremist group in Iraq, all the leftist groups, which had earlier vigorously opposed the Philippines' participation in the Iraq war, joined broad sections of Filipinos (including those overseas) in calling for the immediate withdrawal of Philippine troops from Iraq. Fearful of another mighty political storm over the plight of overseas Filipino workers, President

Arroyo, once one of Washington's most reliable allies in the "Coalition of the Willing," wilted (El Arabiya 2004; Kasarinlan 2004).

Many left-aligned POs/NGOs have managed to engage in leftist and contentious politics despite the bias toward "nonpartisan" (or apolitical) and not too contentious advocacy work of donor agencies funding them. Although funding institutions in general propagate the "strengthen civil society" line, "[n]ot all donor institutions ... are directly or entirely influenced by Putnam's prescriptions" (Howell and Pearce 2001:41). Many of them put stress on grassroots or grassroots-oriented organizations—peasant associations, trade unions, women's groups, and so on, and the NGOs servicing them—not bowling leagues. There is a whale of a difference. According to Huber et al. (1997:328), bowling leagues and choral groups "strengthen civil society without doing much for political participation or class organization." The League of Women Voters strengthens both civil society and political participation, and trade unions and peasant associations strengthen civil society, political participation, and class organization. Moreover, many aid programs promoting a strong civil society such as "people's participation in governance" and "women and development" provide opportunities for militant activism.

Through contentious politics, the emergent leftist parties and groups and allied POs/NGOs have sought to bring the issues and concerns of subordinate classes and groups into the mainstream of public discourse and debate. The engagement of the Marxist-Leninist rejectionist parties in mass movements has still been very much influenced by an antisystemic orientation—"expose and oppose" the "reactionary" state in order to bring it down. The engagement of Akbayan and ABA-AKO, on the other hand, has been transformation oriented rather than antisystemic. In line with its counterhegemonic struggle framework, Akbayan has geared its actions toward changing the balance of power among social classes and groups and eventually transforming the exercise of state power. On the whole, however, the new, leftist groups have been moving toward combining protest with advocacy and "exposing and opposing" with "proposing" alternative projects and policies.

Over the past decade or so, coalitions of POs/NGOs aligned with different new, leftist parties have been slow to arise. In the heyday of coalitions in the late 1980s and early 1990s, POs/NGOs with or without alignments to leftist groups had forged broad coalitions on a variety of issues and concerns—agrarian reform, labor, urban poor, women's issues, human rights, development, U.S. bases, debt, peace, health, environment, and so on.[27] The coalitions were able "to provide important forums to coordinate advocacy work, develop experiences together on campaigns, and to develop analyses and strategies that genuinely cross-cut some of the traditional divisions between the political blocs" (Gershman 1993:159). Most of these coalitions, such as CPAR, LACC, and ULR-TF, no longer exist. Among the factors that brought about their demise were ideological or political differences, perceived ND vanguardism, and the CPP split.

Of late, the emergent leftist forces have tried to develop more collaborative relations among themselves. Factors such as the Lagman killing,[28] differing stances toward pro-Estrada forces and the Arroyo government, and personal grudges, however, have sometimes gotten in the way. Coalitions and common projects with the NDs (reaffirmists) have been rare, because the NDs still basically view the new leftist forces as counterrevolutionaries. Among the old coalitions, the FDC is the only one surviving that still has several political blocs in it—but now excluding the NDs (reaffirmists). The emergent leftist groups and their networks conducted a joint international solidarity conference in August 2001 (Bayanihan International Solidarity Conference 2001). Various new, leftist forces, together with many allied POs/NGOs, coalesced in February 2002 to oppose the deployment of U.S. military "advisers" to train Philippine troops fighting the Abu Sayyaf. They set up the Gathering for Peace, a broad coalition against the presence of U.S. troops in the Philippines and U.S. intervention in Philippine affairs (Gathering for Peace 2002). Most significant, over eight hundred representatives of various new, leftist groups and allied POs/NGOs assembled for a "people's summit" called Alternatiba in November 2003 to forge a new coalition against a governance of elite rule (Alternatiba 2003).

Civil Society as a Laboratory for a Viable Alternative

In the struggle against elite rule, the Philippine Left has often engaged in either armed struggle or contentious forms of open, legal struggle—mass demonstrations, strikes, boycotts, and so on. Since EDSA I, however, emergent leftist forces, apart from persevering with social movements, have pursued the counterhegemonic struggle in another way, a largely noncontentious form: development work. Civil society, in this case, serves as a laboratory for a viable leftist alternative. Development work, being a political concern, is another sphere for popular participation in politics. In usual patronage politics, *trapos* extend privileges or make accommodations to their relatives, benefactors, and friends, often compromising or setting back development endeavors. The *trapos* can resort to popular bargaining and negotiation within a clientelist framework or they can simply make or unmake development decisions without bothering to consult their constituencies. With patronage giving way more and more to predation, development has become almost a pipe dream for Filipinos in many areas. Through their engagement in development work, the new, leftist groups hope to show concretely the contrast between *trapo* and progressive and nonparticipatory and participatory development models. Development work, clarifies Llamas (1996:72), is meant not to be a mere palliative to social ills but to provide "a concrete example of a socialist future."

The few NGOs that existed from the 1950s to the mid-1960s viewed their role in terms of "community development," basically an extension of the Christian ethic of attending to the needs of the poor. Community development work ranged from charity to building sanitary toilets, promoting better nutrition and adult literacy education, and increasing agricultural productivity without changing tenurial systems. With Vatican II and the rise of protest movements worldwide in the late 1960s, however, some community development workers began to emphasize the need to change social structures and encourage people's participation (particularly the participation of the "poor, deprived, and oppressed") in this process of change. The concept of "community organizing" was born, and both NDs and SDs engaged in it. At a time of a worsening political situation in the Philippines, community organizing veered toward mass protest actions—"pressure" or contentious politics (Bulatao 1995:1–3).

Under martial law, NDs and SDs employed community-organizing methods in grassroots organizing in both urban and rural areas, eventually in building progressive "basic Christian communities," community-based health programs, and so on. In the late 1970s, however, the NDs discarded the community-organizing approach, and adopted more "revolutionary" forms of organizing. Programs employing the former approach, especially those of a socioeconomic nature, were seen as tending toward "reformism," "economism," "localism," and "churchiness" (National Peasant Secretariat, Communist Party of the Philippines 1978). Despite the shift to "revolutionary" organizing, NDs continued to pursue "socioeconomic" projects, or at least to solicit funding for such projects without necessarily implementing them. Large amounts of development aid were diverted to the revolutionary underground. Nonetheless, some ND-aligned NGOs, especially in Mindanao, did undertake "socioeconomic work" (SEW) geared toward improving the people's livelihood.[29]

After the fall of Marcos, NGOs engaged in SEW or development work became more numerous, even as POs/NGOs engaged in pressure politics continued to proliferate. Development NGOs, including those that were ND aligned, were able to establish relatively secure bases at the *barangay* (village) level. So-called SEW practitioners insisted that social change is achieved not just through the seizure of state power and the destruction of structures perpetuating inequity and oppression but also through "creating structures and new ways of thinking and of living." They stressed that "the basic activity of SEW is empowerment of people" (Calaguas 1989:9). Horacio Morales, Jr., president of the Philippine Rural Reconstruction Movement, described empowerment as "the process of shifting the balance of social power from one social class or group of classes to another, which may include the shift in economic or political importance between areas or regions, resulting in a new power configuration" (Morales 1990:55). There was growing recognition of the need to shift from too much contentious politics to engagement in projects concretely improving the conditions of the poor and marginalized.

Only late in the Aquino period did the NDs seriously involved in development work gain greater appreciation for their work (Rocamora 1994b:50). By then, however, the CPP was on the verge of a split.

In Rocamora's (1994b:54–57, 60–61) analysis, the CPP split, the worldwide crisis of socialism, and a perceived change in the Philippine political economy pushed development NGOs and the progressive movement as a whole to a strategic reorientation regarding development work. The "irreducible foundation" of the new framework was "a commitment to place the interests and the organizations of poor and oppressed communities as the centerpiece of an alternative society and the strategy for achieving this society." The new paradigm saw a process of building from the ground up. "Simple accumulation of power" at the local level—building more and more POs and more and more livelihood projects—would pave the way for the "complex accumulation of power," which would require doing battle with local elite power structures in different arenas, including elections and governance.

From *barangay*-based, small-scale livelihood and other socioeconomic projects, POs/NGOs engaged in development work moved on to "integrated area development" (IAD), which blended progressive elements of community development and community organizing, covered much wider areas, and was complemented by PO/NGO national advocacy work (Bulatao 1995:9; Rocamora 1994b:62–63). Integrated area development was by no means an original idea of the Left; it was, in fact, a brainchild of the government. The first government IAD projects in the 1970s consisted of an integrated package of infrastructure investments. In the 1980s, the package was broadened to include rural services (such as credit extension and marketing) and institutional strengthening. When progressive NGOs undertook their own IAD in the 1990s, they set growth as well as equity as their aims. The concept of institutional strengthening was itself broadened to include training in popular participation, governance, and empowerment, as well as more traditional skill building (Bulatao 1999:12–13). Community organizing was a crucial component of the NGOs' IAD strategy, facilitating the formation of POs and the training of PO leaders. Other important elements of the strategy were socioeconomic work and effective resource mobilization and management

(Francisco 1995:91). The concept of IAD soon became "sustainable integrated area development" (SIAD), as the POs/NGOs involved in it felt that the question of ecological balance had to be more adequately addressed (Bulatao 1999:12–15).

The IAD/SIAD programs have increasingly become joint endeavors between POs/NGOs and governmental organizations (GOs). For many community organizers, especially those who had experienced repression under Marcos, working with the government as a partner did not come easily. They were accustomed to dealing with the government as an adversary. For a time, some of them seemed to be gripped with "a 'primordial fear' of being co-opted by the government"(Francisco 1995:87). Gradually, however, they realized that they had to work with GOs if they wanted to achieve their development goals fully. "Somehow," Tomasito Villarin (2000:32), executive director of the Institute of Politics and Governance (IPG), points out, "a political-developmental framework that defines project objectives within the broader objective of changing power relations and building up a just, equitable and humane society is needed. NGOs do not exist in a vacuum nor does the implementation of development projects."

Initial IAD/SIAD programs have come up with fairly encouraging results. In Antique Province, for instance, seven years of the Antique Integrated Area Development (Aniad) resulted in the development of some organizational systems in participating POs; greater assertiveness of POs in demanding proper services and greater government responsiveness to community needs, including basic services and affordable credit; increased government recognition of the role of POs/NGOs in local development; improved land tenure arrangements for many farmers; widespread adoption and adaptation of ecologically sound, integrated pest management; and increased appreciation of the role of women. Nonetheless, Aniad assessments showed that much work still had to be done, as the economic situation of many households had not structurally changed; land tenure arrangements for many other farmers had not improved; "critical consciousness and awareness were limited to a few people"; and most POs still came up short in reach, quality and stability or durability (Vandenbroeck 1998:5–6, 44).

Despite a growing number of success stories of PO-NGO-GO cooperation, state manipulation of development initiatives from civil society remains a problem. According to Putzel (1998:100–2), NGOs endeavoring to deliver services to the rural poor have had to compromise with the state and in many cases have ended up legitimizing deeply flawed government programs. Moreover, in some cases the state, after adopting certain programs originating in NGO grassroots work, has perverted their original "people-oriented" thrust.

The emergent leftist parties and groups, in varying degrees, are all engaged in development work. Akbayan appears to have gone much farther than the others in this arena, especially with regard to IAD/SIAD. Furthermore, Akbayan has seized on the opportunities opened by the Local Government Code of 1991, which provided for decentralization and PO/NGO participation in local governments to promote "people's participation in governance." Akbayan and allied NGOs have conducted trainings all over the country on *barangay* governance including *barangay* development planning and budgeting through participatory rural appraisal (see chap. 5). Extending Gramscian counterhegemony beyond civil society, Villarin (2000:32) contends that POs/NGOs engaging with the state should always view it as a "non-monolithic institution" and treat it as an "arena of struggle."

Civil Society as a Counterweight to the State

The ouster of Marcos by people power in 1986, with a prominent role played by cause-oriented groups, essentially followed the same "civil society against the state" logic of counterweight civil society that characterized the antiauthoritarian struggles in Eastern Europe and Latin America. In the early 1990s, when counterweight civil society gained some adherents in the Philippine Left, however, it seemed to lack sting. Build or resurrect civil society? Philippine civil society was already flourishing. In fact, Canadian Embassy officials had already described Philippine NGOs as "the most organized and well-developed NGO community in the world" (Goertzen 1991). The Philippines is now reputed to have the third-largest PO/NGO community in the developing world, behind Brazil and India, and the largest in per capita terms (Clarke 1998a:193, 200–201). Pit civil society against the state? There were still human rights violations, but the state was not as repressive as it had been under Marcos. Moreover, the Aquino and Ramos administrations enjoyed the support of large sections of civil society.

Those in the Left who did try to pursue counterweight civil society managed to expose government abuses, wrongheaded government policies, the usual graft and corruption, bureaucratic foul-ups, and so on—but nothing so serious as to lead to a confrontation between civil society and the state. For the emergent leftist groups, the actual value of counterweight civil society seemed to be more in terms of helping stamp out whatever vestiges of Stalinist thinking still remained within their ranks. But then along came "*jueteng*-gate," a scandal that implicated President Joseph Estrada in a nationwide racket of the popular but illegal numbers game. Soon enough, all sorts of groups called for his resignation or ouster.

In January 2001, people power toppled the boss-president Estrada after impeachment proceedings against him collapsed. Known as EDSA II, this marked the high point of the engagement of the emergent leftist forces in civil society and of their coalition efforts. Unlike in EDSA I, when the bulk of the Left missed out as a result of their boycott of the presidential elections, practically all leftist forces—the emergent ones as well as the mainstream NDs and SDs—participated in EDSA II. Several coalitions were involved in what Reyes (2001) loftily describes as "an uprising of civil society." The NDs formed their own Erap Resign Movement.[30] The emergent leftist forces joined the much larger and broader coalition, the Congress of Filipino Citizens 2 (Kompil 2), which took its name from the first Kompil, which fought the Marcos dictatorship. "Kompil 2 as a broad, loose and pluralist coalition," observes Reyes (2001:10), "held fast to its identity as a civil society opposition movement distinct from the political opposition formed by traditional opposition political parties. Requests by politicians to join the coalition were politely turned down. But party-list groups were allowed to participate in recognition of their grassroots nature and transformative politics." Maintaining unity within Kompil 2 proved a trying task. Unlike most groups that focused on Estrada's ouster, PMP and the POs/NGOs aligned with it were critical not just of Estrada but of Vice President Arroyo as well and advocated for a more radical position: Resign All! PMP and allied groups initiated another coalition bearing such a position, People's Action to Remove Erap, but remained in Kompil 2.

Both EDSA I and II were uprisings of civil society that overthrew a corrupt president. Indeed, Marcos and Estrada were infamous for their corrupt, patrimonial, and plundering ways. In the sense that EDSA II was directed at overthrowing a corrupt *regime,* it can very well be argued that it too was in the nature of "civil society against the state" and hence, a variant of counterweight civil society. Somewhat bolstering this argument is the fact that civil society rose up against Marcos because he was a dictator *and* a crook.

Associational, counterweight, and hegemonic civil society and the traditional concept of "mass movement" all contributed to EDSA II. Many members of the middle class were involved in organizations and groups of the associational civil society type. Despite the apolitical character of neo-Tocquevillean associational civil society, the middle class came out in full force in EDSA II. The middle class may even have comprised the majority at EDSA II, although the greater part of those in the mass protests all over the country leading up to EDSA II came from the lower classes (Bautista 2001:7–9). Influenced by the traditional concept of mass movement, the CPP would certainly have wanted, if it could, to mobilize civil society to overthrow not just the Estrada regime but the entire "reactionary" political system. For some of the emergent leftist forces, however, EDSA II merely constituted a tactical shift of emphasis from hegemonic civil society to counterweight civil society.

After EDSA II, it was back to hegemonic civil society. Not much had really changed; EDSA II maintained the elite democracy that EDSA I had installed. The oligarchic elite had quickly come back to roost. According to Törnquist (2002:chap. 7), "middle class democratization" (featuring EDSA I and II) and the "idealist crafting of civil society democracy" in the Philippines had produced a superficial and unstable democracy. David (2002) remarks bluntly: "It is ... foolish for civil society to think it has any hold on the [Arroyo] administration it helped put in power. The political rules and structures are unchanged. This is still a government of the elite."

In May 2001, EDSA III, the revolt of the pro-Estrada masses, came as a quick and jolting reminder that Philippine civil society was still a very much divided lot and that the Left had failed to reach large sections of the poor and marginalized. Despite all the allegations of corruption and plunder leveled against Estrada and his being labeled as a *trapo*, the masses still identified with him because in their view he treated the poor with dignity and compassion, he spoke their language, and he made them feel that he was one of them and for them: *"Si Erap ay para sa mahirap"* (Erap is for the poor).[31] Bautista (2001:36) explains why patronage and populist politics held sway at EDSA III.

> For as long as the poor do not share the fruits of development, their marginalization and lack of opportunities will make them vulnerable to the machinations of traditional politicians. For as long as they live sub-human lives, desperation will force them to pin their hopes on ineligible candidates created by television and cinema. For as long as they do not experience mobility, an undeveloped sense of efficacy will prevent them from critically holding their leaders accountable for their actions. For as long as they remain poor, therefore, the democratization process will be severely constrained.

The Reassertion of Hegemonic Civil Society

In a relatively short period, the emergent leftist parties and groups in the Philippines have made considerable progress in their engagement in civil society—in contentious politics as well as in development work. Due to the influences of associational and counterweight civil society, however, many activists and members of the new leftist forces have fallen for, as well as disseminated, some misconceptions about civil society. The most common is that civil society is innately good, almost like motherhood / fatherhood and apple pie. Another is that a strong and vibrant civil society ensures or strengthens democracy. A third is that POs and NGOs are at the very core or at the helm of civil society. Many POs and NGOs have become so enamored with civil society that they parade themselves as civil society organizations or present themselves as representing or even *being* civil society. Anna Marie Karaos (2001) observes that in EDSA II many activists kept using *civil society* to refer to anti-Estrada groups.[32] Such assertions have apparently brought results. "In the Philippine context," writes Jose Magadia (1999:255), "the civil society label focuses on two main types of voluntary societal organizations, the NGOs and the POs. This is the convention used and accepted by these organizations themselves, as well as the media, academe, church, business, and government." The misconceptions are by no means prevalent only in the Philippines, and they have been roundly criticized (see Carothers 1999b:18–22).

At first glance, it would seem to be not such a bad idea for the emergent leftist forces and the POs/NGOs aligned with them to ride on the "good" image of civil society. There are deeper implications, however. Civil society, as Rodan (1996a:22) rightly points out, is in fact "the locus of a range of inequalities based on class, gender, ethnicity, race and sexual preference." To view civil society in the inegalitarian Philippines as good is to render oneself blind to the fact that like the state, civil society is dominated by the oligarchic elite. The POs/NGOs may well be the most politicized, vocal and militant sector in Philippine civil society, but they are definitely not the most powerful.

Rivera (2002:476) puts POs/NGOs and the social movements on the list of the most politically significant actors in the Philippines' "dense network of civil society organizations," but the list also includes "the highly influential Catholic church … and various organizations allied with the church; the powerful business groups led by the Makati Business Club which includes the country's top corporations and other business groupings such as the Bankers' Association of the Philippines (BAP) and the Employers Confederation of the Philippines (ECOP); the *Iglesia ni Kristo* (Church of Christ), a tightly organized and disciplined local church group with a track record of voting as a single bloc for their candidates of choice; the mass media, arguably the freest in the region; … and charismatic religious movements." (According to Gretchen Casper [1995:3–4], the Marcos regime, by forcing the Catholic Church to play an active political role against it, inadvertently guaranteed that this social institution would continue to intervene in politics in the postauthoritarian era despite the constitutionally-mandated separation of church and the state.) Miranda (1991:161–63) includes politico-economic clans among the most powerful groups in civil society.

Rivera and Miranda forgot to mention criminal syndicates, which thrive in a patrimonial oligarchic state or boss democracy, and, with their connections to *trapos* of Estrada's ilk, certainly have political clout. Indeed, how can one account for the country's 350,000 loose firearms (Bengco 2003) and eighteen murders per day (*Manila Times* 2003)—*Bowling for Columbine*, Philippines? "[M]ost of the 'actually existing' civil society," remarks Törnquist (2002:53), "reflects the combination of religiously backed liberalism, commercialism, and feudal-like bossism."

Although EDSA I and II overthrew dictatorial and corrupt regimes, in place of them, the "uprisings of civil society" could only install an elite-dominated democracy or arguably a less corrupt regime. From the radical democratic perspective, the counterhegemonic forces of the subordinate classes and communities were still too weak to wrest political, intellectual, and moral leadership from the dominant forces and to build a new national-popular collective will. Philippine civil society, as long as the oligarchic elite wields ideological and cultural hegemony in it, simply cannot be expected to transform an elite-dominated democracy into a more participatory and egalitarian one.

At its July 2003 congress, Akbayan forcefully reasserted the hegemonic civil society position.

> Akbayan employs the strategy of combining a determined struggle for ideological and cultural hegemony, establishing building blocks through radical reforms and sustained organizing and constituency building in local communities, sub-classes and sectors and institutions. ... A determined struggle for ideological and cultural hegemony involves a persistent campaign to critique the social and political order and espouse the alternative one, ensuring that such is the framework of tactical battles, developing the internal capacity for discourse and debate, and winning the battle of discourse in the cultural centers of society like the academe, the media, the churches, parliamentary debates and indigenous centers of local discourse.
>
> (Akbayan National Congress 2003:9)

Far from restricting their activities to civil society, the emergent leftist forces have ventured into the arena of the state or political society—elections and governance—and made initial, albeit very modest, gains. Akbayan, ABA-AKO, Abanse Pinay, AMIN, PM, and Sanlakas won seats in the Lower House of Congress through the party-list system in the 1998, 2001, and/or 2004 elections. Akbayan and Sanlakas also scored some victories in village, municipal, city, and provincial elections.

As the Philippine experience has shown, associational and counterweight civil society are of limited usefulness and may even pose encumbrances to the deepening of democracy in postauthoritarian developing states. By presenting an idealized picture of a "good" civil society, they both gloss over or minimize the gross inequalities and the very real conflicts that exist in civil society. Since the third wave of democratization, a good number of developing countries have succeeded, over a decade or two, in constructing or reconstructing civil societies, some of which are already dense and vigorous. Hence, building or resurrecting civil society, as counterweight civil society emphasizes, may no longer be suitable as a main thrust in these third-world democracies. Counterweight civil society may be relevant in certain instances of corrupt, even if democratically elected, regimes, but the argument for people power uprisings can hold only for extreme cases. In calling for the "strengthening" of civil society but ignoring the balance of power within a polity, associational civil society may serve to maintain or even fortify the rule of an entrenched politico-economic elite in highly inegalitarian and corruption-plagued countries. To get somewhere in building social trust and social capital (as Putnam defines it), perhaps one should first address social justice—and punitive justice for the rascals plundering government. Last, associational and counterweight civil society, by deemphasizing political parties, may prevent subordinate classes and groups from availing themselves of the institutional means to challenge the powerful parties of patronage and patrimonialism of the elite.

John Keane (1998:6) uses the term *civil society* as a somewhat neutral "ideal-typical category … that both describes and envisages a complex and dynamic ensemble of legally protected nongovernmental institutions that tend to be non-violent, self-organizing, self-reflexive, and permanently in tension with each other and with the state institutions that 'frame', constrict and enable their activities." Perhaps, Philippine civil society may eventually move toward this normative definition. A definition, however, is different from an argument. Compared to associational and counterweight civil society, the hegemonic argument is more cogent. The gross social inequalities and high levels of corruption in the Philippines do justify a combative counterhegemonic stance by those working for the consolidation and deepening of democracy and the rule of law.

In a good number of postauthoritarian developing states, hegemonic civil society may have greater relevance than associational and counterweight civil society. The former takes fully into account what the latter two gloss over—the gross inequalities of wealth and power, and the conflict within civil society, and the importance of political parties. The transformation of an oligarchic democracy into a more participatory and egalitarian one can be promoted not so much through the strengthening of civil society, as through contestation within it.

4

The Left, Elections, and the Political Party System

SINCE COLONIAL TIMES, members of the elite have dominated the Philippines' political party and electoral systems. The country's main political parties, representing factions of the elite, have been essentially nonideological organizations that lack coherent political programs and mainly promote personal and factional political ambitions and goals (*Philippine Daily Inquirer* 2004). They have weak membership bases and operate only during election time. Political turncoatism is a venerable tradition (Miranda 1991:159). Post-Marcos parties, in particular, have reflected the inchoate character of the Philippine political party system.[1] Far from being stable, programmatic entities, they have in practice proven to be not much more than convenient vehicles of patronage that can be set up, merged with others, split, resurrected, regurgitated, reconstituted, renamed, repackaged, recycled, or flushed down the toilet anytime. After over a century of playing and dominating the electoral game, members of the elite have so mastered its many tricks that they have turned it, to borrow from C. B. Atim (1989:2) into a game of "perpetual musical chairs in which different bourgeois factions jostle for the right to mismanage the country and plunder its wealth." As in pre-martial-law times, post-1986 elections have focused on the candidates' personalities rather than issues or ideology, and they have been marred by the proverbial three Gs—guns, goons and gold. At least 147 people were killed in connection with the May 2004 national elections (Macaraig 2004), making them the bloodiest since 1986. Instead of having a well-developed political party system notes Belinda A. Aquino, the Philippines seems to have retrogressed. "We have institutionalized the wrong things like vote buying, cheating, flying voters, the birds and the bees, fraud, gaudy entertainment, mudslinging, violence, intimidation, manipulation, tampering with ballot boxes, and other unsavory practices, which are played out with impunity." (Aquino 2004:5).[2]

According to Putzel (1999), Philippine democracy remains weak and shallow because of the mismatch between formal political institutions (free elections, universal suffrage, free expression, etc.) and the entrenched informal institutions of patronage politics that still govern behavior. Deepening democracy, he argues, entails going against the grain of traditional informal institutions and establishing political parties based on programmatic politics. With the fall of Marcos and the restoration of formal democratic institutions, some space has been created in which new political actors can challenge the control of political clans and engage in issue- not personality-oriented politics.

In fighting the oligarchic elite, the Left has taken advantage of this political space. After mostly boycotting elections under Marcos, leftist parties and groups have participated in postauthoritarian electoral and parliamentary processes. With the entry of leftist parties advocating a new politics into the electoral arena, there were bright hopes in some quarters, especially in the Left's support base, that the Left would be able to bring the demands of the poor and marginalized into the electoral and parliamentary processes and to break the stranglehold of elite parties on Philippine politics. There were expectations among some of those nauseated with *trapo* ways that the leftist parties would force the traditional parties to define their positions on issues more clearly and thus foster a more issue-oriented politics. Perhaps the Left would help bring about a change from an inchoate to an institutionalized political party system and contribute to the deepening of Philippine democracy. Unfortunately, for the most part, the Left has not been able to live up to such hopes and expectations.

In this chapter, I discuss the electoral challenge of the Left—communists and the CPP-aligned NDs, as well as SDs and independent socialists—to the *trapos* and the traditional parties.[3] I argue that the Left has not yet made much progress in breaking *trapo* domination over the post-Marcos political party and electoral systems not so much because of a long-held aversion to electoral politics, as some scholars contend, but more because a sizable part of the Left still holds an instrumental view of democratic processes and institutions. I show, however, that some emergent leftist parties (1) have adopted or are moving toward an integral view of democracy; (2) have made a vital breakthrough in the congressional party-list vote; and (3) are now more methodically entering other electoral contests, particularly at the *barangay* and municipal levels.

Helpful for analyzing shifting views about elections of the Philippine Left are distinctions Kenneth Roberts made in his study of the left in Latin America regarding the responses of leftist groups to formal democratic institutions and processes, which ranged from (1) the outright rejection or boycotting of such processes, (2) an instrumental view of democracy, and (3) an integral conception of democracy (see chapter 2). By no means is the view of or orientation toward democracy in the Philippine Left the sole or the overarching reason for its dismal electoral performance. Structural and relational (Left-state, Left-civil society, state-elite, intra-Left, etc.) factors certainly need to be taken into account, and I bring these into my discussion. The Left's view of democracy and democratic institutions and processes, however, plays a crucial role, as it determines to a large extent how the Left approaches or confronts these structural and relational factors.

The Left and Elections before EDSA I

Elections have long been one of the weakest spots in the Philippine Left. This is so not only because the elite has always seen to it that there is no level playing field but also because during a certain period a large section of the Left chose to boycott these "bourgeois" exercises and fight in other arenas. According to David (1997:144–45), one of the main reasons why the Left has never won power in the Philippines is the "deeply entrenched tradition of refusal by progressive elements to engage in electoral struggles." A review of the Left's involvement in elections, however, reveals that the left-wing aversion to electoral politics is not as deep as is often portrayed. This "tradition" actually dates back only to 1968 and the founding of the

Maoist CPP. Most members of the CPP during the Marcos period were in favor of boycotting of elections, but other leftist groups, particularly the SDs, often opposed these boycotts. And there were times in the pre-1986 period when the CPP itself, or sections of it, seriously considered, or even engaged in, electoral politics.

The early leftist parties such as the PKP and the Sosyalistang Partido ng Pilipinas (SPP) in the American colonial period participated in elections. From its very founding in 1930, the PKP (precursor of the CPP) declared its intention to participate in elections "under its own banner." In 1931 the PKP presented its own candidates for political office, including PKP leader Crisanto Evangelista, who ran for the Senate. Government authorities, however, refused to give the PKP rally permits and dispersed its rallies when it persisted. The illegalization of the party and imprisonment of its leaders in October 1932 precluded participation in the next few elections (Hoeksema 1956:88, 102, 125).[4] In 1934, SPP chairman Pedro Abad Santos, a former two-term assemblyman, ran unsuccessfully for the governorship of Pampanga. The Republican Party, the SPP, and the Toilers League (a legal front for the outlawed PKP) formed the Coalition of the Oppressed Masses and backed the candidacy of Republican Gregorio Aglipay for president and communist Norberto Nabong for vice president in the 1935 elections (Allen 1985:14–15, 88; Pomeroy 1992:91). Aglipay and Nabong were routed. The Popular Front, which included the PKP and the SPP, fielded candidates in the local elections of 1937 and 1940 and in the Philippine Assembly elections of 1938. In 1937, the SPP won the mayorship in the provincial capital and another major town of Pampanga, and a majority in eight municipal councils (Tan 1985:34). Abad Santos, the SPP leader, lost again in the Pampanga gubernatorial race, but he nearly tripled the votes he got in 1934. In 1940, the Popular Front increased the number of its winning mayoral bets in Pampanga to nine, and it also won all the council seats in three of the province's biggest municipalities. One of its candidates for provincial board member also made it. Abad Santos failed a third time in his gubernatorial attempt, but this time by a close margin. Apart from its gains in Pampanga, the Popular Front also won the mayoralty or councilorships in four towns in Tarlac and one town in Nueva Ecija (Kerkvliet 1972:142;

R. Constantino 1975:382). The Popular Front also put up candidates for various national positions in the 1941 elections. Evangelista, the chairman of the merged PKP-SPP, headed the roster of senatorial candidates. Vice chairman Abad Santos filed his candidacy for no less than the country's presidency but withdrew a few weeks before the elections after the Popular Front was denied the right to have more election inspectors (Hoeksema 1956:178, 221–22; Tan 1985:36–37).

Participation in electoral politics immediately resumed after the Japanese occupation. In the first postwar election in April 1946, the leftist Democratic Alliance, whose top leaders consisted of progressive intellectuals as well as PKP cadres, forged a coalition with President Sergio Osmeña's Nacionalista Party (NP). The NP-DA coalition lost, but all of the seven DA candidates in Central Luzon for the House of Representatives won convincingly. Upon the convening of Congress, however, the Liberal Party-dominated body unseated six of the seven, alleging that they had resorted to fraud and terrorism during the elections.[5] The situation in Central Luzon, a hotbed of agrarian unrest since the 1920s, further deteriorated. Nonetheless, the PKP did not boycott elections. In 1949, it extended "critical support" to Jose P. Laurel's presidential bid (Saulo 1990:36–43; Lava 2002:94, 102). Only in 1951, at the height of the Huk rebellion, did the PKP actively boycott elections, but it soon regarded this as an error (Lava 2002:163).[6] The PKP did not participate in subsequent elections, not because it opposed them but simply because the party had become too debilitated to make any impact.

When the Maoist CPP was established in 1968, it condemned the PKP for abandoning the armed struggle and pursuing a purely parliamentary line. Elections were taboo. The CPP's founding chairman, Sison, castigated the PKP leadership for falling into "the counterrevolutionary practice of directly participating in the puppet elections" (Guerrero 1979a:37). "To have a few seats in a reactionary parliament, and to have no [revolutionary] army in our country is to play a fool's game," he wrote (Guerrero 1979b:181). Party members were constantly reminded of events in the country's history ostensibly pointing to the bankruptcy of the electoral or parliamentary road, such as the PKP's illegalization in 1931, the DA experience, and so on. The tragic experiences of the "revolutionary" forces in

Indonesia in Sukarno's time and Chile in Allende's time were also often cited to demonstrate the folly of the purely electoral or parliamentary path.

In the main, the CPP and ND forces boycotted elections from 1969 to 1986. Before martial law, the CPP did not always engage in a campaign of "hard" boycotting. In the 1971 elections for delegates to the Constitutional Convention, the official CPP/ND line was boycotting, but legal ND forces in the national capital region were directed to campaign actively for a leftist candidate, Enrique Voltaire Garcia III, who won, nearly topping the Metro Manila vote. After the Plaza Miranda bombing of 1971, the CPP toned down its call for a boycott of the senatorial elections so as to allow for a landslide win for the legal opposition and hasten Marcos's political isolation.

After Marcos imposed martial law, however, the CPP boycott line turned hard. Participating in Marcos's electoral shows was thought to be tantamount to legitimizing his dictatorial regime. In the 1978 elections for Marcos's transition parliament (the IBP), however, NDs in Manila-Rizal decided to participate in the elections, linking up with "bourgeois" anti-Marcos forces and the SDs and putting up a coalition opposition ticket with them. The cadres of the national capital region hoped to take advantage of the "democratic space" opened up by the elections to develop the mass movement into a "revolutionary upsurge" (Executive Committee, Manila-Rizal Committee, CPP 1977:1). Afterward, however, the national CPP leadership roundly criticized the leading CPP cadres in Manila-Rizal for engaging in "reformism" and removed them from their posts for violating the party's boycott policy.[7] In subsequent election boycotts in 1980–84, there was not much questioning about, nor any significant violation of, the boycott policy. *"Rebolusyon, hindi eleksyon!"* (Revolution, not election!) became virtually became an all-weather slogan.

Party leaders, however, made some exceptions during the 1982 *barangay* elections. In many guerrilla zones, NPA fighters and ND cadres and activists were directed to secretly put up or endorse ND or allied candidates for the *barangay* councils to prevent these councils from being mobilized by the government for counterinsurgency purposes. The NDs also fielded or endorsed candidates in some major urban centers to disseminate antidictatorship propaganda and help project some legal mass leaders.[8]

When the antidictatorship movement registered a mighty upsurge after the Aquino assassination in 1983, party leaders mulled over the idea of participating in the national electoral arena at some future period and even of establishing an electoral party. For the 1984 Batasang Pambansa elections, however, the position remained one of boycotting. In preparation for possible participation of the NDs in forthcoming polls, Bayan, the multisectoral coalition of ND organizations and groups, created an electoral struggles commission in 1985. Electoral participation, nonetheless, continued to be viewed with relatively low regard. Sison (1985:2), then in prison, wrote: "[T]he electoral struggle is inferior and merely supplementary to other forms of political struggle. To revolutionaries, it runs fourth to armed struggle, people's strikes and other mass action."

The SDs had fewer objections to participating in elections during martial law. They viewed the polls as a means of weakening the Marcos dictatorship. In the 1978 IBP elections, they went all out. With only eighty cadres, PDSP wrested control of the Laban electoral machinery from the NDs and managed to mobilize 7,400 poll watchers (Hofileña 2002a:10). In subsequent elections, however, PDSP was not able to play as prominent a role due to divisions within the SD ranks. Some SDs in Mindanao helped organize the reform-oriented PDP in 1982, which merged with Laban the next year. In 1984, PDP-Laban won several Batasan seats and a good number of local government posts, especially in Mindanao. By then, however, there were already marked tensions between Laban's old pros, with their traditional politics, and young and idealistic PDP stalwarts, with their "politics of principles" (Gutierrez 1994b:99–100). The PDP soon became just another traditional party.

Bowing to strong domestic and international pressure, Marcos called for a "snap" presidential election in November 1985, to be held in February 1986. Not realizing that the antidictatorship struggle was coming to a head, the CPP once again adopted a boycott stance, even as the other antidictatorship forces rallied behind the candidacy of Senator Aquino's widow, Corazon Aquino, who ran under the PDP-Laban banner. The election, the CPP leadership said, would merely be "a noisy and empty political battle" between factions of the ruling classes; it would be rigged by the "U.S.-Marcos dictatorship," and it would be "meaningless to the broad masses of our people" (Executive Committee, Central Committee, CPP 1985). As expected, Marcos tried to steal the election, but Filipinos, fed up with dictatorial rule, protested in huge numbers. Less than three weeks after the elections, people power deposed Marcos and swept Corazon Aquino to power.

The boycott fiasco forced the CPP Politburo (Politburo, CPP 1986:1–2) to admit that the party had made a "major tactical blunder" and that as a result of the boycott "we lost a lot of our political leverage, impaired our political image built up over the years, and forfeited our leadership of the people when they decisively moved to end the Marcos fascist dictatorship." The CPP leadership further acknowledged:

> As practice has now shown, the snap election and the major events it unleashed constituted the climax of the people's long-drawn struggle against the Marcos fascist dictatorship. During and after the snap election, the historically determined central political struggle was the showdown over the very existence and continuance of fascist rule. The snap election became the main channel for the large-scale mobilization and deployment of the masses for the decisive battle to overthrow the fascist dictatorship.

The Partido ng Bayan Experience

Still smarting from the boycott fiasco of February 1986, the NDs set up Partido ng Bayan (PnB) six months later. Sison, newly released from detention, chaired PnB's preparatory committee and founding congress. In early 1987, the NDs established a women's party, Kababaihan para sa Inang Bayan (Kaiba) or Women for the Mother Country. PnB, Kaiba, Bayan and several other organizations established the Alliance for New Politics (ANP). Advocating a new politics, PnB fielded candidates for both houses of Congress in the 1987 polls. The neophytes expected to win two or three seats in the Senate and around 20 percent of the seats in the House of Representatives, but all of its senatorial candidates lost and only two of its congressional hopefuls were elected. The PnB cited the following factors as responsible for its loss: (1) various institutions of the state and the ruling system had connived to make traditional parties and politicians win; (2) the majority of the population was still influenced by traditional politics and the reactionary system—the masses turned out to be susceptible to vote buying and the middle forces to "reformism"; and (3) the PnB's network was beset by internal problems (such as the lack of accurate data on PnB's mass base and too many mass campaigns on various issues getting in the way of the electoral campaign) and unresolved questions (such as how to view the Aquino government, the place of electoral struggle in the overall struggle, and whether the PnB was participating in elections to win or simply to wage propaganda). The PnB fielded candidates in the 1988 local elections, but the fire was gone. Soon after, it ceased to have a national center and became dormant (Partido ng Bayan 1993:4–19, 30). Kaiba, which won only one congressional seat in the 1987 elections, suffered the same fate. The PnB's two congressmen, as well as Kaiba's congresswoman, eventually joined traditional parties.

Despite PnB's disappointing performance as a national party, the victory of two of its congressional candidates proved that "even less-than-democratic elections at the district level can contribute to the further erosion of authoritarian obstacles to democratization if certain regional conditions are met, [specifically:] ... regional authoritarian elites are either divided or isolated from allies 'at the top'; the democratic opposition is united electorally; and there is a pre-existing alternative outreach network that enhances the political capacity of previously unrepresented groups during and in between elections" (Franco 2001:xxxii).

With PnB's and Kaiba's entry into the electoral arena, it seemed that the NDs had finally overcome their aversion to electoral politics. But their inactivity after the 1988 elections led many to wonder if the NDs were not that serious after all. Had a distaste for electoral politics become too ingrained? Not exactly. Even after the 1987 PnB debacle, the NDs continued to field or at least endorse candidates. They no longer equated the boycotting of elections with being revolutionary or electoral participation with being reformist. The NDs still believed that only a revolution could bring about genuine political and social change in the Philippines and that only those who upheld the primacy of armed struggle could be considered genuine revolutionaries, but they approved of participating in elections and taking seats in Congress as long as these were subordinate to, and in support of, the armed struggle. Assessing the 1987 polls, a CPP Politburo member declared: "The Party viewed the elections as a major but secondary arena of struggle. The tasks in the armed struggle and in the mass movements occupy a higher place in our priorities" (Editorial Staff, *Ang Bayan* 1988:25).

With PnB and Kaiba, the NDs shifted from outright rejection of "bourgeois" democratic institutions and processes to what Roberts has termed "an instrumental view of democracy" and not "an integral conception of democracy." Elections had become a useful tool in the CPP's program to overthrow the "reactionary" Philippine state. Sison (1989:168–69), who in the early 1970s had lambasted PKP's participation in bourgeois elections as counterrevolutionary, now sang a somewhat different tune. "Even if by fraud and terrorism the reactionaries deprive Partido ng Bayan of electoral victory," remarked Sison, "the party still serves a good purpose by exposing such fraud and terrorism, by taking advantage of splits among the reactionaries, by promoting the national democratic line, and, of course, by winning seats that can be won." To the PnB, participating in the reactionary elections was but a means to do away with them: "The people will continue to participate in reactionary elections for as long as their time in politics is not yet up, for as long as the people have not yet realized through their own experience that these elections are rotten and bankrupt, and that there are more effective means for change they can pin their hopes on." (Partido ng Bayan 1993:13, translated from Filipino).

Upon Sison's intercession, the PnB was reestablished in mid-1991, and it participated in elections the following year. After its poor showing in 1987–88 and subsequent inactivity, however, PnB had acquired a loser's image. Worse, according to one observer, the NDs were actually split three ways on the elections: (1) *"Rebolusyon, hindi eleksyon!"* (2) participation as a tool for propaganda and education, and (3) "all-out" participation (Gershman 1992:5). When PnB endorsed—somewhat belatedly—the presidential bid of Senator Jovito Salonga (Liberal Party) in 1992, the candidate himself did not acknowledge PnB's support and his campaigners refused to work with PnB activists. Salonga lost badly—he ended up sixth among seven presidential candidates. Two senatorial, 4 congressional and 622 local candidates endorsed by PnB won (Partido ng Bayan 1993:37, 42). The overwhelming majority of them, including some NDs, however, had run under the banners of traditional parties. "Hardly anyone wanted to run under PnB—it was the kiss of death," recalls Loretta Ann "Etta" Rosales, PnB president in 1991–92 and Akbayan congressperson since 1998. "PnB should not have been revived. After the elections, we buried it very gently."[9] Despite PnB's demise, the NDs still found it useful to participate in elections, but their instrumental approach toward them became increasingly cynical. Throughout the 1990s, the NDs, apart from supporting the candidacies of certain allies, used elections for "fund-raising"—collecting "contributions" and "permit-to-campaign" fees from various candidates, especially those campaigning in NPA guerrilla zones (Cala 1995:3; Mogato 2003).

Prior to the big debate and split in the CPP in 1992–93, voices within the broad Left and within the ND ranks had called on the revolutionary movement to change its outlook over elections. In the light of dramatic domestic and international changes, particularly the downfall of the Marcos dictatorship and the collapse of Soviet socialism, Bisig member Rene Ciria-Cruz (1992:10–12), for instance, entreated the CPP to work for a negotiated settlement with the government and to take the parliamentary road. University of the Philippines professor Temario Rivera (1992:50) urged the NDF to engage seriously in legal electoral politics for three reasons: (1) the restoration of the electoral process made active support for armed struggle more difficult; (2) the poor prospect of receiving external material support for the armed struggle necessitated developing a much broader base; and (3) in order to democratize its political practice and flesh out a system of accountability, the movement had to practice a form of representative democracy. A Bayan official J. V. Bautista (who later became a Sanlakas congressperson), complained of the Left's "ideological ambiguity" over elections, which stymied its ability to unite behind a common strategy (Gershman 1992:5). Others attempted to go a bit deeper into ideological or strategic questions. Extending the Gramscian argument on counterhegemony beyond civil society into the realm of political society, Eric Gutierrez (1994b:105), a member of the Volunteers for Popular Democracy, urged fellow NDs to view elections not merely as a process for the reproduction of the dominant classes and their form of rule but as "'sites of struggle,' which the Left must wrest from the dominant classes in the process of countering their hegemony."

Walden Bello (1992:5), then a U.S.-based ex-ND and one of the main organizers of the FOPA conference, advocated that the Left take electoral struggle as one of the central arenas of change. Bello cited political culture as an important factor: "[O]ne major failing of the Philippine progressive movement has been its underestimation of popular political culture and how much elections play in this, how people see elections as the only form or source of political legitimacy. And unless you are tried and tested in the electoral battle, you're not accorded legitimacy." Unlike the other electoral advocates, Bello's stance shifted from the instrumental to the integral view of democracy, the third response in Roberts's typology.

> To automatically approach the elections as an outside political force and condemn the whole thing or to just have very tactical approaches to elections and to formal democratic processes, I think, will condemn us to be forever marginal in this culture. ... In our studies of democracy, power and transformation, rather than conceive of an unbridgeable gulf between formal democracy and substantive democracy, we would like to see how substantive democracy can be pushed within the tradition of formal and elite democracy so that there is a continuation in some way, as well as having some elements of a break.

The CPP debate and split between the reaffirmists and the rejectionists afforded many leftists the occasion to reexamine their views on electoral and parliamentary struggle. In the course of repudiating Maoism, particularly the Maoist tenet of the primacy of armed struggle over all other forms of struggle, the rejectionists developed a greater appreciation for the various forms of political struggle, including the electoral struggle. The mass movement and electoral struggle ceased to be seen as being merely in the service of the armed struggle. In castigating Stalinism, particularly a Stalinist one-party dictatorship, the rejectionists embraced political pluralism and truly competitive elections. In the 1993 FOPA conference, representatives of the rejectionists, Bisig, and other leftist groups put together a new vision and program for the Philippines, which highlighted the role of the electoral struggle in the Left's overall strategy: "The [progressive] movement must be able to contend in different political arenas, but especially under a regime of elite democracy, in the electoral struggle, which is, whether we like it or not, the current source of legitimacy on who governs. This ability to compete electorally must include evolving an organization that can compete with the political parties of the elite in terms of electoral mobilization and mass outreach" (Bello 1993:21).

Twists and Turns in the Evolution of a New Electoral Formation

The evolutionary process of coming up with a formation of the Left that could compete with the parties of the elite had actually already begun earlier. As mentioned in chapter 3, there were already some leftist groups and individuals within as well as outside the ND and SD ranks who, after the PnB's dismal performance in 1987–88, wanted to take the electoral struggle more seriously. They refused to take the CPP's very tactical view of elections and to move along with PDSP's rightward drift.

In their efforts to intervene meaningfully in the 1992 general elections, the popdems, Bisig, and Pandayan went through a complicated and excruciating process, experimenting with various forms of organization. First, they tried to build a national Center-Left coalition through Project 1992. When this failed due to a lack of support from mainstream NDs and SDs, they spearheaded Project 2001, a very broad coalition that drew POs, NGOs, and PO/NGO networks from all over the country. The coalition worked hard to "raise political consciousness," lobby for electoral reforms and develop a "people's platform." It was stymied, however, on the matter of giving actual support to specific candidates, as some NGOs refused to go to such an extent. The popdems, Bisig, and Pandayan ended up turning themselves, virtually at the eleventh hour, into a loose nonparty formation, Akbayan, which endorsed the Salonga-Pimentel tandem as well as some other progressive candidates from the national to the local levels.

Akbayan fared just as badly as PnB in the 1992 elections—both had endorsed mostly the same candidates. The loss of the Salonga-Pimentel ticket, however, was particularly hard on Akbayan. Unlike PnB, it had formally been a part of the LP-PDP coalition. The PnB crowed that Akbayan had been reduced to a mere "support appendage" with no say in crucial decision making in the LP-PDP coalition and that the "broadly-based NGO electoral movement" Akbayan had counted on had failed to deliver (Partido ng Bayan 1993:52).

By the time of the 1995 congressional and local elections, the CPP had already split, and the rejectionists mainly gravitated toward two multisectoral alliances, Sanlakas and Siglaya. Both alliances supported "progressive" candidates running under traditional parties or as independents. So did the three groups that had gathered under Akbayan in 1992—the popdems, Bisig, and Pandayan. Some of the candidates endorsed by the emergent leftist groups did win, but their victories were due to a combination of factors, not simply the progressive vote. Sanlakas performed creditably in Metro Manila, where five out of seven congressional candidates and a good number of local candidates it backed made it. Bisig did fairly well in several local contests, especially in General Santos City, where the mayoral candidate it endorsed won (Cala 1995:3). In a number of cases, the new, leftist groups backed rival candidates. In Pasig, this proved disastrous, as a traditional politician edged out two leftist congressional candidates, one supported by Sanlakas, the other by Siglaya.

Those within the Left who had been thinking of setting up a new electoral party did not do so before the 1992 and 1995 elections because they doubted that a new party would have a winning chance. Participating in elections without one's own party, however, had grown most wearisome. A PO-NGO coalition such as Project 2001 could not be expected to endorse candidates. A nonparty formation in an electoral coalition with *trapo* parties (such as LP-PDP) ended up becoming a mere appendage of the latter. Many of the Left-endorsed winning "progressives" who ran under *trapo* parties or as independents in 1992 and 1995 moved away from the popular movements upon assuming office and soon imbibed—or laid bare—the thinking and ways of patronage politics.

The new, leftist forces saw an opening when In early 1995, Congress passed the Party-List System Act in early 1995. The act, which President Ramos promptly signed into law, provided that 20 percent of the seats in the House of Representatives be reserved for representatives of labor, peasants, urban poor, indigenous peoples, women, and other marginalized sectors elected through a party-list system. The emergent leftist forces believed that the leftist parties would have good chances of winning since the new law barred the five biggest parties from participating in the first party-list vote.[10] Wurfel (1997:19–30), among other scholars, has lauded the party-list system as a "major innovation" and "an essential asset for reforming the fundamental character of the Philippine political system." However, he sees some deficiencies in the law itself and many difficulties in its implementation.[11]

The emergent leftist groups saw the party-list system, despite all its deficiencies, as an excellent political opportunity. Thus, for the first party-list vote (held as part of the general elections of 1998), they organized or refashioned themselves into electoral parties or "sectoral organizations" and tossed their hats in the ring.[12] Many ex-cadres and ex-activists of ND, SD and other leftist backgrounds became politically active again. The PDSP was the only leftist party of long standing to sign up for the party-list elections. The tripartite Akbayan revived itself, this time as a political party, and with a fourth "little pig," Siglaya. Some popdems and Pandayan members, however, did not join the new party. Sanlakas registered for the party-list vote as a sectoral organization. The NDs (reaffirmists) did not participate in the first party-list vote due to their inability to agree on whether they would field candidates or not.[13] Thanks to the party-list system, the emergent left groups scored a double breakthrough. They finally managed to build new electoral formations distinct from those of the *trapos* and with no strings attached to the CPP. Moreover, amid the voters' great confusion as to what the party-list system was all about, some of the new formations registered their first, albeit modest, wins: ABA, AKO, Abanse Pinay, Akbayan, and Sanlakas each won a seat in the House of Representatives.

The Instrumental versus the Integral View of Democracy

As the 2001 congressional and local elections neared, leftist parties and groups vigorously prepared to compete once again in the party-list vote. Each of the incumbents hoped to garner the maximum number of seats that a party could get under the party-list system: three. As a way around this three-seat limit, Sanlakas, with the prodding of the newly established Marxist-Leninist PMP, decided to divide itself in two: Sanlakas and a new electoral party, the Workers' Party (PM). The leftist parties that lost in 1998 (e.g., PDSP, Pinatubo, AMIN, and Abanse Bisaya [renamed Atin]) got ready to try again. Bandila, the SD multisectoral alliance of the mid-1980s, resurrected itself for the party-list vote. New groups with many ex-NDs, such as Asakapil and Alternative Action, surfaced. Comelec judged the poor old Democratic Alliance a nuisance and disqualified it. What would later turn out to be the most significant development in the Left's participation in the 2001 elections, however, was the emergence of Bayan Muna, the electoral party that the NDs established in September 1999 to replace PnB.[14] In the midst of the preparations for the 2001 elections came the "*jueteng* scandal," in which then President Estrada was accused as having taken "kickbacks" from the illegal numbers game, *jueteng*. Virtually all of the leftist groups participated in the campaign for Estrada's ouster, and, unlike in People Power I, they were in the thick of People Power II. Seven leftist parties managed to translate their mobilization capabilities into post-EDSA II electoral victories, but most of their representatives had to wait a long time before they could be proclaimed.[15] The neophyte Bayan Muna topped the party-list race and garnered the maximum three seats. Akbayan increased its seats to two, but got its second seat only after one and a half years. One seat each went to AMIN, ABA,[16] PM, Sanlakas, and Abanse Pinay, though their representatives were installed less than a year before the end of their three-year terms.

Bayan Muna marked a more determined contestation by the NDs in the electoral field. Instead of entering the contests in both houses of Congress, as PnB did in 1987, the ND electoral party focused on the Lower House and only on the party-list polls. Bayan Muna, however, did not constitute a departure from the NDs' post-EDSA I instrumental attitude toward "bourgeois" democratic institutions and processes. As early as December 2000, before Estrada had fallen, the CPP leadership had instructed its leading party committees in a memo on the May 2001 elections "to bring down the U.S.-Estrada regime and comprehensively advance the anti-imperialist, antifeudal and antifascist struggle." The CPP memo listed four additional tasks: (1) to build up further the momentum of protest actions and mass struggles, (2) to intensify the revolutionary armed struggle, (3) to forge close ties with legal progressive forces, and (4) to expose the "reactionary character" of the elections (Executive Committee, Central Committee, CPP 2000:2–4, translated from Filipino).

The NDs have attributed Bayan Muna's success mainly to their grassroots machinery, their high-profile role in People Power II, and their skillful alliance work. Bayan Muna's president, Congressman Satur Ocampo, remarks, "One factor that made it easier for Bayan Muna to carry out its campaign, as compared to Partido ng Bayan in 1987, was the fact that EDSA II intervened. Bayan Muna had been able to take a leading, a very significant participation in that process, which resulted in a situation where Bayan Muna, though not formally, was regarded as an ally of the [Arroyo-led] People Power Coalition [PPC]." Bayan Muna negotiated with twelve of the PPC's thirteen senatorial candidates, getting their endorsement for Bayan Muna in the party-list vote in exchange for Bayan Muna's support for their senatorial bids. The allied candidates provided Bayan Muna with campaign materials, sample ballots, and other forms of support.[17] Ostensibly to keep some distance from *trapos*, Bayan Muna refrained from campaigning on the same stage as the PPC senatorial candidates. At the PPC's *miting de avance* (final campaign rally), however, Ocampo himself showed up and was one of the speakers. In that single symbolic event, the PPC-Bayan Muna alliance, never officially declared, was made plain.[18] Having to campaign for mostly *trapo* senatorial candidates was compromise enough. But at the local and district levels, Bayan Muna struck deals with *trapos* of all stripes—pro-Arroyo, pro-Estrada, and "independents"—and sometimes even with rivals for the same position. One scribe commented that Bayan Muna topped the party-list vote by riding on the machinery of the traditional politicians with whom it had allied itself (Go 2002:14).

Even as Bayan Muna solicited support in cash or kind from *trapos* and other sources, the CPP-NPA collected "permit to campaign" (PTC) fees more extensively from politicians wanting to campaign in "red areas." The CPP's December 2000 memo had explicitly stated: "Expand the implementation of the PTC. The PTC contains a tactical alliance part as well as a part for asserting revolutionary political power" (Executive Committee, Central Committee 2000:3, translated from Filipino). The PTC fees ranged from ₱50,000 or two M-16 rifles for mayoral candidates in small towns to ₱500,000 to ₱1 million for senatorial candidates. The CPP-NPA is said to have raised ₱50 million from local candidates in the 2001 elections (Mogato 2003:20–21). Other leftist parties—PDSP, Akbayan, and Sanlakas—complained that in many places NPA guerrillas, while actively campaigning for Bayan Muna, harassed their members and campaigners. An ex-ND aide of a traditional politician commented that the NDs had given the three Gs a new meaning: guns, guerrillas and gold.[19]

Some of the emergent leftist parties and groups, such as Akbayan, ABA and Abanse Pinay, have from the start taken an integral view of democracy. They hold that formal democracy is valuable in its own right, to paraphrase Huber et al. (1997:323), because "it makes deepening towards more fully participatory democracy and progress towards increasing equality possible." Even while Akbayan was still being formed, it came up with a clear-cut position recognizing the Philippines' democratic institutions and processes while at the same time expressing its desire to transform formal democracy into a more participatory and egalitarian one. As Joel Rocamora (1997a:2), the Akbayan president in 2001–3, stated early on: "The party will operate within existing constitutional processes while seeking to change them to make them more democratic. The contradiction between the form and substance of elite rule, between political democracy and social disparity presents a substantial opportunity for a political party that will engage in mainstream political processes to advance a redistributive agenda."

In its political platform, the Akbayan National Congress (1998a:7) declared: "We believe that the restoration of constitutional democracy in 1986 was an important achievement of the antidictatorship movement. The reestablishment of the institutions of democracy during the Aquino presidency consolidated this historic step. … But formal democracy is not enough. We cannot have political democracy for long with an undemocratic economic system. … Asset reform is not just a matter of social justice or laying down a domestic market base for sustained economic growth, it is also imperative for deepening democracy." And further: "The long term goal of Akbayan is to facilitate, and to directly organize greater popular participation in politics. Not just formal, pro-forma participation, but effective participation. Not just through elections, but through other processes of government."

Akbayan's acceptance of constitutional democracy, however, does not mean that it completely rules out extraconstitutional forms of struggle. The party takes a proactive stance toward political crises, convulsions, and ruptures, given the Philippines' propensity toward these, as shown by the First Quarter Storm of 1970, and the series of EDSA uprisings in 1986 and 2001.[20]

The position of PMP vis-à-vis democratic processes appears to be somewhere between Bayan Muna's instrumental view and Akbayan's integral view. Rejecting the Maoist protracted people's war strategy, PMP struggles for "democratic reform" and regards "the open and unarmed mass movement as the primary mode of struggle" in the postauthoritarian era (Ramirez 2002a). Furthermore, PMP participates in elections by backing the candidates of allied electoral parties and other progressive candidates. On the basis of some of its pronouncements, PMP would seem to take an instrumental position. Like the CPP, PMP regards elections and Congress as "bourgeois" and sees the value of participating in them mainly in terms of helping build up the strength of the popular forces for a revolutionary denouement—a "people's democratic revolution." Mass struggles are seen by PMP as expanding, deepening and ultimately maturing into a people's uprising—"a plebian-[led] not patrician-led people's uprising like the three previous EDSA's" (Ramirez 2002b). The central task of this democratic revolution would be "to establish the revolutionary government of the workers and peasants, and of other democratic forces and parties that actively participated in the people's revolution." The democratic revolution would be part of a greater process of socialist revolution (Partido ng Manggagawang Pilipino 2002:4, 16).

For parties coming from ND roots such as PMP (as for the CPP), the crucial distinction vis-à-vis their electoral and parliamentary work has traditionally not been between the instrumental and integral views of democratic institutions and processes but between revolutionary and reformist politics. This is in line with precepts in the traditional form of Marxism-Leninism emphasizing the armed capture and "smashing" of the bourgeois state. Engaging in electoral and parliamentary struggle is deemed revolutionary if this is geared toward the eventual overthrow of the "reactionary state" and reformist if it is not. The view of PMP appears to be changing, however. "There has often been a tendency to draw too sharp a distinction between reform and revolution," remarked one PMP leader, "We do not wish to fall into that."[21] An implication of this is that PMP may be moving to a position similar to Akbayan's on "moments." "Struggles for democratic reform" would cease to be simply geared for that one "grand moment" of cataclysmic seizure of power and thus would be more appreciated for their intrinsic merit.

Local Elections

Since 1998, media attention to the Left's participation in electoral politics has tended to focus on the party-list ballot. The Left, however, has also been busy elsewhere. Well aware of the limitations of the party-list system, leftist parties and groups have fielded candidates in other electoral contests, such as those at the local (municipal or city) level.

Wurfel (1997) views the party-list system as being "[i]n the long run … the best hope for the transformation of the *trapo* system into one with more programmatic parties, more responsive than at present to the needs and concerns of the majority of the people—the workers, farmers, and fishermen." He seems to suggest, however, that to stimulate political reform, a majority, or at least a more substantial number of legislators, would have to be elected through a party-list vote—in effect a shift to a system of proportional representation. In the short term, such a prospect does not appear to be likely, as a shift to proportional representation requires a constitutional amendment.

Victories in the party-list ballot constituted a breakthrough for several emergent leftist parties and groups in 1998 and for the NDs in 2001. But overall the party-list system in its current form has not made much of an impact on the *trapo* system. Traditional politicians representing different factions of the elite still constitute the overwhelming majority in both houses of Congress, and they continue to operate as before. Under the Party-List System Law, 50-odd of about 258 seats in the Lower House are supposed to be allocated to representatives of the marginalized sectors. However, only 14 of these seats were filled in 1998 and 20 in 2001, because of loopholes in the law and Comelec's poor implementation of it. In future Congresses, even if all party-list representatives manage to get installed, they will still be very much in the minority.

To project themselves nationally, leftist parties need to win at least one seat in Congress through the party-list system, but in the years to come the crucial electoral battle for the leftist parties and groups may no longer be the party-list ballot but the local elections. Pouring all of one's energies into the party-list vote, it is argued, merely perpetuates the system of *trapo* control of Congress and the political system. Thus, before leftist parties can really put up a strong challenge in the main congressional, senatorial, and presidential contests, they have to build up their strength from below, particularly at the municipal level.[22]

In electoral strategy, the Philippine Left can take a leaf from the Latin American Left's playbook. In the 1980s, leftist parties chalked up victories in local elections in many Latin American countries. According to Jonathan Fox (1995:15–19), local politics became "the most viable arenas where the Left can compete for power, experiment with progressive reforms, and learn how to govern." Leftists in elected local posts undertook major "good government" reforms and at times succeeded in sweeping away entrenched traditions of corrupt clientelism. "Local government," Fox observes, "provides the opportunity to begin to construct states that listen and deliver."

From the local, the leftist parties built up toward the national. By the 1990s, the Left had become the main *legal* opposition at the national level in a number of countries (Brazil, Uruguay, and El Salvador). In 2002, the Workers' Party came to power in Brazil.

Among the Philippine leftist parties, PDSP has perhaps been the most aggressive in competing in local and other non-party-list electoral contests. In fact, it has supported or fielded candidates at various levels since 1986. Unlike most leftist groups, PDSP has had no problems in accepting the democratic institutions and processes of the postauthoritarian Philippines. Its early electoral forays had little impact, as most of the candidates it supported ran mainly under traditional parties. It fared badly in the first party-list elections, placing sixty-third out of 123 groups. After party chairman Norberto Gonzales, Jr., secured a Cabinet post in the Arroyo government, however, his party's electoral fortunes improved. In 2001, PDSP again did poorly in the party-list vote (forty-fifth out of 162 parties), but it bagged one congressional seat (Abra Province) and many local positions. By 2002, PDSP had more than a hundred elected officials, some of them recent party recruits. In a regional Socialist International forum hosted by PDSP and keynoted by Arroyo, the party delegation included thirty-nine local government officials, mostly mayors, governors, and vice governors (Pablo 2002). It is difficult, however, to gauge the party loyalty of PDSP's elected officials, since many of them ran mainly under traditional parties or on *trapo*-dominated tickets. And whether these officials are indeed undertaking SD or progressive programs needs to be evaluated.

The party has had to come a long way. "During the dictatorship period," explains PDSP chairman Gonzales, "our party was a cadre party. We had a tough education program, heavy on ideology, philosophy. After February 1986, there was a debate: remain a cadre party or become a mass, electoral party? We opted for the latter. We became more liberal towards those who wanted to enter the party. Because of the shift, however, we lost some former cadres."[23] After having been active in the anti-Marcos coalitions headed by Benigno Aquino in 1978 and Corazon Aquino in 1986, the SD groups (PDSP, Kasapi and Pandayan) and their allies were amply rewarded with positions in the Cory government. With better access to funding, the

SDs greatly expanded their development NGO work (Rocamora 1993:10). Frictions soon arose, however, within the SD ranks on whether the stress should be on work in the government bureaucracy or the mass movement. Kasapi, Pandayan, and PDSP established the Demokratikong-Sosyalistang Koalisyon (DSK) to foster SD unity, but it proved to be short-lived. Through its alliances with traditional parties and politicians, PDSP has tried to get into the corridors of power, hoping that from there it would be easier to approach and recruit good, independent-minded politicians into the party.

Other leftist groups have been very critical of PDSP's and Gonzales's ways; in fact, many in the other leftist groups do not regard PDSP as belonging to the Left anymore. Before the collapse of the DSK in 1991, the other SD groups in the coalition had strongly reacted to PDSP's "high-handed and undemocratic methods" and questionable dealings with *trapos* and right-wing labor and peasant associations. Since then, PDSP has distanced itself even farther from the other leftist groups and worked even more closely with *trapos*.

Some leftist parties and groups—Akbayan, Bayan Muna, and Sanlakas—have put up candidates in the local elections, but they have done so in a most curious fashion. Often a candidate who was a bona fide member of a leftist party ran under a traditional party in the local polls, while at the same time campaigning for the leftist party in the party-list vote. In effect, he or she was affiliated with two parties—*trapo* and leftist! Where the candidate's main allegiance lay was open to question. The leftist parties tolerated this dual-party affiliation since they believed they did not yet have the wherewithal to field successful leftist or progressive candidates without some backing from a *trapo* party.

Unlike most leftist parties, Akbayan emphasizes participation in local elections. Rocamora (2002:7) explains: "This is both a matter of principle and practical politics. We participate in elections initially at the local government level where we have the resources to win and only slowly build up to the national level. Given the people's alienation from a political system dominated by upper class groups, restoring a sense of effective participation—the essence of radical democracy—can be best done at local government levels." Among the leftist parties, Akbayan seems to be the most successful in local elections. In 2001, it elected eighteen mayors and over a hundred other local officials.[24] Many of these elected officials, however, are "unconsolidated," as Akbayan has to compete with the traditional parties in influencing them and gaining their primary allegiance. A small number of Akbayan candidates for local posts, however, did run solely under Akbayan's banner.

In contrast to Akbayan's approach, Bayan Muna focused on the party-list elections and officially fielded only a handful of local candidates in 2001. Two official candidates for councilor—one each in Caloocan City and Davao City—won.[25] Many more NDs ran and won under traditional parties, however. For its part, Sanlakas, having registered as a sectoral organization and not a party, could not put up candidates of its own in the local polls. In some areas (Rizal, Bohol, and Davao Oriental), however, I found Sanlakas members who were elected to local posts running under traditional parties.

"Barangay" and Sangguniang Kabataan Elections

In the Philippines, "local elections" are associated with municipal, city, and provincial elections. Although the *barangay* is the Philippines' basic geographical unit and its government structure is a local government unit too (i.e., the lowest unit of governance in the Philippines), its elections, however, are held separately from those at other local levels. The Sangguniang Kabataan (SK), or Youth Council, which is elected by *barangay* youths at least fifteen and below eighteen years of age, has separate elections too.[26] In the 1970s and 1980s, the *barangay* councils and the Kabataang Barangay (Barangay Youth), the precursor of SK, did not have much clout. When Marcos was in power, he easily manipulated them. With the passage of the Local Government Code in 1991, however, certain powers (such as making ordinances, imposing taxes, and soliciting loans) were devolved to the *barangay* councils. *Barangays* received bigger internal revenue allotments, and the *barangay* captain and council members got regular salaries or honoraria, allowances, and various benefits. Since 1991, *barangay* and SK elections have become much livelier contests.

While there have undoubtedly been candidates with a public service orientation, there have also been many of the *trapo* sort, who run for access to a bit of power and money—including patronage from higher politicians, gifts and bribes from local businesses, kickbacks from government projects, or percentage shares from illegal activities such as *jueteng* (Patiño 1999:2)—and for the opportunity to move up the political ladder.

Despite the provisions of a Marcos era law that stipulates that *barangay* and SK elections be "nonpartisan,"[27] they have, in fact, been very partisan. Mayors, governors, congresspersons, and other local officials, as well as aspirants to these positions, have always been intensely involved in the *barangay*/SK elections and the subsequent municipal- and provincial-level Liga ng mga Barangay (League of Barangays) and SK Federation elections. Why? The *barangay* organization plays a crucial role, and the SK organization a supporting role, in determining the outcome of their own bids in subsequent local and congressional elections. Indeed, the *barangay* organization can be an electoral machine or serve as its backbone. The July 2002 *barangay*/SK elections were a preparation for the May 2004 local and congressional elections. In one town I visited, it seemed as if the *barangay* captains practically carried the day in the mayoral contest of 2001: in all the *barangays*, the candidate supported by the captain won in the *barangay* concerned. Another reason why mayors and governors get so involved is that the Liga and SK Federation presidencies mean two votes in the municipal council and the provincial board. The mayor or governor sometimes needs these two votes to secure a majority in the council or board, or, in the case of a petty local autocrat, to ensure that there will be no opposition. I came across an interesting case of a mayor in Salcedo, Eastern Samar, who employed the dynastic approach to get a majority in the municipal council. He had three first-degree relatives on the council: a councilor elected at large, the Liga president, and the SK president. Precisely because *barangay*/SK and Liga/SK Federation elections are of great importance to their own political future, many mayors and mayoral aspirants closely oversee the campaigns of their candidates or even call the shots. It would sometimes seem, in fact, that it is the mayor or the mayoral aspirant himself who is running. Alberto Agra

(1994:26), former executive director of the Institute of Politics and Governance, sums it all up: "[B]arangay officials are cuddled and financially supported by higher local and national government officials in furtherance of the latter's perpetuation in power."

Perhaps in an attempt to break loose from the "nonpartisan" provision, the Comelec allowed local officials, acting individually or in their own personal capacity, to campaign for their candidates outside their own *barangays* in the July 2002 *barangay* elections. Ilocos Norte governor Ferdinand R. Marcos, Jr., the son of the late dictator, welcomed the move, saying, "While barangay elections are supposedly nonpartisan, we all know that has not been the actual case. Higher officials do interfere in them. ... [Comelec] is merely recognizing what has actually been happening all along" (Galing 2002, partly translated from Filipino).

Since the Marcos period, as mentioned earlier, the CPP-NPA has put up or endorsed candidates in *barangay* elections to frustrate the government's counterinsurgency moves, engage in political proselytization and project open mass leaders. The CPP-NPA's instrumental view of *barangay* elections contrasts with that of emergent leftist parties, such as Akbayan, which see the potential for developing participatory democracy. According to Rocamora (2000a:5), the creation of *barangay* government units under the 1991 Local Government Code opened "the possibility of lowering the center of gravity of Philippine politics from the town and city centers where elites dominate to the level of the barangay." Now that the *barangays* had some ordinance-making powers and funds, their politics could stop being only an adjunct of town politics. "The Local Government Code," he adds, "also provides for barangay assemblies with limited legislative powers where all barangay residents can participate, the only form of direct democracy available in the existing political system. Barangay governments are obliged to formulate barangay development plans through the creation of a barangay development council with provisions for NGO and people's organization participation. These institutional arrangements open up the possibility of a broadly participatory political process." In 1996, several NGOs that later aligned themselves with Akbayan responded to a request from some PO leaders who wanted to run in the May 1997 *barangay* elections and put together a course on electoral campaign management for the candidates. Since then, Akbayan and allied NGOs have moved on to the nitty-gritty of participatory *barangay* governance.

Like all of the *trapo* parties, many of the major leftist parties have participated in the *barangay*/SK elections by fielding or endorsing candidates—without unfurling their banners, of course. Since all parties have to keep up the pretense of being nonpartisan, it is virtually impossible to get accurate data on just how many candidates of leftist parties won in the *barangay*/SK elections in 2002, but we do know that a significant number of candidates from the Left won in the 1997 *barangay* elections. A partial tally indicates that over a thousand candidates identified with the political groups that later formed Akbayan and Sanlakas (i.e., as Comelec-registered entities) won positions, including almost two hundred candidates for *barangay* captain (Patiño 1999:2).[28] The tally did not cover candidates of the ND movement.

The CPP-NPA's policy on *barangay* elections has remained basically unchanged. The contest for control of a good number of the country's *barangays*, particularly in the hinterlands, between government forces and the CPP-NPA continues. In the July 2002 *barangay* elections, the military declared many NPA areas as "hot spots," after receiving numerous reports of CPP-NPA involvement. Bayan Muna expressed concern about the military's assessment, asserting that the hotspots were actually areas where it had a strong following and well-established mass organizations (Canuday 2002). The CPP claims that the NPA now operates in 8,500 barrios (*barangays*) or 18 percent of the total number of Philippine barrios, and that the number of barrios where the NPA operates increased by 71 percent from 1980 to 2001 and by 28 percent from 1994 to 2001 (Liwanag 2002:2). The military has come up with a higher figure for NPA-influenced barrios. "If the military is to be believed," writes one journalist, "the number of New People's Army rebels is on the rise and about a fourth of barangays nationwide could be controlled by the leftist Bayan Muna if barangay elections were held today" (Hofileña 2002b:21).

With all the stakes involved for both *trapos* and the CPP-NPA, it is no wonder that *barangay*/SK elections have become as violence-marred as other elections. At least eighty-seven people were killed and forty-five injured in 183 violent incidents in connection with the *barangay*/SK elections in 2002. Comelec officials reported 26 incidents on election day itself, including 2 shooting cases, 2 cases of ballot snatching, the burning of a school and a ballot box, and the discovery of ready-made ballots. The day after the elections, President Arroyo thanked Filipinos for "our generally peaceful elections" (Burgonio and Roque 2002). Election-related violence is often mainly attributed to *trapos*. According to a Comelec commissioner, however, the NPA committed most of the election-related violence during the 2002 *barangay*/SK polls (Dancel 2002).

Moving into the Main Electoral Arena

For all its the Left's successes at the local and *barangay* levels, many leftist parties and groups still train their primary attention on the party-list ballot. In the electoral fight against the *trapos*, however, it is the "regular" electoral contests—local, congressional by district, senatorial, and presidential—and not the party-list ballot that are the main arena in the electoral fight against the *trapos*. It is in the regular elections that a candidate of alternative politics comes face to face with the heart of *trapo* politics—with patronage and guns, goons, and gold. In the 1998 party-list elections, the leftist parties and groups did face some challenges from the *trapos*, mainly through the latter's surrogates. In 2001, however, their main rivals were definitely not the *trapos*.[29] In practice, Bayan Muna treated the other leftist parties as its main rivals in the party-list ballot and vice versa. Bayan Muna's leftist rivals encountered more problems with NPA guerrillas than the *trapos'* goons.[30] Only in the other electoral contests were the leftist parties mainly up against the *trapos* and *trapo* parties and their dirty tricks. Incidents of Left versus Left are bound to be repeated in future party-list elections; Left versus *trapo* will prevail in regular elections where the Left fields candidates.

The Left, through its participation, in elections in the past seven decades, however sporadic, has accumulated an appreciable amount of experience in running electoral campaigns and dealing with *trapo* tricks. Drawing from this experience, many leftist parties and groups have devised guides and training kits on electoral campaign management, poll watching, how to prevent election cheating, and so on, which have proven effective in helping some progressives defeat *trapos*, even in places where the latter employed the entire regalia of guns, goons, and gold. But before the Left can become a formidable electoral force, much more needs to be done. Leftist parties and groups could conceivably counter the *trapos'* demagogic or populist appeals with good issues and platforms and check the *trapos'* use of fraud and terrorism through vigilant poll watching, media liaison, and mass mobilization. The *trapos'* arsenal, however, includes the exploitation of traditional patron-client relations and other personalistic ties, the artful use of pork barrel and related tactics—weapons that often are more effective than fraud and terrorism in the electoral arena. *Trapos* build and develop clientelist ties with their supporters not just during elections but as part of their daily routine, whether in or out of public office. Many of them are good at maintaining personalistic styles and appropriating local traditions and practices. "The fact that we now construe song and dance, handshakes, attending weddings and wakes as 'traditional' in a negative way," notes Patrick Patiño (1999:3), "shows how thoroughly so-called *trapos* have appropriated these traditions to their advantage." The Left, in other words, would have to combat a most pervasive and pernicious *trapo* political culture—the world of nepotism, cronyism, distorted *kumpadre-kumare* (extended kinship) relationships, *lagayan* (bribery), *palakasan* (influence peddling), *weather-weather* (the spoils system), "boss" culture, and so on.[31]

A widespread and particularly baneful practice in *trapo* political culture is vote buying. Frederic Charles Schaffer (2003:1–2) found that in the May 2001 national elections, one out of every ten Filipinos was offered money or material goods to vote for a certain candidate and that seven out of every ten took the bribe. The poor who accepted money had a mixed set of motives; almost a third said that they needed it. A psychographic study on voter behavior conducted by the Institute for Political and Electoral Reform (IPER) (2004: 27–30) came up with much higher figures: 48 percent of voters were offered bribes, and 75 percent of those offered bribes accepted them. The most common explanations of those who got the money were that they felt powerless to prevent it, that it was a fact of life, that their lives remained miserable, and that the money would benefit them.

In the course of my fieldwork, I discovered that leftist parties and groups experienced particular difficulty in trying to counter vote buying. In most of the many places I visited, such as Bohol, Eastern Samar, Albay, and Davao Oriental, I found that vote buying had become the rule, not the exception, and that payoffs were getting bigger and bigger with every election. Candidates who refrained from vote buying often lost. Thus, many candidates who were otherwise well-meaning and public service oriented, including some progressive candidates, succumbed to the practice, accepting it as a fact of Philippine politics. Voters seemed to have grown inured to the practice, as it was widely held that politicians were in government mainly to enrich themselves, their relatives, and close friends and it did not really matter who won. For many voters, elections at least provided the opportunity to make some easy money. In 1987, an ND activist asked some peasants in a "consolidated" NPA guerrilla zone why they had sold their votes instead of voting for PnB. "We give ourselves to the revolution 364 days of the year," replied one, "Give us just this one day."[32]

Kerkvliet (1995: 408–9408–9;. 1996:137, 152–61) points out that while many Filipinos use elections to advance personal and factional interests and capture the spoils of government and see elections as battles fought with guns, goons, and gold, others struggle to make elections be about legitimacy, fairness, and democratic processes. He cites cases in the past, such as the elections in 1947–53 and the fateful snap presidential polls of 1986, when voters guarded ballot boxes, monitored the counting of votes, and stood their ground, even as armed men and officials tried to scare them off. Elections, he notes, have themselves become a struggle, a contest, about "the meaning and purpose of elections."[33]

In her study of the 1992 elections in a hacienda area in Murcia, Negros Occidental, Rosanne Rutten (1994) examines the candidates' campaign pitches, particularly the "cultural" frames used in wooing hacienda workers, as well as the response of the workers, who had been supportive of the CPP-NPA before. Rutten observes that the candidates used both the "patronage frame" of traditional politicians and the "oppression frame" of new politics. The workers, who had been socialized to two apparently contradictory cultural frames, responded positively to both. They evaluated the candidates on the basis of both frames, participated in both clientelist and new politics, and recognized the legitimacy of both. Rutten's finding suggests that the contest over the meaning of elections, far from being a competition between mutually exclusive opposites, is a much more complicated affair.

Such complexity is also discussed in a study by Raul Pertierra (1995b), which delves into electoral politics in Zamora, Ilocos Sur. He notes the inconsistency between political support and voting behavior. He also observes that during the 1986 presidential elections many voters of Zamora expressed their moral support for Aquino but nonetheless cast their votes for Marcos. He relates this to the remark of a Catholic activist after PnB's poor showing in 1987 that the NDF had the support of the Filipino people but not their votes. In Pertierra's analysis, two views of elections are recognized in the Philippines: elections as "an expression of a political will in which case they are both representative and participative" and as "an instance of domination where they are used simply as a means for structural reproduction and legitimation" (Pertierra 1995b:21). Political or moral support for Aquino (in Zamora) and the NDs failed to translate into votes, as the view of representation and participation gave way to the realities of reproduction and legitimation.

The leftist parties and groups have themselves contributed to the blurring of the distinction between *trapo*/patronage politics and new politics by forging alliances with *trapo* parties or individual *trapos* and by letting or even encouraging their members or close allies to run under *trapo* parties and coalitions. Such practices may indeed be necessary compromises that the leftist parties have to make in order to build themselves up and challenge the *trapos*. If the more democratically oriented leftist parties truly want their anti-*trapo* message to be as sharp as possible, however, they will have to put an end at some point to de facto dual-party membership (*trapo* and Left!) and adopt a more judicious alliance policy.

For the Left to be capable of truly breaking the hegemony of *trapos* in Philippine electoral politics and help bring about an institutionalized political party system, those with an integral conception of democracy will have to gain the upper hand over those with an instrumental view—within the electoral Left at the very least. The instrumentalists tend to put a hedge around electoral engagement because they do not really believe that the Philippine political system can be changed (except by violent overthrow) or that the majority of the *trapos* can be electorally defeated. As more leftist candidates win and are exposed to the hard realities of actual governance, more left-leaning activists, parties, and groups may well shift to the integral view. In the CPP's case, perhaps only a negotiated political settlement with the government—at present, truly a long shot—could make it budge from its instrumental outlook. With the CPP still fixated on "total victory," Bayan Muna and other ND electoral parties will likely move to an integral conception of democracy only if they are able to exercise considerable autonomy.

5

The Left's Engagement in Public Office and Governance

WORKING IN PUBLIC OFFICE AND GOVERNANCE, even more than elections, are fields of endeavor that the Left in the Philippines has spurned for a long time. During the Marcos dictatorship, leftists—NDs and SDs—often looked with disdain on comrades and allies who accepted government appointments, regarding them as having capitulated to the regime. When Marcos liberalized somewhat and allowed elections to be held starting in 1978, the NDs were very critical of those in the traditional opposition who ran in these elections and took office, contending that these oppositionists were helping to legitimize the regime and its "rubber-stamp" Parliament. After the fall of Marcos, many in the Left continued to shun government work, as they looked on the new order as a fake democracy or merely the return of "elite" or "bourgeois" democracy. They viewed the government as being corruption ridden, dominated and run by *trapos*, who represented an oligarchic elite that preyed on it. Hence, government office was a dirty job.

The Left has taken some time to get used to the idea of having some within its ranks working in government. Upon assuming office, President Aquino appointed some leftists and progressives to government positions. However, they did not get much support for their reform initiatives from a fragmented progressive movement, and some got co-opted into *trapo* politics. The most prominent progressives left government (Rocamora 2002:3). Although some candidates of the leftist PnB did win in the congressional elections of 1987 and the local elections of 1988, PnB became inactive soon after the 1988 polls and thus did not gain much experience in government work. The Left has since, and especially over the last six years, become more involved in government work. The major factor, of course, has been the victory of some candidates of leftist parties and groups in the party-list vote and local and *barangay* elections in 1997–2004. The engagement of leftist parties in public administration is still very modest, but it shows signs of growing rapidly in the coming years.

The Left's engagement in public office and governance has to be viewed within the context of the general run of Philippine public administration. In a patrimonial oligarchic state like the Philippines, "governance by patronage" or the "patrimonial approach" toward public office and governance predominates. Under governance by patronage, writes Randolf David (2004), "[g]overnment office is treated as nothing more than booty." Public officials extend public welfare benefits mainly to those whose "gratitude" will be translated into votes on election day. As an alternative to traditional public administration, revisionist neoliberals have been propagating a model of governance—"new public management"—that features efficiency, decentralization, competitive markets, accountability, and public-private partnerships (see Konrad Adenauer Foundation 2000).

In chapter 2, I discussed how leftist parties and groups coming from the ND tradition moved from the outright rejection (or boycott) of processes and institutions of elite or bourgeois democracy to an instrumental view of these processes and how some leftist groups moved on to an integral view of democracy and democratic processes. The instrumental-integral distinction holds not just for elections (which I traced and examined in chapter 4) but for formal institutions of the state as well: the legislature, the executive branch, local governments, and so on. In this chapter, I trace the development of the Left's government work—from virtual nonengagement to substantial engagement since the fall of Marcos. I cover the work of leftist parties and groups in Congress and some departments and agencies of the executive branch and their work in local government units at the *barangay*, municipal, and city levels. I discuss the response of leftist forces to two developments that have had a significant impact on government work in the postauthoritarian era: coalition politics and government decentralization. Toward the end of this chapter, I present four contending strategic perspectives on or approaches to public office and governance—two from the Right (the patrimonial and revisionist neoliberal approaches) and two from the Left (the revolutionary and radical democratic perspectives).[1] In the Philippines' contested democracy, the radical democratic perspective represents a creditable leftist alternative to the patrimonial approach to public office and governance of the country's oligarchic elite. However, those bearing this perspective face great odds. Apart from having to do battle with the patrimonialists, they are also up against the "new managerialists" (revisionist neoliberals) who now overwhelmingly dominate the governance and development discourse in the Philippines.

The Left in Congress

According to Kenneth Roberts (1998:18), a leftist party that has an instrumental view of democracy participates in democratic processes and institutions for "political proselytization, aiming not so much to gain access to government office as to spread its message, expand its organizational networks, and develop a critical consciousness among popular sectors to hasten the dawning of a revolutionary situation." The PnB was clearly in this mode. In the elections in which it participated, its primary concern proved to be to conduct propaganda for the revolutionary movement. Winning was secondary. In its early electoral bids (the 1987 congressional and 1988 local elections), PnB performed far below the NDs' expectations (see chap. 4). Its dismal initial showing was compounded by its failure to provide leadership and direction to winning candidates—two congressmen and eighteen local officials—and other winning progressives who had run under traditional parties but still identified themselves or worked closely with the ND movement. The party did not seem to care much about work in government. "After the 1987–88 elections," remarked Etta Rosales, the PnB president in 1991–92, "the PnB leadership did not even bother to take care of those who won, to consolidate the party's modest victories."[2]

From the start, there had always been doubts about how serious a political project PnB was. Its erratic operations soon after the 1987 debacle tended to reinforce these doubts. The National Council did not meet; the party's executive officers ran the show. A PnB leader served as the link and "political officer" to the congressmen and their staffs, as neither of the two PnB congressmen was in the core of the party leadership. The party did recruit and assign some ND cadres and activists to work in the staffs of the two congressmen. This arrangement, however, proved most inadequate. "We were often clueless on the big scheme of things," comments Ka Dencio, a former staff member. Reflecting just how little importance the NDs then attached to the electoral struggle and especially to government work, PnB "practically dissolved itself" after the 1988 elections.[3] The party closed down its national offices and ND cadres and activists assigned to it were shifted to other lines of work (Partido ng Bayan 1993:59). "PnB was just a label for an experiment," says Ka Dencio. "When the experiment failed, PnB was discarded like a disposable napkin." Despite being left to their own devices, the two PnB congressmen consistently took left-wing positions on national issues (land reform, militarization, U.S. bases, etc.). The abandoned PnB congressmen and local officials eventually joined traditional parties.[4]

"If progressives want to play a significant role in governance," writes IPD's Jennifer Albano (2001:20) in retrospect, "they must take part in the formal institutions of the state." When the Left returned to Congress through the party-list vote in 1998 and 2001, it took the work in the legislature more seriously. The leftist parties that made it in the party-list voting—ABA, Abanse Pinay, Akbayan, AKO, Sanlakas, and later Bayan Muna, AMIN, and PM—are more involved in what their congresspersons are doing, whether pushing for bills and resolutions, issuing press statements and delivering privilege speeches, or appropriating funds for projects. The congresspersons themselves are among the core leaders of these parties. While earnest about their work in Congress, these leftist parties and groups do not necessarily share the same framework or perspective. In the main, those coming from the ND tradition view the work in Congress merely as a means of advancing the revolutionary struggle, while those from the SD and "mixed" traditions basically take an integral view of democratic processes and institutions.

With Bayan Muna, the NDs have worked much more determinedly to win at the polls than they did with PnB in 1987–88 and they are now apparently much more engaged in congressional work than before. Still adhering to the concept of "protracted people's war," however, the NDs remain in the instrumentalist mode. Thus, in essence, Bayan Muna is the same as PnB. The NDs' main objective continues to be political proselytization—at the hustings during the election campaign and in the halls of Congress after the elections.

In a statement released after the 2001 elections, the Central Committee of the CPP (2001) reiterated that electoral struggle and legislative work are secondary to revolutionary armed struggle and the open mass movement and clarified their roles as follows.

> [E]lectoral struggles and work within the reactionary parliament do carry importance for the progressive and democratic forces. It is our fundamental and principal duty to expose the rottenness of the reactionary system and fight it simultaneously from within and from without, project the revolutionary alternative and point to the path that leads to it. Along with this, we may take advantage of the space and opportunity provided, in order to achieve tactical gains for the people and the progressive and democratic movement. This, while we maintain strict vigilance and resist being enticed and gobbled up by the rotten system.

In the light of Bayan Muna's main function of political proselytization, the party's three representatives in the Twelfth Congress (2001–4) were most prolific in issuing press statements, outstripping even the most publicity oriented among other congressional representatives.[5] The Bayan Muna representatives also filed or cosponsored many bills and resolutions. The media releases and filed bills and resolutions were mainly in the nature of exposing and opposing "the rottenness of the reactionary system" and defending the NDs' mass base. The largest number of press statements and resolutions, for instance, had to do with denunciations of, or inquiries into, alleged human rights violations committed by government forces engaged in military operations against the CPP-NPA and with opposition to the U.S.-led "war on terrorism," which targets the CPP-NPA, among other groups, in the Philippines. Bayan Muna also devoted much attention to such matters as corruption, consumers' issues, women, labor, and globalization. In an interview, Congressman Satur Ocampo admitted that his party did not really expect most of its bills to be passed.[6] The House approved some Bayan Muna resolutions, but most of these were merely calls for inquiries and investigations into abuses and irregularities. Not all of Bayan Muna's interventions were of the "expose and oppose" type. For instance, Bayan Muna congresswoman Liza Masa was one of the principal sponsors of a bill that was enacted into law to combat trafficking in persons, especially women and minors. The articulate and personable Ocampo, a well-respected journalist in pre-martial-law days and a high-profile NDF negotiator after the fall of Marcos, has been most effective in promoting the party and attracting allies.

While rejecting protracted people's war, other parties and groups of the ND tradition, such as PMP and electoral parties aligned with it, retain a revolutionary perspective. In 1994, when the CPP had just split, Lagman (1994:59), who later founded PMP, agreed with the CPP that "revolution is war." He criticized the CPP, however, for waging a revolutionary war even when the proper conditions for transforming revolution into war, or political into military struggle, had not yet developed. Chiding CPP chairman Sison for earlier dismissing participation in parliament as "a fool's game," Lagman argued that the conditions in Russia in Lenin's time were a lot worse than present-day conditions in the Philippines and yet the Bolsheviks had participated in elections and worked in the Duma (Parliament) for several years as part of their efforts to accumulate strength and set the stage for revolution. "Lenin played a 'fool's game' for several years," wrote Lagman, "never calling for a revolutionary war until the conditions for such a war arose."

Renato Magtubo (1998:2–3), who represented two PMP-aligned electoral parties in the House of Representatives (Sanlakas in 1998–2001 and PM in 2003–4), has been most consistent—and more forthright than the Bayan Muna legislators—in treating Congress mainly as a venue for revolutionary proselytization. From the outset, he said that he was in Congress "to try to articulate society's cry for change—profound social change" and that he was a leader of the militant BMP, whose "main objective is a political revolution, a workers' revolution to overhaul the capitalist system." With regard to bills and resolutions, Magtubo did not make much of a mark. However, the in-your-face privileged speeches of the political maverick proved controversial, often drawing angry responses from other representatives. In April 2000, Magtubo and Akbayan's Rosales hogged the headlines for exposing a big payola scheme in the House of Representatives that implicated their fellow representatives in the House—a most blatant case of *trapo* corruption. Going much farther than Rosales, Magtubo (2000:3–4) practically labeled the House of Representatives "a den of thieves" and "a stinking pigsty" and virtually accused his colleagues of "lying through their teeth." Reacting to threats of expulsion from the House, Magtubo defiantly rejoined: "You cannot intimidate me. *Hindi ako nag-iisa!* [I am not alone!] I belong to the real majority—the toiling masses of our people." And he warned: "Those who hinder the road to reform only pave the way for revolution."

The stance of PMP and allied electoral parties vis-à-vis government work, however, appears to be changing. In the Twelfth Congress, PM and Sanlakas became more involved in pushing for reforms, especially those in support of workers. In late 2003, for instance, PM representative Magtubo and Sanlakas representative Jose Bautista pressed for the passage of a bill seeking to increase the retirement pay of workers in the private sector (Cruz 2003).

Leftist parties of the mixed ND-SD tradition (like Akbayan) and the SD tradition (like ABA-AKO) have an integral conception of democracy and recognize the intrinsic value of formal democratic processes and institutions such as elections and Congress. Akbayan participates in these processes avowedly to "achieve concrete gains for the people and to weaken elite rule" (Akbayan National Congress 2003:9) and not merely to engage in advocacy or propaganda for some far-off revolutionary change. "The contradiction between the form and substance of elite rule, between political democracy and social disparity," says Rocamora (1997a:2), "presents a substantial opportunity for a political party that will engage in mainstream political processes to advance a redistributive agenda." Akbayan aims to make Congress a more democratic institution and hopes to eventually move it from elite domination to popular control. Espousing a program-based politics, Akbayan seeks to do away with the practices of personality- and patronage-based politics such as corruption and horse trading in the policy-making process (Rocamora 1997b:23).

As a neophyte legislator, Congresswoman Rosales (2003b:1–3, 12) of Akbayan actively participated in a number of committees and authored or cosponsored dozens of bills and resolutions covering a wide span of concerns. In recognition of her good work, at least in part, the House leadership appointed her the chairperson of the Committee on Civil, Political, and Human Rights at the start of her second term. Two years into Rosales's second term, four bills principally authored by her—notably the Absentee Voting Law—and six bills coauthored by her were enacted into law, and twenty more (two authored and eighteen co-authored) were passed by the House. In addition, twenty-four resolutions she filed, plus ten coauthored, had been passed by the chamber. Her legislative and advocacy work were related to human rights, labor, agrarian issues, women, overseas Filipinos, education, political and electoral reform, and national sovereignty. With Rosales as head of the Party-List Caucus and chair of the Subcommittee on Party-List and Sectoral Representation, the party-list representatives took common positions on Party-List System Law amendments. Often sought for interviews by the mass media, the articulate Akbayan representative has become one of the country's most visible legislators. In an editorial, a Philippine daily newspaper, *Today* (2001), paid her a rare compliment: "Forget the others. The only party-list member who has been of any real service to our country is Etta Rosales."

Coalition Politics: Dangers and Opportunities

Coalition politics, asserts Patricio N. Abinales, has become "the defining feature of political warfare" and "a new way of governing" in the Philippines. Since the fall of Marcos, "big tent" alliances that draw together forces from the Right, Center, and Left have replaced political parties as the means by which groups and individuals aspire to and wield power. Though ideologically opposed, the forces temporarily set aside their differences and unite for a common objective such as the election of a presidential candidate. Once in power, they apportion among themselves the top positions in the government bureaucracy. "Under leaders capable of balancing the interests of these disparate forces," observes Abinales (2001a:154–61), "coalition politics can considerably benefit governing. But the marriage between coalition politics and stable governing also has a limit. Under less-than-competent leadership, a coalition can unravel and affect the ability of a regime to govern, as was the case under President Estrada."

According to Felipe B. Miranda (1993), a political scientist and commentator, coalition politics was a major policy thrust of the Ramos administration. In the name of "national unification," Ramos systematically recruited pliant politicians, including even "treasonous" figures of the Marcos dictatorship, into "rainbow" coalitions and endeavored to integrate rebel groups—military rebels, as well as communist and secessionist insurgents—into the main body politic. Citing surveys by the Social Weather Stations, Miranda points out that there was broad political support for such "ultra-comprehensive coalition politics" … "a popular belief that a political consensus must be forged among all sectors of Philippine society for the country to progress." This attitude, he declares, "underscores the desperation of a people who in the last two decades had been systematically blocked in the pursuit of national development."

Of course, *trapos* and their parties dominate the big tent coalitions. Wary about being co-opted or manipulated by the *trapos*, leftist parties and groups have actually often been unenthusiastic about these coalitions or at best ambivalent towards them. None, except PDSP, has formally or officially joined these coalitions.[7] The "representatives" of the left in the coalitions are usually individual personages who are close allies, former leaders or nonleading members of leftist parties. Prominent leftists Horacio Morales, Jr., and Edicio de la Torre, both former leading NDs and popdems, did not belong to any political party when they joined Estrada's coalition.[8] While in government, they worked closely with such leftist groups as Akbayan and AMIN until the start of the "Oust Erap" campaign.

The brief, hard-luck stint of leftists in the Estrada administration has shown the pitfalls of participating in big tent alliances. While the leftists and other "state reformists" performed relatively well and maintained "isles of state efficiency" (Abinales 2001a:158), it was clientelist politics as usual in other departments, and the president and his cronies engaged in patrimonial plunder. In Törnquist's

(2002:42, 60, 63) analysis, Morales and De la Torre had followed the "pragmatic argument" that "leading democrats should make their way to the top by drawing on the 'traditional' clientelist and populist clout of certain leaders." The grand experiment "to boost Estrada and use his strength to expand and promote radical reforms ... ended in outright failure." Morales and De la Torre's decision "to stay on the sinking ship" in the hope of increasing their influence on the captain should he survive the storm was a costly political mistake.

According to Martin Tanchuling, the executive director of a rural development NGO, the appointment of progressives to high government positions has quite often led to frictions and strains between different leftist groups and allied POs/NGOs trying to influence the appointees' policies and programs. One such divide has been that between groups coming from the ND tradition and those from the SD tradition. Sometimes, he said, the rivalries, which have even affected the appointees' choices in the hiring of personnel, no longer seem to be much different from the *trapos'* "weather-weather" jockeying for influence.[9]

Leftist participation in big tent coalitions, however, has not been all negative. Although the 1986 Constitutional Commission, whose members were all appointed by President Aquino, was dominated by members of the elite, the leftists (NDs, SDs, and independent leftists) and liberal progressives on the commission managed to have a good number of progressive provisions included in the draft charter. The "Freedom Constitution" ratified in February 1987, contained an expanded bill of rights and certain "protectionist" provisions on the national economy and patrimony. Leftist parties and groups are themselves now availing themselves of provisions on the role and rights of POs/NGOs, the introduction of the party-list system, government decentralization, and so on, whether for revolutionary proselytization or for the transformation of an elite-dominated democracy into a more participatory and egalitarian one.

The appointment of reform-oriented progressives, including some popdems and SDs, to key positions in the Department of Agrarian Reform during the Ramos and Estrada administrations encouraged land reform advocates within both civil society and the state to pursue a "*bibingka* strategy" in land reform implementation, combining initiatives by "state reformists" from above with mobilizations of POs/NGOs "from below."[10] Thanks in large part to this symbiotic interaction, the post-Marcos Comprehensive Agrarian Reform Programme (CARP), against most expectations, registered significant accomplishments in counteracting strong landlord resistance to agrarian reform and in facilitating land redistribution to poor peasants. By the end of 1999, the program had succeeded in redistributing 4.84 million hectares of land, or about 60 percent of its target, directly benefiting about 2.1 million rural poor households (Borras 2001).[11]

Despite the Morales-De la Torre imbroglio, some leftist parties and groups have remained open to the idea of progressives, even their own members, taking up posts in the executive branch of the government. Representative Leonardo Montemayor of the ABA gave up his seat in Congress to serve as Arroyo's secretary of agriculture, but he was eased out in a Cabinet reorganization a year later. As a member organization of the Barangay-Bayan [Village-Municipal] Governance Consortium (BBGC), also known as the Batman Consortium, Akbayan continues to adhere to a "dual-power strategy," which consists of "building strong, autonomous POs taking on sectoral issues and concerns" and working with "progressives in government (or putting in some of our own)" (Villarin 2001:2).[12] In Rocamora's view (2002: 9), it was fine for progressives to work within the Arroyo regime and pursue reforms as long as "the overall impact of the regime's policies has not reached a point where we are obliged to call for Arroyo's ouster" and "the balance of power within the cabinet continues to provide maneuver space for our allies within government." Arroyo remained vulnerable to PO/NGO advocacies, in Rocamora's assessment, because there were reformers in the Cabinet and key agencies and because POs/NGOs could draw support from the church and big business on some reform issues.

Apart from supporting progressives in government, since 2001, Akbayan has actively worked for the appointment of several of its members to certain government positions. Under Arroyo (as under Estrada), several Akbayan members took up positions in the National Anti-poverty Commission (NAPC). Created by virtue of the Social Reform and Poverty Alleviation Act of 1998, the NAPC coordinates and oversees the implementation of the government's Social Reform Agenda (SRA), develops and promotes microfinance schemes, and acts as the lead agency of Kapit-Bisig Laban sa Kahirapan (Kalahi), or Linking Arms against Poverty, the Arroyo administration's strategic program for poverty reduction. According to the NAPC vice chair for Basic Sectors and Akbayan leader Oscar Francisco (2003), the commission would intensify its efforts, among others, in securing funds for CARP from the "coconut levy" and the "Marcos wealth"; in successfully carrying out the Community Mortgage Program for the urban poor; in promoting community-based enterprise development; and in effectively implementing laws supporting or protecting poor fishermen, senior citizens, the handicapped, and indigenous peoples.

Since 2001, the inclusion of the left in big tent coalitions has not been limited to the executive branch of government. For their participation in EDSA II and their support for the successful bid of Jose de Venecia for the speakership of the House of Representatives, leftist parties such as Bayan Muna and Akbayan were included in the majority bloc of the House, which was dominated by Arroyo's PPC. Thanks to their being in the majority bloc, Bayan Muna and Akbayan had better access to project funds, and Akbayan's Rosales was appointed chairperson of the Human Rights Committee. Neither party had to toe the line of the Arroyo administration; in fact, both became increasingly critical. Yet they were not expelled from the majority bloc nor sanctioned. Keeping them in the "majority" may have been a preemptive move on the part of the administration. It is very possible that the House leadership preferred these leftist parties to remain as an "in-bloc" opposition rather than letting them forge a potentially powerful coalition with the *trapo* opposition.

Through careful and judicious engagement with big tent coalition politics, democratic leftist parties and groups can conceivably go beyond merely supporting or placing a number of progressives in government. The looseness of big tent coalitions provides a democratic leftist party with possibilities for drawing progressives in government together, creating progressive groups and blocs within both the executive and legislative branches of government, and eventually recruiting some of these progressives into the party.

The Left and Decentralization

Although the Left, in general, has long spurned working in government, the revolutionary Left has long been *getting into* local government. Since the Marcos era, says former CPP Politburo member Ricardo Reyes, the CPP-NPA has tried to win over many *barangay* officials, and even entire *barangay* councils, to its side, recruited a good number of these officials into its ranks, and supported or even put up candidates in *barangay* elections. This has been a common practice, especially in CPP-NPA guerrilla zones. Links with *barangay* officials and candidates, however, have been of a clandestine nature. The CPP-NPA's objective in such involvement in *barangay* politics has not been to turn the councils into models of good government but to neutralize them or render them inutile and prevent them from being used for "counterinsurgency" and to tap individuals or the councils themselves for various needs of the revolutionary movement such as material support and intelligence work on the "enemy." Its involvement in *barangay* government or governance, hence, has not been real engagement. "The CPP did not have any idea of local governance," remarked Reyes. "It did not really care much for the *barangay* councils. The stress was on building barrio [*barangay*] revolutionary committees as an alternative organ of revolutionary power. No matter how hard it tried to build these revolutionary committees, however, it did not succeed much." In the urban areas, the objective was different. During the Marcos era, for instance, getting into the *barangay* council was found to be useful in certain cases in "helping build an antidictatorship front." There have been no indications of any significant change in the CPP-NPA's policy of neutralizing the *barangay* councils.[13]

It may be said that the Left's engagement in local government in the post-Marcos period began with President Aquino's appointment of some leftists to "officer in charge" positions soon after EDSA I or with the electoral victories of some PnB candidates in the 1988 local elections. These were times, however, when the Left was still quite disoriented in the light of the 1986 boycott fiasco. Thus, PnB and other leftist groups failed to provide much direction or leadership to the leftists who had been appointed or elected to local government posts. The latter were largely left to fend for themselves, especially after PnB closed its national offices. Serious engagement of the Left in local government came later, through a circuitous route, and it started at the *barangay* rather than the municipal or city level.

In the late 1980s and early 1990s, emergent leftist groups, together with POs and NGOs aligned with them, engaged more seriously in development work, even as they continued to be actively involved in "pressure" or contentious politics—rallies, marches and other protest actions. Among these new, leftist groups were the popular democrats (or popdems), Bisig, and Pandayan—three "political blocs" that, together with Siglaya, formed the political party Akbayan in January 1998. From small-scale, *barangay*-based development projects, the popdems, Bisig, Pandayan, and allied POs/NGOs soon moved on to "integrated area development" (IAD) or "sustainable IAD" (SIAD) projects covering much wider areas. In pursuing these projects, the new, leftist groups and allied POs/NGOs increasingly had to deal with *barangay* and municipal LGUs, coordinate with them, and eventually work on joint projects with them. Thus, the IAD/SIAD experience eventually led to greater PO/NGO and LGU interaction. From development work, the emergent leftist groups and allied POs/NGOs moved on—naturally, as it were—to greater engagement in both local governance and local government work and developed a different concept of governance. Several developments facilitated this process. The most important was the passage of the Local Government Code of 1991, which provided for decentralization and the transfer of power to local governments. Another was that international donor agencies provided funds and new ideas for PO/NGO participation in local governance (Rocamora 2000a:4).

The Local Government Code has been praised as a "landmark" piece of legislation (Eaton 2001:114) and "a revolution in governance" (Rood 1998). Despite her elitist background, President Aquino had pushed hard for decentralization, the most important policy departure of her entire administration, wanting it to be part of her legacy of democratization. For several years, the LGC bill languished in Congress. It was only toward the end of Aquino's term that the LGC was enacted. Hoping to gain her crucial endorsement for their electoral bids, Congress members rushed to have it approved (Eaton 2001:116–18).

In what has been described as "one of the most ambitious decentralization attempts in Asia" (Eaton 2001:106), the code devolved to local governments the responsibility for the delivery of basic services, as well as certain regulatory and licensing powers; increased their share in taxes; and provided various incentives for local governments to become more entrepreneurial (Brillantes 1996:87). In just four years, seventy thousand national government employees were transferred to local organizational structures, and the share of local governments in internal revenue allotment increased from 11 to 40 percent. "The decentralization programme has proceeded steadily, if not always smoothly," assessed Mark Turner (1999a:118), "and there are certainly indications that real gains have been made in promoting local autonomy and enabling local government to run more of their own affairs in cooperation with NGOs and the private sector." Others have even been more praiseful. "Perhaps nowhere else in the world," gushed a panel of scholars, "has decentralization of the political system proceeded as rapidly as in the Philippines."[14]

In the Latin American experience, decentralization did not necessarily involve the democratization of local governments. "If a local government is already democratic and responsive to its citizens," Fox (1995:16) observes, "then the outcome is promising. If not, then decentralization can reinforce patronage politics or even authoritarian rule at the local level. Some decentralization programs create new concentrations of elite power while others actually do decentralize control. But despite these diverse outcomes, decentralization did pave the way for left victories at the local and regional levels."

In theory, at least, the decentralization program in the Philippines provides better conditions for the Left since it includes some democratization features. The code not only devolved certain powers of the national government to local governments; it also introduced some forms of direct democracy, as well as the participation of POs/NGOs in local special bodies such as the local development councils and the bids and awards committees (Pimentel 1994:93–5). "Decentralization," writes Alex Brillantes, Jr., (1994:584), "is a modality of democratization, ... a major strategy to empower the previously marginalized sectors of society." A "rapid field appraisal" of decentralization conducted by Associates in Rural Development, Inc., in 1996 noted growing popular participation in local governance (Turner 1999a:112).

The initial reaction to the code from the Left and the PO/NGO community was far from enthusiastic. Many POs/NGOs were indifferent. Others dismissed it as just another medium for state co-optation, providing only token representation for marginalized groups (Villarin 1996:1–2). POs/NGOs had achieved some successes in their development work, while corruption, patronage, and bureaucratic red tape had blunted the development efforts of local governments. Why bother to work with local governments (Soriano 1992:16)? A different view surfaced within the emergent left, however. Pandayan peasant leader Vic Fabe (1992:84) saw opportunities for much more grassroots organizing and mobilization against the abuses of local officials. Men Santa Ana (1992:3, 9), then executive secretary of the Freedom from Debt Coalition, argued that the LGC was "a forceful instrument to change the political power equation" and "a powerful tool for people's organizations to carry out their political and development agenda on the ground." He warned, however, that if the code were to be implemented without people's participation, the elite and the *trapos* could exploit it to consolidate their political and economic turfs. He urged POs/NGOs to take into account the code's impact on the struggle for local power and to "slug it out." For Bisig, the LGC provided an opening for POs/NGOs to participate actively in local special bodies, including such important ones as the local development councils. Bisig eyed the possibility of achieving immediate tangible gains at the grassroots level by combining the collective action of POs and work within local government structures (Valte 1992:5).

Through 1992, POs/NGOs, especially those in the CODE-NGO, took an active part in regional consultations and a national POs/NGO conference on local governance. The participating POs/NGOs, including many aligned with ND and SD groups, formed the National Coordinating Council on the Local Government Code, a broad coalition of twenty-three national PO/NGO networks. Endorsing the code, the conference participants took up the challenge of active partnership with local governments. To counter moves of some officials to do away with the code's basic POS/NGO empowering provisions, the participants called on the government to ensure its full implementation.[15] In the first few years of the implementation of the code, the council actively campaigned among both member and nonmember POS/NGOs to become accredited with local governments and take an active part in local governance. According to Villarin (2000:2), however, the initial participation of POS/NGOs in governance was mainly at the regional and national levels and consisted mostly of "conferences and media-hugging activities praising NGO-LGU partnerships."

The Left and "Barangay" Governance

In November 1996, seven NGOs closely identified with the popdems, Bisig, Pandayan, and Siglaya decided to work together to assist PO leaders in the NGOs' respective project areas who were intending to run in the May 1997 *barangay* elections by providing them with training in electoral campaign management (Bulatao 2000b:191).[16] Many of those who took part in the trainings did win.[17] The newly elected *barangay* leaders asked the NGOs' help in running their *barangays*. In a conference convened by the IPG, the nine NGOs that participated agreed to conduct trainings on *barangay* governance. They soon produced a "Barangay Administration Training Manual" (Batman) and used it for initial trainings (Villarin 2003:3).[18] Many other newly elected *barangay* officials expressed interest in the Batman trainings and joined in. Meanwhile, members of the nine NGOs became actively involved in the formal establishment of Akbayan and subsequently in the party's campaign to win seats in Congress through the party-list elections in 1998. In the course of conducting Batman trainings, the NGOs involved realized that *barangay* governance—and local governance in general—had a lot more training needs. Thus, Batman became a much bigger and longer-term program. The consortium of NGOs involved in local governance endeavors officially became the Barangay-Bayan Governance Consortium in 1999, but its comic-book nickname stuck. Since the original Batman trainings, the NGOs involved in the Batman Consortium have developed other training courses, including the

Basic Orientation for Barangay Governance (BOBG) for *barangay* officials and community PO leaders; the provincial-level Barangay Governance Trainers' Training; and the Direct Action for Local Governance Seminar (Dialogs), an orientation seminar on the Local Government Code for NGO-PO-LGU partners. The crowning achievement of the consortium, however, has been the Barangay Development Planning through Participatory Resource Appraisal (BDP-PRA), which promotes active community involvement in the local development planning process (Villarin 2003:4; Rocamora 2000a:3).

Tomasito Villarin, IPG executive director, and Rocamora, Akbayan president in 2001–3 and former IPD executive director, have described the BDP-PRA process. Prior to the actual planning in BDP-PRA, the Batman NGO trains PO leaders and LGU officials as local community facilitators in an intensive one-week course. This trainers' training ends with the formation of participatory resource appraisal (PRA) teams, which take charge of the planning process, each team consisting of a facilitator, a documenter, and a process observer. The BDP-PRA proper begins with social or community preparation and then moves on to data gathering and analysis, problem prioritization, the setting of the community vision, mission, goals and strategies, and the writing up of a draft five-year development plan. It concludes with the formal adoption of the plan by the *barangay* council (Villarin 2004:20–23). The BDP-PRA process involves "poverty mapping, [i.e.,] identifying the poor in the barangay, and analyzing why they are poor." This exercise serves to curb the infrastructure project orientation of most development planning in the Philippines (Rocamora 2000a:4).

BDP-PRA is a Philippine adaptation of an approach to participatory development planning known as participatory rural appraisal (PRA), which spread in many developing countries in the 1990s. In PRA, local people undertake their own appraisal and analysis. They make maps and models, walk transects and observe, investigate and interview, score and diagram, present and analyze information, and plan. It contrasts with traditional methods of inquiry, which tend to impose and extract. "[W]hen it is well done," Robert Chambers (1994:1266) notes, "local people, and especially the poorer, enjoy the creative learning that comes from presenting their knowledge and

Figure 5.1 *Key steps in the BDP-PRA process*

1	**Social preparation**	Identifying local POs, NGOs, and other nongovernmental stakeholders who are willing to participate in the BDP-PRA.
2	**Community orientation**	During the *barangay* assembly, members of the local community are given an orientation about the project, its objective, its relevance to them, and so on.
3	**Data gathering**	Through PRA, community facilitators trained earlier will gather community data (demographic, socio-economic, historical, etc.).
4	**Data analysis and interpretation**	The community designs a problem tree based on the data gathered.
5	**Problem prioritization**	The process whereby participants reason out and argue which problems will be prioritized based on criteria they set.
6	**Cross-sector validation**	Comparative discussions of the problems posed by the different sectoral groups of the BDP-PRA.
7	**Community vision-mission setting**	A highly graphic and visual process of defining what the community would like to be ten years from the present.
8	**Goals and objectives setting**	A problem tree is made into an objective tree; a community goal is defined and specific objectives are identified.
9	**Identifying indicators of development**	Each set of objectives will have indicators that are qualitative, quantitative, and time bound.
10	**Strategy formulation**	The community defines what strategies to pursue, usually after an external and internal environmental scan.
11	**Comprehensive five-year development and annual investment/ operations planning**	Five sectoral groups under the BDP / MDP standard format define these plans.
12	**Plan presentation with the *barangay* assembly**	The packaged plans are presented to the *barangay* assembly for approval.
13	**Approval and formal adoption of the plan by the legislative council**	A formal resolution is passed by the legislative council and later an ordinance for implementing the plans will be adopted.
14	**Setting up the monitoring and evaluation system**	The *barangay* development council and the municipal technical working group are trained on how to establish a project-monitoring and evaluation system.

(From Villarin 2004:23)

their reality. They say that they see things differently. It is not just that they share knowledge with outsiders. They themselves learn more of what they know, and together present and build up more than any one knew alone. The process is then empowering, enabling them to analyze their world and can lead into their planning and action." Compared with data taken through traditional means, information shared by local people through PRA has been marked by "high validity and reliability."

Usually, BDP-PRA includes planning for raising *barangay* funds and actual fund-raising as well. "Because the barangay budget is almost always inadequate," Rocamora (2000a:4) explains, "the development plan includes a strategy for accessing additional funds. Batman assists the process with a pilot project to provide a seed fund of ₱100,000 (US$2,500) which can be accessed by the barangay only if they manage to generate funds from other sources. Batman also assists by organizing 'pledging sessions' where higher level government officials and ODA [official development aid] and other foreign funding agencies are brought together to listen to barangay officials make a pitch for financial support for their projects."

Still other programs of the Batman Consortium are the women in governance training program, electoral and political education, and organizational development and strengthening. Thanks to the women in governance trainings, an increasing number of Batman POs/NGOs have developed and integrated gender-focused programs in their local governance work (Sumaylo 2004:221). The consortium also engages in policy advocacy at the local and national levels, such as campaigning for community-based antipoverty programs and strengthening the Local Government Code (Villarin 2004:15).

By 2000, the member NGOs of Batman had increased to thirty-five, mostly local NGOs. The following year, however, the consortium suffered a serious setback when Gerardo Bulatao, a leading and influential member of both Akbayan and the consortium, withdrew from both in the wake of the controversial elections for party-list candidates at the 2001 Akbayan congress. Together with several supporters, he established a new NGO, Empowering Civic Participation in Governance (ECPG). Moreover, he convinced a good number of NGOs to withdraw from the Batman consortium and set up a new one, the Local Governance Citizens' Network (LGCNet).[19] Both consortiums have grown since then. By the end of 2003, the Batman Consortium's membership roster included sixty NGOs and three national POs. The Batman NGOs have worked in more than 2,500 of the country's 45,000 *barangays*, of which 1,200 have undertaken BDP-PRA. The 2,500 *barangays* are spread out in 28 of the country's 79 provinces, 167 of 1,496 municipalities and 16 of 83 cities (Villarin 2004:8; Rocamora 2004:335).

Akbayan is the lone political party in the Batman consortium (Villarin 2000:29). Its involvement in Batman marks the first, and thus far the only major engagement of a leftist party in local governance—open and legal, not "underground" governance—since the late 1930s and early 1940s.

Assessing Batman's Work at the "Barangay" Level

Rocamora (2000a:5–6) describes Batman as a governance and development project of Philippine POs/NGOs whose goal was to set in motion a series of political activities at the *barangay* level that would enable elected *barangay* officials to make full use of the Local Government Code in providing economic and political services to their constituents, maximize economic gains for *barangay* inhabitants, and strengthen local communities and increase their capability to negotiate their economic and political relations with the larger society. He saw it as a way to change a patronage-permeated political culture. According to him, public goods and services in the prevailing "currency" of political relationships are transacted privately—politicians provide jobs, money, and so on to individuals, who give their political support in turn. With a strengthened *barangay* governance system, relations between *barangay* leaders and municipal-level politicians could take on the elements of negotiation, and "the introduction of another mode of relations with municipal elites should, over time, erode personalism and move local politics from exchanges of private goods to exchanges of public goods."

Villarin (2000:1–4) highlights Batman's role in promoting "democratic participation in governance," portraying it as "a movement of NGOs, people's organizations, political blocs, progressive local government officials and a progressive reform electoral party promoting good governance through participatory approaches in local governance." He contends that "governance is essentially an issue of power," and that democratic participation in governance is "a collective effort of citizens to negotiate from the state rights already mandated but effectively denied them because of an imbalance in power relations" and "an attempt to change certain institutional arrangements, power relations and hierarchical structures."

Preliminary findings of an assessment of the impact of Batman interventions in local politics point to creditable gains in the promotion of both participatory democracy and development at the *barangay* level. Hawes (2000:20) cites the following "rather remarkable impacts" of the Batman approach.

- Residents have begun to more fully understand their rights as citizens and to engage in oversight of the local governments.
- More important, citizens have also demonstrated that they recognize their responsibility for improving local governance by volunteering their time and talent.
- Local government elected officials are beginning to acknowledge that they are accountable downward to the community rather than upward to their political bosses and allies.
- The very limited resources available at the local level are increasingly being invested in priority projects identified by the community that address local needs for better services and improved livelihoods. Most notably, prestige projects such as basketball courts, *barangay* halls, and waiting sheds that bear the names of the elected officials are seldom identified as high priorities when planning and budgeting are done in a participatory fashion with high levels of community involvement.
- The best local governments are also beginning to realize that if they want to improve service delivery they must have community participation in agenda setting and the implementation of projects. This collaboration mobilizes additional labor and contributions from the community that multiply the impact and extend the reach of whatever could have been accomplished without citizen participation.

Although Batman has made considerable progress in furthering participatory democracy, it does have some weaknesses. One crucial weak spot is popular political education, particularly in fostering greater awareness of how patronage politics directly affects the lives of *barangay* residents and how it can be combated. Despite greater popular participation in local governance in areas covered by the program, clientelist thinking and behavior have persisted or even continued to hold sway. This has been most apparent at election time. In many Batman areas, non-*trapos* still fared badly against *trapos* in the 1998 and 2001 polls, as residents continued to behave and vote as before. Most telling for me, however, was that in most Batman *barangays* I visited in 2002 vote buying during the *barangay* elections was just as bad as in previous elections, or worse.[20] My field visits did confirm that Batman has helped *barangay* leaders become more resourceful and enterprising in raising funds for their projects, especially through the "pledging sessions." I observed, however, that staffers of Batman NGOs had not gone on to explain "moving local politics from exchanges of private goods to exchanges of public goods." A bit of patronage politics thus managed to creep back in, as municipal, provincial, and national officials approached for "pledges" were quick to use the opportunity to grandstand and try to make funding beneficiaries feel indebted for the grace bestowed on them. To change power relations even at the local level, "people's participation in governance" apparently needs to be complemented with an ideological and cultural struggle against patronage politics.

Another weakness has been the delay in moving up to municipal and city governance. As its official name indicates, the Batman Consortium's work was supposed to be scaled up from the *barangay* to the *bayan* (municipal) level. It took some time, however, for the consortium to do so. Batman's—and Akbayan's—engagement in local politics had centered on "democratic [or people's/citizens'] participation in governance." Democratic participation in governance is in line with the objective of transforming an elite-dominated formal democracy into a more participatory and egalitarian one. Since governance lends itself best to direct people's participation at the *barangay* level, it was but fitting that Batman should start at this level. Those involved in Batman, on seeing *barangay* residents actively involved in the day-to-day activities of the *barangay*, were very much buoyed up by its apparent success. Batman NGOs and Akbayan poured their energies into reaching out to as many *barangays* as possible and to achieving proficiency in participatory *barangay* governance. Absorbed in horizontal development, they on the whole kept postponing Batman's vertical development and forgot about the vacuum in political leadership at the municipal / city level. Another factor for the delay in scaling up was that the Batman NGOs and Akbayan tended to be restricted by the Batman frame of democratic participation in governance, which had a particular emphasis on direct democracy. Although it was perhaps adequate for *barangay* governance, it did not suffice for municipal / city governance, where one already had to reckon with a civil bureaucracy and much more representative democracy.

Despite these weaknesses, Batman has not slipped into the pitfall of "localism" that seems to have beset PRA projects in some developing countries. Mohan and Stokke (2000:249), while viewing PRA as a positive trend in development theory and practice, warn of the tendencies to essentialize and romanticize "the local" and detach it from broader economic and political structures. Akbayan and the POs /NGOs involved in Batman and BDP-PRA have managed to avoid localism because of their involvement in social movements and the state arena (elections and governance) at various levels—local to national.

The Left and Municipal/City Governance

In 1997, while other Batman NGOs focused their energies on trainings on participatory *barangay* governance and development planning, the Institute for Political and Electoral Reform (IPER), an NGO aligned with Siglaya and later Padayon, pioneered in trainings on *municipal* governance and development planning. Municipal officials in pilot areas were well satisfied with the trainings. Due to financial constraints, however, IPER could not sustain the initiative and had to suspend it indefinitely in 2000.[21]

Although there were some leftist or "progressive" candidates at the municipal and city levels who were elected in 1998 and 2001,[22] the leftist parties and groups did not attend to them upon their assumption of office as much as the parties did to winning congressional candidates in 1998 and 2001 and as Akbayan did to winning *barangay* candidates in 1997 and 2002. When I did my field research in April-November 2002, it seemed to me that as far as government work at the municipal/city level was concerned not much had changed since the PnB period. As in 1988, the post-PnB leftist parties (Akbayan, Sanlakas, Bayan Muna, etc.) had taken a stance of nonengagement or minimal involvement in municipal/city governance. I observed that leftist or progressive municipal/city officials were largely left to their own devices in performing their governmental functions. In some places, local structures of leftist parties—such as Akbayan's divisions in the Iranun areas of Maguindanao, in southeastern Samar, and in Daraga, Albay, and Bayan Muna's chapter in Davao City—did endeavor to become much more engaged in municipal/city governance. Until then, none of the left parties or groups had come up with a national program or orientational framework on municipal/city governance similar to that of Batman's/Akbayan's on *barangay* governance.

Local leaders and members of leftist parties tended to treat progressive municipal/city officials—even those who had already joined the party—not as fellow party members or potential recruits but simply as allies, usually approaching them only to ask for some form of support for a mass action or campaign, for a PO/NGO project, or simply for humanitarian assistance. While the progressive officials grappled with such major municipal concerns as the revamping of a corrupt and inefficient bureaucracy, improvement in the delivery of basic services, increasing municipal revenue, and comprehensive planning and budgeting, local leaders and members of leftist parties did not help them out. Either they were too preoccupied with other concerns or they felt that municipal governance was out of their depth. Given that the progressive officials worked in a *trapo*-dominated milieu and many of them had in fact run under traditional parties, the leftist parties ran the great risk of losing these officials (or their main allegiance) to the traditional parties by default, as PnB had in the late 1980s.

It must be borne in mind that the development of the ties between a leftist party and a progressive LGU official usually goes through a complicated process. Leftist party activists "spot" a progressive official or a potential ally in the course of interacting with him or her in connection with a mass campaign, a development project, participatory governance, and so on. They then try to forge a closer relationship with him or her through frequent follow-up and by working on joint endeavors. The official usually belongs to a traditional party, but such affiliation does not prevent the leftist activists from working closely with him or her. Sometimes, the leftist party recruits the said official into the party, but he or she does not break off with the traditional party. In effect, the official has a dual-party affiliation—traditional and leftist. Since leftist parties are commonly viewed as not having the wherewithal to win elections, the politician usually still runs in elections under one or the other traditional party. Thus far, none of the leftist electoral parties has stringently enforced single-party affiliation on politician members.

Although Sanlakas/PM and Bayan Muna have a number of municipal/city officials, they remain largely uninvolved and unengaged in municipal/city governance. This is not because they want to boycott "bourgeois" municipal/city government institutions and processes. Municipal/city politics simply lies outside of their current priorities. It appears that, for both Sanlakas/PM and Bayan Muna, Congress (through the party-list system) is more important as it serves as a much more powerful medium for political proselytization. Several times in the period between April 2002 and January 2003, I visited Angono, Rizal, a municipality whose mayor was a member of Sanlakas, and Guinobatan, Albay, a municipality whose mayor was a member of Bayan Muna. Both mayors seemed to be performing very well in public office, but neither Sanlakas nor Bayan Muna seemed to be very involved or engaged in government work and governance.

While still vice mayor, Gerardo Calderon observed that many painters and sculptors lived or often came to Angono, a picturesque, foothills town along Laguna de Bay. He noted, too, that two acclaimed national artists had actually come from the town. When Calderon ran for mayor in 1998, he presented his vision of the "Angono dream"—turning the municipality into "an artists' paradise and a tourists' haven" through a "holistic concept of local

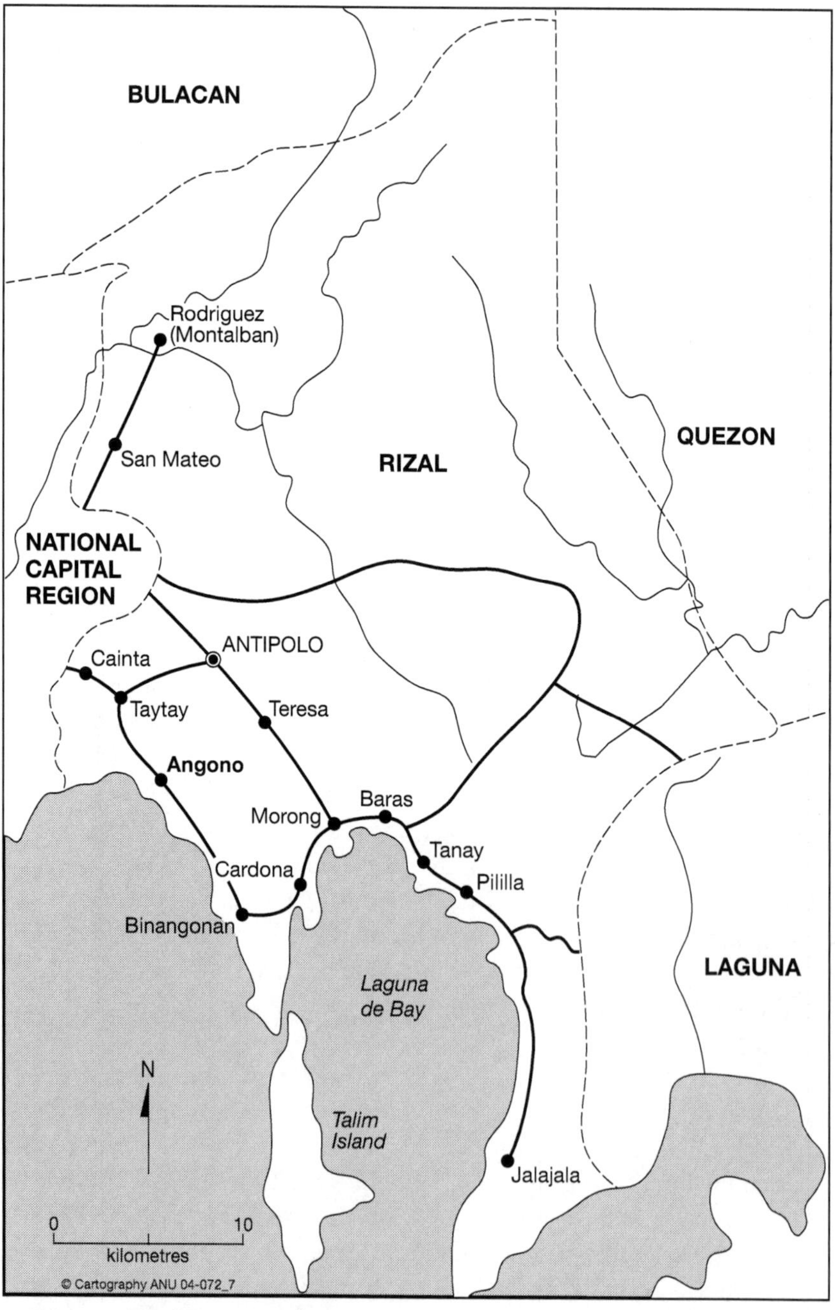

Map 5.1 Rizal Province, showing Angono

governance anchored on LGU-NGO partnership."[23] He won by a slim margin, running under the Nationalist People's Coalition (NPC). Under Calderon's leadership, the new municipal government immediately carried out improvements in infrastructure and service delivery and promoted the cultural development of Angono. It extended various forms of support to artists in various fields—painting, music, sculpture, native artistic traditions, and so on. It undertook the identification and preservation of historical sites, as well as the revival of colorful traditional celebrations. Calderon promoted people's participation in governance, regularly holding consultations with local neighborhood associations and organizations of tricycle drivers, fisherfolk, women, artists, and others. Soon, Angono was winning awards for "outstanding municipal peace and order, and as the "cleanest and greenest" municipality in the entire province. With much increased revenues, Angono was promoted to "first-class municipality" in 2001. Calderon won reelection in 2001 by a wide margin. When I visited Angono in 2002, I was surprised to find a tidy little town with art shops, galleries, and ateliers, as well as restaurants with different types of cuisine. Calderon personally brought me to an area that was being turned into a forest park, and from a distance he pointed out to me the site of a lakeside park being developed. In 2003, Angono's municipal government became one of the recipients of the national Galing Pook awards. The Galing Pook Foundation, which gives out the awards in recognition of outstanding achievements in local governance, cited Calderon and his colleagues for turning Angono's potential as an "artists' haven" into a reality.

With its base among the workers of Yupangco Cotton Mills, Sanlakas vigorously campaigned for Calderon and his local slate in 1998. Sanlakas members watched the vote counting closely and guarded the ballot boxes overnight. Despite several power outages, they stayed put. Calderon acknowledges that had it not been for the vigilance and courage of the Sanlakas activists he would have lost. Apart from Calderon, two other Sanlakas members, both candidates for councilor, were elected. Calderon also appointed some Sanlakas members to local government posts. Sanlakas was very supportive of Calderon's initiatives. Neither the local chapter nor the provincial committee of Sanlakas, however, played much of a role in trying to shape the conduct of local governance in Angono. The members of the local chapter of Sanlakas were much more involved in the activities of the local chapter of KPML, the urban poor coalition. In 2001, both Sanlakas and PM supported Calderon and his local slate, but due to miscommunications, PM members did not campaign for two Sanlakas candidates for councilor, who won nonetheless. After the elections, the engagement of Sanlakas/PM in local governance in Angono continued to be minimal.[24]

Bicol, where Guinobatan, Albay is located, is a region in which the CPP-NPA has been very adept at playing the "bourgeois" electoral game, for instance, supporting *trapos* that pay a "revolutionary tax" or helping to unseat *trapos* who have become too entrenched. It is also a region where the NPA has been most assiduous in enforcing PTC fees. Guinobatan, an inland municipality with a rugged terrain, is a well-known hotbed of CPP-NPA dissidence.

Belonging to a prominent family in Guinobatan, Christopher Flores was an ND student activist in the 1980s. After college, he took

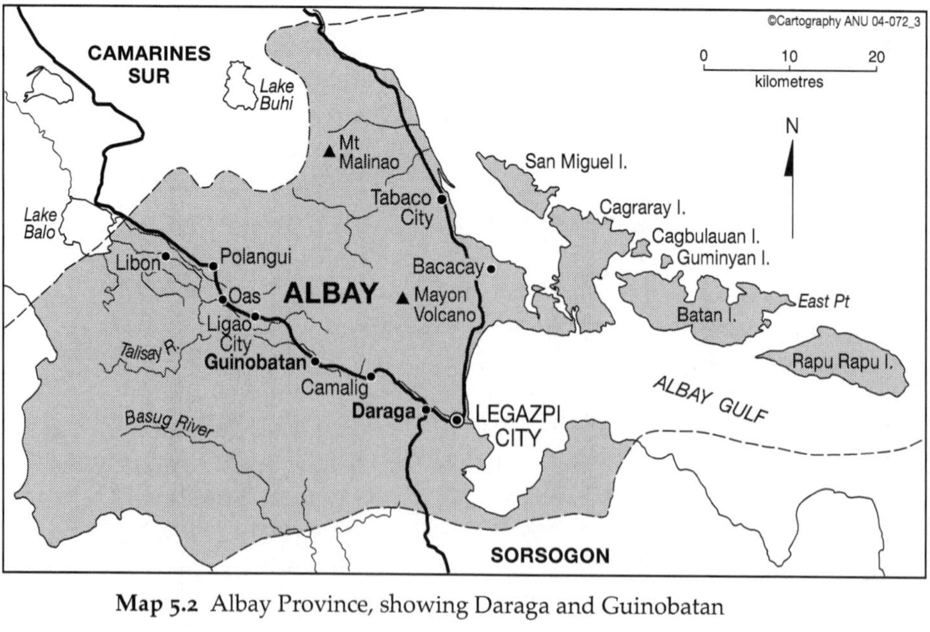

Map 5.2 Albay Province, showing Daraga and Guinobatan

care of the family business concerns. Although he ceased to be active in the ND movement, Flores remained sympathetic to it. On the prodding of his father, a judge, he entered local politics in 1995, running for municipal councilor and winning easily. While serving in the municipal government, Flores was appalled at the extent of the corruption within it. He could not do much about it, as he and another councilor were just two in the opposition. Since 1956, two political families had controlled the town's politics. In 1998, Flores ran for mayor under Estrada's Laban ng Makabayang Masang Pilipino (LAMMP), or Struggle of the Nationalist Filipino Masses, campaigning on a platform of good governance. Despite CPP-NPA support, Flores lost—by a mere 159 votes—in elections marked by extensive vote buying and vote-counting irregularities. In 2001, Flores tried again, this time running under Aksyon Demokratiko, and with the support of Bayan Muna, which had just been set up. He joined Bayan Muna and campaigned for it in the party-list vote. Once again, Flores adopted a platform of good governance. The incumbent used the "red scare" against him, but this did not work. Flores won by a convincing margin.[25]

Flores undertook a clean-up of the municipal government and tried to institute transparency. In the process, he unearthed various ghost projects and many other irregularities. He encountered stiff opposition from some municipal employees, who remained very loyal to the previous administrations and considered him an outsider. Guinobatan came to have a new municipal development plan and comprehensive land-use plans after over a decade of having none. These featured area development and economic integration of the highlands. Flores was particularly good at finance generation, managing to get funding for municipal projects from various government agencies and Congress. He managed to pay off the ₱23 million debt accumulated by past administrations.

Bayan Muna had a chapter in Guinobatan, but it seemed unable to define clearly what it should be doing after elections. Although Flores and two councilors were members of Bayan Muna, it played no role in actual governance. Flores promoted people's participation in governance, but only traditional civic organizations signed up for the Municipal Development Council and other local special bodies.

"We tried to get groups in the countryside to participate but they refused," commented Flores wryly. "They did not want to register as they had to submit lists of their members."[26] (In the "red zones," the CPP-NPA organizes the peasants, women, youth, and others into cells and groups that support the revolutionary movement, but these are, of course, of a clandestine nature.)

A negative point in Flores's administration, however, was the unstable peace and order situation. At the time that I visited Guinobatan, two telecommunications firms had just shut down their operations there due to NPA harassment. For refusing to pay the revolutionary tax, the NPA had killed the landowner of one firm's relay station and had attempted to blast the other firm's tower. "Since Flores took over," declared a local official, who was very critical of the mayor, "there have been fourteen of such shooting incidents. The NPA collects monthly dues from big establishments in the town center, and it 'asks' 5 to 10 percent from contractors for projects implemented in the highlands. During elections, the NPA threatens voters and demands PTC— ₱15,000 to ₱20,000 from candidates for councilor, ₱50,000 for mayoral candidates. Because of all these, investors are reluctant to invest." He virtually accused Flores of conniving with the CPP-NPA: "Our problem is that we have a mayor who serves two governments."[27]

An exception to Bayan Muna's noninvolvement in municipal/city governance is Davao City, where the local chapter has been very much engaged in the legislative and advocacy work of Councilor Angela Librado, one of only two "official" Bayan Muna candidates who won in the 2001 local elections. Librado has been very active in articulating the ND movement's positions on various national and local issues—power price hikes, the government's "war on terrorism," U.S. troops in Mindanao, women's rights, globalization, and so on.[28] It must be borne in mind however, that Davao City is the Philippines' third largest metropolis (after Metro Manila and metropolitan Cebu) and is thus important as a center for political proselytization.

In its early years, Akbayan, like Sanlakas/PM and Bayan Muna, did not engage much in municipal and city governance. In December 2002, however, the party took the decisive step to undertake serious engagement, holding the "First Political Meeting of Akbayan LGU

Officials," a conference attended by selected Akbayan municipal, city, and provincial officials from different parts of the country. Akbayan's national officials elucidated the party's platform for change and good governance and its electoral framework. In turn, the LGU officials explained the main issues and concerns that confronted them in their respective municipalities, and the changes and reforms that they were working on. Since the conference served as a venue for discussion on scaling up participatory governance initiatives from the *barangay* to the municipal/city level, a good part of the discussion dwelled on "citizen participation in local governance."[29]

Since the December 2002 conference, Akbayan and allied POs/NGOs have become more involved and engaged in municipal/city government and governance concerns. To formulate a more comprehensive framework for the party's engagement in local governance, Akbayan's Government Affairs Committee has endeavored to draw lessons from the pioneering efforts of local chapters that had grappled with municipal/city governance in 1998–2002—as well as individual LGU officials who were Akbayan members (as in Banaybanay, Governor Generoso, and Victoria).[30] A big help to Akbayan is that the Batman Consortium has now drawn up a more comprehensive framework for its engagement in local governance, one that goes beyond "democratic participation" and addresses municipal and city governance more squarely. The consortium, for instance, is now designing programs to expand the "fiscal space" to assist municipal and city LGUs in coming up with innovative tax and nontax revenue measures to beef up their limited resources. Among the programs are those for creating more self-liquidating public services such as public markets and potable water systems. The consortium is moving with more resolve into urban governance, putting stress on the role of the urban poor themselves. Looking beyond the municipal level, the consortium is now also promoting "inter-LGU [intermunicipal] development cooperation programs using sustainable integrated area development models that tap common resource base like coastal waters, common topographical and environmental characteristics, and culture" (Villarin 2003:7–8, 18–20). As part of its efforts to learn from the experiences in participatory local governance in other countries, Akbayan sent a six-person delegation all the way to Brazil in February 2003 to study participatory local governance in several cities governed by the left-wing Workers' Party (PT). The delegation, which included PO/NGO representatives, as well as LGU officials, studied various aspects of local administration, such as participatory budget preparation and tax administration and reform, and visited several local government projects, such as housing and river rehabilitation projects, and different NGOs (*Bohol Sunday Post* 2002). It is much too early to assess the impact of Akbayan's engagement in municipal/city government work, but one very noticeable result is that Akbayan's LGU officials, many of whom tended to play down their links with the party before, now more openly identify themselves with it.[31]

Contending Perspectives in Governance

In his study on local politics and the Left in Peru in the 1980s and early 1990s, Gerd Schönwälder (1998:76–77) notes the emergence of two clashing strategic perspectives of the Peruvian Left's involvement in local politics. The "revolutionary approach" holds that the Left should make local government serve mainly as a venue for ventilating popular demands, which are deemed "unfulfillable" under the existing order, to build a political movement capable of overthrowing the state. The "radical-democratic perspective" postulates that leftist intervention in local politics "should serve to demonstrate its capacity to govern within the existing political institutions while opening them up to popular participation from below." The two strategic perspectives of the Peruvian Left's involvement in local politics correspond with two of what Roberts has described as the Latin American Left's three conceptions of democracy. Schönwälder's revolutionary approach jibes with Roberts's "instrumental view of democracy," and the radical-democratic perspective is consistent with the "integral view of democracy."

If Schönwälder's categorization were to be applied to the Philippine situation, it can be said that Akbayan's engagement in local politics hews to the radical-democratic perspective. That Akbayan does indeed take this perspective is beginning to be acknowledged

(Rocamora 2004:345–46).[32] The NDs can be said to take the revolutionary approach on the basis of using local governments, particularly at the *barangay* level, not really for ventilating popular demands, as Schönwälder puts it, but for "neutralizing" them and using them in other ways (gathering material support, intelligence work, and so on) in the service of the revolution. It is not clear where Sanlakas stands, as there has not been much actual engagement in local government work—or not enough data about such engagement at least. In the Philippine context, Schönwälder's two strategic perspectives, like Roberts's categories, can be applied to the Left's engagement in *government work and governance as a whole* and not just local government. Leftist parties such as Bayan Muna adhere to an instrumental view of democracy and to a revolutionary approach to government work and governance, treating governmental institutions and processes mainly as instruments for furthering the revolution. In recognizing the intrinsic value of democratic institutions and in working for progressive and participatory governance, Akbayan has essentially taken an integral view of democracy and a radical-democratic perspective vis-à-vis government/governance.

By no means does the Left have a monopoly on alternatives to the current "governance by patronage" or the "patrimonial approach" toward public office and governance of *trapos*, who are associated with the Philippines' oligarchic elite. Development specialists identified with the likes of the World Bank and advocates of "new public management" have been propagating a model of governance and development that puts an emphasis on sound management to produce an efficient, noncorrupt and accountable public administration (Konrad Adenauer Foundation 2000; Leftwich 1993; Desai and Imrie 1998). The World Bank, the quintessential neoliberal institution, has changed its pitch from "less government" to "good governance" (Törnquist 2002:21). The "revisionist neoliberals" continue to emphasize market deregulation but now also put stress on institutional reforms and social development, with a special niche for the participation of "civil society" (Mohan and Stokke 2000:248). With the solid backing of Western donor organizations, the "new managerialism" has overwhelmingly dominated governance and development discourse in the Philippines—in academe, state institutions, and civil society. Books and articles extolling "best practices in local governance,"[33] as well as awards given out to model local governments promote the outlook and standards of the new managerialists on good governance.

In more recent years, revised neoliberal thinking in relation to governance has been extended to, and has suffused, the decentralization discourse. By decentralizing government, declared the World Bank (1999:107, 121–2), localization nourishes responsive and efficient government. In typical technocratic fashion, the bank argues that the success of decentralization depends on its "design," and equates successful decentralization with improved government efficiency and responsiveness and the "accommodation" of potentially explosive political forces. It encourages the "harnessing" of civil society to bring about more effective and responsive governance.

The term *governance* has traditionally been equated with *government*—the formal institutions of the state and the state's coercive power (Stoker 1998:17). In the last twenty years or so, however, *governance* has evolved. Whereas *government* refers to "the institutions and agents charged with governing," *governance* is now taken to mean "the modes and manner of governing."[34] *Governance* is now used in many ways. "In developing countries," notes Gerry Stoker (1998:18), "governance has entered the policy arena. For the World Bank it is at times reduced to a commitment to efficient and accountable government. Others use it more broadly ... to recognize the interdependence of public, private and voluntary sectors in developing countries."

In accordance with their emerging radical democratic perspective, Akbayan and allied POS/NGOS have opted for the broader concept of governance. During the December 2002 conference of Akbayan LGU officials, one of the main discussants elaborated on governance as a relational concept—governance as a relationship between civil society and the state—and stressed the challenge for civil society to become more engaged in governance matters, as well as for local governments to increase their responsiveness.[35] A Batman workbook states: "The interaction and cooperation of people's organizations, non-governmental organizations and the private sector with government in crafting policies and in implementing programs define what governance is" (Institute for Strategic Initiatives and Institute of Politics and Governance 2002:2).

Mohan and Stokke (2000:249) compare the "new" Right (revised neoliberal) and "new" Left (post-Marxist or radical democratic) conceptualizations of development. (In the main, the comparison actually holds true for the two perspectives' conceptualization of governance as well.) Both the "new" Right and the "new" Left believe that "states or markets cannot and should not be solely responsible for ensuring social equality and welfare growth" and organizations of civil society, particularly at the local level, can and should play a role. The revised neoliberal model, however, is a top-down approach, merely geared to increasing the efficiency and accountability of government institutions. Moreover, it adheres to a "harmony model of power," which envisages the empowerment of the powerless as coming about without really touching the power of the powerful. The "new" Left position is the opposite. "The radical notion of empowerment," write Mohan and Stokke, "focuses on 'bottom-up' social mobilization in society as a challenge to hegemonic interests within the state and the market. ... Power is conceptualised in relational and conflictual terms. Hence, empowerment of marginalized groups requires a structural transformation of economic and political relations towards a radically democratised society."

Like many other developing countries, the Philippines has had well over a decade of the revisionist neoliberal prescriptions on good governance and new public management. Despite tremendous financial backing from Western donor institutions, however, the revisionist neoliberal paradigm on governance has been an abject failure. The persistence—or rather the worsening—of corruption, plunder, oligarchic patrimonialism, and bossism attests to this. The Philippines' elite-dominated democracy allows for a number of revisionist neoliberal state reformists to exist in a sea of *trapos*. There will always be some of the Galing Pook type—honest public servants managing isles of state efficiency, transparency, and accountability. Once their three terms are up,[36] however, it's back to *trapos* again. Why? There is no reform-oriented party to carry on what they started. The new managerialists do not challenge the traditional parties, the convenient instruments of the oligarchy for patronage and patrimonialism. Almost all of them, in fact, are members of traditional parties. While many of the new managerialists (like the "young Turks" in the Liberal Party) have earnestly tried to reform the traditional parties, their efforts have always come to naught, as the *trapos* are too well entrenched. They have often ended up condoning the patrimonialists' behavior or being swallowed up by the system. The *trapos* welcome the neoliberal state reformists, as it is good for the former's image to be seen in the latter's company. The traditional parties woo the do-gooders, and once they get them, they put them on show as the poster children for good governance.

Revisionist neoliberalism may not work, but it poses great problems for Akbayan and its allied POs/NGOs. Akbayan's framework vis-à-vis government work and governance, while clearly moving toward a radical democratic perspective, has not taken full shape. A crucial missing element is a sharp delineation between Akbayan's framework and the revised neoliberal perspective. Akbayan members have often mouthed such terms as *good governance, civil society, people's participation in governance, transparency,* and *accountability*—which just happen to be the favorite buzzwords of revisionist neoliberals—without making a clear distinction between their and the neoliberals' concepts of them. Thus, to some extent at least, Akbayan and its allied POs/NGOs have played right into the revisionist neoliberals' hands. It is no wonder that Western donor agencies promoting the revised neoliberal agenda have been most willing to fund seminars and training sessions on "good governance" and "people's participation in governance." Akbayan has started to recognize the dangers of not drawing a clear delineation. "[W]ithout consciousness of the distinction," states Rocamora (2004:332), "the danger of cooptation or the related pitfall of opportunism, of being used while taking money from neo-liberal local governance projects is great. At the same time, it will be difficult to identify areas of convergence with reformers who may operate within a neo-liberal frame but who work on projects such as anti-corruption, which is a common concern. Finally, without discourse maps for navigating the white waters of local governance discourse, we cannot maximize the empowerment potential of local governance projects such as the BBGC."

For Akbayan, forging alliances with state reformists should not be too hard. The much bigger challenge is recruiting state reformists and eventually securing not just their main but their sole party allegiance. Akbayan has been moving deeper into a milieu (local politics) in which the revisionist neoliberal perspective has a much stronger influence than the radical democratic perspective. Unless it makes a sharp distinction between the two, Akbayan may end up, in most cases, helping prepare the LGU officials attending its seminars and training sessions to convert to revisionist neoliberalism, which, after all, provides certain perquisites. Apart from the being backed by many donor agencies, revisionist neoliberalism, Philippine style, affords politicians the convenience of joining a traditional patronage party, switching parties and coalitions every so often, and availing themselves of the support of powerful clans and personages.

Counterhegemony in the State Arena

Leftist parties and groups in the Philippines have moved, in varying degrees, from nonengagement to engagement in government work and governance. They have tangled with *trapos* aligned with the oligarchic elite. They have worked closely with state reformists. They have forged tactical alliances with sections of the *trapo* community and even the ruling coalition in certain situations, as in placing state reformists in important government positions. Responding, again in varying degrees, to two developments that have had a major impact on government work and governance in the postauthoritarian era—coalition politics and government decentralization—the leftist groups seized on the opportunity to further their revolutionary or radical democratic ends. In the process, however, they have exposed themselves to the dangers of being manipulated or co-opted not just by *trapos* but also by revisionist neoliberals, and they have at times been used by them.

While Philippine decentralization has provided for openings for popular participation in governance, leftist groups have to take into account its actual impact, overall, in furthering democratization. Summarizing several initial assessments of the Local Government Code vis-à-vis popular participation, Rood (1998:129–30) notes that the code has advanced democracy at the local level, produced a mind-set promoting participation, enhanced the legitimacy of political action by NGOs, and increased the participation of women in governance. With regard to the impact of NGO and PO participation in local governance since the passage of the code, Terrence George (1998:250) declares: "NGOs are strengthening the hand of development-oriented local and national officials and are weakening elite families' hold on both civil society and the state." Hawes (2000:3–4, 21) observes that, with LGUs acquiring a major share of total government revenues and greater control over natural resources and local development planning, the code has introduced "a radical redistribution in the control over vital resources." Despite predictions of many that this redistribution would only foster a new generation of local bosses, most LGUs were acting responsibly in utilizing their new powers and resources. He cites a much better informed public as one reason for this behavior. Analyzing the structural impact of the code, Hawes enthuses that it has brought about "a dramatic change in intergovernmental relations [that] is further breaking down the clientelistic basis of Philippine politics."

There are, however, more circumspect voices. "Despite the profusion of NGOs and POs over the past fifteen years,' writes Hutchcroft (1998b:40), "they still have a long way to go before they can be considered to have significant and lasting influence on the conduct of local government and politics. Despite their successes on particular fronts and in particular localities, the cumulative impact of these nontraditional actors is decidedly weak in comparison to the formidable networks of power enjoyed by the traditional structures that they are confronting." Eaton (2001:101) reports that since approving the code legislators have attempted "to reverse and then circumvent decentralization since it threatened their status as brokers claiming personal credit for negotiating fiscal transfers from the center." He also says that traditional actors in Philippine political society have consistently and effectively moved to undermine new participatory roles for NGOs and to sideline them from the policy-making process (Eaton 2003:470–71).

As the Batman experience shows, the Local Government Code has given a tremendous boost to people's participation in governance. But the deepening of democracy in the Philippines requires much more than elements of participatory governance. In terms of breaking elite rule, the code has barely scratched the surface. The surest sign that democratization of local politics still has a long way to go is that traditional parties of patronage and patrimonialism are the ruling entities in *almost all* of the country's municipalities, cities, and provinces. The POS/NGOS may have gotten a say in local governance in a good number of areas, but at the end of the day the *trapos* still call the shots.

Vis-à-vis deepening democracy, the decentralization experience of the Philippines appears to parallel that of Indonesia, whose decentralization laws include some democratization features. "Not only have local parliaments [in Indonesia] been significantly empowered," observes Hans Antlöv (2003:78), "but many ordinary people have started to engage in dialogues on the future of their home towns and villages." Among the various mechanisms for political participation are citizen forums, village councils, social movements and mass organizations. Vedi Hadiz (2003:130) maintains, however, that the ones who have thrived best under Indonesia's new democratic institutions are still those within predatory networks of patronage—"[t]hose with money and those capable of deploying an apparatus of violence."

The deepening of democratization in the Philippines may hinge a lot on which approach toward government / governance eventually gains predominance: the currently dominant patrimonial approach of the oligarchic elite or one of the alternatives—revised neoliberal, revolutionary, or radical democratic. As an alternative to the patrimonial approach, the revolutionary approach seems to constitute a dead end. Leftist parties that take the reins of local government cannot keep blaming the national government for local ills, nor keep promising a substantial or appreciable improvement in the people's livelihoods after some far-off or indeterminate victory of the "revolution." The Peruvian experience has shown that "leftist local governments cannot escape responsibility for governing, that is, they cannot forgo the difficult task of trying to find workable solutions for the urgent needs of the popular majorities within the framework of the existing political institutions" (Schönwälder 1998:97). At the national level, it is conceivable that revolutionary proselytization and mobilization could indeed hasten the dawning of a revolutionary situation. As long as lower classes, marginalized groups, and their allies have not broken the ideological and cultural domination of the oligarchic elite, however, the latter will continue to maintain its hold on economic and political power. The political upheavals of February 1986 and January 2001 that ousted Marcos and Estrada, respectively, were indeed people power uprisings, yet they installed elite-dominated regimes.

With the initial achievements and gains made in congressional work, as well as in LGU work and governance at the *barangay*, municipal, and city levels, there is reason for some optimism in the prospects of the emergent radical democratic perspective. To an appreciable extent, adherents of this perspective (such as Akbayan) have indeed been able to promote popular empowerment and bring about concrete improvements in the people's well-being, especially at the grassroots level. However, if Akbayan and its allied POs/NGOs want to be much more effective in their efforts to bring about radical political and social change, a lot more needs to be done. Leftists in government, working closely with leftists in civil society, will have to bring the fight against elite rule and the *trapos'* instruments of patronage (including traditional patron-client ties) well into the ideological and cultural spheres too. The emergent radical democratic framework in government/governance itself will have to be more fully developed and sharpened and posited within Akbayan's counterhegemonic strategy.

Those who hold the radical democratic perspective are up against not only the *trapos* but also revisionist neoliberals, who present themselves as state reformists but work in unholy cohabitation with the *trapos*. For some time now, revisionist neoliberals have been spreading ideas of good governance and people's participation in governance that give the illusion that empowerment of the powerless can be achieved without touching the power of the powerful. It is surprising that the Philippine leftist groups that hold the radical democratic perspective, which have been very active in the movement against neoliberal globalization, have failed to recognize this crucial fight against neoliberalism on the home front, and have even, to some extent, unwittingly helped propagate the revised neoliberal concepts. The danger of erosion and co-optation cannot be underestimated. In the assessment of James Petras (1999:34), almost all leftist groups, including former revolutionary groups, that have engaged in electoral politics and entered political office, have succumbed to a globalist ideology. His assessment may be too sweeping, but he probably is not entirely wrong.

6

Special Areas of Concern: Popular Political Education and Working for Political Reform

IN PREVIOUS CHAPTERS, I discussed the engagement of the emergent leftist parties and groups in mass movement and development work, elections, and public office and governance—all in relation to their fight to end elite rule in the Philippines. In this chapter, I deal with two special areas of concern. The first, popular political education, does not really fall under any of the areas of engagement mentioned earlier, but has a great bearing on all of them. It has much to do with whittling down the ideological and cultural domination of the elite over the masses in the Philippines' contested democracy. The second concern, working for political reform, has moved from being advocacy of "the parliament of the streets" to an endeavor conducted both outside and *inside* the legislature since the entry into Congress of some representatives of new, leftist groups through the first party-list vote in 1998. This shift indicates the intensification of the efforts of the emergent Left to build counterhegemony.

Leftist parties and groups in the Philippines, in general, regard "raising the level of political consciousness of the masses" as one of their fundamental tasks. In fact, they consider popular political education as absolutely essential for the success of their political endeavors—mass mobilizations, development projects, electoral campaigns, and participatory governance. In conducting popular political education, some new, leftist groups and their allied POS/NGOS have discarded the traditional teacher-student approach and moved to a dialogical form of pedagogy, which they regard as more participatory and liberating. Dialogical "pop-ed," based on Freirean pedagogy, has made some contributions in such areas as development work, participatory governance and gender education. Like old-style political pedagogy, however, popular education (known as "pop-ed") has thus far not proven to be effective in combating clientelist and patronage politics. There appears to be a problem in the way the dialogical approach has been applied, particularly in posing problems and finding generative themes. More important, cadres and activists of new, leftist parties and groups continue to be strongly influenced by the viewpoint of "raising the masses' political consciousness"—a top-down and not truly dialogical framework.

In trying to break elite hegemony, some of the emergent leftist parties and groups have paid special attention to working for major political reforms. Given the highly skewed distribution of the country's wealth and power, the new leftist groups and their allied POS/NGOS have pushed for reform measures fostering the fuller participation and representation of marginalized or unrepresented sectors of the population (such as the party-list system and "absentee voting" for overseas Filipinos), as well as those curbing elite domination and manipulation of political processes and institutions (such as election modernization[1] and a ban on political dynasties.)[2] The new, leftist groups joined broad movements that opposed the attempts of Presidents Ramos and Estrada and Speaker De Venecia to have the Constitution amended, seeing these moves as self-serving or benefiting vested interests. Since 2002, however, some leftist groups have declared that they are for constitutional reform—though through an elected constitutional convention, not a constituent assembly.[3] For its part, Akbayan, favors a shift to a parliamentary form of government with a system of proportional representation to significantly lessen the use of patronage and guns, goons, and gold in elections. In the course of pushing for political reforms, some of the new, leftist groups appear to have become more skilled and sophisticated in combining legislative work, mass actions and campaigns, and lobbying.

Popular Political Education

From basa-talakay to dialogical encounter

Philippine leftists have long recognized the importance of mass or popular education—that is, political education—as a tool in "arousing, organizing, and mobilizing" the masses in the struggle for fundamental political and social change. During the pre-martial-law period, ND and SD activists conducted teach-ins and discussion groups (DGs) in schools, communities, and public places, discussing Philippine history, the major ills plaguing the country and their ideas on an alternative society. In their efforts to "politicize" the masses, the NDs claimed to follow the Maoist tenet of the "mass line." In practice, however, the pedagogy was far from being "from the masses, to the masses."

Tracing the development of mass or popular political education in the Philippines, Roy Loredo (1999) observes that leftist activists (primarily the NDs) in the late 1960s and early 1970s used the *basa-talakay* (read then discuss) method and mixed education with propaganda. They did learn to talk in the masses' language and became good propagandists and organizers. What the activists imparted, however, was *their* message or analysis without really learning from the masses. They had turned into "efficient transmission belts from the revolutionary centers of power to the periphery, the revolution's cogs and wheels" (Loredo 1999:78). Under martial law, leftist activists shifted to an evocative approach to popular political education—they strove to draw out and structure the masses' views and insights. In the last few years of Marcos's rule, amid political crisis, mass education sessions turned very lively. All through this time, however, the NDs' revolutionary line and their propaganda-education framework remained basically unchanged. After the 1986 people power uprising, a section of the ND movement, the popdems, began to see popular education in a different light. They regarded it as a tool for the masses' liberation and empowerment. Strongly influenced by Paulo Freire's ideas on the "pedagogy of the oppressed,"[4] the popdems viewed popular education no longer as a process in which a teacher imparts knowledge to a student but more as a dialogical encounter between the two, with each learning something from the other. Furthermore, they saw popular education no longer as a mere echo of a political program but as the creation of new knowledge, including a rethinking of the political line. And instead of looking only at the content and method of popular education, as NDs had tended to in the past, the popdems took cognizance of the importance of the learning context. They thus adopted a "context-content-method framework."

The new orientation of popular education actually took form in the course of two consultations organized by the popdems in August 1986 and April 1987 that were billed as Popular Education for Popular Empowerment (PEPE) I and II, respectively. Popular educators from various POs/NGOs participated in the two consultations.[5] Afterward IPD established a team to take care of PEPE's secretariat functions. Its PEPE program evolved into a separate NGO, which continued to provide pop-ed services to POs/NGOs, primarily by developing the capacity of grassroots educators to respond to their constituencies' needs (Garcia 1999a:115–19). In 1992, the popdems established the Education for Life Foundation (ELF), an NGO that engaged in grassroots leadership formation mainly through *paaralang bayan* (folk schools), and was guided, like PEPE, by the new pop-ed orientation (Abes 1998). Since 1993, popular educators coming from various POs/NGOs from all over the country have gathered thrice (1993, 1996 and 1999) for the "Daupan Popular Educators' Festival" to exchange experiences and insights in popular education, assess their work, and set directions for the future (Garcia 1999a:117–8; Fajardo 2000).

The mainstream NDs and the other leftist groups did not adopt the popdems' pop-ed framework. They continued with their usual propaganda-education sessions, albeit sometimes conducted in an evocative style. Participation in elections starting in 1987 did not bring about any change in the mainstream NDs' mass education orientation.

In 1991, leftist groups and left-aligned POs/NGOs involved in Project 2001 (including the popdems) engaged in "voters' education"—"raising political consciousness among the voter population." This meant "educating (and at times, re-educating) voters to adopt a more issue-oriented rather than a personality-centered attitude towards elections" (Abad 1991). Apart from participating in Project 2001, Pandayan initiated the formation of a coalition called Citizens for Meaningful and Peaceful Elections (Compel), which encouraged many organizations, mostly church based, to undertake voters' education in their parishes and constituencies (Gutierrez 1994b:112).

On the basis of the 1995 psychographic study on voter behavior of IPER, which showed that fraud, especially vote buying, was a common occurrence in Philippine electoral politics, the Consortium on Electoral Reforms (CER) likewise launched a campaign for voters' education in 1997–98 (Consortium on Electoral Reforms and Institute for Political and Electoral Reform 1997:14–15).

With the continuing virulence of vote buying and other fraudulent acts in Philippine elections, the voters' education efforts of various civic and religious groups, as well as of the new, leftist groups and their allied POs/NGOs, can be said to have been largely ineffective in addressing the problems of patronage and clientelism. "Political education seminars, voters' education—we in the diocese conducted a lot of them, but they were all for nothing," bewailed a priest in Davao Oriental. "After the seminars, those who attended, even the lay leaders, accepted the money offered them."[6] Tailored for the preelection period, voters' education tended to treat these problems merely as election-time occurrences and not as part and parcel of everyday politics. Furthermore, it tended to revert to the traditional "banking" method of pedagogy; worse, it adopted a moralistic tone. Well-meaning advocates of clean and peaceful elections, often of middle-class background, lectured the masses on what they should do without much regard for social and historical context. With voters' education, even the popdems, the initiators of dialogical pop-ed, fell back, at least to some extent, to the old ways.

Voters' education appears to be strongly influenced by the notion of "civic education," which, according to Thomas Carothers, has been a common feature of U.S. democracy assistance portfolios to the developing world and has largely tended to focus on elections in recipient countries. Carothers (1999a:231–33) assesses the results of civic education efforts as disappointing. He writes:

> The experience of many civic education efforts points to one clear lesson: short-term formal instruction on democracy that presents the subject as a set of general principles and processes generally has little effect on participants. Such information is too abstract and usually too removed from the daily lives of most people ... Moreover, civic education in many transitional countries is negated by the actual practice of politics. It is hard for people to accept that a national legislature is a valuable body with important charge of representing their interests when they see every night on their televisions endless squabbling

> sessions of a corrupt, feckless parliament. Teaching them that elections are essential to democracy has little effect if the only elections they know are manipulated by a dominant party to entrench its power still further.

In a study on class divisions and electoral reform in the Philippines, Frederic Schaffer (2001:19) offers this critique of voters' education programs:

> Clean election reform in the Philippines ... has a class dimension. Reformers are drawn disproportionately from the middle and upper classes, while those targeted for reform—"education" in the language of the reformers—are the poor. The project of reform, looked at in this way, is an effort to discipline the poor, to inculcate them with the values of the better-off. There are at least two ways in which this class character of reform frustrates the larger project of deepening Philippine democracy. First, some among the Catholic poor (who make up the bulk of the voting population) find the political education they receive from the Church to be alienating, the result of which is to discredit its attempts to clean up the electoral process. Second, voter education campaigns crafted by those in the middle and upper classes misunderstand the nature of practices among the poor they wish to reform. These campaigns, at least with regards to vote buying, are ineffective and offensive, one consequence of which may be to further estrange the poor not only from the rich, but from democracy itself.

Problems in pop-ed

During my fieldwork in 2002, I noted some problems in the popular political education work of the emergent leftist parties and groups. In Akbayan areas, I immediately perceived a language problem. In all of the Akbayan areas I visited, there was a dearth of popular education materials in Filipino or other local languages. This simply meant that Akbayan's grassroots educators had to translate verbally to the masses whatever printed material (in English) they were using. Explaining concepts was hard enough; the absence of popular education materials in the vernacular made it even more so. From her own experience, one Akbayan member working with PEPE illustrated how concepts could get garbled in translation.

> Translation is a challenge because Akbayan is offering alternatives that people are not very familiar with yet. I remember in Bataan, when we interviewed people about their ideas on *kapangyarihan* [power], they referred to it as "dirty," "controlled by the big people in politics," and "used by the rich." When asked what for them is *pagsasakapangyarihan*,

> the Tagalog equivalent that we in the NGOs use for "empowerment," most of the respondents had difficulty in describing it. They did not equate this with their efforts for change. One respondent even said, "This is a trespassing on my very person." Another said it was "constriction and control of what I want."[7]

Another problem was that the emergent leftist parties and groups afforded only superficial treatment of Philippine political culture. Particularly weak was the discussion on the ideological and cultural weapons wielded by the oligarchic elite to maintain its hold on economic resources and political power. The 1990s saw the publication of many excellent studies on Philippine political culture and particular aspects of it—clan politics, voter behavior, pork barrel, everyday politics, corruption, bossism, and more.[8] Some of these emanated from academe or the media, but others were produced by left-aligned NGOs such as IPD, IPG, and IPER. I noted, however, that the findings of these studies were not well incorporated in the popular education materials of the new, leftist parties and groups. In Akbayan's case, there had been a fair amount of interest in, and discussion of, political culture during the party's formative stage (see Montiel 1997:111–23). At its founding congress, Akbayan adopted a cultural platform in which it recognized corruption, nepotism, political violence, and money politics as elements of Philippine political culture that had specific historical and institutional sources, and it expressed confidence in the Filipinos' capacity to reshape the political culture and move away from patronage politics (Akbayan National Congress 1998c:2–3). Some leading Akbayan figures attempted to build an Active Citizenship Foundation (ACF) as an NGO that would conduct orientation and political education seminars. They believed that "a change in political culture ... essentially involves reorientation in consciousness, value systems and behavioral patterns." The ACF project fell through, however, as Akbayan got caught up in various mass campaigns and other immediate concerns. Akbayan's education committee tried to fill the gap, but it became too busy attending to the political education needs of the Akbayan members themselves.

What particularly struck me about the conduct of popular political education during my fieldwork, however, was the decline of the dialogical pop-ed approach. I had thought that in terms of popular empowerment, as well as effectiveness in combating patronage politics, the dialogical approach would clearly be superior to the traditional lecture or "banking" style of pedagogy. Did not dialogical pop-ed mean that the masses would discuss themes and analyze events on the basis of their own experiences and in their own language, that they would thus understand and internalize concepts better, and that they themselves would decide on their course of action? The dialogical method did show up in some Batman endeavors, particularly BDP-PRA, but only to some extent. On the whole, the emergent leftist parties and groups did not make much use of it, and they often resorted to the usual lecture style of instruction. "In Akbayan," writes Cecilia Soriano, "there is indeed an intent for dialogue. But activists in many NGOs and political groups (and not only in Akbayan), feeling comfortably assured that they work on behalf of the people, have been complacent in their political education work. The needed rigor and patience for dialogue are sometimes forgotten. Educators have also been lax in questioning their own assumptions about democracy, development and local governance. There is a need for self-reflexivity among educators."[9]

"Pop-ed," I found out, had undergone a crisis of sorts. After the third Daupan festival (1999), those engaged in dialogical pop-ed voiced doubts about the efficacy of their approach. Popular educators affiliated with Daupan, declares Loredo (1999), were no longer sure that pop-ed was what the people really needed. According to him, pop-ed in the Philippines tended to be defined by international and local donor agencies, not by the people themselves. Oriented toward a "globalized" context, popular educators no longer responded to the actual needs of small communities. Pop-ed followed a "flavor of the month" pattern—the emphasis or theme of education work depended on what programs donor agencies were inclined to fund (Fajardo 2000).

In my fieldwork, I discerned that one problem with pop-ed had to do with the way the dialogical approach was being applied. Dialogical education involves, as Freire (1996:60, 85) puts it, "the posing of the problems of human beings in their relations with the world" and "the investigation of generative themes."[10] Instead of helping the people discover generative themes, popular educators often came with their own themes—or rather, the flavor of the month themes espoused by donor agencies such as sustainable development, good governance, people's participation, and gender education. The situation could have been remedied if popular educators had moved on through a dialogical process to the masses' "generative themes." However, popular educators often stuck to the familiar themes. Moreover, they tended to remain within the "positive" or "harmony" framework of most donor agencies on these themes and to avoid dealing squarely with "negative" or "conflictual" concerns such as domination, clientelism, and patrimonialism. Popular educators missed countless opportunities to conduct "problem-posing education" on patronage politics. By "problems," I refer not just to cases of big-time corruption, fraud, and political violence but also to the many instances when patronage politics reared its ugly head in local everyday life—at baptisms, weddings, and funerals; on billboards along newly-built roads and on bridges and public school buildings; and in the long lines of people seeking jobs or emergency help at the municipal hall (or a government official's house). Posing these problems could very well have stimulated the reflection-action process on patronage and clientelism.

A much more profound problem with pop-ed, and, in fact, with the popular political education efforts of the emergent leftist parties and groups in general, is that they have basically remained within the "consciousness-raising" mode and are not truly or fully dialogical in essence. Historically, leftist cadres and activists in the Philippines, whether communist, socialist, or social democratic, have engaged in mass education, pop-ed, "politicalization," or "conscientization," as well as in propaganda activities, in order to "raise the masses' political consciousness." The presumption has always been that the political consciousness of the masses (or of the majority of them) is backward. Philippine leftist cadres and activists, including those using more dialogical pop-ed approaches, have never really abandoned the consciousness-raising viewpoint.

Thinking in terms of consciousness-raising is a remnant of vanguardism that has long been criticized by theorists of "everyday politics." In a study on the relations between "political commissars" and peasants in revolutionary movements, James Scott (1979) observes that there has often been a lot of tension between the "great tradition" espoused by the radical intelligentsia, such as the modern creeds of nationalism and communism, and the "little tradition" of the peasant masses, reflecting their grievances and aspirations, often concerns that are purely local and immediate and bound to local custom. Noting that radical elites have often tended to impose their concepts and views on the peasants and to ignore the latter's views, he remarks:

> There is more than a trace of unwarranted arrogance in the assumption that only the party embodies "true historical consciousness" and that the vision of justice and order found among the peasantry are examples of "partial" or "false" consciousness. The concept of a vanguard party which has a monopoly on reality not only obviates the need for democracy in the revolution but it overlooks the very real possibility that the consciousness of the rank-and-file may not be inferior but simply different. A recognition that the values of a revolutionary peasantry are distinguishable from those of the party can form the basis for collaboration and learning rather than a one-way exercise in "consciousness-raising."[11]

Akbayan and its allied POs/NGOs have made some achievements and gains in dialogical pop-ed, especially in relation to issues of development, participatory and gender. It would seem, however, that for a deeper and more empowering pop-ed, they would have to address patronage and clientelism in a more head-on and sharper way, bearing fully in mind that the *trapo* frame has succeeded in intermeshing with popular culture in many ways. Organizers and activists of the emergent leftist parties would have to develop their skills, not just in problem posing and evoking generative themes but also, borrowing from Scott, in allowing the "little tradition" of the masses to percolate up and not just the "great tradition" to percolate down. Moreover, the new leftists would have to produce a lot more pop-ed materials that are in the languages of the masses and that, among other things, promote a deeper understanding of political culture.

Working for Political Reform

The party-list law: a breakthrough for the emergent left in political reform

After the fall of Marcos in 1986, the Left was slow to move into the realm of working for political reform. During the sessions of the Constitutional Commission (ConCom) in 1986, some leftist groups supported proposals put forward by leftist and progressive commissioners, but the NDs in general were lukewarm toward the process of the making of a new constitution. After all, the NDs espoused revolution not reform. In the February 1987 constitutional plebiscite, the NDs campaigned for a rejection of the new charter, while emergent leftist groups such as the popdems and Bisig pushed for a "critical yes." When the bill for the Local Government Code was introduced in Congress shortly after the ratification of the new Constitution, leftist groups did not pay much attention to it. Even for those that were open to working for reform, the passage of the code seemed much too tall an order. The 1987 Constitution contained many provisions on decentralization and local autonomy—twenty-one provisions in all (Villarin 1996:61)—but these needed enabling legislation. Since the granting of Philippine independence in 1946, national politicians had always managed to block or significantly water down measures providing for the devolution of power to local governments. By what some viewed as a historical accident, Congress passed the code in October 1991. According to Eaton (2001:114–18), members of the Lower House, after doing nothing about the code for more than four years, rushed to see it through in 1991 in the hope of getting the electoral support of President Aquino, who regarded decentralization as "the linchpin of her administration," and of House Speaker Ramon Mitra, a presidential aspirant who himself was seeking Aquino's "anointment." Leftist groups played no significant role in the approval of the code.

The first stirrings in political reform advocacy among the emergent leftist groups occurred at about the same time that the Local Government Code was being rushed for approval. The leftist groups and POs/NGOs involved in Project 2001 included "lobbying for electoral reforms" as one of their tasks (Abad 1991:11). Mainly on

Pandayan's initiative, Project 2001 and supportive NGOs held a conference on electoral reforms and participation to try to build consensus on amendments in the election code among other objectives (Gutierrez 1994b:111–12). Pandayan also became actively involved in organizing forums on major political reform issues such as the Local Government Code, the party-list system and the shift to a parliamentary form of government (see Macuja 1992). Meanwhile, the NDs established an NGO to work for political and electoral reform, IPER. At this time, the NDs were still locked in an intense debate on strategy, including the role of electoral struggle and parliamentary work in the overall strategy. When the ND movement split in 1992–93, the members of IPER aligned themselves with the "rejectionists," and later joined Siglaya.[12] The leftist groups involved in Project 2001 and the first Akbayan (then a nonparty formation) came together immediately after the 1992 elections and conceived of IPG as a political institute that, apart from serving as a think tank, would coordinate electoral and local governance programs (Santos 1997a:10). When IPG was being formally established in 1994, Prof. Francisco Nemenzo, Jr., a Bisig political council member, urged the new, leftist forces to take up the struggle for electoral reform as a strategic concern and change the balance of forces in the electoral landscape. Following his advice, the IPG resolved to "push for electoral reforms as a strategic agenda, both as a movement-level agenda and as a political advocacy agenda" (Institute of Politics and Governance 1994:11).

As discussed in chapter 5, the emergent leftist groups seized the opening provided by the Local Government Code to promote participation in governance and deepen democratization. The code had another effect on the new, leftist groups: its passage helped inspire and embolden them to push for other political reforms. If a progressive bill of major significance such as the code could make it through a den of *trapos*, then perhaps some others could make it through too.

The emergent leftist groups turned their attention to a new election code proposed by the Comelec (then still headed by a very reform-oriented chairman, Christian Monsod) and certified as an urgent bill by President Ramos himself. The proposed code was intended to replace the Omnibus Election Code of 1985, passed when the dictator Marcos was still in power. A product of extensive consultations with various political parties, legal practitioners, NGOs, and local Comelec workers, the proposed code sought to modernize the electoral process and institute sweeping electoral reforms. Of particular concern to the new leftist groups were provisions designed to curb elite domination and dirty *trapo* tricks in the electoral process (such as election modernization, a ban on turncoatism, and a ban on political dynasties) and to ensure greater participation and representation of marginalized or unrepresented sectors of the population (such as the party-list system of representation, the election of sectoral representatives in local councils, and "absentee voting" for overseas Filipinos). Some NGOs aligned with the new leftist groups joined the Kilusang Mamamayan para sa Repormang Elektoral (Kumare-Kumpare) or People's Movement for Electoral Reform, a coalition of thirteen networks coming from various sectors that campaigned for the passage of the new election code (see Formilleza 1994; and Yorac and Agra 1994:69–74). The leftist groups themselves, however, did not go all out for the proposed code. Although they regarded it, on the whole, as progressive, they were not fully convinced about the importance or even the merit of all the reform measures contained in it. They decided to campaign only for a number of particular reforms in the proposed code: election modernization, the party-list system, local sectoral representation, and the ban on dynasties among others. Top priority went to advocacy for the party-list system. Like decentralization, the party-list system (for choosing 20 percent of the members of the House of Representatives) was already mandated by the 1987 Constitution but needed enabling legislation. A bill for this purpose had been filed in the House of Representatives as early as 1991 (Eighth Congress) and refiled the next year (Ninth Congress). The emergent leftist groups and their allied POs/NGOs saw the party-list system as affording grassroots organizations and alternative parties the opportunity to gain seats in a legislature dominated by the traditional political parties (Bukluran sa Ikauunlad ng Sosyalistang Isip at Gawa 1996a:86; Institute for Political and Electoral Reform 1995b:10).

The proposed election code encountered great resistance in Congress. Many legislators apparently found provisions such as the ban on dynasties detrimental to their own interests (Carlos 1998:82). Ostensibly to facilitate the code's discussion and approval, legislators filed separate bills for certain provisions (Formilleza 1994). Ramos and the Comelec, some of whose members were due to retire in early 1995, had hoped to see the proposed election code enacted before the May 1995 elections. As 1995 approached, however, hopes that the code would be approved in time for the elections dimmed. The PO/NGO networks pushing for electoral reform and the new, leftist groups persisted in lobbying for some of the bills for specific electoral reforms.

For the party-list bill, the lobbyists expected rough sailing in Congress, especially in the Lower House, which was going to be directly affected by the reform measure. No major resistance within the two chambers materialized; legislators debated more on specific provisions of the bill. The intense lobbying by party-list advocates, including such new, leftist groups as Bisig, Pandayan, the popdems, Sanlakas, and Siglaya, bore fruit. Toward the end of 1994, both houses of Congress approved their respective versions of the bill. As the two houses discussed how to reconcile the two versions, the party-list lobbyists pushed for banning the five biggest parties in the first three party-list elections, a provision contained in the House version but not in the Senate version. In the end, the bicameral conference committee agreed to a compromise: a ban on the five only in the first party-list vote (Abelardo 1998:8–10).[13]

The proposed election code never made it. Among the bills for specific electoral reforms, only one—the party-list bill—was enacted into law before the 1995 elections, but it could only be implemented in 1998. The Party-List System Act was quite a comedown from all the sweeping reforms that the proposed election code, if approved, would have brought. For the new, leftist groups and their allied POS/NGOS, however, the enactment of the party-list law constituted their first major victory in the struggle for political and electoral reform.

Campaigning for automated elections, the Empowerment Bill, and local sectoral representation

After the May 1995 elections, the new, leftist groups and their allied POs/NGOs continued working with coalitions and groups such as Kumare-Kumpare and the National Citizens Movement for Free Elections (Namfrel) for the passage of other electoral reform bills, especially those on election modernization, absentee voting, and local sectoral representation. The electoral reform advocates put election modernization—the automation or computerization of vote counting and canvassing—at the top of their list. In past elections, counting and canvassing had been a long, tedious process—lasting several weeks for elections at the national level—and they were very vulnerable to fraud, especially the practice of *dagdag-bawas* (addition-subtraction). Cheating during counting and canvassing was a common occurrence and seemed to be getting even worse. Former Comelec chairman Monsod (1997:29) himself noted that *dagdag-bawas* "occurred in 1995 on an unprecedented scale heavily in favor of one side." The electoral reform advocates believed that computerization would bring about a vote-counting process that would be much faster and less prone to error or fraud (Kilusang Mamamayan Para Sa Repormang Elektoral 1997). After failing to get election computerization approved in time for the 1995 elections, they now sought to hold the first computerized national elections in 1998.

Immediately after the May 1995 elections, Congress approved an act authorizing the Comelec to test computerized vote counting and canvassing in the 1996 elections in the Autonomous Region of Muslim Mindanao (ARMM) and to conduct public demonstrations of it. The pilot program was a success, as attested to by the House Committee on Suffrage and Electoral Reforms and groups such as Namfrel. After this, however, Congress moved too slowly. By the time the legislature passed the Election Modernization Act in December 1997, it was too late to put the automated system fully in place for the May 1998 national and local elections. Only the ARMM areas had computerized counting and canvassing in these elections. Due to the rushed implementation of the system, however, the Comelec made printing and procedural errors and had to do manual recounts in some of the areas covered.

The fight for electoral automation did not end with the approval of the Election Modernization Act. In the 2001 elections, vote counting and canvassing were again done manually. The Comelec, bogged down by infighting, had failed to put a computerized system in place, although it had had three years in which to do it. Electoral reform groups led by Namfrel called for the impeachment of Luzviminda Tancangco, the chairperson of the Comelec's modernization committee, for gross negligence and inefficiency and the betrayal of the public trust. Her most controversial move was the awarding of a contract for a voters registration and identification system to a private firm at a cost that was far beyond the budget. The ₱6.5 billion contract, according to a ruling by the Supreme Court, was "illegal and against public policy" (Concepcion and twenty-two other complainants 2002). Akbayan and AKO, whose leaders signed the formal complaint submitted to the House of Representatives, participated actively in the impeachment campaign. Despite the hard lobbying by the electoral reform groups, however, the House threw out the motion for Tancangco's impeachment.

Vote counting and canvassing in the 2004 elections again were manual. This time, the entire Comelec was to blame. In January 2004, a month before the start of the election campaign, the Supreme Court ruled that the Comelec's awarding of a ₱1.3 billion contract for vote counting machines to another private firm violated the law and the Comelec's own bidding rules. In addition, the court found the machines vulnerable "to election fraud on a massive scale by means of just a few key strokes." It was the second time in less than two years that the court voided an election modernization contract. "The illegal, imprudent and hasty actions of the commission have not only desecrated legal and jurisprudential norms, but have also cast serious doubts upon the poll body's ability and capacity to conduct automated elections," the Supreme Court declared (Tubeza 2004). A survey conducted by the Social Weather Stations later indicated that 58 percent of voters perceived corruption as having been involved in the awarding of the contract (Marfil 2004).

Electoral reform groups had no choice but to set their sights on a new date for computerized elections: May 2007. This would be just months before the tenth anniversary of the Election Modernization Act.

In 1996–97, even as the emergent leftist groups and allied POS/NGOS were in the thick of the campaign for the approval of the Election Modernization Act, they became involved in another campaign for political reform—the passage of the "Empowerment Bill." A provision in the Local Government Code stipulated that Congress should undertake a mandatory review of the code at least once every five years. Taking cognizance of this provision, POS/NGOS aligned with Bisig, Pandayan, the popdems, and Siglaya took the lead in forming the NGO-PO Working Group on the Local Government Code Review, anchored by IPG. The Working Group decided to engage the official review process, as well as to conduct a parallel PO/NGO process (Institute of Politics and Governance 1997:16). It followed a course of programmatic demand making. After over a year of conducting studies and consultations, the IPG drafted the Empowerment Bill, which Senator Juan Flavier and Representative Florencio Abad filed in the Senate and House of Representatives, respectively. According to Kaisahan executive director Villarin (1997:123), the bill sought "to broaden, enhance and institutionalize NGO-PO participation in local governance by way of amending the 1991 LGC in the following selected areas: declaration of policy, rules of interpretation, mandatory consultations, role of NGOS-POS, sectoral representation, recall and disciplinary action, local special bodies, and initiative and referendum."

The Working Group did not restrict its work to just Congress and the PO/NGO community. In preparation for the congressional review, it held a series of consultations with the Department of Interior and Local Government (DILG) and with the Leagues of Provinces, Cities, and Municipalities in the Philippines. The Working Group managed to convince DILG to pick the Empowerment Bill as the main source on issues related to people's participation in drafting the executive branch's proposed amendments to the code (Institute of Politics and Governance 1997:18). The group failed to get the endorsement of the Leagues for the bill as, in IPG executive director Soliman Santos's (1997b:11–12) assessment, this would have meant sharing local power with local communities. On the important question of local sectoral representation, the group managed to get the support of the League of Provinces and the League of Cities but not the League of

Municipalities. Significantly, however, the Working Group succeeded in forging "a strategic alliance for local autonomy and people's empowerment" with the leagues in April 1997. The two sides agreed to support "the decentralization thrust in resource mobilization, basic services and regulatory functions, and control supervision over local offices/officers," as well as "the democratization thrust of people's participation in local governance." They achieved consensus on many points in the following areas: national-local government and interlocal government relations, devolution, regulatory powers and franchising authority, local resources and funds and local taxation, local development corporations and enterprises, human resources development and public accountability, and local boards and special bodies. And they called on Congress to give the review due attention and give priority to amendments enhancing decentralization and democratization (Leagues of Provinces, Cities and Municipalities in the Philippines and the NGO-PO Working Group on the LGC Review 1997:151–53).

The official code review process proved most frustrating. Congress did not actually conduct the review, even though it was supposed to be mandatory. The Empowerment Bill got only as far as the first reading. In preparing for the review, however, the POs/NGOs involved in the Working Group gained some valuable experiences, especially in the drafting of a legislative bill and in the links and dialogue with the leagues. With the 1998 elections fast approaching, the Working Group decided to put off campaigning for the code review and the Empowerment Bill and concentrate on working for the approval of one of the main features of the Empowerment Bill, local sectoral representation—but as a separate bill.

The Local Government Code actually provides for the election of sectoral representatives—one from the women, one from the workers, farmers, and fisherfolk, and one from another marginalized sector (e.g, the urban poor, indigenous cultural communities, and disabled persons)—in all municipalities, cities, and provinces. This provision was never implemented, however, as Republic Act 7887, passed in February 1995, stipulated enabling legislation for such an election to be held. The new, leftist groups and their allied POs/NGOs viewed local sectoral representation as a local version of the party-list system, another instance of affirmative action, ensuring that marginalized sectors would be able to express their own concerns and needs and to participate in local development planning and lawmaking (Santos 1997b). They also saw it as a means of breaking elite domination in local politics. IPG declared, "With a plurality of voices in a democracy, especially in democracies dominated by a ruling minority, we must ensure that the marginalized have a venue for participation in governance" (Institute of Politics and Governance 1999:3).

Saligan drafted a bill providing for the manner and date of the election of local sectoral representatives and succeeded in getting several legislators from both houses of the Tenth Congress to sponsor the bill. Electoral reform groups, including the new leftist groups and the PO-NGO Working Group (coordinated by the IPG), lobbied hard for the bill's passage, hoping to get it approved in time for it to be made part of the 1998 national and local elections. The bill was scheduled for deliberation but got caught in the legislature's recess. In the Eleventh and Twelfth Congresses, several legislators, among them party-list representatives Montemayor (ABA) and Rosales (Akbayan), filed a revised version drafted by Kaisahan and the Local Governance Policy Forum. The bill's lobbyists got wide support from the League of Municipalities of the Philippines and the NAPC Basic Sectors' Council. Despite this, Arroyo did not give the bill priority status. In June 2003, the House of Representatives of the Twelfth Congress finally passed House Bill 5781, a consolidated version of three bills, including Rosales's. The Senate bill languished, however, because Senator Edgardo Angara, the chairperson of the Committee on Constitutional Amendments, Revision of Codes and Laws, refused to hold a committee hearing.[14] For the first election of local sectoral representatives, the electoral reform groups had no choice but to look toward May 2007, just as for the first computerized elections.

Opposing cha-cha but opening to a shift to a parliamentary system

The system of government, particularly the issue of the presidential versus the parliamentary system, has been under debate in the Philippines since the late 1800s, at the time of the first Philippine Republic. Presidentialism versus parliamentarism featured prominently in the discussions and debates of the constitutional conventions of 1935 and 1971 and the constitutional commission of 1986. In 1993, just six years after the ratification of the new Constitution, the issue came back to the fore. The House of Representatives, apparently with the backing of President Ramos, passed a resolution calling for the convening of Congress into a constituent assembly to amend the 1987 Constitution, particularly to change the Philippine system of government from a presidential to a French-style parliamentary one (Abad 1997:48). Ramos, who had said he favored a parliamentary system during the 1992 election campaign, was constitutionally barred from running for reelection.

The new, leftist groups wondered whether to support a parliamentary system. It was a much more complicated political reform measure to tackle, and it was fraught with risks. Unlike the Local Government Code and the Party-List System Act, which were laws for the implementation of certain provisions in the 1987 Constitution, a shift to a parliamentary form of government required a constitutional amendment. Opening the door to a single amendment in the Constitution also meant opening the door to other charter amendments or even to a revision of the entire charter—for better or for worse.

The initial reaction within the ranks of the emergent leftist groups was mixed. Some members urged that the Left support the shift to a parliamentary system on the grounds that this would promote greater engagement and intervention of "progressives" in electoral politics (see Parreño 1993). Others wanted the new Left to participate in the presidential-parliamentary system debate but not to become too closely identified with a particular position (Rocamora 1997b:24). Soon the political blocs of the emergent Left took different stands. Bisig and the popdems opted for the parliamentary system, believing that this would strengthen the political party system in the country. Pandayan and Siglaya adopted a more cautious noncommittal stance, as they did not want themselves to be put in an awkward alliance with administration advocates or to be used by officials wishing to extend their terms (Hofileña 1997:163).

Public discussion and debate on a shift to the parliamentary system and on charter change picked up tremendously and came to a head in the second half of Ramos's term. Shortly after the 1995 elections, pro-Ramos forces, as well as many elected officials who could no longer run again due to term limits, intensified their efforts to effect a constitutional change. The House Committee on Constitutional Amendments convened public hearings on the presidential-parliamentary system issue. The National Security Council (NSC) produced a draft constitution, which provided for a parliamentary system. Exposed by the media, the draft charter became controversial, as critics charged it with exhibiting "authoritarian tendencies." In December 1996, pro-Ramos groups started gathering signatures for a "people's initiative" to amend the Constitution to remove the one-term limit on the presidency. They then formally organized themselves into the People's Initiative for Reform, Modernization and Action (Pirma).[15] Viewing the one-term limit as a safeguard against future dictators, prominent EDSA I figures such as Corazon Aquino and Cardinal Sin led a broad movement to oppose "cha-cha" (charter change). The Left—the NDs and the emergent leftist groups—sensed the danger of a return to authoritarian rule; thus, virtually the entire spectrum of the Left went all out in campaigning against cha-cha. In March 1997, the Supreme Court threw out a petition of Pirma on the "people's initiative" on the grounds that there was still no implementing law for this (Rocamora 1997c:90–133; Hofileña 1997:134–69). Even as Pirma appealed the decision, pro-Ramos forces tried another route for constitutional change: the convening of Congress as a constituent assembly. In September 1997, on the twenty-fifth anniversary of the imposition of martial law, five hundred thousand people packed into Luneta Park in Manila to oppose cha-cha. Two days later, the Supreme Court rejected Pirma's appeal (Suh and Lopez 1997). Due to strong public opposition, the House was forced to abandon its push for a constituent assembly. Ramos's cha-cha ground to a halt.

Although the Left opposed Ramos's cha-cha, some of the emergent groups did not rule out the possibility of working for charter change at a more propitious time in the future. Bisig, Pandayan, the popdems, and Siglaya—all of which were against cha-cha—took a strong pro-parliamentary system stance when they formally banded together to form Akbayan. During its founding congress in January

1998, Akbayan castigated the presidential system and argued for a switch to the parliamentary system.

> The presidential system has generated a policy formulation process dominated by horse trading, by politician interference in policy implementation. It has also generated political parties that cannot play the role they should play in policy formulation. Without political parties with distinct programs and stable membership, policy formulation cannot be removed from the circuits of horse trading. ... We believe that a parliamentary form of government and a party list electoral system will generate political parties better able to perform the function of identifying interests and opinions in society, shaping these opinions into a coherent program and facilitating policy formulation in government.
>
> (Akbayan National Congress 1998a:3–4)

Akbayan also advocated the adoption of a system of proportional representation—in effect, a party-list system for electing the entire membership of the legislature, not just a small part of it—to remove the highly personalized character of Philippine elections, shift the focus to political parties, and gradually eliminate money politics and the use of violence. Going beyond the presidential-parliamentary system debate, Akbayan decided to promote discussions on the issue of changing from a unitary to a federal form of government, taking cognizance of the central government's neglect of the people of Mindanao (Akbayan National Congress 1998a:9–12). A shift from unitary to federal, like that from presidential to parliamentary required a constitutional amendment.

Constitutional change became a big issue once again barely two years after the defeat of Ramos's cha-cha. In his state of the nation address in August 1999, President Estrada proposed convening Congress as a constituent assembly to amend constitutional provisions purportedly restricting the flow of investments and technologies into the Philippines, particularly those prohibiting foreign ownership of land and limiting foreign equity in local businesses. The broad movement against cha-cha revived. Many did not trust a *trapo*-dominated Congress, acting as a constituent assembly, to restrict itself to economic reforms and leave term limits and antiauthoritarianism safeguards untouched. To allay such fears, Estrada came up with a two-part reform process, which he called the Constitutional Correction for Development (Concord). In the first part,

Congress as a constituent assembly would take up economic reforms and eventually submit amendments for approval in a plebiscite coinciding with the 2001 elections. In the second part, a duly elected constitutional convention would tackle political reforms. This would only be convened, however, after the end of his term in 2004. To justify his proposed economic reforms further, he stressed that Concord favored the poor and would allow him to move his poverty eradication program beyond rhetoric to action (Editorial Board, *Governance Brief* 1999:1–2; Office of the Press Secretary 1999). Critics of Estrada's charter change initiative remained unconvinced. Opposition to Cha-Cha II did not abate. In January 2000, amid the discord, Estrada was forced to shelve Concord (Sprague and Lopez 2000). The "Oust Erap" campaign that culminated in Estrada's fall in January 2001 spelled the end for Concord.

The Left's opposition to Estrada's Concord had gone much deeper than just a distrust of a constituent assembly. "The national patrimony provisions of the constitution that President Estrada wants to remove," Akbayan (1999:1) stated, "are among the few remaining defenses of our economy against unruly globalization." Padayon (1999:1) charged that Concord would "completely open the Philippine economy to global forces in one stroke." Chairman Filemon Lagman of the PMP lumped Concord together with such other "anti-poor and anti-people policies" of Estrada as "the continuous privatization of state-owned corporations and the further liberalization of our economy in favor of imperialist globalization" (Bukluran ng Manggagawang Pilipino 2000:1).

Notwithstanding its strong anti-Concord position, Akbayan and its allied POs/NGOs again did not rule out constitutional change. In fact, Akbayan (1999:1) urged that the matter be immediately addressed: "[I]f constitutional reform can be re-framed within a participatory and democratic process, if cha cha is undertaken within an elected Constitutional Convention, the challenge of constitutional reform should be confronted now. We must prepare for the struggle on the substantive issues of constitutional reform as soon as possible."

Campaigning for suffrage for overseas Filipinos

Prior to 1998, the emergent leftist groups and their allied POs/NGOs waged the fight for political reform from outside Congress, mainly through "the parliament of the streets." In lobbying for reform bills, they even went to the extent of drafting bills for legislators. With the victory of some new, leftist parties and groups in the first party-list elections in 1998, the terrain changed a bit. Now the left groups could fight for reforms from both outside and inside the legislature. As mentioned earlier, the groups' representatives in the Lower House endorsed or sponsored political reform bills such as the empowerment and local sectoral representation bills. They also spoke out on matters related to the implementation of reform laws already enacted such as the Election Modernization Act and the Party-List System Act. The first political reform bill passed by Congress in which a new leftist party's representative played a major role in its enactment was the Overseas Absentee Voting Act, a law providing for a system of voting for overseas Filipinos (OFs).

In 2000, the government's Commission on Filipinos Overseas estimated that there were 7.38 million Filipinos abroad, roughly 10 percent of the Philippine population. Spread out in over 180 countries, the overseas Filipinos included 2.99 million migrant workers, 2.55 million immigrants, and 1.84 million with irregular status (Syjuco 2002:1). By sending money to their families in the Philippines—$6 to $8 billion annually in bank remittances (Akbayan 2004:2) and billions of dollars more through other means—OFs contributed a great deal to the Philippine economy and helped keep it afloat in times of crisis. The government hailed them as modern-day heroes. Yet OFs did not enjoy suffrage. The 1987 Constitution expressly stipulated that Congress should provide a system for absentee voting for Filipinos abroad, but after more than a decade the legislature still had not come up with an enabling law. The House of Representatives had approved the absentee voting bill during the Ninth and Tenth Congresses, but the Senate had not (Opiniano 2001).

Soon after one of its members was elected to Congress, Akbayan decided to make absentee voting a priority. After examining the six House bills on overseas voting then pending, Akbayan concluded that the bills put too many restrictions on the OFs' right to vote (the exclusion of immigrants, exclusion from the party-list ballot, etc.). Thus, in her first year in Congress Akbayan Representative Etta Rosales joined the Committee on Suffrage and Electoral Reforms and filed her own bill on absentee voting. "Apart from their significant contribution to the Philippine economy," stated Rosales (1999:1–2) in her bill, OFs "represent a political and social bloc, whose exposures to various cultures, to different concepts and practices of democracy, to new technology, make them a distinct sector that has yet to be tapped to work towards the overall development and transformation of our country." Rosales took an active role in arranging a series of consultations by members of the Committee on Suffrage with OF organizations in Western Europe and Asia. She worked closely with organizations such as the Manila-based Kapisanan ng mga Kamag-anak ng Migranteng Manggagawang Pilipino, Inc. (KAKAMMPI) or Association of Families of Overseas Filipino Workers and Migrant Returnees, and the Netherlands-based Platform of Filipino Migrant Organizations in Europe, which campaigned hard for the passage of absentee voting and organized "advocacy visits" by delegations of OFs.[16]

Both houses of Congress produced their respective consolidated versions of the absentee voting bill in 2000, and both versions awaited floor deliberation. Rosales was all set to present the consolidated Lower House bill for a second reading in the House when the "*jueteng*-gate" scandal exploded. The impeachment proceedings against President Estrada and the turbulent events leading to his ouster in January 2001 upset the Congress timetables completely and dashed all prospects of the absentee voting bill being approved by the Eleventh Congress (M. Sison 2001). After EDSA II, the absentee voting lobby, as Ellene Sana, KAKAMMPI advocacy officer and Akbayan member, glumly assessed, was "back to square one."[17]

Not quite. The momentum of the absentee voting campaign had built up. As KAKAMMPI and the Platform organization plugged on, the ranks of the campaigners swelled. Among those that signed up were large OF organizations and networks such as the U.S.-based National Federation of Filipino-American Associations (NaFFAA) and eLagda and the Saudi Arabia-based Overseas Filipino Workers'

Congress; dozens of country- or city-based OF organizations; and international solidarity formations such as the Netherlands-based Philippine-European Solidarity Centre and the Solidarity Philippines-Australia Network). In March 2000, the overseas voting advocates founded the Global Coalition for the Political Empowerment of Overseas Filipinos (Empower). In a ringing manifesto published in several OF community newspapers, Empower, speaking on behalf of OFs, demanded "our inalienable right to vote" and called on President Arroyo, the political parties, and all prospective legislators to prioritize and ensure the passage of an absentee voting law. The absentee voting advocates campaigned through e-mails, e-groups, and Web sites, and posted letters and postcards, faxes, and text messages targeting the administration and Congress, as well as influential personages and groups in the media, church, academe, POs/NGOs, and so on. Soon many opinion articles, letters, and editorials pushing for or endorsing absentee voting appeared in the major dailies. Appeals from OFs were aired in the broadcast media. The Catholic Bishops' Conference of the Philippines (CBCP) issued statements urging the government to give priority to the enactment of an absentee voting law. In August 2000, the campaigners organized a much bigger "advocacy visit." Through the coordination of Empower, KAKAMMPI, Platform and eLagda, more than fifty representatives of OF and local support organizations lobbied the administration and Congress, making sure of extensive media coverage. Some OF leaders threatened a "remittance boycott" in the event that the government did not act on their demand for suffrage.[18]

The truly global campaign of the OFs had a tremendous impact. In her first state of the nation address, Arroyo asked Congress to enact an absentee voting law. Legislators fell all over themselves in jumping on the absentee voting bandwagon. Eleven senators and eighteen representatives filed their own bills on the issue. In August 2001, Arroyo, congressional leaders, Comelec, and foreign affairs officials warmly received the representatives of organizations advocating absentee voting and publicly committed themselves to an OF suffrage law. Political catalysis was reaching a climax.

The two houses of Congress passed their respective versions of the absentee voting bill in August 2002. The campaigners were greatly dissatisfied with the House version, which was essentially a pilot bill. It excluded immigrants, allowed OFs to vote only in the presidential and vice-presidential contests, disallowed personal campaigning, and limited the effectiveness of the law to the 2004 elections (Jimenez 2003:33). Representative Rosales herself was not too happy with the limitations inserted in the House version, but she felt confident that something could still be done in the bicameral conference committee.[19] In the endgame, the campaigners trained their barrage on the bicameral committee. House members who had pushed for the limitations relented. The bicameral committee approved a version without the restrictive provisions, and Arroyo signed it into law in February 2003.[20]

Akbayan had been actively involved in the campaign for the absentee voting bill. In both the Eleventh and Twelfth Congresses, Representative Rosales was in the thick of the debates on the bill. At the time of the campaign, Akbayan did not yet have chapters abroad (except in Greece), but this did not deter the party. Akbayan members and supporters in Manila-based OF support organizations reached out to allies and contacts in Filipino communities abroad.[21] The OFs themselves and their support organizations in the Philippines were mainly responsible for the enactment of the absentee voting law. Akbayan's main contribution had been to help in the OFs' realization and unleashing of their power.

Con-Ass versus Con-Con

Despite the failed attempts of Ramos and Estrada to implement constitutional reform, the issue of charter change refused to go away. Groups in Mindanao such as Kusog Mindanaw and Lihuk Pideral-Mindanaw, which in 1999 had already started pushing for a shift to a federal system of government, intensified their campaign after the May 2001 elections. More organizations, as well as some respected scholars and personages not limited to those from Mindanao, joined their ranks. Federalism's advocates, mostly coming from the provinces, believed that Manila-based bureaucrats were too biased in favor of "imperial Manila," and were hampering development efforts in areas outside of the national capital region. The federalists likewise believed that a federal system would be the best territorial method of addressing the Muslims' demand for self-governance and would thus help bring about a just and enduring peace in war-torn Mindanao (Quimpo 2001a:280). The issue of charter change hit the front pages once again in April 2002 when Jose de Venecia, Jr., Speaker of the House of Representatives, apparently with the support of most House members, espoused constitutional reform, particularly a shift to a parliamentary system, through a constituent assembly. He announced that he was calling a national summit of all political parties the next month to discuss charter change and other issues. Some critics of De Venecia charged that the move to amend the Constitution was a ploy to eventually get himself installed as prime minister. However, prominent opponents of previous charter change initiatives, such as Corazon Aquino and Cardinal Sin, kept silent this time.

Most leftist groups jettisoned De Venecia's cha-cha initiative, just as they had rejected Ramos's and Estrada's. The NDs adopted an outright anti-cha-cha stance. Some leftist groups, however, clarified that they did not oppose charter change per se. In a joint press statement, leaders of Sanlakas, PM, and BMP declared, "There is no doubt that the Constitution should be changed for it is a reactionary charter that has served more the interests of the elite rather than [those of] the people. Yet while we believe that the Constitution must be changed, we oppose the proposed method for the Cha-Cha. … Instead of a constituent assembly, a nonpartisan Constitutional Convention must be called and vested with the power to draft an entirely new charter" (Fortaleza, Magtubo and Briz 2002). Unlike most of the other leftist groups, Akbayan decided to "support cha-cha through the only possible democratic and participatory process, an elected constitutional convention." It would work for "a shift to a parliamentary form of government, proportional representation elections and a federal system" even as it would "defend the 1987 constitution's progressive provisions" (Akbayan Executive Committee 2002:3). Akbayan further decided to engage De Venecia and his followers in debate and to try to convince those gravitating toward a constituent assembly to go for a constitutional convention instead. Thus, representatives of Akbayan, working closely with a group of NGOs called the Consortium on Constitutional Reform

(CCR), participated actively in De Venecia's "all-parties" summit project, both before and during the summit.

The First Philippine Political Parties Conference assembled heads and representatives of national and regional/local parties and party-list groups. However, some parties—both traditional, such as Laban ng Demokratikong Pilipino (LDP), or Struggle of Democratic Filipinos, and PDP, and left, like Bayan Muna—did not attend. Akbayan representatives actively pushed for an agenda on political and electoral reforms that they had worked on with CCR. Surprisingly, they managed to persuade the conference participants, including the representatives of traditional parties, to agree to certain leftist positions. The participants, for instance, acknowledged the following in the summit declaration (Representatives of political parties 2002:4–5).

➢ "Rent seeking and crony capitalism diverted national resources from productive economic activities and discouraged the rise of an entrepreneurial class. Factionalism, patronage and bossism, along with the failure to adopt decisive policies to help the economy and the people to cope with the challenges and consequences of globalization, contributed to the crisis in our economy, with the result that social inequity and mass poverty incidence in our country are the highest in East Asia."

➢ "A weak party system makes government vulnerable to the dictates of powerful interest groups in politics and the economy. Dealmaking and trading favors to build fragile coalitions behind candidates and programs elevate operators rather than statesmen to positions of power and authority in the state."

➢ "While we must adjust our nationalism to accommodate a progressively globalizing world economy and politics, we cannot entrust the protection of our country and the advancement of our economic interests to foreigners, foreign governments or multilateral institutions."

The representatives of proadministration parties, however, managed to get the gathering's support for President Arroyo's Medium-Term Philippine Development Plan, which leftist groups had earlier criticized of being neoliberal and top-down. Although the representatives of Akbayan and a few other party-list groups were not able to convince all the conference participants to drop the idea of a constituent assembly altogether, the body recognized that "there is a strong sentiment in support of a Constitutional Convention" (Representatives of political parties 2002:5).

Soon after the political parties' conference, however, the House leadership reverted to its constituent assembly position. De Venecia stepped up his cha-cha campaign, and he managed to win over many opposition lawmakers in both houses of Congress. Obviously hoping to gain the support of the federalists for his cha-cha initiative, De Venecia called for a shift to a federal form of government. In January 2003, Sen. Edgardo Angara, the main proponent of a constituent assembly in the Upper House, very nearly succeeded in wresting the Senate presidency from Sen. Franklin Drilon.

Akbayan and other Con-Con (constitutional convention) advocates became increasingly concerned with the moves of the Con-Ass (constituent assembly) forces, which included four major political parties representing the political elite. In Akbayan's analysis, the Con-Ass forces wanted to change the system of government so that members of the House of Representatives would become the fulcrum of a new, parliamentary, political system (Rocamora 2003b:2). To try to stop the Con-Ass steamroller, Con-Con advocates banded together into a coalition in November 2002. The Citizens for Con-Con 2004 (CFC 04) consisted of three major formations: the Consortium for Constitutional Reform, a loose group of NGOs and political groups (including Akbayan) committed to working for charter reforms; the Citizens' Movement for a Federalist Philippines, the main alliance of federalist groups; and Kilusang Pilipino, a multisectoral organization of concerned citizens. The coalition launched a campaign for a Con-Con in 2004, with the election of delegates to be held simultaneously with the May 2004 general elections (De Roma 2002:4–5). In January 2003, soon after the failed "Senate coup," the tide began to turn against the Con-Ass camp. Senator Drilon, who in April 2002 had been for Con-Ass, solicited fourteen signatures in the Senate for a Con-Con in 2004 resolution. Corazon Aquino and Cardinal Sin, moral leaders of the movement against Ramos's and Estrada's cha-chas, declared their opposition to Con-Ass. President Arroyo, who had announced in December 2002 her decision not to run in 2004, spoke out for a Con-Con too (Rocamora 2003a:1). The politically influential religious groups Iglesia ni Kristo and El Shaddai opposed charter change, saying that the people would interpret any move to change the Constitution, with the 2004 elections fast approaching, as an attempt by those in Congress to advance their vested interests. When the House passed a resolution in March 2003 calling for Congress to convene a Con-Ass, several networks of POs, NGOs and new leftist groups joined forces for an even broader movement, the People's Coalition against Con-Ass, with CFC 04 at the core (Institute for Popular Democracy 2003a:1–2, 2003b:1). Throughout the rest of the year, the Con-Con advocates kept up with their campaign for a Con-Con in 2004.

The Con-Ass versus Con-Con contest of 2002–4 ended with neither side really winning. In January 2004, De Venecia and the House of Representatives dropped their Con-Ass position and acceded to a Con-Con (Pablo 2004). By then, however, with four months to go before the elections, there was no more time left to work out a Con-Con bill and have it passed by both houses of Congress. The Con-Con advocates did manage to block Con-Ass, but they fell short of their main objective: a Con-Con in 2004.

Although Akbayan had been among those in the forefront of the campaign for a Con-Con, the whole issue of charter change proved a most contentious one within the party itself. There were members who felt that Akbayan should have rejected De Venecia's cha-cha initiative from the outset. Others criticized weaknesses in the way Akbayan leaders had dealt with the *trapos* at the political parties' summit, particularly in letting the endorsement for Arroyo's medium-term development plan slip through. Defending Akbayan's engagement in the cha-cha issue, Rocamora (2003b:3), the party's chairman in 2001–3, stated: "[I]f we had chosen to oppose cha-cha from the beginning, we would not have been in position to oppose and to succeed in opposing Con-Ass."

Whittling away at elite rule through the fight for political reform

For over a decade now, the emergent leftist groups and their allied POs/NGOs have been engaged in the fight for political reform. In the main, the reform measures pursued have been geared toward promoting people's participation and affirmative action for marginalized sectors and toward weakening oligarchic domination and manipulation of democratic processes and institutions. The groups' actions for political reform are reflective of an overall effort to build a counterhegemony movement against the oligarchic elite and to transform an elite-dominated democracy into a more participatory and egalitarian one.

Since 1995, important political reform measures have been passed—adoption of the party-list system, election modernization, and absentee voting. The new, leftist forces contributed, to varying degrees, to the enactment of these measures, and their contribution to the processes of other political reforms appears to be steadily increasing. Despite the many limitations of the party-list system, IPER executive director Ramon Casiple (2003:5) acknowledges that it has given marginalized and underrepresented sectors "a genuine doorway into the halls of power, albeit a small one." As mentioned earlier, election modernization still needs to be implemented. Absentee voting was introduced in the 2004 elections.

Although the emergent leftist groups vigorously opposed the moves for charter change of Presidents Ramos and Estrada and Speaker De Venecia, the hubbub over cha-cha provided an excellent opportunity for broad public discussion of constitutional reform. In 2002, the new, leftist groups joined the broad movement that campaigned for a more democratic and participatory means of charter change: a constitutional convention instead of a constituent assembly. Going farther, right into the substantive issues, Akbayan pushed for a political reform measure that it believed would have a most profound impact on Philippine patronage politics: a shift to a parliamentary form of government with a system of proportional representation.

In going about their work for political reform, the emergent leftist groups have acquired a wealth of experience and developed some skills and sophistication. Prior to 1998, these groups and their allied POs/NGOs pressed for reform from outside Congress by rallying in the streets and by lobbying. Employing programmatic demand making, they approached legislators and other government officials, endorsing or proposing bills and a few times even drafting them.

After the first party-list ballot in 1998, they began to participate directly in the deliberations and debates in Congress. They learned how to formulate and carry out plans and tactics on multiple fronts, how to combine and weave mass actions in the streets, how to utilize various forms of advocacy—lobbying in person or sending letters, e-mails, faxes, and so on, sometimes even from abroad—and how to debate on the Congress floor.

In the years ahead, the efforts of the emergent leftist groups to achieve political reform are likely to continue to be directed toward fostering people's participation and breaking elite domination and manipulation. The political reform agenda of the new, leftist groups will probably include measures that they have worked on in the past but that remain unenacted or unimplemented. Somewhere at the top of the list will be the passage of local sectoral representation and the long-delayed implementation of election modernization. Also high up in the agenda will be a measure to amend the party-list law to insure that the seats allotted by the Constitution for party-list representatives are filled.[22] Likely to be filed again are the antidynasty and antiturncoatism bills, which are supposed to be simply enabling measures of constitutional provisions but which the *trapos* have strongly resisted and successfully blocked in the past. The new, leftist groups will probably bide their time and, before really pushing for these, make sure they can muster massive support.

After figuring prominently in three successive administrations, the cha-cha controversy is bound to erupt again within the next few years. It is likely to be in the nature of another Con-Ass versus Con-Con clash. In the event that the deadlock between Con-Ass and Con-Con advocates is broken and the constitutional reform process (whether Con-Ass or Con-Con) does begin, the focus of the new leftist forces' endeavors in political reform will probably move to bigger issues such as the shift to a parliamentary system with proportional representation.

7

Party Work at the Municipal Level

To DISTINGUISH THEMSELVES from traditional parties, the emergent parties of the left have endeavored, among other things, to build grassroots-based party organizations. This chapter discusses how one of these parties, Akbayan, has done this, particularly at the municipal and city levels. I focus on the municipal / city level because members of elite political families, as well as traditional parties, directly hold power usually at this level rather than in *barangays*. I first examine how Akbayan opened up new areas for the party's expansion and study its engagement in civil society, elections, and governance at the municipal / city and to some extent the *barangay* levels; look into how it builds local party units; and, finally, make a schematic presentation of how Akbayan builds a political-electoral base at the local level. This chapter also includes case studies of Akbayan's engagement in civil society, elections, and governance.

In my fieldwork in 2002, I chose to go to municipalities and cities in which leftist parties had fielded or endorsed local candidates that had won. I wanted to examine the leftist parties' engagement not just in the mass movement and elections (both party-list and local) but also in local government work and governance, and the interweaving of these engagements, plus the setting up of the local party organization. I covered a good number of municipalities and cities and a few "belts" (clusters of municipalities with some common or shared characteristics). The municipalities and cities I covered in which Akbayan endorsed or fielded winning local candidates were Los Baños and Victoria in Laguna Province; Daraga, Albay; Sulat, Eastern Samar; Jagna, Bohol; Surallah, South Cotabato; Davao City; and Cotabato City. The belts with Akbayan or Akbayan-endorsed local officials were southeastern Samar (specifically the municipalities of Guiuan, Mercedes, Salcedo, and Hernani), the western part of Davao Oriental (Banaybanay, San Isidro, and Governor Generoso), and the Iranun areas of Maguindanao (Buldon, Matanog, and Barira).

Among the salient findings of my field research on Akbayan's political work at the municipal / city level were the following.

- In opening up new areas for expansion, Akbayan has not just relied on the usual NGO-PO combination (or the "civil society route") but has also employed other methods—the now more common "LGU route" and, in Muslim areas, "clan-based" organizing.
- Although Akbayan came from the "mass movement" tradition and continues to be very much involved in contentious politics, much more of the party's energies at the local level has actually been devoted to local governance (especially people's participation in governance), development work, and preparing for elections.
- Akbayan has successfully devised means for foiling or countering various forms of *trapo* dirty tricks during elections; however, it still has not developed effective ways to stop vote buying and NPA harassment.
- Akbayan's engagement in development work has converged with its engagement in local governance; programs such as SIAD and BDP-PRA have contributed immensely to Akbayan's deepening engagement in local governance.
- In many areas, local party activists, too preoccupied with their particular tasks and concerns, have failed to give due attention to building and strengthening the party organization.
- The process of transforming a *trapo*-controlled area into an Akbayan political-electoral base calls for integrated efforts in civil society, the LGU, and party building.

Opening Up New Areas for the Party

When Aksyon / Akbayan started out, its members came mostly from left political blocs (Bisig, the popdems, Pandayan, and Siglaya) and the POs/NGOs and social movements aligned with, or sympathetic to, these blocs. In areas where the political blocs had already been engaged in organizing work, their chapters and units became, or were integrated into, Aksyon/Akbayan chapters. Usually a local chapter of a political bloc had a network of local POs/NGOs allied with it. Bisig, Pandayan, and Siglaya (later replaced by Padayon) maintained themselves as political blocs within Aksyon/Akbayan.

In its formative years, Aksyon/Akbayan opened up many new areas—municipalities or *barangays* where no chapters or units of the party or the political blocs existed—mainly via the civil society route: Akbayan members working with an Akbayan-aligned NGO or national PO federation simply combined party organizing with PO organizing or PO/NGO-related work. To local residents, they usually introduced themselves as NGO personnel and initially did only NGO-related work. Only after a period of local integration would they identify themselves as Akbayan members and engage in political organizing. Akbayan took the traditional civil society route in expanding to several municipalities in southeastern Samar (the lower half of Eastern Samar Province) and to the municipality of Victoria in Laguna Province.

Apart from the "purely" civil society method for opening new areas, Aksyon/Akbayan, usually with NGO assistance, also developed the LGU route, which combines party organizing with work within local governments or with programs involving partnerships between POs/NGOs and LGUs. Training programs related to *barangay* governance, conducted in coordination with allied NGOs such as Basic Orientation on Barangay Governance (BOBG) and Barangay Development Planning through Participatory Resource Appraisal (BDP-PRA), have proven to be particularly helpful in Akbayan's expansion efforts. Akbayan was the first political party to conduct training programs for good governance and people's participation in governance at the *barangay* level on a national scale. In many regions (e.g., Southern Mindanao, Eastern Visayas, and Bicol), the LGU route has turned out to be Akbayan's principal means of moving into new areas.

To expand into the communities of Muslims and indigenous peoples in Mindanao, Akbayan has employed clan-based organizing, a method that it picked up from armed rebel movements. In the late 1980s, CPP-NPA cadres in Maguindanao discovered that the Moro National Liberation Front (MNLF), and later the Moro Islamic Liberation Front (MILF), had mainly worked through the traditional clan structure in organizing their units and base support. The CPP-NPA tried clan-based organizing in communities of Muslims and *lumad* (non-Muslim indigenous peoples) in the Central Mindanao Region (CMR) with some success, but the regional party organization broke away from the CPP-NPA in 1993 during the party split. Rejectionist cadres from Mindanao introduced the clan-based method in Akbayan.[1]

Recruitment into Akbayan is a relatively easy process. A person who wishes to join only has to be a registered voter, to be endorsed by the chapter to which he or she will belong, and to complete the party's basic orientation seminar, usually a one-day affair, which consists of discussions on the national situation and Akbayan's constitution and program. The most crucial point is whether the new recruit becomes a truly active member.

Engagement in Civil Society at the Municipal/City Level

Moving from one area to another in the course of my fieldwork, I observed that Akbayan's engagement in civil society at the local level—organizing POs, promoting popular movements, development work, preparing for elections, and so on—was indeed mainly directed at the poorer classes and marginalized sectors. In most of the rural areas I visited, the emphasis was on peasants or fisherfolk. In Davao City and plantation areas in Davao del Sur, Akbayan and its allied NGOs put stress on organizing industrial, transport, and plantation workers.[2] Local PO organizers who were also Akbayan organizers in Daraga, Mercedes, and Victoria, were particularly successful in building women's POs.[3] In Paquibato, a rural district of Davao City, and in San Isidro, Akbayan, in coordination with the Pandayan-aligned NGO Pambansang Kilusan ng mga Samahang Magsasaka (Pakisama) or National Movement of Farmers' Organizations, assisted peasants in building cooperatives.[4] Akbayan was very much involved in integrated area development in the Iranun areas of Maguindanao.[5] By working among peasants, workers, women, fisherfolk, and the urban poor and in Moro communities, Akbayan could indeed lay claim to being a party of and for the poor and the marginalized. However, I found Akbayan surprisingly weak in the community- or *barangay*-based youth sector, and, as far as I had observed, it had not yet significantly ventured into organizing work among non-Muslim indigenous peoples.

Styles and methods of doing grassroots work varied from place to place, depending a lot on which political bloc was involved and with which NGO or PO federation Akbayan was working. On the whole, Akbayan activists appeared to be adept at conducting political education or skills-training seminars and workshops. Despite their limited resources, local Akbayan organizers often managed to keep a good balance between such "sweeping" activities and follow-up, "solid" organizing work. Building a people's organization usually proceeded on a sectoral basis, except in the case of cooperatives. Multisectoral federations or coalitions of these organizations emerged—for instance, Ugnayan-Los Baños and Ugnayan-Victoria—in areas where a number of local POs had already been set up. Or PO leaders and local officials formed councils, such as the Bicol Grassroots Leaders for Empowerment and Development (Biglead) in Daraga.

I did come across, however, some areas where PO building seemed not to have made much progress. Despite the fact that leftist parties and movements in the Philippines had been very much associated with POs, there were Akbayan areas with hardly any progressive POs. Akbayan had been active in Surallah and Jagna for several years, yet almost all of the local societal organizations in these two municipalities were of the traditional type (religious, civic, school, or sports associations). Why were there hardly any progressive POs? In Surallah, one factor was a relatively weak Akbayan chapter. The Akbayan organization in Jagna, however, was relatively strong and active. Probing deeper, I found that Akbayan had expanded to Surallah and Jagna mainly through the LGU route and that Akbayan members in Jagna had been recruited mainly from political society (the *barangay* and municipal governmental structures and the traditional political parties), not civil society.[6] Furthermore, I found that in some areas opened via the LGU route, Akbayan and its allied NGOs had not been able to work out programs for community organizing to complement or immediately follow BOBG and BDP-PRA trainings.[7]

Regional and local NGOs that were usually based in regional and provincial centers, extended support services to grassroots organizing, the popular movements, and development and local governance-related work. I observed that the regional and local NGOs with which Akbayan worked closely were one or a combination of the following types: (1) peasant NGOs, which assisted in organizing peasants, fisherfolk, and rural women and youth and were active in advocacy for agrarian reform and rural development; (2) labor NGOs, which helped organize urban and farm workers and advance the trade union movement; (3) development NGOs, which promoted programs ranging from simple livelihood projects to SIAD programs; and (4) local governance-related NGOs, which conducted trainings and seminars on progressive good governance, people's participation in governance, and so on. Because of the increasing demand for support services, more and more development and governance NGOs were being set up on the provincial or even subprovincial level. Moreover, the distinction between development and governance NGOs tended to disappear as development NGOs ventured more and more into governance-related concerns and governance NGOs ventured into development work. I found no local NGOs specifically for the women's movement. Governance-related NGOs took care of seminars on "women in governance," and development NGOs handled "gender and development." Neither were there regional or local NGOs for the youth and student movements.

In line with the thrust of "democratic participation in governance," Akbayan and its allied POs/NGOs have worked for the accreditation of local POs/NGOs with the government bodies concerned, for more joint undertakings between POs/NGOs and LGUs, and for the participation of POs/NGOs in local governance, especially in the local special bodies of LGUs such as the local development councils and the local prequalification, bids, and awards committees. In some areas, however, I observed that the participation of POs/NGOs in local governance was still quite limited. In San Isidro, for instance, the leaders of peasant cooperatives aligned with Akbayan were not very active in local development planning. Sounding somewhat apologetic, the representative of a local servicing NGO, who was also an Akbayan officer, explained that the cooperatives concerned still had not had seminars on democratic participation in governance.[8] In some other areas, however, the problem was the opposite: POs/NGOs had become so assertive that they sometimes made demands that even progressive local officials, including some Akbayan members, found far beyond the local government's ability to meet.[9]

As is to be expected of a political party that came out of social movements, Aksyon/Akbayan has been very much engaged in, and identified with, "pressure" or contentious politics. In such major urban centers as Metro Manila, Metro Cebu, and Davao City, Akbayan and POs/NGOs linked with it have frequently launched mass protest or advocacy actions over a wide range of national and local issues. By no means, however, has Akbayan's pressure or contentious politics been limited to major urban centers. In 2000–2001, local activists and members of Akbayan and its allied POs/NGOs in such remote places as Guiuan and Governor Generoso, for instance, launched a series of mass protest actions to stop the environmentally destructive practices of a mining firm on Manicani Island (a part of Guiuan municipality) and logging companies in Governor Generoso.[10]

Many Akbayan activists and members, especially in urban areas, tend to see their party as being mainly in the mass movement mode, a party whose political activities revolve around mass actions and campaigns, especially of the protest or advocacy type. This self-perception, it turns out, is not too accurate. In the course of studying Akbayan's activities at the local level, I noticed that Akbayan cadres and activists in many areas did *not* devote much time and effort to pressure or contentious politics and were in fact much more involved in such concerns as development work, local governance (especially people's participation in governance), and preparing for elections.

On closer examination, I discerned a difference in priorities in urban and rural civil society work. Cadres and activists in major urban areas tended to put the stress in their civil society work on contentious types of actions, while those in rural areas (except some plantation areas and agrarian reform "hot spots") stressed development work and people's participation in governance. Urban activists were often called on, and felt compelled, to articulate and project the party's positions on national, sectoral, and local issues and developments. While they were centers of the mass movement, urban areas also played a significant role in a noncontentious aspect of Akbayan's politics: as national or regional hubs in the party's efforts vis-à-vis development work and local governance. Both urban and rural activists paid attention to preparing for elections, but rural activists seemed to have more time for this, as they did not have to engage in mass protest actions as often as their urban counterparts did.

It was but logical for contentious types of actions—rallies, marches, pickets, and so on—to gravitate toward urban centers, where the main institutions and offices of government, the churches, academe, and the mass media were located. I noted, however, that many Akbayan cadres and activists were not too conscious about, and sensitive to, the difference in urban and rural priorities. Moreover, I observed that the time and energy of Akbayan national leaders often tended to be drawn to, and caught up in, the exciting, fast-paced contentious politics of the major urban centers, sometimes at the expense of the mundane, slow, and not too contentious concerns of those working in the rural areas. This was especially true during times when "urgent" national issues and developments, which called for decisive and sharply formulated responses, came in quick succession.

Electoral Engagement at the Municipal/City Level

In its first electoral bid in 1998, Akbayan mainly focused on the party-list ballot, although it also fielded or endorsed some candidates in the local elections. Local activists and members of Akbayan were most eager to campaign and speak to voters about the party's platform of new politics, but they were hobbled by the Comelec's failure to conduct a good informational campaign on the party-list system. "We ended up spending much more time, money and energy explaining what the party-list system was all about," complained one campaigner. The voters' lack of understanding of the party-list system, however, was not just a problem of Akbayan.

All the parties and groups in the system were in the same bind. In raising funds and winning votes, local Akbayan campaigners relied on the networks of POs/NGOs aligned with, or supportive of, the party; the communities serviced by various projects of these POs/NGOs; and allies within the church, civic groups, and the business sector. In areas where Akbayan and its allied NGOs had conducted trainings on participatory *barangay* governance, as in Los Baños and Daraga, Akbayan also managed to harness the support of some *barangay* and municipal officials.[11] Like other leftist parties and groups, Akbayan campaigners fretted about the possible dirty tricks of *trapos* and their surrogate parties and groups. It turned out however that the threat the *trapos* posed in the party-list vote had been overestimated. *Trapos* interested in becoming congresspersons had apparently preferred to pursue the traditional route—elections by congressional district. In some areas, votes for Akbayan were not counted, but in many cases this had less to do with *trapo* tricks than with confusion about, or exasperation with, the party-list system among public school teachers designated to do the counting.

In 2001, Akbayan aimed to get the maximum three congressional seats in the party-list vote; at the same time, it fielded or endorsed more candidates in the local elections. Akbayan tapped its usual networks of POs/NGOs and supporters. This time, however, Akbayan had many more allies among *barangay* and municipal officials, thanks in good part to the Batman and IAD/SIAD programs. Since the Comelec still had not come up with a proper informational drive on the party-list system, local Akbayan campaigners once again had to do this themselves. In almost all of the rural municipalities I visited during my fieldwork, Akbayan or Akbayan-endorsed candidates informed me that they had had to contend with the dirty tactics of their *trapo* opponents—vote buying, "flying voters" (voting nonresidents), tampering with election returns, and so on. Guerrillas of the NPA harassed local Akbayan campaigners in several of the places I visited, including Daraga, Surallah, and Davao City (particularly Paquibato district), telling them to stop campaigning for Akbayan.[12] The guerrillas also ripped off Akbayan posters. Although local Akbayan campaigners tried to thwart or neutralize the *trapos'* dirty tactics and NPA harassment, they were not always successful.

Since 2001 was the second foray of Akbayan into both the party-list ballot and local elections, it would have been logical to expect it to be much better prepared. But most of the places I visited showed signs of inadequate or last-minute preparations. First and foremost, I could hardly find any written evidence of systematic investigations into local politics and power dynamics—profiles of major politicians, politico-economic clans, and factions at the local and provincial levels; their political party and coalition affiliations; links to provincial and regional kingpins and national politicians; sources of funds; and so on. Nor was there much evidence of thorough searches for prospective progressive candidates at the local level. Key local cadres or "operators" could rattle off a lot of information and analysis, but since most of this was unwritten not much filtered down to the mass activists and campaigners. According to an Akbayan leader, quite a number of party members are still very much used to the "oral tradition."[13] Good studies of local politics and power dynamics would probably have helped Akbayan not just in mounting stronger challenges to *trapos* in local elections but also in identifying potential Akbayan supporters in the party-list vote and in exploring possible synergies between its party-list and local election campaigns. For proper planning and preparation, the studies of local politics and power dynamics could have been done long before election time.

In several places I visited, I noted that in the months and weeks before the deadline for filing of candidacy Akbayan did not take an active part in, or even attempt to influence, certain crucial decisions of local politician-allies or even of local politicians who were already Akbayan members: whether to run; for which position; under which party, coalition, or slate, or as an independent; who should or should not be included in a slate; whom to approach for financial support; and so on. It seemed to have forgotten that it was a political party that could and should assert itself on such matters. Since Akbayan was vying with *trapo* parties for the primary allegiance of these politicians, it could very well have lost some of them by default.

Knowing that the Comelec had made such a mess of the information drive on the party-list system in 1998, Akbayan could have encouraged civic-oriented groups, especially those that maintained a nonpartisan stance, to help with voters' education before the election campaign period. And, knowing that the CPP-NPA considers all non-ND leftist parties and groups to be counterrevolutionary, Akbayan could have anticipated that with the entry of Bayan Muna into the electoral arena the CPP-NPA would threaten and harass its activists and campaigners (among others). Hence, it could have prepared a forceful political response well in advance.

I found no evidence of long-term financial planning for the elections in any of the areas of study. Planning began a few months or weeks before the election campaign or during the campaign itself.

According to some Akbayan members I interviewed, one of the factors responsible for the inadequacies or belatedness of the preparations for the 2001 elections was that, as in 1998, Akbayan held its national congress just a few weeks before the start of the campaign season. The January 2001 congress could indeed have been held much earlier. However, I attribute the inadequate or last-minute electoral preparations mainly to something else: a strong proclivity within the Philippine left toward short-span, short-preparation mass actions and campaigns. Leftist parties and groups can and do plan certain mass campaigns months or even over a year in advance. In response to urgent political or social developments, however, they often feel compelled to come up with mass protest or advocacy actions as promptly as possible. Many urban-based or urban-developed activists and members of leftist parties and groups have become so inured to the quick-reaction type of mass actions and campaigns that they have developed a tendency to treat all mass activity in the same manner: on the quick. Elections are no exception. For many leftist activists, the election campaign has turned into just another "quickie" mass campaign. They forget that, although the actual election campaign does not last very long (from one and a half to three months), it requires long preparation. The quickie mentality of leftist activists contrasts with the more premeditated outlook of many *trapos*, who see politics as a means to power and wealth and right after one election start planning for the next. Against such calculating opponents, progressive candidates who have prepared late risk getting thrashed.

Akbayan's two congresspersons and over a hundred local officials indicate that notwithstanding the deficiencies in electoral preparations, the party did manage, in a fair number of areas at least, to thwart or neutralize the *trapos'* dirty tactics and NPA harassment and to achieve some modest victories. Drawing lessons from its electoral experience since 1997, Aksyon/Akbayan has designed and refined training modules on election campaign management and poll watching and come up with possibly more effective ways of preventing fraud, coercion, and violence. To try to counter both *trapo* tricks and NPA harassment in the 2004 elections, for instance, Akbayan joined hands with a number of societal organizations, as well as other political parties, in launching a campaign for free, honest, and peaceful polls called Compact for Peaceful Elections, and seeing to it that this would be a truly grassroots campaign and not just a middle-class and urban-centered one.[14] It will take much, much more than just a campaign, however, to fight vote buying and the culture of influence peddling, unequal favor exchange, and dependence that *trapos* have propagated for decades.[15] Perhaps only sustained popular political education, in the nature of "dialogical encounters" with the masses, can uproot the pervasive and harmful influences of patronage politics.

In many of the areas I visited, I noted some confusion as to whether Akbayan was actually fielding or merely endorsing certain local candidates. I discovered that this had something to do with under which party the candidate chose to run. Akbayan had campaigned for three types of local candidates: (1) non-Akbayan members who ran under traditional parties or as independents, (2) Akbayan members who ran under traditional parties or as independents, and (3) Akbayan members who ran under Akbayan. Strictly speaking, only those in (3) could really be considered as Akbayan fielded. Within Akbayan's ranks, however, those in (2) also tended to be seen as such. In 1998, a good number of local candidates of types (1) and (2) had won. There were a few of (3), however, who were elected, as in Culion, Palawan, for instance.[16] Prior to 2002, the distinction between fielding or merely endorsing local candidates did not seem to matter much since Akbayan was still unfamiliar with municipal governance and could not provide much political direction or guidance to winning candidates, whether fielded or endorsed.

Akbayan leaders did not have qualms about Akbayan members running under traditional parties. They believed that the party, in the process of building itself up to mount a strong challenge to the *trapos*, would have to go through a phase in which some members, in effect, would have dual party membership—Akbayan and *trapo*. However, when and how the practice of dual-party allegiance would end was not clear.

Engagement in Municipal/City Governance

As mentioned in chapter 5, Akbayan remained largely unengaged or only peripherally engaged, in municipal and city governance in 1998–2002, even though some progressive local candidates who were sympathetic to it, or even members of it, had won in the 1998 and 2001 elections. Until December 2002, the progressive LGU officials performed their governmental functions without much help from Akbayan. Certain initiatives of Akbayan and its allied POs/NGOs—SIAD projects, programs related to participatory *barangay* governance, PO/NGO participation in local special bodies, programs on women in governance, and so on—did intersect with municipal governance but did not get into the main run of it. Some Akbayan chapters and divisions (such as those in Los Baños, Daraga, Banaybanay, Governor Generoso, and southeastern Samar), however, strove to learn the ropes of good, progressive governance at the municipal level by themselves.

In the course of my fieldwork, I observed that Akbayan's engagement in development work was no longer limited to working with progressive societal organizations but was getting more and more intertwined with local governance, both at the *barangay* and, however limited initially, at the municipal level. It used to be that in undertaking development initiatives leftist groups and their allied POs/NGOs avoided linking up with LGUs for fear of being caught up in government bureaucracy or being co-opted by the *trapos*. Akbayan and its allied POs/NGOs realized, however, that for their SIAD and other development initiatives to really succeed they needed to work more closely with LGUs. Thus, more and more the development projects became joint PO/NGO/ Akbayan and LGU projects. Akbayan's engagement in development work was no longer just limited to the realm of civil society but now extended to the state. Programs related to people's participation in governance, especially BDP-PRA, further reinforced the LGU aspect of development work. In working with LGUs on development projects, Akbayan and its allied POs/NGOs gravitated toward, and later more actively sought out, progressive LGU officials—local "state reformists." In the process of cooperation, relations between Akbayan and these officials drew closer. Not surprisingly, many of them joined the party.

One of the notable early recruits from the ranks of municipal officials was Vice Mayor Jose Learto Otig, a former diocesan priest, of Banaybanay, Davao Oriental. As a priest, Otig had been very much involved in church social action and oriented toward serving Vatican II's priority sectors—"the poor, deprived, and oppressed." When personnel of the Bisig-linked People's Alternative Development Center (PADC) first met Otig in 1998, they were very much impressed with his progressive politics. They invited him, together with other local leaders of Banaybanay, to a Batman training seminar in Lake Sebu, South Cotabato, in which some leading Akbayan figures were resource persons. With his wholehearted support, Banaybanay became one of the pilot areas of BDP-PRA in Mindanao. Otig joined Akbayan and organized a chapter in Banaybanay. Invited to join PADC's board of directors, he was eventually elected board chairman. In 2001, Otig, touted to be a very strong mayoral contender, ran again for vice mayor instead because of poor health.[17] He succumbed to a heart attack in September 2003.

Throughout 1998–2002, the pressure built up for a more serious and comprehensive engagement of Akbayan in municipal/city governance. The number of Akbayan members and allies among local state reformists was fast increasing as a result of Akbayan's engagement not just in the mass movements and elections but also—and especially—in local governance and development concerns such as BDP-PRA and SIAD. Attracted to Akbayan's program of new politics, these local state reformists strove to inject new politics in their own work in government and looked for political direction and leadership. As early as 1999, Akbayan and the POs/NGOs involved in Batman had already seen the need to scale up Batman's ambit from *barangay* to municipal/city governance. Only in late 2002, however, did Akbayan decisively do so, as was explained in chapter 5.

The case studies presented in chapter 5 and in this chapter demonstrate very clearly that state reformists in local governments (*barangay*, municipal, and city) are not a rarity at all. Despite the odds, some reform-oriented candidates do win elections, and once in public office they do strive to undertake reforms and practice good governance. A leftist or left-leaning state reformist is no longer a rarity either. When a new, leftist party such as Akbayan enters the local scene, it does manage to link up and work closely with reform-oriented politicians and even to recruit a good number of them into its ranks. And Akbayan has sometimes succeeded in having old-time activists elected to public office.

Recruiting a local state reformist or getting one elected is but one step. The tug of war with *trapos* for the state reformist's allegiance is far from over—especially when he or she joins Akbayan under a dual-party (*trapo* and Akbayan) arrangement. Surrounded by *trapos*, a state reformist can become corrupted. Or he or she can be influenced mainly by, or even converted to, new managerialism. Since new managerialists usually join or remain in *trapo* parties for reasons of political expediency, a state reformist converted to new managerialism can end up being used by the *trapo* parties and perpetuating or even strengthening the prevailing system of patronage and patrimonialism.

The local public officials mentioned in the case studies all endeavor to pursue good governance or participatory governance, but whether this is more in line with the new managerialist, radical democratic, or some other perspective in governance is not clear. Given the predominance of "new public management" in the governance discourse in academe, government circles, and development NGOs, it is likely that the local officials cited have imbibed at least a bit of new managerialist thinking. As mentioned earlier, only lately have leading Akbayan members become more conscious of the various competing theoretical perspectives in governance and of the importance of making distinctions among them. For as long as the patrimonial and/or new managerialist perspectives continue to have a strong influence on local politicians who have joined Akbayan, and for as long as the party has not developed a radical democratic or left alternative perspective, it cannot rest assured that it has fully won them over.

Case Studies of Akbayan's Engagement in Municipal/City Politics

The focus on Akbayan's electoral engagement

GOVERNOR GENEROSO, DAVAO ORIENTAL, AND JAGNA, BOHOL: RUNNING UNDER A TRADITIONAL PARTY. Akbayan expansion into Governor Generoso, Davao Oriental, and Jagna, Bohol, basically followed the LGU route. In late 1998, personnel of PADC contacted Jerry Dela Cerna, whom they had heard was a very "propeople" and "nontraditional" politician. In 1998, Dela Cerna, a former diocesan priest with no prior experience in electoral politics, had run for mayor of one of Davao Oriental's most remote towns, Governor Generoso, and narrowly lost. Like Otig, Dela Cerna had been very much involved in church social action for the poor. He had also been very active in the environmental movement, organizing mass protests against illegal logging in Davao Oriental. PADC arranged for Dela Cerna, together with other local leaders in Governor Generoso, to attend Batman trainings in Davao City in 1999. Meanwhile, two Akbayan members, both former NDs working with the Center for Politics, Governance and Development (CPGD) in Tagbilaran, Bohol, invited a former colleague, Exuperio "Eksam" Lloren, together with other local leaders of Jagna, a small port town in southeastern Bohol, to a Batman "trainers' training" seminar in 1999. Lloren, a former student activist, NPA commander, and political detainee who later opted to run for public office "to continue working for the masses," had been elected *barangay* captain in 1997 and Jagna municipal councilor the next year. Convinced by Akbayan's platform of new politics and participatory governance, most of the Batman seminar participants in Tagbilaran and Davao, including Dela Cerna and Lloren, joined the party and proceeded to push for participatory governance in their respective municipalities.[18]

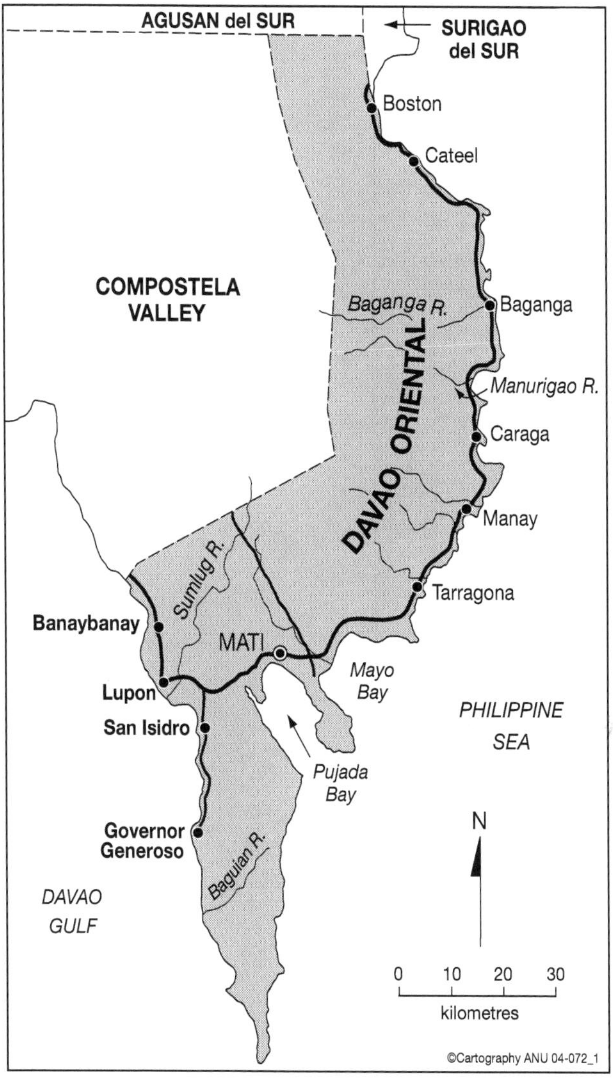

Map 7.1 Davao Oriental Province, showing Banaybanay, Governor Generoso, and San Isidro

In 2001, fresh Akbayan recruits Dela Cerna and Eksam Lloren ran for mayor in their respective towns, Governor Generoso and Jagna, going up against powerful opponents. Dela Cerna ran against Perfecto Orencia, the elder brother of the incumbent mayor, Vicente Orencia (of the PMP),[19] who, after three terms, could no longer run for reelection. V. Orencia had defeated Dela Cerna in a closely fought contest in 1998 that, Dela Cerna's supporters claimed, had been marred by vote buying, harassment, and cheating. (The Comelec eventually excluded election returns from two *barangays* because of irregularities.) V. Orencia's stint as mayor had been tainted by several unsolved, apparently political killings, including those of a municipal councilor and municipal planning and development officer, who both had questioned certain financial irregularities in the local bureaucracy, and a *barangay* captain who had opposed illegal logging operations. P. Orencia had the backing of the great majority of the municipal councilors and *barangay* captains in Governor Generoso.[20] Lloren faced the incumbent mayor, Marciana Ocmeja Tsurumi (PDP-Laban), who was running for a third term and had most of the municipal councilors and the barangay captains on her

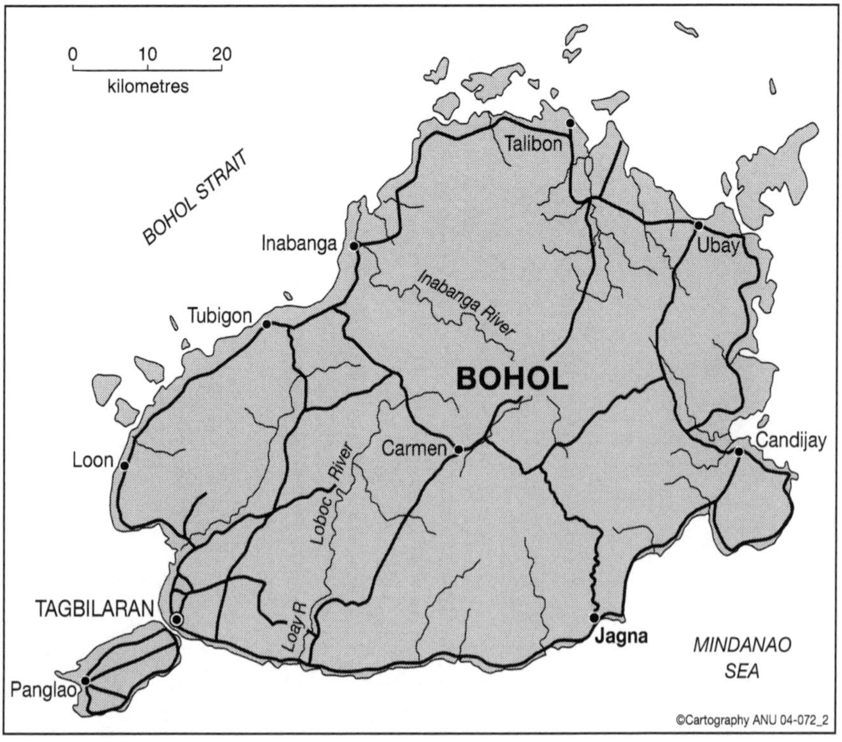

Map 7.2 Bohol Province, showing Jagna

side. Tsurumi had trounced Eksam's brother, Senen, in the 1995 mayoral contest, and her candidate for the Liga ng mga Barangay presidency had defeated Eksam by a single vote in 1997. Eksam was one of the "Concerned Citizens of Jagna" who had filed a complaint against Tsurumi with the ombudsman in 1996 on alleged irregularities in the delivery of construction materials for some local projects.[21]

Akbayan did not play much of a role in the decisions of Dela Cerna and Lloren to run for mayor or on the choice of party under which to run. Dela Cerna had intended to make another bid for the mayorship even before joining Akbayan. With Akbayan in Bohol still very weak, Lloren had made the decision largely by himself.[22] Both Dela Cerna and Lloren opted for the party of President Arroyo, Lakas-NUCD,[23] and the ruling coalition, PPC. Neither really entertained the idea of running under Akbayan, although both fully endorsed Akbayan in the party-list ballot. Up against powerful opponents, both felt that they needed the backing of an established party.[24] Lakas-NUCD had its appeal as a party identified with the administration and EDSA II. But probably the deciding factor for Dela Cerna and Lloren was that their opponents did *not* go with Lakas-NUCD and chose parties of the opposition instead. Lakas-NUCD, which was looking for candidates with good chances of winning against P. Orencia and Tsurumi, picked them.[25] Dela Cerna and Lloren consulted local Akbayan members, all fresh Akbayan recruits too, in forming the slate of candidates for the local elections. Higher organs of Akbayan had no hand in this—indicating again that the party was still grappling with what it should be doing vis-à-vis local elections.

With vigorous engagement during the election campaign period, Akbayan managed to make up for its earlier shortcomings. Akbayan was at the very core of the campaigns of Dela Cerna and Lloren and their respective municipal tickets. The Dela Cerna and Lloren tickets actually relied on two campaign machineries or networks: the one that revolved around the traditional party and the one that revolved around Akbayan. Because Dela Cerna, Lloren, and many of their colleagues had run before, they already had traditional party networks. Lloren also benefited from the support of a former mayor who had lost to Tsurumi in a comeback bid in 1998. In Governor Generoso, the Akbayan network was virtually synonymous with Barog Katawhan, a multisectoral PO that Bisig members had helped organize in December 2000, a few months before the start of the election campaign. Since August 2000, PADC had been conducting political education seminars in different *barangays*. Barog recruited many of those who had attended. When the election campaign started, Barog went all out for Dela Cerna and Akbayan. Its members joined Akbayan.[26] In Jagna, the Akbayan organization consisted mainly of those who had come from the Batman seminars. Since CPGD had run out of funding, it had not been able to do follow-up work, such as PO organizing, in Jagna. To assist Lloren and Akbayan in Jagna, the Manila-based IPG deployed a senior cadre, who immediately arranged for electoral campaign management training for Lloren's campaigners and took charge of strategic planning.[27] Toward the latter part of the campaign, Akbayan arranged for poll-watching seminars for Dela Cerna's and Akbayan's campaigners.

Both Dela Cerna and Lloren strove to conduct platform-based campaigns, emphasizing the need for good governance, transparency, and new politics. They decried the retarded development of their respective towns and put the blame for this squarely on the incumbents' lack of clear development plans and on rampant graft and corruption.[28] "Lloren represented a new system of politics," observed retired judge Bernardo Salas, "one of idealism, decency, a commitment to do something good, an aspiration for the town to develop ... a rejection of patronage."[29] The development programs that Dela Cerna and Lloren outlined put the stress on poverty alleviation, on improving the livelihoods of the masses—the peasants, fisherfolk, and, in Governor Generoso, the *lumad*. For the protection of small fisherfolk as well as the environment, for instance, Dela Cerna vowed to fully implement the law banning commercial fishing in municipal waters, thus earning the ire of local fishing magnates, who had been flagrantly violating the law. As advocates of participatory governance and popular empowerment, Dela Cerna and Lloren pushed for greater participation of POS/NGOS in local special bodies of the LGU, such as the local development councils, and more cooperative ventures between the LGUS and POS/NGOS.

Dela Cerna, Lloren, and several others on their tickets actively campaigned for Akbayan and explained its platform to voters, but they respected ticket mates who supported, and campaigned for, other party-list groups.

The campaigns of Dela Cerna and Lloren had the usual evening rallies, house-to-house visits, leafleting, campaign jingles, and so on. In Governor Generoso, Barog / Akbayan, with chapters in all twenty *barangays*, campaigned aggressively. When word got around that certain logging interests were reportedly offering financial support to some councilors if the municipal council approved an application for an Integrated Forest Management Agreement that would have circumvented the logging ban, Barog / Akbayan staged a rally in front of the municipal hall and threatened to campaign against those voting in favor of it. The application was rejected.[30] In Jagna, Lloren's campaigners came up with imaginative, high-impact forms, such as caravans of jeepneys, motorcabs and motorcycles, which traversed the municipality from end to end, and a multimedia *miting de avance* with simultaneous big-screen showings. They also conducted several straw votes in the course of the campaign. What turned out to be the single biggest issue was Tsurumi's plan to put up a new public market (to replace the old one, which had burned down) in a less convenient site, a decision made without much public consultation.[31]

Dela Cerna's and Lloren's opponents used the "red scare" to frighten voters. Lloren managed to turn the "rebel" label into something positive by arguing that many of the Philippines' heroes had once been branded rebels. With the help of Lakas-NUCD provincial leaders and Akbayan national officials, he managed to foil a plan unearthed by his supporters to have him arrested for supposed links with the CPP-NPA. Tsurumi invited a well-known anticommunist crusader from Cebu to speak at her *miting de avance*. In Governor Generoso, the red baiting directed against the ex-priest Dela Cerna was more indirect—it was Akbayan that was branded as "communist."[32]

On election eve and election day, Dela Cerna's and Lloren's supporters closely monitored goings-on in their areas. They watched for possible election irregularities before and during the voting and during the counting. Because of the vote buying, both Governor

Generoso and Jagna were awash with money. "It was more than Christmas," remarked the owner of a small pharmacy-store in Jagna. "We ran out of powder, lotion, sanitary napkins, ice cream. Some of the peso bills still had stickers on them."[33] In Governor Generoso, there were numerous reports of harassment or coercion during the voting and of attempts at fraud, particularly ballot switching, during the counting.[34]

With thirteen thousand Jagna residents casting their ballots, Lloren won by a comfortable margin of almost 2,000 votes (7,423 versus 5,532). His running mate and five candidates for councilor on his slate emerged victorious too.[35] In Governor Generoso, Dela Cerna also made it, but just barely. On the basis of precinct-based counting, he had won by over 900 votes. At the municipal hall, however, the figures that came in did not tally with the precinct count. Nonetheless, in the end he still came out ahead by a slim margin—725 votes (7,817 versus 7,092).[36] Fearing that the election could yet be stolen, Dela Cerna's supporters adamantly demanded that the local Comelec official immediately proclaim him as the winner. They refused to leave the hall. Finally, at 2 a.m. the next day, Dela Cerna was proclaimed the winner. Only four others on his ticket (the vice mayor and three councilors) won.[37] In both Governor Generoso and Jagna, Akbayan topped the party-list vote, garnering over 2,000 votes in each.[38]

VICTORIA, LAGUNA: RUNNING UNDER AKBAYAN. Victoria was one of the few municipalities in the entire country where Akbayan fielded—not just endorsed—candidates for local government posts in the 2001 elections. The fielding of Akbayan candidates in Victoria largely resulted from a local initiative and did not really proceed from some well-laid plan coming from upper levels of the party organization.

Akbayan started organizing in Victoria using the traditional NGO route. In February 1999, the Bisig-linked Center for Agrarian Reform Empowerment and Transformation (Caret) assigned two community organizers, who were also Akbayan members, to Victoria, a fifth-class municipality and one of Laguna's poorest. The two organizers helped local women, peasants, and fisherfolk set up or reinvigorate

POs. In the original plan, a municipal federation would be formed once there were enough POs, and this would be followed by Akbayan organizing. In the latter half of 2000, however, the Caret tandem undertook Akbayan organizing earlier, in preparation for the May 2001 congressional and local elections. By early 2001, there were Akbayan chapters in all the nine *barangays* of Victoria. By then too, there were sixteen POs, new or newly reactivated, mostly *barangay* based. In April 2001, the POs forged a federation, Ugnayan ng mga Mamamayan Tungo sa Kaunlaran ng Victoria (Ugnayan-Victoria) or People's Coordinating Council for the Development of Victoria. In the flurry of the electoral campaign, the distinction between Akbayan and Ugnayan-Victoria became somewhat blurred, a problem that took some time to iron out after the elections.[39]

When community organizers of Caret sought accreditation for their NGO with the local authorities in Victoria in 1999, they sought the help of Restituto Cacha, then a municipal councilor. A physician by profession, Cacha was well known in the municipality for extending free medical service to indigent residents. Cacha managed to convince members of the municipal council, some of whom were wary of "leftist" groups, that Caret was a development NGO and not a communist front organization. Through the Caret organizers, who were also Akbayan members, Cacha got to know about Akbayan. Invited to an Akbayan political education seminar in Antipolo, Rizal, Cacha learned more about the party and its programs for people's participation in governance. Convinced about Akbayan's participatory approach, he joined the party and assisted Caret's PO organizing efforts. He also helped to organize a province wide Akbayan "basic orientation seminar" in Victoria, drawing some local leaders who had supported him in previous elections. Afterward they too joined Akbayan.[40]

For some time, Cacha, a three-term councilor, had been contemplating making a bid for the vice mayorship. When he decided to go for it, he did not feel that he needed the backing of an established party. In his first and third electoral attempts, Cacha had run under traditional parties—the Kilusan ng Bagong Lipunan (KBL) or New Society Movement, and LAMMP, respectively. In his second attempt, however, he had run as an independent—and still won. Why shouldn't a party of the new politics be able to make it?[41] Akbayan provincial leaders agreed to his proposal of a local Akbayan ticket with himself as candidate for vice mayor, eight of his allies (mostly political greenhorns) for councilor and no candidate for mayor. Since the Caret / Akbayan organizers did not know local politicians well, they largely left it to Cacha to pick the Akbayan slate.[42] In the rush to meet the deadline for filing candidacy, he was not able to conduct more extensive discussions or consultations with the Akbayan-PO/NGO network.[43]

Three parties contested the Victoria local elections: PPC, LAMMP and Akbayan. The PPC fielded a complete slate and LAMMP a slate without a vice-mayoral candidate. The contest for vice mayor still turned out to be a three-cornered fight, because the PPC, unable to decide on an official candidate, had two competing for the post.[44] The Akbayan slate carried a platform of participatory governance and transparency in public office. Apart from Akbayan chapters in the different *barangays* of Victoria, Ugnayan and its affiliate organizations campaigned for the local Akbayan slate and for Akbayan in the party-list vote. Cacha and company raised funds mainly from local sources. The Akbayan national secretariat helped primarily in terms of posters and leaflets and with trainings on campaign management and poll watching.[45] Since the formation of the Akbayan slate had not been the result of extensive consultations, support within the Akbayan-PO/NGO network for individual candidates on the slate varied greatly.[46] "We really lacked resources," said Akbayan organizer Nick Soriano. "We had to go all the way to the Akbayan headquarters in Quezon City to print our leaflets and small posters with the Risograph machine. Black and white, no pictures. We couldn't afford mobile loudspeakers … or [hiring] vehicles, for that matter. Doc [Cacha] didn't even have a car of his own."

Despite heavy vote buying by their opponents, Cacha scraped through with a winning margin of just three hundred votes (out of twelve thousand cast) and two Akbayan candidates for councilor also made it. In Cacha's analysis, the split in the PPC camp in the vice-mayoral contest contributed to his victory. Because of its feisty anti-Estrada stance during the time of EDSA II and III, Akbayan lost the party-list votes of local Estrada supporters, who comprised a sizable portion—possibly even a majority—of Victoria's population. Nonetheless, as in Governor Generoso and Jagna, Akbayan came in first in the party-list balloting in Victoria, garnering two thousand votes.

SULAT, EASTERN SAMAR: UP AGAINST GUNS, GOONS, AND GOLD. On the way from Sulat, Eastern Samar, to Tacloban, Leyte, in June 2002, I hitched a ride with Mayor Javier Zacate, who was with his driver and two bodyguards. When I boarded the mayor's land cruiser, I was somewhat taken aback on seeing several high-powered rifles lying around in the vehicle. It took me a while to get used to finding a new politics politician traveling with so many guns. But having stayed at Zacate's residence and interviewed him and several others, I knew and understood why he was well armed.

Zacate had first been involved in the ND movement as a student activist in the early 1980s, and later engaged in urban poor, trade union, and peasant organizing and in mass campaign management and was briefly with the NPA. When the ND movement split in 1992–93, Zacate did not join the reaffirmists or the rejectionists, but he maintained close ties with the latter. Having gained some experience in electoral campaign work in Mindoro in 1992, he served as the campaign manager of a congressional candidate in Eastern Samar in 1995. He weighed the possibility of running for public office himself.[47]

In 1998, Zacate made his first bid for the mayoralty of his hometown, Sulat, a fifth-class municipality that had experienced hardly any growth for years. He faced a formidable opponent, the incumbent, Thelma Baldado, whose husband had been Sulat mayor in the Marcos period and whose other relatives were "all over the place" in the local government bureaucracy.[48] (The local government was practically the only major source of employment in the municipality.)[49] Zacate headed the local slate of NPC, which had earlier been looking for a plausible candidate to face Baldado (the Lakas candidate). He did not endorse any party or group in the party-list ballot, but both Sanlakas and Akbayan supported his candidacy.[50] Having closely studied the dirty tricks resorted to by *trapos* in the 1992 and 1995 elections, Zacate felt confident that he would be able to sufficiently thwart attempts to use such tricks against him.

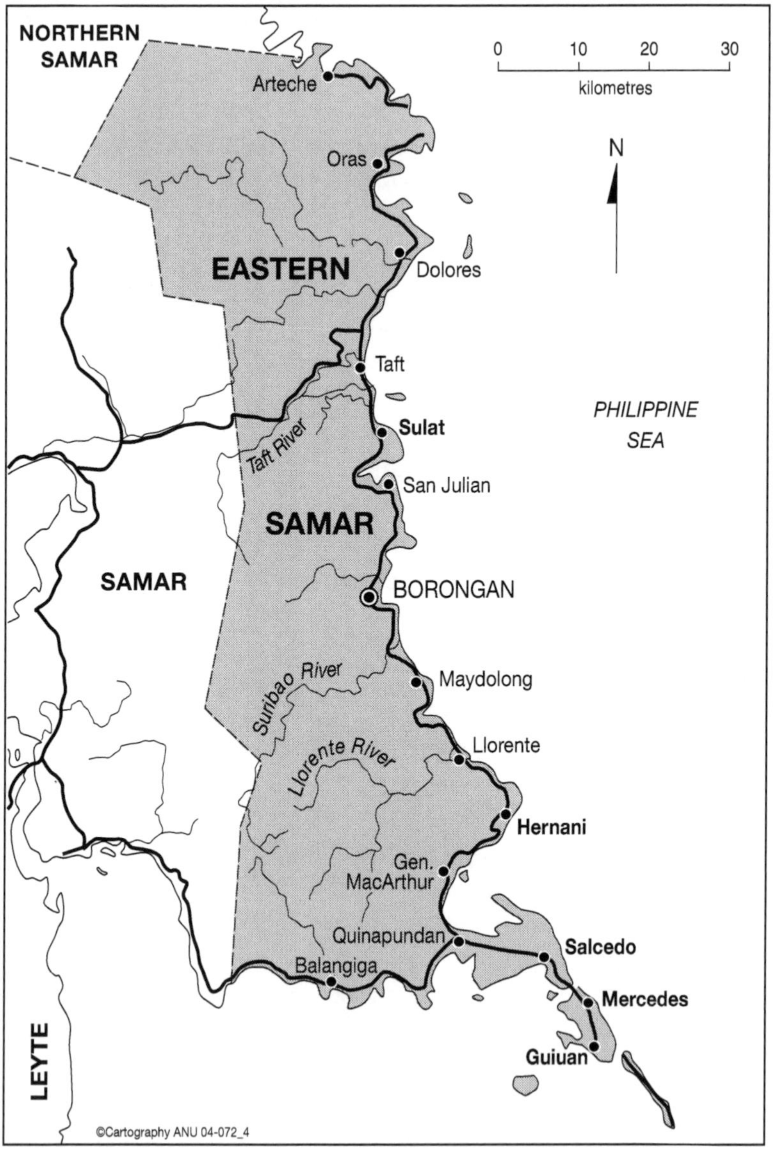

Map 7.3 Eastern Samar Province, showing Guiuan, Hernani, Mercedes, Salcedo, and Sulat.

During the campaign, Zacate (2001:1–3) criticized Baldado's lackluster performance and various anomalies under her administration and put forward a program for agricultural, fisheries, and ecotourism development anchored on "people empowerment."[51]

Baldado countered by raising the communist bogey, charging that Zacate was an NPA commander. On the night before the elections (often regarded as *ora de peligro*, the "hour of danger"), there was extensive vote buying, with certain *barangay* officials reportedly disbursing the money themselves. On election day, it was found that six hundred official ballots were missing, and Zacate's camp feared that the missing ballots would be used for *lanzadera*.[52] It was during the counting, however, that much of the fraud took place: ballot switching, misreading of ballots, doctoring of election returns, and so on. In several precincts, there were more ballots than voters and some ballots without the official seal. Zacate's campaigners believed that some teachers and certain Comelec officials were directly involved in the cheating. Baldado won by over two hundred votes.[53]

Zacate filed a protest. He hired handwriting experts from Manila. There was abundant evidence of fraud: the same handwriting on a series of ballots, fine penmanship on many ballots from areas where most residents had poor penmanship, and the use of ballpoint pens different from those officially issued. In September 1999, Zacate received unofficial word that Comelec had finished recounting and he had won the election by just one vote. In the midst of the Zacate camp's celebration, just a few hundred meters from his house, some of Baldado's followers stabbed one of his key campaigners to death. Zacate was inducted as mayor the next month.

Baldado appealed and also filed a petition for writ of certiorari,[54] questioning the execution order of the Regional Trial Court. She lost her appeal; Zacate's winning margin even increased—to 138 votes. But she won the certiorari and was reinstated as mayor in November 2000. Instead of pursuing the legal case, Zacate decided to concentrate his efforts on a rematch—the 2001 elections—only half a year away. Long before the elections, the Zacate camp prepared itself by holding several seminars (lasting several days) on poll watching, reviewing all the dirty tricks used against them in the 1998 elections, and brainstorming over ways and means of countering them.

In March 2001, just before the start of the electoral campaign, Zacate, his brother, and a cousin were arrested in Quezon City for alleged involvement in the kidnapping for ransom of a Chinese businessman in Antipolo. The arrest was all over the national media. The three were brought to a safe house and tortured. Through the intercession of some national politicians, however, they were set free a few days later. The charges were dropped. "It was a setup," Zacate remarked. "I had received warnings several days before that I would be arrested, but I did not know for what. A few hours before our arrest, a lot of people in Sulat were already being told to watch the evening news broadcast."[55] In Zacate's analysis, the attempt to implicate him in a kidnapping case was very much related to a scheme to link him with the NPA, which is known to have engaged in kidnapping for ransom in the past.

At the start of the campaign, T-shirts appeared all over Sulat with the slogan "No to KFR [kidnapping for ransom]!" Zacate's camp immediately came up with its own T-shirt—one with a cat and the slogan: "Sawa na ang pusa sa paksiw!" (The cat is fed up with *paksiw* [a dish of recooked, leftover meat]). The "No to KFR!" ploy backfired. Zacate's arrest and torture had drawn sympathy for him, and his T-shirt clicked. A catchy campaign jingle with the slogan "Javier ato!" (Javier fight!) caught on. Before Zacate's *miting de avance,* his supporters came up with a show of force—a big torchlight parade that passed through the town's main streets.[56]

On election day, Zacate's supporters were much better prepared and vigilant, thanks to the poll-watching seminars. An alert Comelec registrar discovered two identical sets of official ballots; he immediately had one set burned in front of the town plaza. On the whole, Zacate's camp managed to frustrate other attempts at cheating, except for vote buying. During the counting, Zacate received word of the presence of sixteen unidentified armed men in a certain area. He immediately alerted the Philippine Army. In light of the killing of one of his supporters the year before, Zacate had had the foresight to request the deployment of a truckload of soldiers to keep the peace. The unidentified armed men quietly withdrew.

The election was another close contest, this time with Zacate as the victor. The winning margin at the end of the election day count was more or less the same as before—over two hundred votes. This time, however, the result went unchallenged.

DARAGA, ALBAY: UP AGAINST "GUNS, GUERRILLAS, AND GOLD." The first members of Aksyon/Akbayan in Daraga, Albay, a scenic town adjacent to Legazpi City and at the foot of Mayon volcano, trace their initial exposure to the new politics to a seminar on electoral campaign management and *barangay* administration conducted by a Metro Manila-based popdem NGO, the Education for Life Foundation in 1997. One of the earliest in the Batman series, the seminar was mainly intended for candidates in the *barangay* elections, but it also drew some leaders of community organizations. After the elections, the participants, including some winning candidates, intensified PO building and endeavored to implement people's participation in governance. With Akbayan members in Daraga taking the lead, the regional organization of Akbayan for Bicol was set up in Pili, Albay, in December 1997, a few weeks before Akbayan's national founding congress.[57]

With the support of a multisectoral people's organization, Bicol Grassroots Leaders for Empowerment and Development (Biglead), and allied organizations, Akbayan topped the party-list ballot in Daraga in 1998. In the 2001 elections, Akbayan-Daraga tried to go a bit farther. Apart from campaigning once again for Akbayan in the party-list vote, it endorsed the candidacy of Marlene Magayanes for municipal councilor. Magayanes, an urban poor organizer and a leading figure of both Biglead and the local Akbayan, ran under the local Lakas-NUCD ticket headed by the incumbent mayor. With her NGO background, Magayanes stressed participatory governance and development in her platform. Before the electoral campaign, Magayanes and Akbayan-Daraga prepared themselves for contending with the *trapos'* guns, goons, and gold. In the actual campaign, however, their main tormentors turned out to be a different force: the NPA.

On the very first day of the campaign, four armed men, who identified themselves as NPA guerrillas, stopped Magayanes and some of her fellow candidates from proceeding with a campaign rally in Barangay San Vicente Pequeño. "Pay your 'permit to campaign' fee," one of the armed men demanded. The "fee" he stipulated ranged from ₱250,000 and two cell phones for the mayoral candidate to ₱10,000 for candidates for councilor. The guerrillas hit out at Akbayan, denouncing it as "pseudo-leftist" and its president, Joel Rocamora, a former ND, as "a traitor to the movement." They then told everyone to go home. Magayanes's teammates did, but she continued campaigning. A week later, a bigger NPA group, with high-powered rifles, chanced upon Magayanes and company campaigning in Barangay Bigao. Four of the armed men approached Magayanes's group and told them to disperse, saying that something untoward might happen if they did not. Once again, the NPAs let loose a tirade against Akbayan and Rocamora. They told Magayanes, "If you want to continue campaigning, you should resign from Akbayan." Magayanes and her assistant argued with them. One of the men pointed a gun at Magayanes. The guerrillas also threatened to handcuff the two women and bring them to the NPA camp. The barangay residents and Magayanes's fellow candidates became fearful for her. The crowd broke up.[58]

At a campaign rally in Barangay Anislag, the NPAs, who were in the vicinity, did not present themselves. However, they summoned one of the candidates and told him that Magayanes should not be allowed to speak. She still addressed the rally, but her fellow candidates were all nerves. After Anislag, Magayanes, yielding to the pleas of her ticket mates, did not join campaign sorties to the southern *barangays*, reputed to be NPA areas, anymore.[59]

Guerrillas from the NPA harassed Akbayan campaigners in different *barangays* in Daraga, even threatening some of them. They forbade the putting up of Akbayan posters and banners, and they ripped off or tore down those that were put up. Once they stopped a jeep, confiscated Akbayan campaign leaflets, and burned them. Fearing for their safety, Akbayan supporters stopped campaigning openly in or near NPA zones or avoided them altogether.[60] Those who dared to go into these areas sometimes had to tone down their campaigning. A group of campaigners once toured several municipalities of Albay in a hired jeep; they were playing the Akbayan jingle. When the jeep entered a certain part of the town of Manito, however, the driver switched off the loudspeaker despite their objections.

One of those whom the NPA particularly harassed was Adelia Macinas, a *barangay* councilor of Inarado. Once Macinas was called to a meeting at the house of another councilor, which was in a remote area. There two armed NPA guerrillas gave the familiar harangue against Akbayan, Rocamora, and Magayanes and demanded that Macinas resign from Akbayan. When she continued campaigning for Akbayan after the meeting, unidentified men shadowed her and her family. Right in front of Macinas and other Akbayan members, the unidentified men removed, defaced, or burned Akbayan posters that the former had posted in public places. Macinas remained uncowed. "Even if they had chopped me into bits, I would have continued," she recounted. Her defiant stance did not sit well with other *barangay* council members, who did not want trouble with the NPA, and her own husband, who feared for her. (In the 2002 *barangay* elections, the NPA campaigned heavily against Macinas and she lost her reelection bid.)[61]

While openly campaigning against Magayanes and Akbayan, the guerrillas made no bones about their being for Bayan Muna and certain local candidates identified with the NDs. Succumbing to NPA pressure, many of the local candidates, including Magayanes's ticket mates, paid the "PTC fee" and put Bayan Muna on the party-list slot in their sample ballots. Many of those who had earlier agreed to vote for Akbayan shifted to Bayan Muna.[62]

Magayanes still came in third among the eight winning candidates for councilor. Bayan Muna was first in the party-list vote in Daraga; Akbayan was a poor second.

The focus on Akbayan's engagement in local governance

LOS BAÑOS, LAGUNA: ENGAGEMENT IN "BARANGAY" AND MUNICIPAL GOVERNANCE. Neither Aksyon/Akbayan nor any of the political blocs aligned with it were involved in the initial grassroots organizing in Los Baños, Laguna, a town sixty-three kilometers south of Metro Manila and a center for scientific research. In 1995–98, the Evelio B. Javier Foundation, a development NGO, undertook a project in Los Baños called "Promoting Local Initiatives for Democracy and Justice" (Prodem), with funding from USAID, to enhance the capability of LGUs and facilitate citizen participation in local governance. Prodem workers helped build POs and eventually a coalition of seventy-nine local POs/NGOs called Ugnayan ng mga Samahang Pamayanan ng Los Baños (Ugnayan-LB) or Coordinating Council of Community Organizations of Los Baños. They also propagated

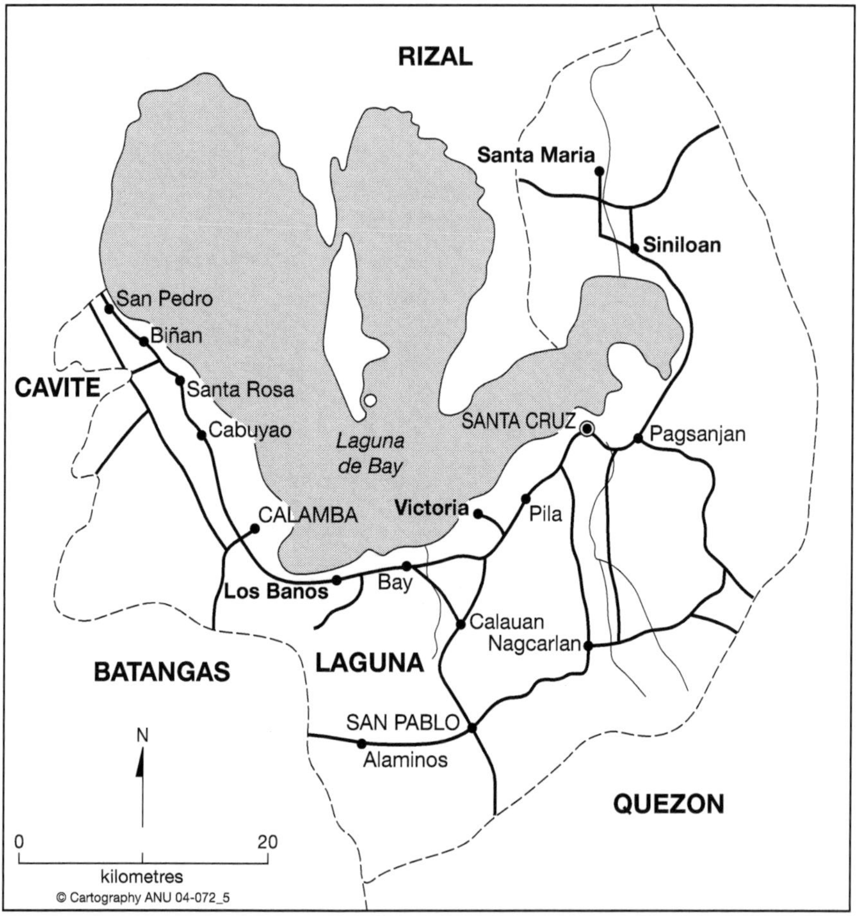

Map 7.4 Laguna Province, showing Los Baños and Victoria

participatory development planning. In 1997, the Los Baños LGU and Ugnayan-LB collaborated in drawing up the town's twenty-five-year comprehensive development plan—"a milestone in LGU-NGO/PO relations" (Martinez 2001:15–18). The Metro Manila-based, Aksyon-linked Institute of Politics and Governance (IPG) helped Prodem workers train local officials and residents to do community-based development planning. In the process, some Prodem workers, *barangay* officials and leaders and members of Ugnayan-LB and its affiliate POs/NGOs joined Aksyon. After the Prodem project finished, IPG helped to establish the People's Institute for Local Governance Advocacy and Research (Pilar) to continue assisting local government officials and residents in capability building and promoting participatory governance in Los Baños and to extend similar services to other municipalities in Laguna.[63]

Unlike its predecessor, Prodem, which had assisted in LGU capability building at the municipal level, Pilar, the Los Baños-based NGO aligned with Aksyon / Akbayan, focused on capability building at the *barangay* level. Soon after it was established in July 1999, Pilar undertook BOBG and BDP-PRA trainings and PO building in three pilot areas (one *barangay* each in Los Baños, Bae, and San Pedro). Pilar signed memorandums of agreement with *barangay* LGUs whereby the former would facilitate development planning activities and the latter would mobilize the various sectors of the community. From the pilot *barangay* of Tadlac, Pilar extended its trainings and organizing work to the thirteen other *barangays* of Los Baños.[64] The emphasis in Pilar's organizing efforts per *barangay* depended on the particular characteristics of the *barangay*. In lakeside Tadlac, the focus was on women and fisherfolk; in Bagong Silang, atop Mount Makiling, it was on farmers, women, and youth. Alongside Pilar's efforts in PO building, Akbayan organized party chapters in BDP-PRA areas.[65]

The *barangay* captain of Tadlac illustrated just how much of a difference a participatory process of development planning had made. "In the past," he recalled, "only the *barangay* captain and the *barangay* council were involved in making the *barangay* development plan. We were told before that 90 percent of Tadlac's [adult] residents were fisherfolk. Our old plan was based on that. BDP-PRA showed that the percentage was much lower: 42 percent!"[66]

For the upland farmers of Bagong Silang, BDP-PRA proved crucial to the very survival of their community. The University of the Philippines, which managed the Makiling Forest Reserve, had formulated a twenty-five-year master plan for the conservation of Mount Makiling without involving them in the planning process. They feared that an accreditation process for determining "legitimate" forest occupants stipulated in the plan could lead to undue demolitions and resettlements, especially in areas deemed critical. The *barangay* officials and residents of Bagong Silang seized on the opportunity provided by the BDP-PRA process to fight for their inclusion in the management of the Makiling Forest Reserve and in the control of its resources and to show their ability to draw up concrete measures for protecting the forest through sustainable resource use (Castillo 2004:117–40).

Of the local officials, one who was very supportive of Prodem's and Pilar's initiatives was Caesar P. Perez, *barangay* captain of Batong Malake. Under twelve years of Perez's leadership, Batong Malake had become a bustling and commercially successful *barangay*.[67] Well respected by his peers, Perez had been elected president of the *barangay* captains of Los Baños and then of the entire province. In the course of working closely with Prodem and Pilar, Perez came into contact with members of Akbayan who were involved in these NGOs. He joined Akbayan in late 2000. In the 2001 elections, Akbayan endorsed Perez for mayor and Matilde Erasga, a local leader of the women's movement and Akbayan member, for municipal councilor. Both ran under the PPC banner and campaigned for Akbayan in the party-list vote. During the campaign, Perez's supporters stressed his performance in public office. Various irregularities marred the elections: tampering with voter lists, which resulted in many "flying voters," as well as disenfranchised residents; and vote buying. Nonetheless, Perez, who was popular among both the middle class and the masses, and who played it clean, won by a wide margin over the incumbent mayor and vice mayor. Akbayan topped the party-list vote in Los Baños, as it had in 1998. Erasga, however, lost.[68]

As mayor, Perez has remained an "action man."[69] He has provided loans for new businesses and established a public employment service for residents looking for jobs.[70] A columnist in a national newspaper (Adriano 2003) praised Perez for "localizing good governance," crediting his administration for upgrading the quality of elementary and high school education, as well as of the health service; improving traffic flow; and maintaining peace and order through such measures as better street lighting, a campaign against drug traffickers, and improved police visibility and capability. He also complimented Los Baños for having the cleanest roads and public markets in Laguna, apparently the result of the municipal LGU's novel antilittering drive, which involved deputizing "environmental enforcers." Building on the success of this campaign, the municipal LGU, in coordination with other government agencies and POs/NGOs, drew up a municipal waste management and waste segregation plan and an environment management system, including the cleanup of creeks and tributaries (Perez, Faylon, Pantua, and Valdez 2002). Through frequent visits to *barangays* and consultations with *barangay* leaders, such as Ugnayan sa Barangay (Linking with the Barangay), Perez has kept in close touch with his constituency. In 2000, President Estrada proclaimed Los Baños, which is said to have the most holders of doctorates per square kilometer in the country, a "science and nature city." Perez has drawn up major programs to develop the municipality, including the establishment of a "one-stop-shop science and technology center."[71]

After Perez's victory, Pilar continued to implement BDP-PRA and Akbayan to build a political party base in the *barangays*. By November 2002, nine out of Los Baños's fourteen *barangays* had finished their five-year development plans, each consisting of a thick volume with illustrations and graphs. After BDP-PRA, Pilar conducted other trainings on such topics as gender and development and organized *barangay* enterprise development planning seminars. Perez sought the assistance of Pilar in drawing up a five-year municipal development plan, which would basically adhere to the twenty-five-year development plant formulated with Prodem's assistance but identify clearer short-term targets.[72] Although a few Akbayan members who were also in Pilar were regularly in touch with Perez and some Akbayan-linked POs/NGOs participated actively in the municipality's local special bodies, Akbayan-Los Baños itself still had not really gotten into the thick of municipal governance. In running the municipal LGU, Perez basically worked with his own team without much assistance from Akbayan or PPC. With Akbayan and Batman NGOs scaling up from *barangay* to municipal governance in various parts of the country, Akbayan-Los Baños resolved to engage more fully in municipal politics, as well as to undertake organizing in academe, in church circles, and among professionals.[73]

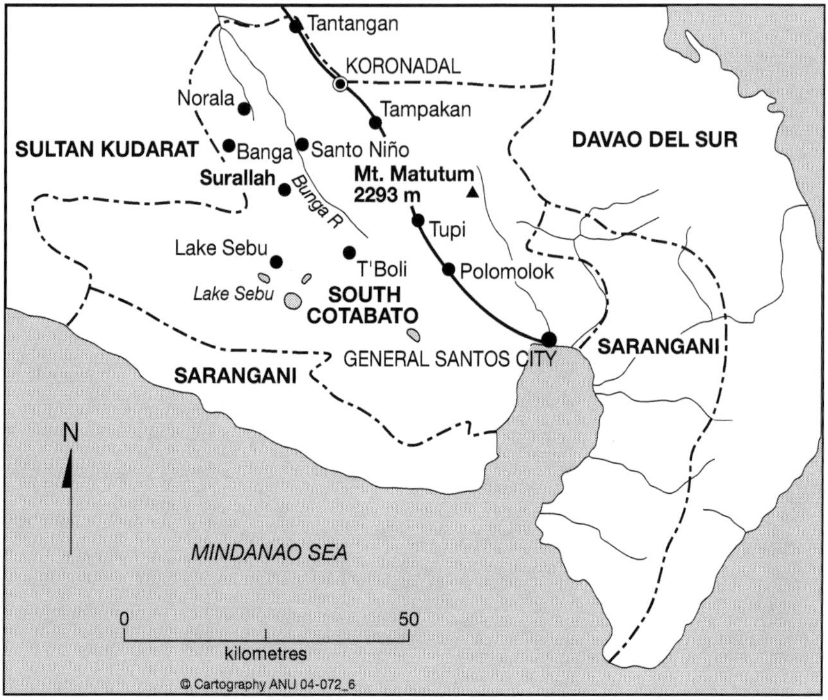

Map 7.5 South Cotabato Province, showing Surallah

SURALLAH, SOUTH COTABATO: ASSISTING A MUNICIPAL LGU IN PARTICIPATORY GOVERNANCE. Whereas Akbayan's engagement in local governance in Los Baños had proceeded from the *barangay* to the municipal level, it was the reverse in Surallah, South Cotabato.

In the Akbayan founding congress of January 1998, one of the delegates from South Cotabato was Romulo O. Solivio of Surallah,[74] a fast-developing agricultural town that aspired to become the province's agro-industrial center. A mechanical engineer and rice mill owner, Solivio had been involved in the ND movement during the Marcos period. After EDSA I, he turned to local politics. He was elected municipal councilor in 1988 and ran unsuccessfully for mayor in 1992 and 1995. Akbayan supported Solivio in his third mayoral bid in 1998. Running under NPC, he was elected, together with his running mate and five of the eight candidates for councilor on his ticket.[75]

In February 1999, Solivio learned about participatory *barangay* development planning through a SIAD conference sponsored by Kaisahan and several other Batman NGOs (Iszatt 2002:5). A few months later, the Surallah LGU launched the Barangay Integrated Area Development Program (BIADP), which aimed "to develop and strengthen the communities and institutions through a process which encourages local initiatives and active participation of the people in carrying out development activities." Solivio's "flagship program" sought to make Surallah's seventeen *barangays* "the center-piece of development." Among BIADP's major features were BDP-PRA, resource mobilization for *barangay* development, and integrated delivery of services to the *barangays*.

Kaisahan and Building Alternative Rural Resource Institutions and Organizing Services (Barrios), a newly established local NGO based in General Santos City, assisted the Surallah LGU in conducting BDP-PRA in all of the municipality's seventeen *barangays* in June-September 1999. The one-week planning process in each *barangay* involved *barangay* and *purok*[76] officials and representatives of sectoral groups and ended with the five-year development plan being presented to a *barangay* general assembly for approval. Six months later, as a follow-up to BDP-PRA, Kaisahan and Barrios facilitated a visit of Surallah municipal and *barangay* officials to Toboso, Negros Occidental, and Alimodian, Iloilo, two early BDP-PRA areas, for on-site learning from the latter's experiences in participatory local governance. Furthermore, to help the *barangays* raise funds for their development projects, the two NGOs, in coordination with municipal LGU staff, conducted a three-day training seminar on project proposal making.[77]

In April 2000, Surallah organized an innovative resource mobilization program called the "Participatory Barangay Development and Local Governance Fair 2000." Nina T. Iszatt (2002:9) has described the event.

> [E]ach barangay set up its own booth in the municipal plaza, creatively decorated to display its five-year development plan, mission-vision of the barangay, project proposals, visual aids such as the Resource Map, which had been made during the planning, and local produce. Potential funders including Congressional Representatives, Provincial and Regional national line agency officials and NGOs,

> wandered around inspecting the hard work of the barangay residents, meeting with them and pledging to finance their projects. In a fiesta-style atmosphere, the barangay residents and officials had the opportunity to "talk to higher officials" in order to market their project proposals. At the end of a tiring day a total of ₱67,370,500 worth of pledges was announced.[78]

Another Solivio novelty, "Barangayan 2000," billed as "an integrated delivery of various services of the LGU to the *barangays*," also had a festive air. Municipal officials and personnel from the different departments of the LGU trooped into a *barangay* to deliver services to the people—staying there for three days and two nights. An LGU official recalled:

> Practically the entire LGU joined the *barangay* visit and practically the entire *barangay* came to meet us. We integrated with the people. We explained to them what the municipal government was doing. We discussed with them. We gave free medical and dental services, free toilet bowls, free seedlings, free iodized salt, free branding of carabaos and horses, free birth registrations, even free weddings. There was food for everyone. Since not all of us could be accommodated in the people's houses, some of us just slept on the stage of the plaza grandstand, on benches, tables, anywhere.[79]

On the basis of his performance, Solivio thought that his reelection in 2001 was assured. "Surveys showed that he would win," remarked a municipal councilor. "He lowered his guard."[80] Solivio's opponent capitalized on an increase in stall rental fees at the newly reconstructed public market, which had incensed many local traders, and on alleged irregularities in LGU dealings with a certain contractor.[81] Regular LGU personnel, who had suffered "culture shock"[82] over the demands and hectic pace of Solivio's participatory, grassroots-focused politics and who found Solivio "too strict," campaigned against him. As in the past, massive vote buying and some intimidation of voters marred the elections. Solivio lost by just 589 votes (out of 23,000 votes cast). Although he came out ahead in twelve of the fifteen rural *barangays*, he fared terribly in the vote-rich *poblacion* (town center).[83]

Throughout Solivio's term as mayor of Surallah, Akbayan's engagement in both municipal and *barangay* governance was at best incidental. The Akbayan organization in Surallah itself was weak, loose, and unconsolidated. Many of the NGO trainers and facilitators who assisted in BIADP were Akbayan members, but they themselves did not engage in Akbayan organizing in Surallah. They had presumed that Solivio and some former NDs working closely with him would take care of this. Unfortunately, the latter did not formally sign up with Akbayan.[84] Several leftist parties and groups competing in the party-list vote—Akbayan, AMIN, Sanlakas, and in 2001 also Bayan Muna—had solicited Solivio's support. Fully aware that much of Surallah was part of CPP-NPA guerrilla territory and not wanting to be dragged into conflict between the reaffirmists and the rejectionists, Solivio and his associates opted to take a neutral stance.[85] During the 2001 electoral campaign, tensions between the ND and other leftist groups heated up. Guerrillas of the NPA harassed Akbayan campaigners in various parts of Surallah. Bayan Muna members tried to increase their influence in Solivio's campaign machinery. Reacting to anti-Akbayan statements made by one of Solivio's associates, some Akbayan members freshly recruited by Akbayan organizers from Koronadal campaigned for Solivio's opponent.[86]

Apart from the serious weaknesses in party building, there were also shortcomings in community organizing. For all its creditable innovations in participatory governance, BIADP was still basically a top-down project. It lacked a crucial element: grassroots POs making their own initiatives and interacting with the municipal and *barangay* LGUs. Akbayan and the Batman NGOs involved in Surallah had apparently overlooked this. The municipal LGU could not possibly have been expected to take on the function of building POs.

SALCEDO, EASTERN SAMAR: ENGAGEMENT IN MUNICIPAL GOVERNANCE WITHOUT BDP-PRA. Akbayan took the traditional "civil society route"—combining party organizing with PO/NGO work—in expanding to several municipalities in southeastern Samar, the lower half of Eastern Samar, one of the most impoverished and neglected provinces in the central Philippines. Starting in the mid-1990s, some former ND activists, who were in touch with NGO-based Akbayan members in Manila and Tacloban, Leyte, organized *barangay* health workers and women's health associations in the municipalities of General MacArthur, Salcedo, and Mercedes for a government project on traditional medicine funded by the United

Nations Development Programme (UNDP). In the middle of the 1998 electoral campaign, the ex-NDs decided to join Akbayan, and they campaigned for it in the party-list vote and for some progressive candidates in the local elections. Immediately after the elections, some of the personnel of the traditional medicine project, which had just ended, set up Pneuma, Inc., to continue the organizing work and trainings. From a health NGO, Pneuma evolved into an NGO promoting "popular empowerment and development" and moved into other concerns, including local governance, agrarian reform, rural development, and environmental protection. With the assistance of the Pneuma staff, Akbayan later expanded to the nearby municipalities of Guiuan, Hernani, Quinapondan, Balangiga and Llorente, all in southeastern Samar, but this time by combining party building with both PO/NGO and LGU work.[87]

In the fifth-class municipality of Salcedo, one of the local candidates whom Akbayan supported in the 1998 elections was an Akbayan member, but she ran under a coalition of traditional politicians. Midwife, community organizer, and Akbayan member Mardonia Duran ran for municipal councilor on the ticket of Vice Mayor Melchor "Mega" Gagante (Lakas-NUCD), who challenged Mayor Alfredo Sumook for Salcedo's top post. In elections tarnished by heavy vote buying, Gagante, a semiretired businessman who wanted to devote the rest of his active life to public service in his hometown, lost by just fifty-two votes.[88] However, Duran, a scion of a well-respected family in Salcedo, won comfortably. Although five of the eight councilors-elect were on Gagante's ticket, two defected to Sumook's camp soon after the elections.

The opposition councilors tried to push for development-oriented legislation but got nowhere. The Dazo-Sumook clan had dominated local politics in Salcedo since the Marcos era (see Macale 2001:3). Blighted by years of mismanagement and corruption under more than twenty years of this dynastic rule, Salcedo had become a rural backwater. Mayor Sumook had no development plan[89] and, although Salcedo had much unutilized land suitable for rice production, had no interest in agriculture at all. He assigned the municipal agriculturist to clean markets and to plant trees and cut grass in the watershed area.[90]

Despite the frustrations of working in the *trapo*-dominated municipal government, Duran persisted in trying to change local politics. She worked together with Pneuma personnel in organizing Akbayan chapters in Salcedo. Among those whom they managed to recruit was Joselito Abrugar, a three-term councilor who had been an activist in his student days.[91]

In the Sumook-Gagante rematch in 2001, Akbayan supported Gagante, who ran again under Lakas-NUCD. Running on a platform of good governance and reform,[92] he had agreed to promote people's participation in governance and to support Akbayan in the party-list ballot.[93] In another election marred by vote buying, Gagante won by 426 votes and Duran was reelected, but pro-Sumook councilors retained the majority in the municipal council. Abrugar agreed to become the mayor's private secretary.[94] After the elections, two Akbayan national officials conferred with five mayors-elect of Eastern Samar, including Gagante. Akbayan continued to organize party chapters in Salcedo; two of the new Akbayan recruits were Gagante himself and a young councilor, Esteban Regis, Jr., a former student activist like Abrugar.[95]

With the able help of Abrugar, Duran, and Regis and of Pneuma, Mayor Gagante was able to achieve much in his first year. To increase food production, his administration set up demonstration farms in different *barangays*, acquired modern farm equipment (to be hired out to farmers), repaired long-neglected farm to market roads, strengthened livelihood cooperatives, and developed links with agricultural institutions. Health services were improved through such measures as *barangay* clinics (one *barangay* per week) and the installation of potable water supplies in key *barangays*. To upgrade education, the LGU opened another rural high school, subsidized volunteer teachers, built additional classrooms, and ensured the granting of LGU scholarships on the basis of merit. For environmental protection, the Gagante administration intensified the rehabilitation of a watershed area and a crackdown on illegal fishing. For transparency and public accountability, the LGU put out a newsletter, *Abot-Kamay*, and the treasurer's and accountant's office published the monthly collections (Abrugar 2002:14–16). Gagante was very much open and willing to undertake BDP-PRA in Salcedo. Unfortunately, neither he nor the cash-strapped Pneuma, based in Guiuan, could find funding for it.[96]

Salcedo nonetheless adopted a more modest version of Surallah's "Barangayan," which the municipal government referred to as "visitation." I had the chance join a visitation of Gagante and LGU personnel to the farthest *barangay*, Matarinao, in June 2002. We left early in the morning. The LGU staffers rode on the back of a truck; I rode with the mayor and the municipal health officer (a medical doctor) in an old four-wheel drive vehicle. Soon enough, I realized that an ordinary vehicle would not have made it—the road was in terrible shape. The *barangay* officials and residents welcomed us at the plaza. In a short program, Gagante explained the development thrusts and projects of his administration and heads of departments discussed the functions of their departments. During the open forum, the residents brought up various problems in their locality: lack of jobs, delayed electrification, illegal fishing, lack of health facilities, poor communications, and so on. At noon, we had a hearty—though not sumptuous—meal. Throughout the day, LGU personnel took care of various services and concerns—medical and dental checkups and giving out free medicines, issuance of residence certificates, collection of business and real property taxes, distribution of vegetable seeds, and so on. We traveled back to the municipal hall in the late afternoon. I noticed that the doctor was exhausted after attending to a stream of patients.

Inspired by the national Akbayan conference of LGU officials in December 2002, Akbayan LGU officials in southeastern Samar held their own subprovincial consultations, and those of Salcedo took an active part.[97] By October 2003, Akbayan had twelve barangay-based chapters in Salcedo. Akbayan-Salcedo had not yet made much progress in recruiting *barangay* officials, but it had made some allies among them. While continuing to explore possible funding sources for BDP-PRA, Pneuma facilitated the participation of Salcedo's municipal planning and development coordinator in BDP-PRA sessions in a nearby municipality. He came away impressed. As in Surallah, PO building remained weak in Salcedo, as neither Akbayan nor Pneuma had the resources to deploy a good community organizer.[98]

BARIRA, BULDON, AND MATANOG, MAGUINDANAO: ENGAGEMENT IN INTER-LGU DEVELOPMENT COOPERATION. The Muslim municipalities of Barira, Buldon, and Matanog in Maguindanao Province are inhabited mainly by the Iranun people.[99] Much of the area of the three municipalities had constituted the famed Camp Abubakar, the main camp of the Moro Islamic Liberation Front (MILF) in the 1980s and 1990s. Because of government neglect, corruption, and the war, Barira, Buldon, and Matanog had remained very backward. They all

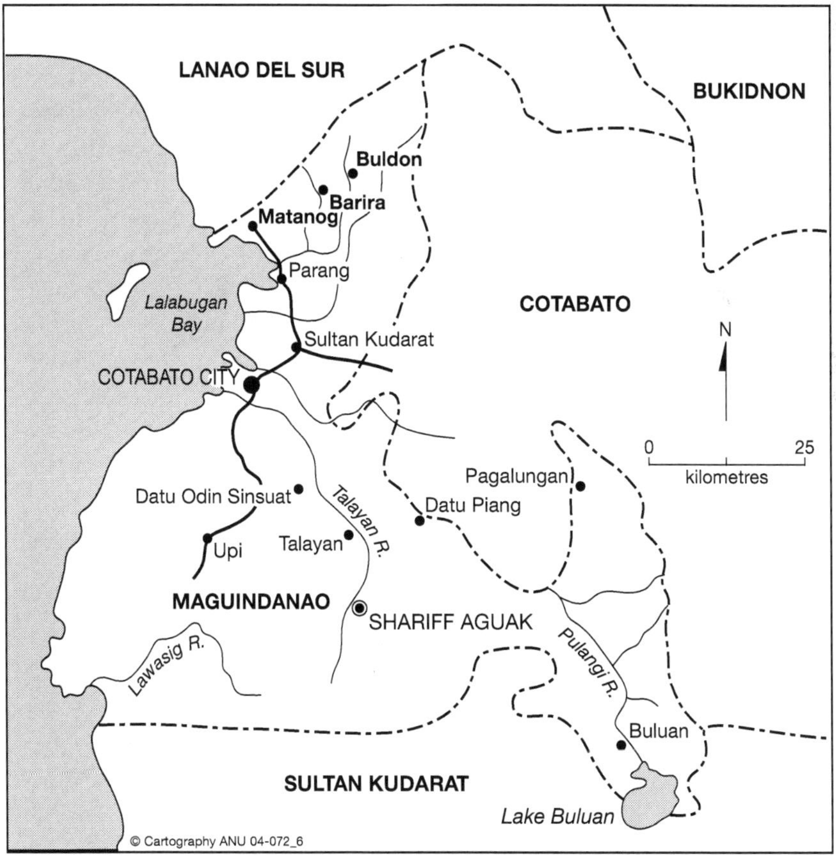

Map 7.6 Maguindanao Province, showing Cotabato City, Barira, Buldon, and Matanog.

(Note: At the time the study was conducted, Maguindanao province had not yet been divided into two provinces: Maguindanao and Shariff Kabunsuan.)

belonged to the sixth-class category—municipalities with the lowest income in the entire country. Since the Marcos period, the LGUs of the three towns had frequently held office in Cotabato City or Parang, that is, wherever the mayor actually lived or spent most of his time. The municipal halls in Buldon and Matanog had often been quiet and nearly empty, with goats peacefully grazing in the yard. On paper, the construction of the municipal building of Barira was supposed to have been finished a long time ago. "Whoever made the report must have taken the photo of another building," quipped an Akbayan organizer.[100]

Akbayan's involvement in Barira, Buldon, and Matanog can be traced to the mid-1990s, when a former CPP-NPA cadre, Roy Delima, then working for a UNDP-funded development project, employed "clan-based organizing," which he had learned in his CPP days, in helping build "agrarian reform communities" (ARCs) in the area. After establishing and developing ties with local MNLF leaders and the Sultan Kudarat Descendants Organization of the Philippines (SKDOP), Delima managed to form a core group consisting of three former MNLF commanders and a *datu* (tribal chief). The group drew entire clans into the ARC project. From the MNLF and SKDOP networks, the group expanded to the MILF mass base, again mainly through bloodlines. When Delima, a rejectionist, joined Aksyon in 1996, he convinced the clans in the ARC project to go with him. They continued with clan-based organizing, this time for Aksyon/Akbayan. The MNLF and the MILF did not mind Akbayan recruiting members from their mass bases. As far they were concerned, there was no conflict of interest—they were armed liberation movements, Akbayan was an electoral party that recognized the right of the Moro people to self-determination.[101]

In the May 2001 elections, Akbayan endorsed the reelection bids of Abolais Manalao (Lakas-NUCD) and Nasser Imam (Kampi),[102] the youthful and progressive mayors of Buldon and Matanog, who in turn supported Akbayan in the party-list vote. Both won. After the elections, Manalao, Imam, and Barira's young, new mayor Alexander Tomawis (KAMPI)—all good friends—often went around together and exchanged notes on their LGU work. In the elections for the legislative assembly of the ARMM in November 2001, the three supported the candidacy of another young, reform-oriented Iranun, Ibrahim Ibay. Also active in Ibay's campaign was the Cotabato City-based lawyer Suharto Ambolodto, executive director of the Institute for Strategic Initiatives (ISI) and the national vice chairperson of Akbayan.[103]

Shortly after Ibay's electoral victory, the three mayors, Ambolodto, assemblyman-elect Ibay, and Maguindanao Provincial Board member Cahar Ibay held a series of meetings to discuss the coordination of their development initiatives. The Iranun LGU officials sensed that they stood a good chance of mobilizing considerable support for their rehabilitation and development endeavors. International and national donor agencies would be only too willing to help the communities in the former Camp Abubakar. Moreover, the Local Government Code encourages LGUs, through appropriate ordinances, to "group themselves, consolidate or coordinate their efforts, sources, and resources for purposes commonly beneficial to them" (Oversight Committee, Philippine Congress 1992:39). They agreed to set up the Iranun Development Council (IDC) as the main vehicle for inter-LGU cooperation, with the Akbayan-aligned ISI, based in Cotabato City, providing support services and acting as its secretariat (Institute for Strategic Initiatives 2002:2).

Without drawing attention to itself, Akbayan became very much involved in the efforts of the LGUs of Barira, Buldon, and Matanog and helped to coordinate their rehabilitation and development plans. Through Ambolodto and the ISI personnel, who were party members, Akbayan played an active role in the IDC's strategic planning, as well as day-to-day administration. Akbayan's involvement in the IDC marked its first engagement in intermunicipal LGU development cooperation.

A week after its formation, the IDC secured the support of President Arroyo and members of her Cabinet, who were then holding a meeting in Cotabato City. In the subsequent months, various forms of support from government agencies did pour in—construction or repair of farm to market roads, access roads, and bridges; new municipal buildings and facilities; day care centers and more shelter units; agricultural implements and plant materials; medicines; and so on. While the development assistance was already coming in, the

IDC, in coordination with ISI, IPG, and government agencies (particularly the Department of Agriculture, the National Anti-poverty Commission, and the Department of Social Welfare and Development), continued to hold development planning meetings to identify needs, gaps, and possible interventions.[104] In July 2002, President Arroyo herself visited the former Camp Abubakar area, declaring it a "peace and development zone" and assuring the local officials that she would extend all her support to the IDC (*Manila Times* 2002).

On the recommendation of ISI, the IDC adopted SIAD as its development framework. In its plan, the IDC envisaged a rehabilitation and reconstruction phase of six to twelve months, followed by the SIAD proper (five years). The SIAD phase would involve the development of the 79,000-hectare area of Buldon, Matanog, and Barira into a progressive agricultural center planted to corn, cash crops, and fruit trees and engaged in integrated sustainable agricultural production. To prepare the LGUs for the SIAD phase, ISI, with funding from the Asia Foundation and USAID, has facilitated local governance capacity-building activities such as basic local governance and BDP-PRA trainings among municipal and *barangay* officials, religious leaders, peasants, women, youth, and LGU personnel. The IDC and ISI hope that the development plans of the thirty-four *barangays* in the area will eventually be integrated into the medium-term development plans of the three municipalities. To complement its engagement with the LGUs, ISI intends to engage in community organizing and thus help build self-sustaining rural organizations and cooperatives (Institute for Strategic Initiatives and Institute of Politics and Governance 2002:52).

As of October 2003, the IDC's performance looked quite impressive. According to Ambolodto, the IDC had managed to attract rehabilitation and development assistance worth a total of ₱240 million since its inception. About 60 percent of the *barangays* had completed the BDP-PRA process. Apart from attracting government support, the IDC had managed to secure the MILF's endorsement through the Bangsa Moro Development Agency, which the government and the MILF had jointly established. Nonetheless, Ambolodto sounded not too content. "Much of the development assistance went into infrastructure. Thus far, the projects have not yet had much impact on poverty alleviation. Perhaps we should have had more of livelihood projects at the start."[105] Despite the IDC's efforts to make the Iranun area a zone of peace and development, it still proved powerless to prevent armed hostilities between political clans in Matanog. In 2002, a series of ambushes and other violent incidents between the feuding Imam and Macapeges clans of Matanog resulted in several fatalities (see *Mindanao Cross* 2002; and Maitem 2002).[106]

Among the LGU officials of Buldon, Matanog, and Barira, Akbayan earned much respect. The three mayors and several other local officials joined Akbayan but were all expected to run under Arroyo's coalition in May 2004. With many of local Akbayan leaders devoting much of their attention to the IDC, however, the organizing of Akbayan chapters at the *barangay* level suffered somewhat.[107]

The focus on Akbayan's engagement in civil society

DAVAO CITY AND COTABATO CITY: REGIONAL CENTERS FOR MASS MOVEMENT AND DEVELOPMENT WORK. Davao City is Mindanao's biggest city and Southern Mindanao's regional capital; Cotabato City is the seat of the Autonomous Region of Muslim Mindanao (ARMM). For Akbayan, Davao City and Cotabato City are not only important centers of the mass movement but also vital regional hubs for its development initiatives.

Davao City has long been a hive of political activism. In the late 1960s and early 1970s, it was the scene of many rallies and marches on land-related issues, as well as on "imperialism, feudalism, and bureaucrat capitalism." During the Marcos era, it became a hotbed of political and armed resistance against the dictatorship. In 1984–85, protesters led by the radical Left—the NDs—paralyzed the entire city several times with *welgang bayan* (a form of general strike). Since the fall of Marcos, the NDs have been weakened in Davao City, but with the CPP-NPA managing to maintain guerrilla zones in the city's rugged hinterland, the NDs continue to be the main leftist force in the city as a whole.[108] Other leftist parties and groups, such as Akbayan, Sanlakas, Partido ng Manggagawa, Alab Katipunan, and POs/NGOs aligned with them, however, have remained active, especially in the *poblacion* and the coastal parts of city.

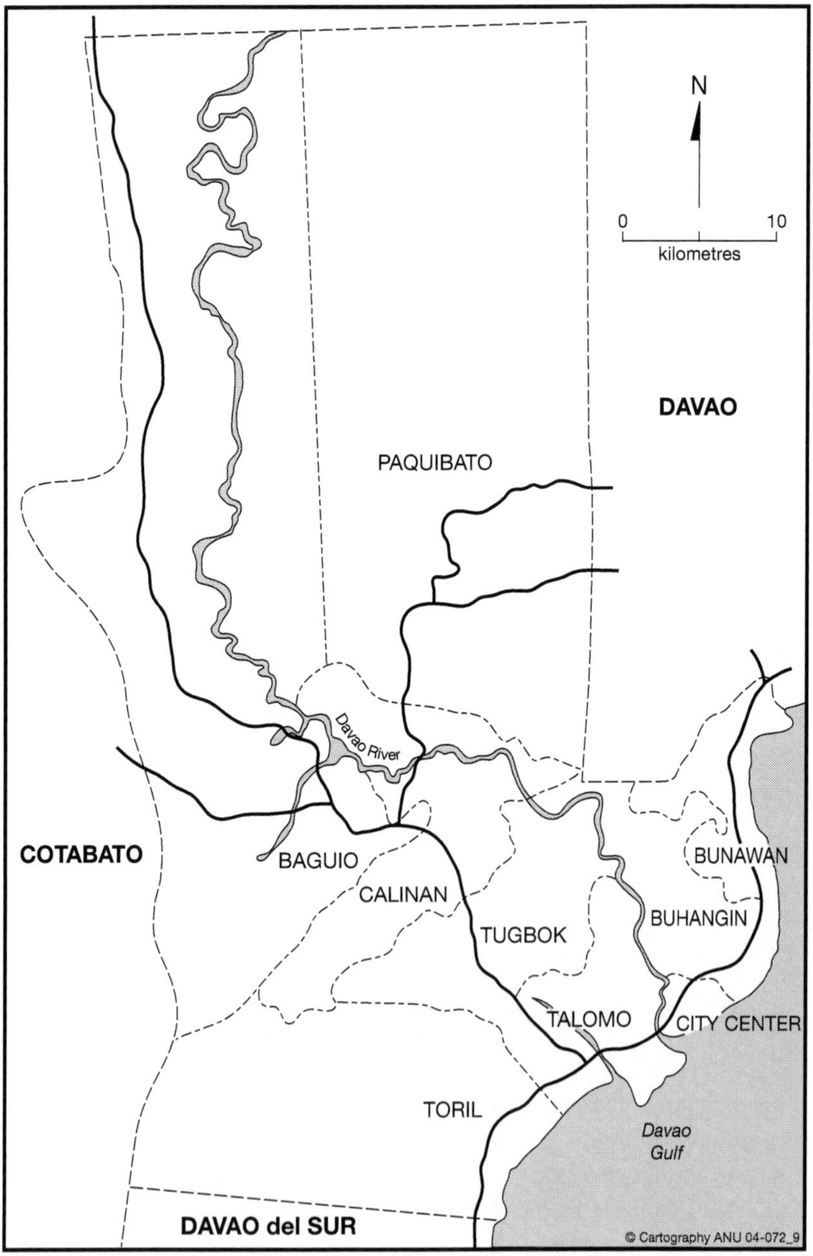

Map 7.7 Davao City, showing its districts.

Akbayan, in particular, appears to have made significant strides in PO building as well as party recruitment among workers, the urban poor, and students. Akbayan and its allied POs/NGOs, often in coordination with other groups of the "democratic Left", have launched mass protest or advocacy actions in the city over a wide range of national and local issues—the war in Mindanao, workers' rights, oil price hikes, land reform, debt, indigenous peoples' issues, human rights, environment, and so on. In annual Labor Day rallies in Davao, Akbayan-linked workers' organizations, particularly those in the local APL and CIU networks, now grouped under the Workers' Council of Davao City, have conducted large mobilizations, outstripping those of the KMU.[109] Akbayan-aligned NGOs based in Davao City serve as regional centers for development work. Until 2003, the PADC, established in 1999, covered the four Davao provinces and Davao City itself.[110] The SIAD Initiatives in Mindanao—Convergence for Agrarian Reform and Regional Development (SIM-CARRD), established in 2001, now serves as a coordinating center for SIAD and other development initiatives in Mindanao and as the secretariat of the Batman Consortium there.[111] Sectoral POs/NGOs aligned with Akbayan, engaged in both contentious politics and development work, such as the labor NGO Learn and the peasant federation Pakisama, also have regional offices in Davao City. Akbayan members in Davao City are also active in the regional formations of such broad alliances of leftist and progressive groups as the FDC and the Gathering for Peace.[112] Akbayan-linked POs/NGOs work closely with Akbayan national council member Peter Laviña, a former newsman who was elected a Davao City councilor in 2001 and reelected in 2004.

In the late 1990s, Akbayan established a strong presence in Cotabato City, with an extensive network of allied organizations (Christian and Muslim) in the urban poor and student sectors. As in Davao City, the local Akbayan organization and its allied POs/NGOs in Cotabato City were very active in mass actions and campaigns on national and local issues. Of particular concern was the issue of the war in Mindanao. Because it is only fifty kilometers away from Camp Abubakar, the MILF's national headquarters, Cotabato City was sure to be greatly affected by the war. Akbayan and its allied

POs/NGOs joined human rights, church, Islamic, and other groups in opposing the government's hard-line position toward the Muslim rebel movements and in undertaking various peace initiatives. When Estrada declared an all-out war against the MILF, a broad coalition of groups, including Akbayan, staged large protest actions in Cotabato City. To assist thirteen thousand families displaced by the war, Akbayan launched a relief and rehabilitation campaign and was one of the few groups that managed to reach far-flung areas.[113] Shortly after the 2001 elections, Akbayan-Cotabato City suffered a serious setback when one of its influential local leaders, Noel Pelonco, a legal consultant for the urban poor who had been elected a city councilor in 1998 and 2001, ceased to be active in the party, and many of his supporters followed suit.[114] With its base in the urban poor communities greatly weakened, Akbayan has not been as active in pressure politics as before. The NGOs linked with it, however, have persisted in their development work, notably the ISI, which, as mentioned earlier, extends support services to development initiatives in the former Camp Abubakar area, and Solidarity for Peace, Empowerment and Equity-Led Development (Speed), which provides trainings on community organizing and democratic participation in governance in different areas in the provinces of Maguindanao, North Cotabato, and Sultan Kudarat.[115]

Building the Municipal/City Party Organization

A strong party organization is crucial if Akbayan is to pursue all its engagements in a wide variety of spheres—contentious politics, development work, elections, governance, popular political education, and so on. At the local level, party units are organized as chapters (with a minimum of twelve members) at the *barangay* level; sections (at least six chapters) at the municipal / city level; and divisions (at least three sections) at the provincial, highly-urbanized city or legislative district level (Akbayan National Congress 1998e:3). Building the party organization, however, has not gone smoothly. To attend to its myriad tasks, Akbayan has only a few full-time personnel. Most Akbayan members have their own jobs or sources of income to attend to. And whether they are full time, part time, or spare time, Akbayan activists have their personal lives to live too. Party members have found it difficult to combine party building with Akbayan's other engagements. In many areas, Akbayan members, too caught up in their particular lines of work, have at times not devoted enough attention to party building.

For Akbayan members working at the local level, the months leading up to the Akbayan congress in January 2001 and then the months leading up to the May 2001 elections were very hectic. In the precongress period, local Akbayan members were involved in their usual engagements in participatory governance, development work, and mass actions. Aside from this, however, they also intensified their efforts in party recruitment, conducting basic orientation seminars and organizational meetings, and they built party chapters, sections, and divisions. Since the number of party units determined the number of delegates to the party congress, local Akbayan activists tried to recruit as many as possible. In many areas, recruitment proceeded in a haphazard manner. Local party members no longer discussed thoroughly the background of each potential recruit before endorsing his or her membership application. Orientation seminars would be poorly prepared. Sometimes, as in Victoria and Governor Generoso, the distinctions between POs and Akbayan became blurred, with members of one thinking that they were automatically members of the other or that membership in one was a prerequisite for the other. This occurred especially in areas where the community organizer also happened to be an Akbayan organizer. After the congress, local Akbayan members immediately had to attend to final preparations for the election campaign. Then the campaign itself arrived.

Local party units conducted postelection assessments and analyses, but after these many of them no longer functioned well. During my fieldwork in 2002, I discovered that some units did not really exist anymore—they had not met for almost a year. While many local Akbayan units were wobbling, the Akbayan-aligned POs/NGOs and the political blocs were very much alive and kicking. The members of these POs/NGOs and the political blocs continued to be active in Akbayan mass actions and activities, but many of them did not belong to an Akbayan unit that regularly met. Some thought that their engagement in mass movements and development work sufficed. Members of POs/NGOs involved in Batman, for instance, considered such involvement to be their work for Akbayan.

Compounding the problem of many nonfunctioning or poorly functioning local party units was the absence of intermediate party organs. In mid-2002, Akbayan had a total of seventy-six divisions. (It was open to question just how functional some of them or their lower units really were.) The national council and the national executive committee had to supervise and coordinate the work of all these divisions directly, as there were no regional bodies of a regular nature to assist them. Mindanao did have its own commission, but this was only a consultative body. With the void in the intermediate bodies, I came across various informal, even unusual, arrangements in the flow of party communications. Instead of passing through normal party channels, directives or other communications from a national party organ would be relayed to someone in a political bloc, NGO, or PO at the national level, then to someone in the latter's regional or local counterpart, and then finally to the local party unit concerned. I wondered if in the process the integrity of the POs/NGOs concerned was not somehow being compromised.

In September 2002, the Akbayan National Council addressed the party's organizational woes. Reviewing the 2000–2001 mass recruitment experience, party leaders acknowledged the lapses committed. They candidly assessed the status of local party units as follows: "[M]embership in the majority of [Akbayan's] divisions have no clear delineation or structuring at the municipal and barangay levels. Moreover, after the 2001 elections, our party units are faced with the problem of inactive party organizations, problematic party leadership, or worse, party units whose members and/or leaders are found to shift their support to other political parties or party-list organizations" (Akbayan National Council 2002:1). In the light of this, the party leadership undertook organizational consolidation. Akbayan conducted a check of all local party units from the *barangay* to the provincial levels. It recertified functioning units, reconstituted ailing ones, and declared nonfunctioning ones dissolved. To prevent a recurrence of the 2000–2001 experience, the National Council stressed diligent compliance with set guidelines on recruitment and the building of party units. Then it embarked on the process of building regional bodies, creating more regional consultative bodies with the view of eventually turning them into regular committees.

The future of the political blocs—Bisig, Padayon, and Pandayan[116]—has been a recurrent topic of discussion within Akbayan. Since the party's founding congress, the ideological and political positions of the three blocs have moved so much closer to one another that it is often difficult to discern what substantial differences remain. Moreover, at least half of Akbayan's current members do not belong to any of the blocs. As mentioned in chapter 2, frictions and disputes have arisen from time to time between members of different blocs or between bloc and nonbloc party members. For instance, some nonbloc members have complained that bloc members put bloc interest above that of the party, that bloc members give preferential treatment to bloc colleagues, or that bloc meetings and activities are an unnecessary extra burden given all the PO/NGO and Akbayan concerns requiring their attention. Bloc members have replied, however, that cases of preferential treatment are overblown. They have argued that the blocs draw lessons and insights from the rich experience of the leftist traditions from which they came; that the blocs on many occasions have taken the lead in tackling major ideological questions; and that differences between the blocs, even if sometimes only on tactical positions and in styles and methods of work, do contribute to livelier discussions and debates within a "pluralist" party. The political bloc question remains hanging, but both bloc and nonbloc party members agree that the resolution of the question depends largely on the development of deeper ideological unity within the party.[117]

Together with organizational consolidation, Akbayan has pursued ideological consolidation. In the first few years of Akbayan's existence (1998–2001), its program for the political education of its members consisted of not much more than the party's basic orientation seminar.[118] This was all to be expected of a new party. But an additional factor for such a low level was that many members of Akbayan, somewhat in reaction to the highly acrimonious polemics between reaffirmists and rejectionists of the preceding years, tended to steer clear of deep discussions and debates on major theoretical questions in leftist politics. Akbayan leaders soon realized that strengthening the party required deeper ideological grounding of its members. They broke with the usual practice of leftist parties of coming up with a party "ideology," as in their view this often ended up being treated as absolute truth. Somewhat influenced by post-modernism, Akbayan leaders opted to build an open-ended "Akbayan narrative." Starting in the second half of 2002, Akbayan leaders promoted deeper theoretical discussions and debates within the party through political education seminars. Initially, the topics included deeper analyses of the national and the international situation, the Akbayan narrative and the party's strategy and tactics. Then the seminars ventured into such discourses as state and civil society, political parties and social movements, reform and revolution, the Philippine political spectrum and comparative ideology, the national question and ethnicity, and ethics and morality in politics. Akbayan's education committee drew up ambitious plans for advanced and specialized courses with education kits. As in popular political education seminars, however, there was a great lack of education materials, especially in vernacular languages. Most of the materials used were drafts; the Akbayan narrative document itself was finalized and approved only at the July 2003 congress. Despite all the limitations, Akbayan members at various levels responded enthusiastically to the political education seminars, which were marked by very lively and extended discussions.

For their operations, local Akbayan units rely mainly on the voluntary efforts of individual members. These units have meager resources and their sources of funds are still quite limited. Many units have tried to be diligent in collecting membership dues.[119] Akbayan has also collected special fees from party members who have secured a public office (through elections or by appointment) with the help of the party. At election time, local party units have often managed to obtain donations in cash or kind (election campaign posters or sample ballots) from politicians and businessmen. From my inquiries with local party leaders, I ascertained that donations or contributions from NGOs or NGO-based individuals also constituted an important source of local party funds. NGOs further assisted local Akbayan units by hiring party "full timers" for part-time jobs or by farming out short-term contractual work to them to help them earn some income.

The Process of Building an Akbayan Political-Electoral Base at the Grassroots Level

One of the ways by which Akbayan can perhaps be best distinguished from traditional parties, as well as from other leftist parties, is the way it operates and conducts itself at the grassroots level. As at the national level, traditional parties at the local level are loose formations revolving around elite clans and factions that rely a great deal on clientelism to maintain their hold on power and shift parties whenever it is convenient. As a party espousing a new politics, Akbayan seeks to build both a solid party organization and a broad political-electoral base at the grassroots level that actively participate not just in elections and local governance but also in the mass movement. Like other leftist electoral parties, Akbayan has been very much involved in contentious politics, the party-list vote, and congressional work. Unlike them, however, Akbayan has also been very much engaged in local politics and development work.

Out in the field, I often could not get a good idea of Akbayan's overall framework in its multisided political work at the local level. Akbayan was into mass movements, contentious politics, development work, elections, government work and governance, party-building, and so on. Still, there was little that had been written about an overall framework or schema. I realized, however, when I tried to put together the data I had gathered, that a framework was emerging. For a more concrete and graphic representation of such a framework, I thought in terms of what Akbayan was doing in its efforts to build a political-electoral base at the grassroots level. Through my interviews and discussions with some members of the Akbayan's executive committee and national council, I was able to piece together how Akbayan envisions this process of base building.[120] As I had been raising questions and sharing my observations and comments in the course of my interactions with them, some of the points they raised already took into account, or were in fact responses to, the problems I had come across during my fieldwork.

Figure 7.1 *Process of building an Akbayan political-electoral base (municipal level)*

Type of Area	Brief Description	Local Government		
		Executive Branch	Legislative Branch	*Barangay* Organization
Yellow area (*trapo* area)	*Trapo*-controlled LGU; weak or politically inactive societal organizations	Mayor *trapo*; civil bureaucracy controlled by *trapo* mayor	Municipal council controlled by *trapos*	LB and BCs very much controlled by *trapos*
Light orange area (expansion area—via LGU route)	TAs or SRs have upper hand in LGU; weak or politically inactive societal organizations	Mayor TA or SR; has won over civil bureaucracy	SRs/TAs occupy seat or seats in municipal council	LB and BCs still controlled by *trapos* but SRs and TAs manage to exert some influence
Light orange area (expansion area—via civil society route)	TT-controlled LGU; emergent societal organizations	Mayor TT; civil bureaucracy controlled by TT mayor	Municipal council controlled by *trapos*	LB and BCs very much controlled by *trapos*
Dark orange area (consolidation area)	SRs have upper hand in LGU; strong and politically active societal organizations	Mayor SR; has won over civil bureaucracy	SRs have majority in municipal council	SRs have upper hand in LB and most BCs
Red area (Akbayan base or bailiwick)	Akbayan is local governing party; strong and politically active societal organizations	Mayor AMU; has won over civil bureaucracy	AMUs have majority in municipal council	AMUs have upper hand in LB and most BCs

Definition of Terms and Classification of Politicians

Trapo. Engages in the politics of patronage, vote buying, fraud, and/or terrorism

Types of *Trapos*

1. ***Trapong-trapo*** (TT). Engages in the worst *trapo* politics; tactical alliance with him or her inadvisable.
2. **Tactical ally** (TA). Engages in the milder, nonviolent form of *trapo* politics, supports certain development-oriented or pro-people initiatives and is willing to work with progressives in certain concerns. If it is still unclear whether a politician is TT or TA, he or she is simply referred to as a *trapo*.

State reformist (SR). Promotes institutional reforms and social development (including people's participation in governance) to achieve good governance.

Types of SRs

1. **Neoliberal state reformist** (NSR). Believes that popular empowerment can be achieved within the existing social order without the need for structural change.
2. **Left or left-leaning state reformist** (LSR). Views popular empowerment as requiring a

Civil Society			Akbayan
People's Organizations	**Nongovernmental Organizations**	**Popular Political Education**	
Few progressive POs in municipality	Few progressive NGOs operating in municipality	No popular political education; voters do not resist / counter dirty *trapo* methods	No Akbayan chapter; no Akbayan members organizing in municipality
Few progressive POs in municipality	Few progressive NGOs operating in municipality	Popular political education initiated; voters resist / counter dirty *trapo* methods to some extent	Akbayan chapter(s) being set up or already set up in one or several *barangays*
Some progressive POs in municipality	One or a few progressive NGOs operating in municipality servicing POs	Popular political education initiated; voters resist / counter dirty *trapo* methods to some extent	Akbayan chapter(s) being set up or already set up in one or several *barangays*
Many progressive POs in area; POs actively participate in rights / welfare issues and governance / development	Several progressive NGOs operating in municipality; NGOs actively participate in rights / welfare issues and governance / development	Popular political education deepening; voters resist / counter dirty *trapo* methods to greater extent	Active Akbayan section
Progressive POs in all major sectors; POs confederated and actively participate in rights / welfare issues and governance / development	Several / many progressive NGOs operating in municipality; NGOs comprehensively service POs; NGOs actively participate in rights / welfare issues and governance / development	Popular political education extensively and intensively conducted; voters effectively resist / counter dirty *trapo* methods	Active Akbayan section with active chapters in all *barangays*

structural change of economic and political relations in society.

Types of LSRs

a. **Non-Akbayan member** (NAM). Engages in new politics but is not an Akbayan member.

b. **Dual-party member** (DPM). Engages in new politics but is a member of both Akbayan and a *trapo* party. His or her primary allegiance may be with Akbayan, with the *trapo* party, or unclear.

c. **Akbayan member, Unhyphenated** (AMU). A full-fledged and solid Akbayan member who is not a member of any other political party. (The term *unhyphenated* is used here in connection with the common practice of *trapos* to run with several party affiliations and endorsements, strung together on campaign materials with hyphens, e.g., LAKAS-NUCD-KAMPI-PPC-Bayan Muna).

Other Abbreviations

LGU = Local government unit

LB = Liga ng mga Barangay (League of *Barangays*)

BC = *Barangay* captain

The base-building process I describe is by no means a comprehensive framework of Akbayan's political work at the local level.

As explained by Akbayan leaders with whom I talked, the party's base building flows from its engagement in both civil society and the LGU, in both the mass movement and local governance and development work. As at the national level, Akbayan wages a struggle against elite hegemony at the local level in both civil society and the state and works for the deepening of democracy in both spheres—"double democratization," to paraphrase David Held. Akbayan aspires to eventually become the governing party in the LGUs where it operates. It also seeks to provide political direction and leadership to organizations and groups in civil society, while fully respecting their autonomy.

In figure 7.1, the process of transforming a *trapo*-controlled area (yellow area) into an Akbayan political-electoral base or a "bailiwick of new politics" (red area) requires integrated efforts in the LGU, civil society and party building. The "features" of yellow, light orange, dark orange, and red areas are idealized representations. They are intended to emphasize what Akbayan leaders see as the need for a relatively balanced and well-rounded development. (A municipality may be considered dark orange if most of its features exhibit such a color, but it may still have one or two light orange features, indicating that there is some catching up to do in these categories.) Two types of expansion areas (light orange) are indicated—one that has been opened mainly via the LGU route and one opened via the civil society route. It must be noted that LGU route expansion areas have an "undeveloped" civil society side; civil society route expansion areas have an undeveloped LGU side. This indicates the need for those working in LGU route areas to do organizing work in civil society too and for those in civil society route areas to get into LGU work.

Akbayan leaders believe that since *trapos* dominate and are very much entrenched in local politics it will be a long and complicated process for Akbayan to dislodge them and become the governing party in a good number of municipalities. First, Akbayan will have to reach out to, and forge good relations with, as many state reformists and potential allies as possible within the municipal and *barangay*

LGUs. It will also have to try to get state reformists and allies elected or appointed to LGU positions. Once a mayor who is a progressive or an ally is elected, Akbayan will have to help revamp or transform the local civilian bureaucracy and put an end to corruption and maladministration. After some time of working closely with state reformists and allies, Akbayan will have to try to draw them away from *trapo* and neoliberal politics toward leftist politics, and to eventually recruit them into Akbayan. Because Akbayan in most areas does not yet have a machine strong enough to ensure the victory of progressives at the local level on its own, it will have to make a tactical compromise: many of these politician recruits will have to go through a period of dual-party membership—a traditional party and Akbayan—and run under a traditional party while supporting Akbayan in the party-list vote. Once Akbayan has achieved enough national stature, it will have to put an end to the dual-party arrangement and ask its politician recruits to choose between the traditional parties and Akbayan.

In Akbayan's engagement in civil society, party leaders believe that it has to take an active role helping build and strengthen POs and NGOs while fully respecting their independence and autonomy. In their view, Akbayan will have to keep close track of the development of societal organizations and to strive to provide political direction and leadership in the mass movements and popular participation in local governance and development work. It will have to make sure that the struggle against elite hegemony in civil society does not lag behind that in LGU work and vice versa. Popular political education that is truly dialogical in character will be crucial in fighting clientelism and dirty *trapo* methods in the ideological and cultural spheres.

Engrossed in their activities in the mass movements, local governance, and development work, Akbayan members in some areas have tended to neglect the building of a solid party organization at the grassroots level. Akbayan leaders have thus stressed the importance of party building—strong chapters at the *barangay* level, sections at the municipal level and divisions at the intermunicipal or provincial level—and the need to integrate party building into political work in both civil society and the LGU.

The process of building an Akbayan political-electoral base is not a simple linear progression. A local Akbayan organization in a "deep orange area" (see fig. 7.1) could commit serious errors or suffer political setbacks and the municipality could very well revert to "light orange" status. Akbayan leaders feel confident, however, that as long as there has been significant effort at well-rounded political work, the local party organization will have the means to get back on its feet. For instance, a major defeat in local elections could result in the virtual destruction of Akbayan's network of progressives and allies within an LGU, but if there is a strong party organization and allied PO-NGO network, they could very well continue with their work, rectify whatever mistakes were committed, and set the stage for a comeback in the next election.

Conclusion

IN THIS STUDY on democratization and the Left in the postauthoritarian Philippines, I have put forward a three-part argument. The first part questions the one-sided and top-down character of predominant interpretations of Philippine politics (the patron-client model, neocolonial/dependency interpretation, and patrimonial/elite-democracy framework), and presents an alternative interpretation combining elite democracy and democracy from below. The Philippines, I argue, is a *contested democracy* in which members of the oligarchic elite seek to maintain a truncated form of formal democracy that they can easily manipulate and dominate (elite democracy) and in which major sections of the poor and marginalized classes, sectors, and communities, together with some allies from the middle and upper classes, struggle for a more participatory and egalitarian democracy (democracy from below). The *deepening of democracy* in the Philippines, the second part of my argument, mainly involves the transformation of an elite-dominated formal democracy into a participatory and egalitarian one, and the process is a struggle of democracy from below versus elite democracy. The third part contends that while the Maoist CPP is an undemocratic force and remains a threat to Philippine democracy, new leftist parties and groups that are democratically oriented have entered into the thick of the fight for democracy from below and are contributing to the deepening of democracy in the Philippines.

Chapter 1 has specifically dealt with the first two parts of my argument, and chapter 2 advances the third. Chapters 3–7 have delved into the Left's political engagements in various arenas or lines of work—civil society, elections, public office and governance, popular political education, work for political reforms, and local work. These chapters expound on the third part of my argument, but they also relate to the first two. The experiences in the different arenas of the Left, particularly the emergent leftist parties and groups, show the complicatedness of the contestation between elite democracy and democracy from below and the problems and difficulties that were or are still being confronted by those working for the deepening of democracy.

In this conclusion, I take up certain salient points that have been touched on in the preceding chapters but need to be synthesized. These have to do with the complexity of the contest over democracy, the difficulties confronted in the deepening of democracy, and the long and continuing process of the democratization of the Left itself. I shall also examine the Philippines' contested democracy and the emergent Left's role in democratization in comparative perspective, adding to comparisons in previous chapters between the Philippines and other developing countries. Last, I explore the prospects for the deepening of democracy in the Philippines and the role the emergent leftist parties and groups could play in this process.

Salient Points Regarding Contested Democracy and the Left in the Philippines

On the basis of the introduction and chapters 1–2 of this volume, contested democracy and the deepening of democracy could still seem somewhat too general and abstract. This is understandable, since the discussion in this early part was largely theoretical. Subsequent chapters, dealing mainly with the Left's engagement in various spheres and lines of work, show contested democracy and the deepening of democracy in more concrete terms. The experiences of the Left, particularly the emergent leftist parties and groups and their allied POS/NGOS, in striving to give form and direction to democracy from below illustrate that the contest over democracy in the Philippines is complicated and that the fight to transform a deficient formal democracy into a participatory and egalitarian one is a tough, uphill struggle.

True to their avowed objectives and priorities, political blocs and groups of the emergent Left engaged in organizing, popular political education, and other forms of "mass work" among the poor and marginalized classes, sectors, and communities and identified with their issues and concerns. The new, leftist groups recruited the great majority of their members from these classes and sectors and built chapters at the grassroots level. In contrast to the traditional parties, which are dominated by the elite, they strove to acquire a truly "mass" character.

In struggling against elite rule, the emergent leftist groups fought in different arenas or lines of work, opening new arenas at crucial periods and striving to master the nuances and intricacies of working in each. They started out in the familiar arena of the mass movement, which increasingly became subsumed under a broader arena known as civil society. In their engagement in civil society, most groups focused primarily on contentious politics, but some went mainly into development work. Traditionally a strong point of the Left, contentious politics was largely directed at fighting elite domination or control of the country's wealth and power. From merely exposing and opposing, the new, leftist groups moved on to proposing and learned to be good at programmatic demand making. In their engagement in contentious politics, the emergent leftist groups sometimes had to compete with the Maoist Left, which sought to instrumentalize the mass movement for its protracted people's war. In the early 1990s, the emergent leftist groups oriented mainly toward contentious politics ventured into development efforts, ostensibly a more "constructive" line of work, or went into it more seriously than before. The new, leftist groups hoped to prove the superiority of their development initiatives to those of the *trapos* and to present concrete evidence of a viable alternative system.

In the midst of the great hurrah for civil society (of the associational type) in the early 1990s, the political blocs and groups of the new Left beat back a strong movement that emerged within their own ranks for an amorphous NGO movement to take the place of a political party. What would be the point of a "strong" civil society if state power ultimately remained in the hands of the traditional parties of the elite? Although the new, leftist groups became fully convinced of the need for a political party to challenge the *trapo* parties, it took them some time to actually found such a party. Due to continuing ideological and political differences, and at times also the personal differences of leaders, the political blocs and groups formed several parties, not just one.

The 1998 general elections provided the emergent leftist parties with their electoral breakthrough—a few seats in the House of Representatives (through the party-list system) and, in the case of Akbayan and Sanlakas, also some positions in a few municipal governments. In subsequent elections, not all of the new, leftist parties managed to retain their seats in the legislature. Only Akbayan managed to increase its party-list seats to the maximum (three) and win more local posts. Meanwhile, the NDs have doubled their seats from three to six by setting up more party-list groups. Despite all the efforts of the leftist parties and groups, *trapo* parties still control 90 percent of the seats in the Lower House of Congress and are still the ruling entities in almost all local governments.

The congresspersons of the emergent leftist parties have been vigorously working for progressive legislation and coordinating closely with POs/NGOs engaged in both mass protest actions in the streets and lobbying. With regard to political and electoral reforms, for instance, the solons of the new, leftist groups have pushed for measures promoting fuller participation and representation of marginalized sectors and for curbing elite domination and manipulation of political processes and institutions. In public office and governance, however, the most notable achievement of the new Left has been at the local level. Seizing the opportunities provided by government decentralization, Akbayan and allied POs/NGOs have undertaken projects in participatory local governance, most especially in development planning, that have produced very creditable results. From the *barangay* level, the groups involved are now moving up to the municipal level. Akbayan has managed to draw and even "recruit" many progressive local officials into its ranks. Such recruitment, however, has a certain degree of ambiguity in the sense that most of the recruited officials still run under traditional parties at election time.

In fighting elite rule, the new, leftist parties and groups have had to contend with the patronage, corruption, fraud, coercion, and violence of the *trapos* and the traditional parties. Perhaps more significant, they have also had to wage battles against the elite in the ideological and cultural spheres. They have had to controvert ideas and notions that democracy equals elections; that democracy can be deepened simply by "strengthening civil society" and promoting "good governance" without actively struggling against the patrimonial elite; that elections are about money and guns, not legitimacy, fairness, and democratic processes. The new, leftist groups have also had to fight against a most pervasive and pernicious *trapo* political culture of nepotism, cronyism, distorted extended kinships, bribery, influence peddling, pork barreling, the spoils system, vote buying, "boss" culture, and so on. Apart from tangling with *trapos*, the new, leftist groups have had to deal with harassment and even violence from the extreme Left, which regards other leftist groups as renegades and counterrevolutionaries.

After *jueteng*-gate, the emergent leftist parties and groups and their allied POs/NGOs were among those at the forefront of the campaign in 2000–2001 for the ouster of President Estrada, who, like Marcos, had become the quintessential symbol of patrimonial politics. Compared to the *trapos* and the traditional parties, however, the new, leftist groups were still very weak. Thus, the leadership of the broad "Oust Estrada" movement passed into the hands of anti-Estrada factions of the elite. EDSA II was people power directed against a corrupt president, but it did not bring about structural change. One section of the elite merely took the reins of power from another one.

The fight against elite rule is a protracted and multisided struggle that is not a simple linear progression. Studies such as those of Franco (2001) and George (1998), as well as case studies presented in this book, show that despite the odds reform-oriented candidates (whether new managerialist, leftist, or whatever) can and do win elections and that reform-oriented public officials can and do manage to undertake efficient and participatory governance. A state reformist winning an election or governing well in his or her first term, however, is not as novel or earthshaking as it is sometimes portrayed to be. In truth, this has happened many times. More crucial is what happens down the road. In a *trapo*-permeated system, victories and gains can prove to be very ephemeral. A state reformist in a traditional party can imbibe *trapo* ways. As was made clear in the PnB experience, a public official belonging to an avowedly new politics party can get persuaded to switch to a traditional party. One in a dual-party arrangement can later turn out to be more loyal to a *trapo* than a new politics party. A traditional party can use the progressives within its ranks as poster children of good governance and give the illusion that the party can shed its *trapo* nature. Reforms undertaken by a new politics official can simply be discontinued or overturned by his or her successor, especially if the latter is a *trapo*. As the process of building Akbayan's political-electoral base at the grassroots level shows, one has to fight the *trapos* in different arenas (civil society, elections, governance, popular political education, etc.) and at various levels (*barangay*, municipal/city, provincial, etc.) and to be prepared to move forward and backward in each arena and level in the protracted struggle against elite rule.

As mentioned in the introduction, Huber et al. as well as Laclau and Mouffe, see the deepening of democracy in terms of a movement from formal liberal democracy to a more egalitarian one. (Huber et al. refer to this egalitarian democracy as social democracy, whereas Laclau and Mouffe call it radical democracy.) In the Philippines, the struggle for an egalitarian society has been most clearly manifested in the struggles of the poor and marginalized classes, sectors, and communities. Due to the wide rich-poor gap, class struggle continues to be the most prominent of the country's social conflicts. The clamor of the poor for social justice remains as strong as ever. For a more equitable distribution of the country's wealth, all the emergent leftist groups argue for some form of socialism-cum-democracy (or an egalitarian democracy) as a long-term goal. In the short term, they have vigorously pushed for such measures as agrarian reform, increased workers' wages, and low-cost housing for the urban poor. Another major conflict involving equality (apart, of course, from national self-determination) has been that between ethnic communities—the "Christian-Filipino" majority on one hand and the Moros and "indigenous peoples" on the other. While upholding the Moros' and indigenous peoples' right to self-determination, the new, leftist groups have advocated federalism or genuine regional autonomy for minority peoples and an end to all forms of ethnic and religious discrimination. Thus far, the emergent leftist forces have not been any more successful than the rebel movements—the Maoist insurgency and Moro secessionist movements—in putting an end to the grave class and ethnic disparities, which in fact have continued to worsen. The women's movement in the Philippines, in which the new, leftist parties and groups have been active participants, has been more successful in pushing for gender equality. Nonetheless, as one well-known feminist has put it, the gains made have been "mostly in the public sphere, not in the private sphere."[1]

According to Huber et al. (1997:324), the deepening of democracy from a formal to a social or egalitarian democracy passes through an intermediate system known as participatory democracy, which has the features of formal democracy plus one other dimension: "high levels of participation without systematic differences across social categories." An egalitarian democracy has all the features of participatory democracy plus "increasing equality in social and economic outcomes."

The Latin American experience appears to bear out the contention that the process of deepening democracy does put the stress, sequentially speaking, on the participatory dimension before the equality dimension. According to Roberts (1998:32–3), the Latin American Left, in working for the deepening of democracy in its region, has directed more attention to the political aspect (i.e., promoting popular participation in the decision-making process) than to the extension of democratic norms to the socioeconomic sphere (i.e., pushing for increased equality in social and economic outcomes). Roberts attributes this to the rise of grassroots popular organizations that are well placed to foster popular participation in local decision-making arenas, as well as to the Left's inadequacies in coming up with a concrete alternative to the capitalist mode of production and problems in instituting democratic controls over the national economy in the era of globalization.

A similar sequence appears to be unfolding for the emergent leftist parties and groups in the Philippines. Their emphasis now is on participatory democracy, which they believe can greatly facilitate the strategic objective of an egalitarian democracy. To describe its "narrative" Akbayan has adopted the slogan "participatory democracy, participatory socialism," which captures the basic elements of its strategic thrusts (Akbayan National Congress 2003). The people power uprisings of 1986 and 2001 provided a major impetus to the push for participatory democracy and popular empowerment in the Philippines—a factor that is absent or not as marked in most countries of Latin America. The new, leftist groups hope to help organize and channel the popular cognition of people power in the toppling of corrupt presidents to political decision-making processes that go on every day from the local to the national levels.

To become positive forces for the deepening of democracy in the Philippines, large sections of the emergent leftist parties and groups have had to undergo a process of democratization themselves. All of the new, leftist parties and groups have had to guard against inducements and co-optation by *trapos* and against the corrosions of *trapo* political culture. Those coming from the ND tradition have also had to break with certain dogmas of traditional Marxism-Leninism and rethink long-held views about the country's "bourgeois" or "elite" democracy. The first major break came during the CPP split when the rejectionists" renounced Stalinism and Maoism, including the concept of a permanent vanguard party. This paved the way for the acceptance by the rejectionists of political pluralism and a plural or pluralist democracy. (Laclau and Mouffe's conceptualization of a "radical *and plural* democracy" therefore has particular resonance for the Philippine Left.) The FOPA conference of 1993 provided the second major break, as certain leftist groups ceased to dismiss post-Marcos democracy as simply "fake" or "bourgeois" and thus worthy only of being dismantled, overthrown, and smashed. They recognized the intrinsic value of democratic processes and institutions and saw the possibilities for transforming a formal democracy into a more substantive one and an elite democracy into a participatory and egalitarian one. Thus, they shifted from an instrumental to an integral view of democracy. Not all the emergent leftist groups, however, have made this decisive shift. Because of the propensity of the Philippines for tumults and ruptures like the EDSA I, II, and III uprisings, some groups still entertain the prospect of a Jacobin-style revolution. Thus, they have tended to straddle the instrumental-integral divide, and this has greatly affected their engagement in civil society, elections, public office, and governance.

The Philippines' Contested Democracy in Comparative Perspective

The developing world is strewn with elite-dominated formal democracies, patrimonial states, weak states captured by strong oligarchic forces, clientelist electoral regimes, boss democracies, semidemocracies and states belonging to various diminished subtypes of democracy. The Philippines is by no means the only deficient formal democracy in which the rule of an entrenched elite is being challenged by popular forces striving for empowerment and social and economic equality. Comparisons of Philippine democracy with democracies in other developing countries would show that the paradigm of contested democracy, where elite democracy contends with democracy from below, is applicable to many other developing countries, especially new or "newly restored" democracies. Comparisons would also be helpful in showing why forces of democracy from below in certain countries would find it more difficult to fight elite rule than would those in other countries.

With regard to elite democracy and its variations, a good number of excellent comparative studies (or studies with incisive comparative sections) have already been published. Three authors who deal with variations of the elite-democracy model (Hutchcroft, Sidel, and Franco), for instance, provide very thought-provoking and useful analyses of different types of patrimonialism (Hutchcroft), bossism (Sidel), and both clientelism and electoralism (Franco). Hutchcroft makes the distinction between the Philippines' "patrimonial oligarchic state" and the "patrimonial bureaucratic states" of Thailand, Indonesia, and Zaire. The elite in the former is a powerful oligarchic class that preys on a weak state bureaucracy, while the elite in the latter is a bureaucratic class that rides roughshod over weak social forces. In Hutchcroft's view, the patrimonial oligarchic state is more obdurate to change than a patrimonial administrative state, as bureaucratic incoherence and the great clout of the oligarchic class hinder reforms. After comparing the Philippine experience with bossism with those of other countries, particularly in Southeast Asia,

Sidel appears to have found additional evidence that links the rise of bossism to electoral democracy and early capital accumulation. Franco came up with her four types of "less-than-democratic regimes"—electoral authoritarian, clientelist electoral, militarized electoral, and demilitarizing electoral—from a review of Latin American transitions in the 1980s. She likened the Philippines' (national) clientelist electoral regime and local authoritarian enclaves to those of Brazil after 1985 and Mexico since 1988.

The Philippines generally fits the description of a "truncated" or "deficient" form of formal democracy in Huber et al.'s typology drawn from Latin American democracies. While it has competitive elections and universal suffrage, it falls short in criteria such as accountability of the state's administrative organs to elected representatives and protection against arbitrary state action. A truncated formal democracy is not new to the Philippines. To some extent, the deficiencies in contemporary Philippine democracy were already present in the early decades of the postcolonial state. Then (as now) the virtual stranglehold on economic and political power of the country's oligarchic elite blocked the attainment of complete formal democracy and its deepening into participatory and egalitarian democracy. Worse, it helped usher in a fourteen-year period of authoritarian rule.

As a truncated or deficient formal democracy, the Philippines may be worse off compared to many Latin American countries. The Philippines suffers from the same defects that afflict the truncated formal democracies of Latin America, as mentioned by Huber et al.: weak accountability, uneven protection of civil and political rights, and patrimonial practices. However, while Latin American democracies generally meet the criteria of free and fair elections, the high incidence of vote buying, other forms of fraud, and violence that attend Philippine elections places in great doubt the actual freeness and fairness of these polls. Huber et al. have warned of the possibility of a vicious cycle of inegalitarian policies in Latin American countries leading to poverty, marginalization, and crime; to the corrosion of political and civil rights; and to a "delegative democracy" with sharply diminished government accountability. With social disparities now worse than in the preauthoritarian and even the early postauthoritarian years, it can perhaps be said that the vicious cycle of inegalitarian policies and stagnation already besets the Philippines.

Because of failings in horizontal accountability and the protection of civil rights, Guillermo O'Donnell (1994) has included the Philippines among the world's "delegative democracies" and Fareed Zakaria (1997) among the "illiberal democracies."[2] As an illiberal democracy, the Philippines would belong to that "diminished subtype" of democracy in which civil liberties are incomplete, as described by David Collier and Steven Levitsky (1997:440–41).[3]

The deepening of democracy, as in the transition to democracy, involves contestation, especially among different classes and class coalitions. Based on their studies of capitalist development and democracy in advanced capitalist countries, Latin America, and the Caribbean, Rueschemeyer et al. (1992:46, 270) and Huber et al. (1997:323) have asserted the centrality of class power to the process of democratization—that democratization was both pushed forward and opposed by class interest, that on the whole subordinate classes fought for democracy and classes benefiting from the status quo resisted democracy, and that this centrality holds for the processes of both achieving formal democracy and advancing toward participatory and egalitarian democracy. A similar contestation has marked the entire process of the deepening of democracy in the Philippines, covering not just the post-Marcos period but the postcolonial era (excluding the interregnum of Marcos's authoritarian rule). Ever since the Philippines gained independence in 1946, there has been a drawn-out struggle between the entrenched economic-political elite and the poor and marginalized classes, sectors, and communities over the meaning and substance of democracy. Parties and groups of the elite have mainly promoted the minimalist concept of democracy, while those linked with subordinate classes have called for civil and political rights, popular participation, and social justice.

In many parts of the developing world, forces of democracy from below are challenging the dominance of the entrenched elite rule in truncated formal democracies. In some of the other postauthoritarian states of Southeast and East Asia, notably South Korea, Thailand, and Indonesia, and in parts of South Asia, movements of poor and marginalized classes, sectors, and communities—workers, peasants, women, urban poor, and so on—have become active again in recent years. The issues they have raised range from labor repression and rights to land, water and forests, all the way to neoliberal globalization. As in the Philippines, the popular organizations and movements have been aided by NGOs, which have largely dedicated themselves to the empowerment of the poor, deprived, and marginalized. Subordinate classes in Southeast and East Asia continue to be largely unrepresented in government, as many grassroots movements have eschewed active engagement in electoral politics and even links to political parties. There are, however, hopeful signs of change (apart from the modest electoral gains of the emergent leftist parties and groups in the Philippines). In South Korea, the left-wing Democratic Labor party has made it to the national Parliament for the first time and emerged as the nation's third-largest party, winning ten seats in the April 2004 elections (Kim 2004). Meanwhile, in South Asia, in the Indian state of Kerala, volunteer organizations headed by the People's Science Movement, with the support of some parties and groups in the Left Front, have successfully spearheaded huge campaigns for civil action and community development cooperation, which have drawn tremendous popular participation, promoted further democratization, and helped improve government performance (Törnquist 1999:146–47 and 2002:102–8).

Latin America appears to be the region where the efforts to transform elite democracy into a more participatory and egalitarian democracy—from below—appear to be making some headway. As in the Philippines, Latin American countries have long been dominated by clientelistic and oligarchic elites. In recent years, virtually all over the region, massive protests of workers, peasants, urban poor, indigenous people, students, and the middle classes have broken out against the neoliberal policies of the 1990s and the corrupt political elite—both of which are widely blamed for worsening poverty and social disparities and recession or even economic collapse. Waves of people power have swept out governments wedded to neoliberalism and tarnished by corruption in Argentina, Peru, and Ecuador. Amid the economic and political turmoil, political parties closely linked to the subordinate classes have reemerged and been revitalized. After chalking up victories and gains in local polls and national legislative elections and learning how to govern in the 1980s and 1990s, parties such as the Fifth Republic Movement, the Workers' Party (PT) and the Frente Amplio (Broad Front) have come to power in Venezuela, Brazil, and Uruguay, respectively. Left and left-of-center parties in Mexico, El Salvador, and Nicaragua now appear to have fair chances of turning from main opposition into ruling party in the next round of elections. For many popular movements and parties in Latin America, neoliberal populism proved too formidable a force to contend with in the 1990s. The recent social explosions in the region, however, may make it harder for demagogic politicians to effectively couple neoliberalism and populism.[4]

Emergent Leftist Parties and the Deepening of Democracy in the Philippines

As in Latin America and elsewhere, the three clusters of power mentioned by Huber et al. (1997)—the balance of class power, the structure of the state and state-society relations, and international power structures—will shape the conditions for the deepening of democracy in the Philippines. The Philippines currently exhibits conditions similar to those of Latin American democracies, conditions that would hinder the deepening of democracy: political and economic power concentrated in a few, weak state autonomy due to dominant class interests, and international pressure for market-oriented but socially inequitable policies. Given the current unfavorable power relations, the Philippines may continue to be a truncated formal democracy for some time, bogged down in the rut of widespread poverty, grave social disparities, and simmering civil unrest. In such an unstable political environment, a comeback of authoritarian rule cannot be ruled out.

Possibilities for the deepening of democracy nonetheless remain. The single most important factor is that the mass movement is very much alive and has manifested in various ways its power, adaptability, resilience—and unpredictability. It has been greatly aided by modern mass media and electronic communications. Over the last few years, the mass movement has succeeded in getting unfair electricity surcharges quashed; thwarted the self-serving moves of leading politicians to amend the Constitution; frustrated the politically motivated moves of certain politicians to impeach the Supreme Court chief justice on flimsy grounds; forced the government to withdraw Philippine troops from Iraq; and, most of all, ousted another corrupt president in another grand display of people power. To be sure, the mass movement has not succeeded in getting many, or even most, of its various—sometimes conflicting—demands, and it has not gotten anywhere near the point of threatening the very continuance of elite rule. Moreover, as EDSA III clearly showed, it can still be vulnerable to clientelist and populist appeals. Democracy from below, however, no longer confines itself to the mass movement. It has branched out into other arenas. And emergent leftist forces are working hard to help give it form and direction.

The early part of this conclusion discussed how the new leftist parties and groups and their allied POs/NGOs have engaged in mass work among peasants, workers, urban poor, and so on; how they have moved into the new arenas of development work, elections, public office, and governance; and how they have had to contend with the patronage, corruption, fraud, and violence of the *trapos* while waging battles in the ideological and cultural spheres as well. I stressed the difficulties that these leftist groups have been experiencing. This, however, is but one way of looking at their endeavors. Although the emergent leftist parties and groups are newcomers to the world of development work, elections, public office, and governance, they seem to have familiarized themselves and adjusted to their environments relatively quickly, and in some respects have even gained some sophistication. As demonstrated vividly by their endeavors for political and electoral reform, the new, leftist parties and groups have learned how to combine their work in various arenas—rallying in the streets, lobbying the administration and Congress, engaging in debate on the floor of the House of Representatives and even waging a worldwide campaign among overseas Filipinos. They are becoming adept at combining active involvement in contentious politics with development work and participatory governance; urban work with rural work; engagement at the national level with engagement at the regional and local levels; countering the *trapos'* guns, goons, and gold with fighting *trapo* political culture; and engaging in political work with party building. The fight against the rule of the oligarchic elite has been turning more and more from a single-pronged attack (i.e., a largely urban-centered mass movement) into a multipronged one and from a political struggle into an ideological and cultural struggle as well. In the Philippines' contested democracy, the struggle against elite rule being waged by the emergent leftist parties and groups is shaping up to be the sharpest expression of the contest between elite democracy and democracy from below.

To become forces for democratization more fully, the emergent leftist parties and groups that still straddle the instrumental-integral divide as regards their view of democracy would have to make the decisive shift to the integral view of democracy. That a decrepit "bourgeois democracy" will be toppled and replaced by a shining new socialist democracy through a "revolution"—a single foundational moment of rupture—is a pie in the sky. There is no completely new order to replace the old order in one swoop. Revolutionary or radical change in the Philippines can only come about through a protracted process with periods of slow, gradual change as well as periods of tumult and rupture. The process cannot but be a movement from an elite-dominated formal democracy to a participatory and egalitarian one. The instrumental view of democracy will continue to serve as a hedge to the engagements in civil society and the state arena of new, leftist groups still influenced by it to some degree. In the drive to build up to a revolutionary climax, the left groups concerned would have to devote too much of their attention and energy to the "expose and oppose" type of contentious politics and too little to development work and local governance. Since Congress serves as a better "propaganda" forum, they would tend to pour almost all of their energies and resources during elections into winning the limited number of party-list seats in the House of Representatives and not attend to building up strength from below by accumulating victories at the local level.

It is certainly politic of the new, leftist parties and group (including those with an integral view of democracy) to take a proactive stance toward political tumults, ruptures, military revolts, coup attempts, and uprisings. The Philippines' truncated formal democracy does have a propensity for these, and radical changes can at times come about only through storms and ruptures. The new, leftist groups, however, would have to guard against becoming too fascinated with, predisposed to, or prepossessed by ruptures. In the first place, undemocratic forces from the extreme Right and the extreme Left, who have no compunction about using or manipulating other groups, do their utmost to create or precipitate political crises and tumultuous situations that they can exploit for their antidemocratic ends. Moreover, a preoccupation with ruptures would lead to less attention being given to other important lines of work such as local governance, development work, and sectoral movements.

From the viewpoint of modernization theory, political instability and disorder in "changing societies"—insurgencies, revolts, coups, uprisings, and so on—are, in Samuel Huntington's words, "in large part the product of rapid social change and the rapid mobilization of new groups into politics coupled with the slow development of political institutions." In complex societies, he argues, achieving a high level of political community depends a lot on political institutions. Huntington particularly stresses the importance of the political party, "the distinctive institution of modern politics," whose function is "to organize participation, to aggregate interests, to serve as the link between social forces and the government" (Huntington 1968:4, 10, 90–91).

Applied not so much to modernization as to the process of deepening democracy in the Philippines, Huntington's argument has important implications for the emergent leftist parties and groups. At present, with the new, leftist parties still quite weak, the opposition to elite rule of the poor and marginalized classes, sectors, and communities cannot but sometimes break out into storms and ruptures, as they do not have political institutions through which they can channel such opposition. If the emergent leftist parties succeed in building a broad political-electoral base among the poor and marginalized, however, and, on the basis of this, chalk up more and more electoral victories, they could succeed in performing the function of organizing participation and aggregating the interests of the poor and marginalized and serving as their representatives in the state arena.

Popular participation, instead of breaking out in ruptures, would come to have an institutional channel. Since peasants, workers, women, and other marginalized groups comprise the overwhelming majority of the country's population, the new, leftist parties could eventually find themselves in power. While taking a proactive stance toward political storms and ruptures, the new, leftist parties should be looking forward, over the long term, to a *decreasing* number of ruptures, as this would be indicative of their own success.

The danger from undemocratic forces—the extreme Right and the extreme Left—should not be underestimated. Despite their very slim chances of getting backing or recognition from foreign powers, disgruntled politicians and military officers have time and again hatched plots to engineer or instigate military revolts, coup attempts, and uprisings. A return to authoritarian rule by ultra-rightist elements cannot be ruled out. The extreme Left—the CPP-NPA—is not anywhere near seizing political power, but for the emergent leftist parties and groups it definitely constitutes the greater and more immediate menace. Apart from assassinating rejectionist leaders such as former NPA chief Kintanar and RPM-P leader Tabara, the CPP-NPA has killed members of rival leftist groups in Central Luzon, the Bondoc Peninsula, and several other places. Moreover, the CPP-NPA has harassed non-ND leftist activists in different parts of the country, especially during election campaign periods. Fortunately, the new, leftist parties and groups have mainly restricted their response to political denunciations, those groups that still have guerrilla units have maintained their restraint, and no all-out war has ensued. The new, leftist parties will have to keep up the political pressure on the CPP-NPA to desist from resorting to further violence in its rivalry with other leftist groups. As the Peruvian experience has shown, intraleftist armed conflict can lead to a carnage as well as the political marginalization of all parties and groups of the Left.

For the CPP-NPA and the NDs, going deeper into the state arena is not going to be easy. If they try to go beyond having a few seats in Congress and really move into local politics—elections as well as public office and governance—they could well find themselves in a truly knotty fool's game. Engaging in local politics, especially local governance, on a national or broad scale would require a lot more personnel and attention than congressional work. Such engagement would have major consequences, such as shifts in the actual emphasis from armed struggle and mass movements to electoral struggle and governance and from revolutionary work in the countryside to work in urban areas and town centers. These would go against the fundamental principles of the Maoist protracted people's war strategy. A contest between "armed struggle" and "political struggle" advocates could arise and split the CPP-NPA and the ND movement yet again. It can, of course, be argued that the CPP-NPA and the NDs could choose to ignore local politics. If they do so, however, the emergent leftist parties and groups, which they regard as renegades and counterrevolutionaries, could make good in this arena and gain strength and momentum.

For the emergent leftist parties and groups, forging a deeper unity has proven be an elusive goal. All of the new, leftist groups have been fighting to transform the Philippines' elite-dominated democracy into a participatory and egalitarian democracy (or socialism and democracy). All of them oppose the rule of the oligarchic elite and the political representatives of this elite—the *trapos*. And all resist the moves and maneuvers of undemocratic forces of the extreme Right and extreme Left to seize power and menace democratic forces. Thus far, however, the emergent leftist parties and groups have managed to forge only tactical alliances, often only on particular issues and concerns. If the new, leftist groups want to become a truly significant force for the deepening of democracy in the Philippines, they will have move into more strategic unities and alliances. For achieving deeper unity, a key question that has to be resolved is the issue of the instrumental versus integral view of democracy. This is, of course, very much related to notions of democracy, the state, revolution, and reform. The emergent leftist groups are now much better equipped for resolving the issue. In a relatively short period of time, they have accumulated an amazing wealth of experience.

Notes

Introduction

1 See Kerkvliet 1977 and Saulo 1990. The communists referred to here belonged to the Partido Komunista ng Pilipinas (PKP), established in 1930, which later adopted a pro-Soviet position in the Sino-Soviet split. A group of young communists who espoused "Marxism-Leninism-Mao Tse-tung Thought," broke away from the PKP and established the Communist Party of the Philippines (CPP) in 1968. Although both parties refer to themselves by both the Filipino and English names, PKP is more commonly used to refer to the old party and CPP to the new Maoist party. With the Pinyin spelling of Chinese names, which has replaced the old Wade-Giles system, the CPP has changed *Mao Tse-tung* to *Mao Zedong*.

2 The percentage of Filipinos who judge themselves to be poor, however, is higher. "Self-rated poverty" surveys of the Social Weather Stations (http://www.sws.org.ph) consistently show that more than half of the country's household heads consider their families to be poor. A Pulse Asia (http://pulseasia.newsmaker.ph.) survey conducted in November 2004 came up with even higher figures: 67 percent of Filipinos regard themselves as poor and 7 percent as very poor.

3 The minimum wage for a worker in Metro Manila in 2004 was ₱250, far below the average cost of living of a family of six, which is estimated to be over ₱460. Outside of the national capital region, the minimum wage represented only 37 to 41 percent of the average cost of living (Committee Affairs Department 2004).

4 Perhaps one of the best symbols of the elite's callousness is the imposing complex of the elite-dominated Congress, which stands right across from a large urban poor community.

5 "There is, in fact," clarifies Paul Hutchcroft (1998a:22), "a certain social mobility at the helm of Philippine society, as new families appear out of nowhere and some of the old families fall by the wayside." In this study, I use Hutchcroft's definition of *oligarchy*, derived from Aristotle: rule of the wealthy for its own benefit, not for the common good. I concur with his view that the Philippine oligarchy is "a social group that is based on wealth and that changes over time."

6 David Kang (2002) notes, in a study on corruption and development in South Korea and the Philippines, that corruption has permeated political life in both countries. Examining why there was economic growth in Korea but not in the Philippines, Kang arrives at this conclusion: "Corruption in Korea, although endemic, was constrained by the collusion of a powerful business class and a coherent state. Each major group was able to benefit from its close relationship with the other, but neither could ever gain the upper hand. Despite each group's constant bemoaning of its counterpart's utter lack of qualifications, each needed and relied upon the other. In contrast, corruption in the Philippines swung like a pendulum. As one group or the other gained predominant power, it would busily set about lining its own pockets, aware that in the next round its fortunes might well be reversed" (2002:20). In the case of the Philippines, Kang mainly describes the elite's behavior in the pre-martial-law period. Pendulum swings, however, have made a comeback in the post-Marcos era (Bello et al. 2004:286–88). This explains, at least in part, why the Philippine elite and the *trapos* (traditional politicians) aligned with them have simply aimed for short-term clientelistic gains and not tried to make their electoral fiefdoms more attractive to outside investment (through better infrastructure, more law-abiding behavior, etc.).

7 Manapat 1991. Manapat's book (*Some Are Smarter than Others*) draws its title precisely from this statement.

8 The abbreviation EDSA stands for Epifanio de los Santos Avenue, the scene of the mammoth rallies during the popular uprisings of February 1986, January 2001, and May 2001. Most political analysts refer to the first two, which ousted Marcos and Estrada, respectively, as people power uprisings, but many refrain from applying the term *people power* to the third, which was in support of the deposed Estrada.

9 In Case 2002:228, William Case does change his assessment: "[I]n falling short on a second dimension of quality, democracy in the Philippines, though stable, must be assessed as unconsolidated."

10 Notable among the few personages who did set up reform-oriented parties are the former immigration commissioner Miriam Defensor

Santiago and the religious charismatic leader Eduardo Villanueva. The feisty Santiago established the People's Reform Party (PRP) in 1992 professedly to fight corruption and promote good governance. She almost won in the 1992 presidential election. After losing again in her presidential bid in 1998, Santiago—and the PRP—joined Estrada's coalition and then shifted to the Arroyo camp just before the 2004 elections. "Brother Eddie" Villanueva, head of the "Jesus Is Lord" movement, put up his own party, Bangon Pilipinas, and ran for president in 2004 on a platform of national moral transformation. Bangon, which has since persisted in campaigning for moral renewal, is perhaps the only significant nonleftist party challenging *trapo* politics. Like traditional elite parties, however, Bangon still mainly revolves around its leader.

11 Given that the bulk of those I interviewed were leftist cadres and activists, a limitation of this study is that their interpretations of the views of ordinary people may reflect biases and selective information.

12 This is different from former president Estrada's Partido ng Masang Pilipino (PMP) or Party of the Filipino Masses.

13 Let me stress at this point that the three major interpretations of Philippine politics—the patron-client, elite democracy, and neocolonial frameworks—are historically embedded (as I will show in chap. 1) and had much relevance and import within their proper historical moments.

14 Huber et al. (1997:340) clarify that their concept of "social democracy" does not refer specifically to the European political movement bearing the same name.

15 Huber et al. (1997:323–24, 330) classify the new democracies of Latin America as formal democracies—in that they meet the criteria of free and fair elections and universal suffrage—but clarify that many of them are "truncated" or "deficient" forms of formal democracy, falling short in other criteria. The Latin American democracies suffer from weak accountability due to powerful presidents and weak legislatures and judiciaries, uneven protection of civil and political rights, and patrimonial practices.

16 Laclau and Mouffe (see Mouffe 1988:103–4) use Gramsci's "collective will" in a metaphoric way only. They reject the notions of a vanguard party and a vanguard class in Gramsci's concept. Besides, as Mouffe explains, collective will, like Rousseau's "general will," can imply too much homogeneity.

1

Contested Democracy: An Alternative Interpretation of Philippine Politics

1 *Cacique*, a term of Spanish origin, refers to the privileged local class.

2 As mentioned earlier, Case (2002:228) has changed his assessment of Philippine democracy from "consolidated" to "unconsolidated" because of its poor quality.

3 According to Hollnsteiner, *utang na loob* may roughly be translated as "debt of gratitude" or "sense of gratitude," while *hiya* embraces the feelings of shame, embarrassment, guilt and shyness.

4 Ando cited John Duncan Powell, who stated in Powell (1970: 412): "It is important to note that patron-client ties clearly are different from other ties which might bind parties unequal in status and proximate in time and space, but which do not rest on the reciprocal exchange of mutually valued goods and services—such as relationships based on coercion, authority, manipulation, and so forth."

5 Scott's studies (1969, 1972b) were not specifically on the Philippines, but he cited the Philippines extensively. In another study, Scott (1972a) acknowledged, somewhat contradictorily, the continued vitality of patron-client ties in Southeast Asia, including the Philippines.

6 Scott later revised his position, saying that machine politics "represent a particular form of electoral clientelism" that involves "the political coordination of favors, patronage, and public contracts" (1977:493).

7 *Pakikisama* roughly translates as "camaraderie" (but with strict reciprocity).

8 Wolters's book was based on his Ph.D. dissertation, "Class Relationships and Political Processes in Central Luzon, Philippines" (1975).

9 The CPP, for instance, labeled all of the country's administrations as "puppets of U.S. imperialism." To underscore Marcos's puppetry, the CPP referred to his government as the "US-Marcos regime" (which later became the "US-Marcos dictatorship"). Although it sometimes used the term *neocolonial*, the CPP preferred the Maoist *semicolonial* (often with *semifeudal* attached to it) to characterize the Philippines. See Pomeroy 1970 for an analysis of neocolonialism from the perspective of the Soviet-aligned PKP and Guerrero 1979a for that of the Maoist CPP.

10 One of these was Dante Simbulan, an early writer on elite politics. See Simbulan 1970:4.

11 For a more detailed account of the "mode of production" debate, see Rojas 1992. Rojas identifies Jose Ma. Sison, Juliet de Lima Sison, and Ricardo Ferrer with the CPP's "semifeudal" position; Merlin Magallona and Rosalinda Ofreneo-Pineda with the "neo-industrialization school"; Jonathan Fast, Jim Richardson, Brian Fegan, Peter Limqueco, Alfred McCoy, and Marshall McLennan with the historical approach of dependency theory; Rigoberto Tiglao with the political economy approach; Alex Magno with the "relative autonomy of the state" approach; and Temario Rivera and Cynthia Banzon Bautista with the "articulation" school.

12 Maria Gloria Cano Garcia (2004) argues that the term *cacique*, as it is used in the Philippines, is an American construction. According to her, *cazique* (the old Spanish spelling) denoted a chieftain or local magnate in Latin America. In applying the term to the Philippines, American officials and scholars "decontextualized" it and gave it a new meaning: "a corrupt system of local government—a cancer—implemented or fostered by the Spaniards in the Philippines" (Cano Garcia 2004:1). She contends that American officials used *cacique* and *caciquismo* to characterize a dysfunctional system that they themselves had established.

13 Hutchcroft (1993:560) uses Stanislav Andreski's definition of *rent capitalism* as a system in which "money is invested in arrangements for appropriating wealth which has already been produced rather than in [arrangements for actually] producing it."

14 Borrowing from James Buchanan, McCoy (1993a:11) explains that "rents are created when a state gives an entrepreneur an artificial advantage by restricting 'freedom of entry' into the market."

15 The three other case studies were Argentina, Guatemala, and South Korea.

16 To come up with a finer categorization of political systems that are neither fully authoritarian nor fully democratic, Franco (2001:5–11) reviews the Latin American democratic transitions in the 1980s and comes up with four possible types of regimes: electoral authoritarian, clientelist electoral, militarized electoral, and demilitarizing electoral. She classifies the Marcos dictatorship as electoral authoritarian.

17 See the preceding discussion of Paredes 1988.

18 All three major interpretations of Philippine politics (including their variants) are actually being proffered as interpretations of *postcolonial* Philippine politics and as continuing to be valid up to the present. As mentioned earlier, a good number of political and social scientists state that the patron-client model has been the predominant paradigm since

1965—and that it still is—through no fault of Landé's. Many of those who still adhere to the neocolonial model insist that it holds true from 1946 (independence) until today (see, e.g., J. Sison 2003). Bello, Anderson and others write about the *restoration* of elite democracy and cacique democracy, saying that the Philippines was / is an elite or cacique democracy from 1946 to 1972 and from 1986 to the present. Hutchcroft declares that the Philippines has been a patrimonial oligarchic state since pre-martial-law times. In this chapter, I have shown the historical embeddedness of the three interpretations and their relevance and significance in particular historical periods.

19 According to Ileto (2001:20), Landé's patron-client paradigm came out at a time of anxiety over the threat of communism. Ileto argues that Landé's model "ought to be seen in the context of mainly Marxist-nationalist challenges to the postwar construction of history and politics."

20 Data are from Gerson 1998:47; and National Statistical Coordination Board 2003.

21 According to Gerard Clarke and Marites Sison (2003), members of the Filipino elite perceive poverty as arising from such factors as the unequal distribution of wealth, corruption, and "traditional" politics. While blaming the "elite" for these problems, members of the elite do not see themselves as part of it. "The Filipino elite," note Clarke and M. Sison (2003:237), "feel a sense of responsibility towards the poor, but this responsibility is met through the provision of assistance on a patron-client basis or through philantrophic activity, rather than a more substantive commitment to redistributive action led by the state."

22 Most Filipinos perceive corruption in government as a serious problem. In a Social Weather Stations survey conducted in December 2000, 36 percent rated the magnitude of corruption in government as "very large" and 36 percent "somewhat large" (Mangahas 2001).

23 The budget deficit of the national government soared from less than 1 percent of the country's gross domestic product (GDP) in 1995 to 5.2 percent in 2002; its debt rose from ₱1.2 trillion or 61 percent of GDP, in 1995 to ₱3.4 trillion, or 77 percent in 2003 (Buenaventura 2004).

24 According to Wallace, the thirty-year average GDP growth rates of selected Asian countries are: China, 7.8 percent; Korea, 6.4 percent; Singapore, 6.3 percent; Malaysia, 5.9 percent; Thailand, 5.7 percent; Indonesia, 5.3 percent; and Philippines, 3.1 percent.

25 See the Haribon web site: http://www.haribon.org.ph/?q=node/view/126.

26 National Statistics Office (http://www.census.gov.ph/data/sectordata/2000/ieoopftx.html).

27 According to Schaffer (2001:4), this is how (certain) columnists in the Philippines' English-language newspapers have referred to the poor.

28 According to a World Bank study (see Doronila 2001b), Estrada's flagship poverty-alleviation program, Lingap para sa Mahirap (Caring for the Poor), benefited the middle and rich classes more than the poor. The study focused on five key aspects of the program: health care, elementary education, water supply, housing, and subsidized rice distribution.

2

Threat to Democracy or Democratizing Force?

1 Hewison and Rodan focus only on the modern countries of Southeast Asia: Indonesia, Malaysia, the Philippines, Singapore, and Thailand.

2 In 1993, President Fidel Ramos derided the communist rebellion as a failure, saying that factional strife was finishing it off (Agnote 1993). In 1995, a U.S. State Department report described the Philippine communist movement as riven by infighting and defeated (*Philippine Daily Inquirer* 1995).

3 In this book, I use the term *progressive* to refer to a person or group of persons that resists arbitrary power (derived from wealth, family ties, or bureaucratic position) and promotes or supports new ideas and social change.

4 More detailed accounts of the PKP and the Huk rebellion can be found in Santayana 1950; Lachica 1971; Kerkvliet 1977; Saulo 1990; Partido Komunista ng Pilipinas 1996; and Lava 2002.

5 In 1972, Marcos promised almost one million hectares of tenanted rice and corn lands for redistribution. By the time of his ouster, he had accomplished only 10 percent of this target (Borras 1998:40).

6 For an account of the PKP's negotiations with Marcos and the changes in its stance toward him, see Pomeroy 1993:73–75.

7 Official CPP documents declare that the CPP founded the NPA, but it was actually Buscayno's guerrilla band that *found* the CPP.

8 For more detailed accounts of the NDs' role in the antidictatorship struggle, see Jones 1989; Rocamora 1994a:chap. 1; Reid 2000:chap. 2; Weekley 2001:pt. 2; Franco 2001:chaps. 4–5; and Boudreau 2004: chaps. 6, 8.

9 For a more elaborate discussion of the three strategic frameworks, see Concerned Communist Party of the Philippines Members 1993; and Tupaz 1991. Omar Tupaz was one of the pseudonyms I used when I was still in the CPP. See also National Democratic Front of Metro Manila-Rizal 1991; Arguelles 1993; and Reid 2000:34–41.

10 The dissenters viewed a mixed economy as an intermediate stage prior to socialism.

11 A more elaborate defense of Stalin can be found in Liwanag 1992b.

12 Many of the most important documents of the CPP debate appear in Concerned Communist Party of the Philippines Members 1993. Others can be found in *Kasarinlan* 8 (2), 1992; and in *Debate*, nos. 5–9.

13 Timonera 1993a; Gloria 1993; Party Organizations in the Visayas 1993; West Mindanao Regional White Area Leading Cadres Conference 1993; Democratic Bloc within the CPP 1994; Melencio 1994; Reid 2000:46–48.

14 See Avendaño 1993a, 1993b; Timonera 1993b, 1993c; Party Organizations in the Visayas 1993; Democratic Bloc within the CPP 1994; and Constantino-David 1997:44.

15 "An Expression of Concern" (with 16 signatories) and "An International Appeal for a Peaceful Resolution of Internal Conflict" (with 108 signatories), which were paid advertisements in the *Philippine Daily Inquirer*, 29 April 1994:28.

16 See Rebolusyonaryong Partido ng Manggagawa—Pilipinas [RPM-P] 1998; and Fortaleza 1999. The RPM-M is affiliated with the Fourth International, which rejects Stalinism and Maoism. The rejectionist groups were not a homogeneous lot. Although they all repudiated Stalinism and Maoism, among other things, they disagreed on strategy and tactics, and their analysis of the Philippine state.

17 The PMP was enlarged after its merger with the Partido Proletaryo Demokratiko (PPD) or Democratic Proletarian Party, and the Sosyalistang Partido ng Paggawa (SPP) or Socialist Workers' Party in August 2002.

18 Interviews with Nilo de la Cruz, head of the peace panel, Rebolusyonaryong Partido ng Manggagawa—Pilipinas, 24 January 2002, in Mandaluyong City; Sonny Melencio, chairman, Sosyalistang Partido ng Paggawa, 5 January 2002 and 25 August 2002, in Quezon City; Manjet

Manalo Lopez, secretary-general, Sanlakas, 1 July 2002, in Quezon City; Ike de los Reyes (pseud.), chair, Rebolusyonaryong Partido ng Pilipinas—Mindanao, 9 March 2002, in Quezon City, and 8 December 2003, in Amsterdam, the Netherlands; Ka Olive and Ka Nicolas (pseuds.), spokespersons, Marxista-Leninistang Partido ng Pilipinas, 8 April 2002, in Quezon City.

19 Sandigan, which never really made much of an impact as an armed group, was disbanded after the fall of Marcos.

20 Remark by Lidy Nacpil, executive director of the Freedom from Debt Coalition, at a forum on "Strategic Left Frameworks for Social Change," in Quezon City, 5 November 2003.

21 Interview with Joel Rocamora, president, Akbayan, and executive director, Institute for Popular Democracy, 17 January 2002, in Quezon City. See also Abao 1997:271. In 1992, Bisig, Pandayan and the popdems forged a loose nonparty alliance called Kaakbay ng Sambayanan (Akbayan) or Ally of the People, which supported the unsuccessful presidential bid of Senator Jovito Salonga. When the three groups and Siglaya banded together to form a new party in 1995–96, they named it Aksyon. The new party had to drop Aksyon, however, because a political party headed by former senator Raul Roco had registered ahead of it with the name Aksyon Demokratiko. In place of Aksyon, the new, leftist party adopted the name Akbayan (but not the longer appellation Kaakbay ng Sambayanan). Not all of Pandayan's members, nor all of the popdems, joined Akbayan. Some Pandayan members joined the Liberal Party, ABA, and AKO. A section of the popdems established a separate party-list group called Pinag-isang Lakas sa Pagbabago (Pinatubo) or Consolidated Power for Change, which fielded candidates in the 1998 and 2001 party-list elections but did not make it to the winning column.

22 Hewison and Rodan (1996) use Michael Bernhard's definition of *civil society*: an autonomous sphere "from which political forces representing constellations of interests in society have contested state power."

23 See http://pulseasia.newsmaker.ph.

24 With regard EDSA II, see Bautista 2001:7–9.

25 In the Philippines, opinion pollsters classify the population as follows: A, the upper class; B, the upper middle class; C, the middle class; D, the poor; and E, the very poor. The number of people belonging to classes A, B, and C is small, usually totaling only 11 to 12 percent. Hence, pollsters often just lump them together when presenting their findings.

26 For a chronology of significant events in relation to the PKP, see Saulo 1990:app. 4.

27 Here I am relying mainly on my personal experience as a CPP cadre doing organizing work among students, workers, urban poor, and "middle forces" during the Marcos authoritarian period. How the CPP went about the step-by-step process of organizing peasants, workers, urban poor, and students is explained in Central Committee, CPP 1972, 1976. CPP organizing of middle forces is elaborated in National United Front Commission, CPP 1982.

28 Regarding the undemocratic workings of the CPP, see Abinales 1988; Tupaz 1992; Bello 1993; Concerned Communist Party of the Philippines Members 1993; Melencio 1994; and R. Constantino 1996:36–38. Regarding PKP, see Nemenzo 1984a, 1984b, 1984c; Kerkvliet 1977:218–33; and Kerkvliet 1996. The undemocratic features of the PKP were not always in the Stalinist mold. Nemenzo (1984c:24) states that before the assumption by Jose Lava of the PKP leadership in 1948, the party operated "like a typical populist movement—loose, slovenly and reckless" (especially after the PKP-SPP merger of 1938). He also points out that after the enactment of the Anti-subversion Law in 1957, the PKP departed from strict "democratic centralism" by adopting a "single-file" organizational policy. This, however, virtually liquidated the party (Nemenzo 1984c:33–36). In another essay, Nemenzo (1984b) states that the Filipino Marxism of the merged PKP-SPP exhibited "millenarian-populist aspects."

29 With regard to patriarchalism, Nemenzo (1984c:15) describes the SPP leader Abad Santos as follows: "He built a mass following by invoking feudal obligations and relied on psychological techniques to motivate his followers. The strongest bond holding the SP together was devotion to 'Don Perico' (an aristocratic title that aptly conveyed his feudal relationship to the party rank-and-file)."

30 For accounts of how the NDs tried to build a broad antidictatorship front under its control and to push for a boycott of the 1986 snap elections, see Jones 1989:chap. 13; Rocamora 1994a:33–41; Weekley 2001:133–38; and Boudreau 2004:chap. 8.

31 On the PKP, see Nemenzo 1984a, 1984c; Jose 1985:83–85; and Kerkvliet 1996:17. On the CPP, see Damazo 2003; Amnesty International 1992:chap. 4; Lawyers Committee for Human Rights 1990:chap. 1; Lawyers Committee for Human Rights 1988:3–20; and Editorial Staff, *Ang Bayan* 1987b.

32 In the case of the CPP, see Bello 1993:13–14.

33 See Arguelles 1995:105–23; Abinales 1996a:154–79; Garcia 2001; and Sarmiento 2003.

34 Asia Watch 1990:43–49; Lawyers Committee for Human Rights 1990:15–16; Santos 2003; Rosales 2003a; Contreras 2004. Asia Watch notes that in CPP-NPA executions, due process seems to be almost nonexistent, and many of those killed are not legitimate military targets. According to the Lawyers Committee, the CPP-NPA's people's courts do not meet the standards set in Protocol II (1977), a protocol additional to the Geneva Conventions of 1949, since they are neither regularly constituted nor independent of the ruling authority and they do not give the defendant the means to present an adequate defense.

35 See Jones 1989:chap. 5; Corpus 1989:chap. 1; and Salonga 2001:chap. 12. According to Corpus (1989:13–16), the Plaza Miranda bombing had been a CPP operation plotted by Sison and a few other CPP leaders and designed to "heighten the contradictions between the two main factions of the ruling class," force the hand of Marcos to take more repressive measures (which he did with the suspension of the writ of habeas corpus and eventually the declaration of martial law), push the middle forces to join the armed struggle, and thus hasten the revolutionary process.

36 The other ND party-list groups are Anak ng Bayan, Suara Bangsamoro, and Migrante.

37 Carlo Butalid, cited in Pascual 2003.

38 I recall that personnel of open organizations sometimes referred to the political officers as "dark lords."

39 Former CPP cadres who had worked extensively in the open legal sphere discussed the experience of legal organizations turning into transmission belts of the party during a conference of PO and NGO leaders in Manila on 6 March 1994 (see PO-NGO Conference 1994). See also Constantino-David 1997:43–46.

40 Both the 1977 and 1982 drafts of the NDF program, as drawn up by the CPP, contained a provision that no single political group would monopolize political power in a national democratic state (see Rocamora 1994a:160).

41 Interviews with De la Cruz, Melencio, Lopez, and De los Reyes.

42 Interview with Rocamora, 17 January 2002. Interview with Victor Gerardo Bulatao, executive director, Empowering Civic Participation in Governance (ECPG), and former member, National Council, Akbayan, 23 January 2002, Quezon City.

43 Ben Reid (2004:31) describes the divergence in this way: "[T]here is a consensus [among SDs and Bisig] that the democratic struggle remains primarily defending and consolidating the gains of the EDSA revolution

against the Marcos dictatorship in 1986. This contrasts with the revolutionary left [e.g., the PMP], which while defending the opening created by EDSA still seeks the replacement of the existing state with revolutionary organs of popular power."

44 Among "emergent" or "new," left parties and groups, I exclude the CPP and PDSP, which are the more established leftist parties, as well as ND and SD parties and groups identified with the CPP and PDSP.

45 Sanlakas representative Renato Magtubo and Akbayan representative Loretta Ann Rosales exposed payoffs to legislators for the passage of the Omnibus Power bill in the Eleventh Congress.

46 See note 17.

47 The engagement of the PMP in the state arena is mainly through the two party-list groups aligned with it, PM and Sanlakas.

3

The Emergent Left's Engagement in Civil Society

1 I also draw from my personal recollection of popdem positions in 1986–87.

2 See, for instance, Rebolusyonaryong Partido ng Manggagawa—Pilipinas 1998; and Partido ng Manggagawang Pilipino 1999.

3 Putnam (1995:67) defines *social capital* as "features of social organization such as networks, norms, and social trust that facilitate coordination and cooperation for mutual benefit."

4 The aforementioned are based on my personal recollection, having been very much involved with the CPP and the ND movement during the Marcos and Aquino periods.

5 See Art. II, Sec. 23; Article X, Sec. 14; and Art. XIII, Sec. 15–16 of the 1987 Constitution.

6 Francisco (1994:2–5) specifically mentions the popdems and some mainstream NDs, but other leftist political blocs working closely with the popdems then were Bisig, Pandayan and Kasapi.

7 It is quite possible that sections within the antiauthoritarian movements of Eastern Europe and Latin America started out by following Gramsci's main argument on building counterhegemony *within* civil society, that they managed to gain dominance in the relatively weak and undevel-

oped civil societies, and that they then shifted to "civil society against the state."

8 By rejecting "totalizing ideologies" and "centralized direction," FOPA departed from Gramsci's adherence to much of orthodox Marxism-Leninism.

9 As the term used here, *contentious politics* is collective action in which "ordinary people, often in league with more influential citizens, join forces in confrontations with elites, authorities, and opponents" (Tarrow 1998:2).

10 *Kabisig* is a Filipino term for "linking of arms," denoting working together.

11 Foley and Edwards (1996:40) apply this only to Civil Society I, but it holds for Civil Society II as well.

12 I wish to thank Silvia Sanz-Ramos Rojo and Joel Rocamora for drawing my attention to Mohan and Stokke's article.

13 Gerard Clarke, cited in Melegrito and Mendoza 1999:247.

14 Chapter 6 contains a critical analysis of the concept of "raising political consciousness."

15 This is the precursor of the political party.

16 In the foregoing paragraph, I draw once again from my experiences in the ND movement.

17 Interview with Reyes, 3 November 2003, in Quezon City.

18 The *bibingka* strategy is discussed in Borras 1999. Morales, a popdem leader, was formerly the president of the Philippine Rural Reconstruction Movement (PRRM), a development NGO.

19 Interviews with Reyes; and Martin Tanchuling, 14 October 2003, in Amsterdam.

20 See the BMP Web site: http://www.geocities.com/bukluran/WhatisBMP.htm.

21 See the APL Web site: http://www.apl.org.ph/APLPrimer/PrimerIndex.htm.

22 Interviews with Wilson Fortaleza, 20 March 2002, in Quezon City; and Marlon Quesada, 8 April 2002, in Los Baños, Laguna.

23 Interview with Quesada. For more on CIU, see its Web site: http://www.ciu.ph/

24 Interview with Fortaleza.

25 Interview with Ike de los Reyes, 8 December 2003, in Amsterdam.

26 FDC Web site: http://www.freedomfromdebtcoalition.org/

27 For a detailed discussion of coalition experiences during this period, see Cala and Grageda 1994; and Magadia 2003.

28 The assassination of PMP founder Filemon Lagman in February 2001 remains unsolved. Among those suspected of perpetrating the murder are the CPP, elements in the AFP, powerful politicians, and crime syndicates. Also being entertained, however, is the possibility that Lagman's murder may have had to do with the fissures of the late 1990s.

29 Here I write from direct experience, having been a leading cadre of the CPP in Mindanao and then in international work. In the late 1970s, the CPP laid out elaborate finance policies and procedures on how such funds should be diverted. Before a project proposal would be submitted to a funding agency, party cadres in the legal organization or program concerned had to get clearance from the party's higher organs on how much of the project funds would actually be used and how much would be "centralized." Projects were categorized—"ghost projects," those to be given "credible reality," and those that were for "partial" or "full" implementation. To ensure that large amounts could be "centralized," budgets were often inflated.

30 Erap is Estrada's nickname.

31 Schaffer 2001:11–15; Maria Christina Astorga, cited by Schaffer. In a study conducted by Schaffer in Barangay Commonwealth, an urban poor community, 4 percent of the respondents understood *trapo* not as a term referring to a certain type of politician but as "a term used disparagingly by the rich to describe the poor, especially those who gathered at EDSA 3."

32 Pro-Estrada forces, in turn, have been very critical of organizations and groups that they perceive as being pro-Arroyo. Late last year a pro-Estrada newspaper referred to the latter as "the mob," "the noisy rabble calling itself the civil society," and "President Arroyo's civil society" (*Daily Tribune* 2003). This shows, at least, that civil society is not always seen in a good light.

4

The Left, Elections, and the Political Party System

1 Mainwaring and Scully (1995:22) describe the problems of an inchoate party system: "Democratic politics is more erratic, establishing legitimacy is more difficult, and governing is more complicated. Powerful economic elites tend to have privileged access to policy makers. In the absence of well-developed institutional checks and balances, patrimonial practices often prevail, and legislatures tend to be weakly developed."

2 In mentioning "the birds and the bees," Aquino refers to the classic imagery in Philippine politics of birds and bees having the ability to vote.

3 In this chapter, I do not delve much into the May 2004 elections, as I did my fieldwork before 2004.

4 The Court of First Instance of Manila actually declared the PKP illegal and sentenced its leaders in September 1931, but the PKP appealed. The Supreme Court upheld the decision in October 1932.

5 Alejo Santos was the only DA congressman-elect who managed to retain his seat. Unlike the other DA congressmen-elect, Santos had run under both the NP and the DA.

6 According to Harold Crouch, the PKP's boycott coincided with a similar "hardening" among other Asian communist parties and may have been influenced by the latter (E-mailed comment from Crouch, 6 July 2003).

7 For an account of the struggle between the CPP's Central Committee and the Manila-Rizal Regional Party Committee over the party's tactics in the 1978 elections, see Jones 1989:chap. 10.

8 Interview with Ricardo Reyes, 3 November 2003, in Quezon City.

9 Interview with Loretta Ann Rosales, 12 January 2003, in Quezon City.

10 A Supreme Court ruling on 26 June 2001 barred them completely from the party-list system.

11 According to Wurfel, the law made a pointless and confusing distinction between sectors and parties and contained loopholes making it possible for *trapo* dummies to sneak in as parties of marginalized sectors. With only several months to go before the first party-list vote, few voters knew about the system or understood how it worked. In addition to failing to conduct a good information drive about the party-list system, the

Commission on Elections (Comelec) also did not come up with a reasonably tamper-proof counting system.

12 Prior to 1997, the emergent leftist groups were only preparty formations or multisectoral alliances that were not formally registered with the Comelec as electoral parties or groups. The PDSP was registered with the Comelec as an electoral party as early as 1987.

13 Interview with Satur Ocampo, 11 January 2003, in Quezon City.

14 Bayan Muna acknowledges "ideological affinity" with the CPP-NPA, but does not categorically admit an organizational link (see Go 2002:14).

15 Comelec reviewed the long roster of party-list groups, deciding which were qualified or not qualified, only *after* and not before the elections. Only five party-list representatives were immediately proclaimed. The fifteen others were sworn in, in several batches, only after prolonged legal tussles.

16 The ABA coalesced with AKO to form the ABA-AKO coalition in July 2003.

17 Interview with Ocampo.

18 It is sometimes argued that traditional politicians woo leftists to give the impression that they too are issue oriented, principled, progressive, or enjoy the support of those who are. Patricio N. Abinales (2001a:154–61) contends, however, that politicians in the Philippines now practice "big tent" politics—forging coalitions that bring together ideologically opposed groups for tactical purposes such as the election of a presidential candidate. In this case, the PPC needed support in the senatorial race, which was a tight contest. Arroyo's support for Bayan Muna was probably also a "confidence-building measure" for government-NDF talks, which were reopened two weeks before the elections.

19 Interview with Ka Dencio, 22 March 2002, in Makati.

20 E-mail communication with Reynaldo Gueco, a leading Akbayan political education officer, 5 June 2003. The First Quarter Storm of 1970 refers to a series of turbulent confrontations in the early part of 1970 between youth and student activists hurling pillboxes and Molotov cocktails and policemen armed with truncheons and automatic rifles.

21 Comment of Ka Miriam during the forum "Strategic Frameworks of the Philippine Left," 5 November 2003, Quezon City.

22 To some extent, this is borne out by the Philippine left's early electoral experience — that of the SPP and the PKP in the 1930s and 1940s. As mentioned earlier, the SPP and PKP never made it in their bids for national and Assembly positions before the war, but they did win in

some municipal contests and were gaining ground. The momentum, however, was broken by the Japanese occupation. The DA's near clean sweep of Central Luzon's congressional seats in 1946 can be attributed mainly to the Hukbalahap's and PKP's roles in the anti-Japanese resistance, but the SPP/PKP's prewar electoral achievements helped to build up to it.

23 Interview with Norberto Gonzales, Jr., 26 June 2002, in Manila.

24 List of Akbayan's local government unit (LGU) officials presented at the Akbayan National Congress, 30–31 July 2003, in Manila. The figures do not include Akbayan-endorsed local officials.

25 Interview with Ocampo.

26 In 2002, however, the *barangay* and SK elections, both already long-delayed, were held simultaneously.

27 Introduced in 1982, the nonpartisan barangay election scheme was designed to give the dictator Marcos's party undue advantage over its rivals (see Carbonell-Catilo et al. 1985:78).

28 The leftist groups involved in the 1997 vote openly talked about the candidates they backed since they were not yet registered electoral parties.

29 Had the major traditional parties really wanted to dominate the party-list vote in 2001 they would have poured more resources into their party-list campaigns. Only two major traditional parties made it to the minimum threshold—good for only one seat each—before the Supreme Court disqualified the big traditional parties from the party-list vote.

30 Interview with Rosales.

31 I do not wish to suggest here that if not for the *trapos'* arsenal of patronage and dirty tricks the poor and marginalized would naturally vote for candidates of the emergent leftist parties. I merely wish to indicate the hurdles they have to overcome in competing with *trapos*.

32 Narrated to me by Ka Dencio, 22 March 2002, in Makati.

33 I actually came up with the idea of "contested democracy" after reading Kerkvliet's "Contested Meanings of Elections in the Philippines" (1996). I reckoned that it is not just the meaning of elections that is contested in the Philippines. Perhaps, and even more important, the meaning of democracy is contested as well.

5

The Left's Engagement in Government and Governance

1 As used here, *government* refers to "the institutions and agents charged with governing" and *governance* to "the modes and manner of governing" (Jessop 1998:30).

2 Interview with Loretta Ann Rosales, 12 January 2003, in Quezon City.

3 Interview with Ka Dencio, 22 March 2002, in Makati.

4 Interview with Ka Dencio.

5 Interview with Ka Dencio.

6 Interview with Satur Ocampo, 11 January 2003, in Quezon City.

7 Although Bayan Muna supported almost all of President Arroyo's senatorial candidates in exchange for her endorsement of its bid in the party-list vote in 2001, it did not officially join Arroyo's "People Power Coalition."

8 Although Morales and De la Torre helped set up Akbayan and many of their fellow popdems became members of the new party, they themselves did not join it.

9 Interview with Martin Tanchuling, executive director of the Philippine Network of Rural Development Institutes (Philnet-RDI), 14 October, 2003, in Amsterdam.

10 The most notable appointees were Secretary Ernesto Garilao and Undersecretary Gerardo Bulatao under Ramos and Secretary Morales under Estrada.

11 Borras's assessment of Morales's reform efforts contradicts Törnquist's point that these were an outright failure.

12 The dual-power strategy is essentially the "*bibingka* strategy," but with a "democratic participation in governance" component, which will be discussed later in this chapter.

13 Interview with Ricardo Reyes, 3 November 2003, in Quezon City.

14 See http://www.aasianst.org/absts/1997abst/seasia/sea82.htm. The panel of Session 82, "Decentralization and Democracy: Exploring the Linkages in the Philippines," consisted of Gary Hawes, Emil Bolongaita, Paul Hutchcroft, John Thayer Sidel and Nereus Acosta. It took place at the 1997 Association for Asian Studies Annual Meeting, Chicago, Illinois.

15 Villarin 1996: 7–10; electronic communication with Maritona Labajo, former secretary-general of Akbayan and former program officer of CODE-NGO, 8 August 2003.

16 The seven NGOs were the Center for Agrarian Reform, Empowerment, and Transformation (Caret), Education for Life Foundation (ELF), Institute for Popular Democracy (IPD), Institute of Politics and Governance (IPG), Kaisahan Tungo sa Kaunlaran ng Kanayunan at Repormang Pansakahan (Kaisahan), Popular Education for People Empowerment (PEPE), and Sentro ng Alternatibong Lingap Panligal (Saligan).

17 According to Patrick I. Patiño, the NGOs identified with what later became the Batman Consortium, supported over 600 candidates for *barangay* posts in 1997. Half of the candidates for *barangay* captain (92 out of 182) and over a third of the candidates for *barangay* councilor (180 out of 450) won. See Patiño 1999:14.

18 The two additional NGOs were the Labor Education and Research Network (Learn) and Small Economic Enterprises Development (SEED).

19 Interview with Bulatao, 27 August 2002. Founded in August 2001, ECPG now assists ABA-AKO and Alab Katipunan in their development work. Established in October 2001, LGCNet was formally incorporated in August 2002 with forty-two member NGOs.

20 I visited ten Batman *barangays* in Banaybanay, Governor Generoso, Surallah, Jagna, and Daraga.

21 Interview with Ramon Casiple, IPER executive director, 26 March 2002, in Quezon City.

22 Some case studies are discussed in Chapter VII.

23 Interview with Gerardo Calderon, mayor, Angono, Rizal, 7 April 2002, in Angono.

24 Interviews with Calderon; Bernardo Balagtas, artist and municipal councilor, Angono, 7 April 2002, in Angono; Lecifina Arce, former secretary, Rizal Provincial Committee, Sanlakas, 10 January 2003, in Quezon City; and Helen Bonga, former chairperson, Angono Multisectoral Organizations, 6 January 2003, in Angono.

25 Interviews with Christopher Flores, mayor, Guinobatan, Albay, 30 October 2002, in Quezon City; Wilber Francis Rontas, action officer, Municipal Disaster Coordinating Council, Guinobatan, 3 November 2002, in Guinobatan; Rodolfo Teope, businessman and former activist, 3 November 2002, in Guinobatan; and Rodrigo Realubit, former activist, 3 November 2002, in Guinobatan; and Beth Oñate, member, management staff, Office of the Mayor, 4 November 2002, in Guinobatan.

26 Interview with Flores.

27 The name of the local official is withheld here, as divulging it could endanger his security.

28 Interview with Angela Librado, city councilor, Davao City, 17 July 2002, in Davao City.

29 Minutes, "First Political Meeting of Akbayan LGU Officials," 15–16 December, 2002, Quezon City.

30 Interview with Carmel Abao, chairperson, government affairs committee, Akbayan, 4 November 2003, in Quezon City.

31 Interview with Abao.

32 Some Akbayan members, who still consider themselves revolutionaries, are not too keen on using the revolutionary-radical democratic dichotomy because they equate revolution with a process of radical transformation involving gradual changes as well as storms and ruptures.

33 See, for instance, two books on "new public management" in a series entitled "East and Southeast Asia Network for Better Local Governments" published by the Konrad Adenauer Foundation and the Local Government Development Foundation in 2000.

34 See note 1.

35 Minutes, "First Political Meeting of Akbayan LGU Officials," 15–16 December, 2002, Quezon City.

36 By law, local officials are limited to a maximum of three three-year terms for the same position.

6

Special Areas of Concern: Popular Political Education and Working for Political Reform

1 In the Philippines, election modernization simply means the shift to automation—or the use of automated counting machines, computer equipment and other appropriate devices—in the process of voting, counting the votes, and canvassing and consolidating election results.

2 The ban on political dynasties is actually constitutionally mandated, but it needs enabling legislation, as the Philippine Constitution provides that

the state shall "prohibit political dynasties as may be defined by law." In various Congresses, bills have been filed stipulating that a person up to a certain degree of consanguinity (second, third, or fourth) to an incumbent elected official be barred from running for public office or succeeding the incumbent.

3 Amendments to the Philippine constitution (ratified in 1987) may be proposed by Congress gathered as a constituent assembly, upon a vote of three-fourths of all its members, or by a constitutional convention, whose members are elected by Filipino voters according to district. Proposed amendments become valid when ratified by a majority of the votes cast in a plebiscite.

4 "[E]very human being," writes Freire (1975:13, 52), "no matter how 'ignorant' or submerged in the 'culture of silence' he may be, is capable of looking critically at his world in a *dialogical encounter* with others. Provided with the proper tools for such encounter, he can gradually perceive his personal and social reality as well as the contradictions in it, become conscious of his own perception of that reality, and deal critically with it. In this process, the old, paternalistic teacher-student relationship is overcome." And further: "Attempting to liberate the oppressed without their reflective participation in the act of liberation is to treat them as objects which must be saved from a burning building; it is to lead them into the populist pitfall and transform them into masses which can be manipulated."

5 This orientation was new in the Philippine context at least.

6 Interview with Fr. Ben Verzosa, assistant parish priest, Banaybanay, Davao Oriental, 10 July 2002, in Banaybanay.

7 Electronic communication with Cecilia Soriano, 12 June 2003. (Some parts translated from Filipino.)

8 Some noteworthy studies dealing mainly or in part with Philippine political culture are: Kerkvliet 1990; Kerkvliet and Mojares 1991; Gutierrez, Torrente, and Narca 1992; McCoy 1993b; Lacaba 1995; Pertierra 1995b; Institute for Political and Electoral Reform 1995a; Alejo, Rivera, and Valencia 1996; Diokno 1997 (three-volume series); Sidel 1999.

9 Electronic communication with Cecilia Soriano, 1 June 2004.

10 According to Freire (1996:83), generative themes "contain the possibility of unfolding into again as many themes, which in turn call for new tasks to be fulfilled."

11 In a later publication, Scott calls for a fundamental rethinking of the Marxist and Gramscian concept of hegemony (i.e., the ideological

hegemony of the ruling class over subordinate classes), arguing, for instance, that "subordinate classes are able, on the basis of their daily material experience, to penetrate and demystify the prevailing ideology" and that "theories of hegemony frequently confound what is inevitable with what is just" (1985:317).

12 Interview with Ramon Casiple, executive director, IPER, 26 March 2002, in Quezon City.

13 In June 2001, the Supreme Court ruled that a party-list organization must represent "marginalized and underrepresented sectors," thereby disqualifying the top five political parties from the party-list elections altogether.

14 Electronic communication with Nina Iszatt, coordinator, Policy Advocacy and Campaigns Center, Kaisahan tungo sa Kaunlaran ng Kanayunan at Repormang Pansakahan, 7 July 2004.

15 *Pirma* is a Filipino word meaning "to sign."

16 Interview with Etta Rosales, 12 January 2003, Quezon City.

17 Electronic communication with Ellene Sana, 6 February 2001.

18 Voting Rights for Filipino Migrants Campaign Central, http://www.philippineupdate.com/vote.htm; Opiniano 2001.

19 Interview with Rosales.

20 Voting Rights for Filipino Migrants Campaign Central, http://www.philippineupdate.com/vote.htm.

21 Interview with Erwin Lara, secretary, House Committee on Suffrage and Electoral Reforms (1994–2001), 3 November 2003, in Quezon City; Akbayan 2004:7.

22 In the Twelfth Congress, party-list representatives managed to work out a consolidated bill for this purpose, HB 5081, but it did not reach floor deliberations.

7

Party Work at the Municipal Level

1 Interview with Roy Delima, chairperson, Mindanao Commission, Akbayan, 31 July 2002, in Digos, Davao del Sur.

2 Interview with Michael Ibañez, secretary-general, Davao region, Bisig, 8 August 2002, in Davao City.

3 Interviews with Marlene Magayanes, municipal councilor, Daraga, Albay, 30 March 2002, in Quezon City, and 5 November 2002, in Daraga; Nick Soriano, community organizer, Center for Agrarian Reform Empowerment and Transformation (Caret), Victoria, Laguna, 5 February 2002, in Victoria, and 29 November 2002, in Quezon City; and Fe Barsaba, municipal councilor, Mercedes, Eastern Samar, 13 November 2002, in Guiuan, Eastern Samar.

4 Interview with Ma. Louise Lampon, area coordinator, Southeastern Mindanao, Pakisama, 6 August 2002, in Davao City.

5 Interview with Delima.

6 Interviews with Benjamin Sumog-oy, executive director, Building Alternative Rural Resource Institutions and Organizing Services (Barrios), and member, Akbayan National Council, 20 November 2002, in Davao City; and Elaine Teope, member, National Council, Akbayan, 18 March 2002, Quezon City. A notable exception in Surallah is the Allah Valley Development Foundation, a social development NGO that assists cooperatives and POs in organizational diagnosis and development planning.

7 In a study of the role of POs and NGOs in local governance, Terrence George notes that in all four of his case study areas "community organizing has played a critical role in the ability of the poor to participate effectively in local politics and to weaken ties with the patrons who have so long shaped their political behavior" (1998:245).

8 Interview with Lampon.

9 Interviews with Jerry Dela Cerna, mayor, Governor Generoso, Davao Oriental, 3 July 2002, in Governor Generoso; and Javier Zacate, mayor, Sulat, Eastern Samar, 16 June 2002, in Sulat.

10 Interviews with Rodel Mercado, executive director, Pneuma, 12 November 2002, in Guiuan, Eastern Samar; and Dela Cerna.

11 Interviews with Conrad Castillo, chairperson, board of directors, People's Institute for Local Governance Advocacy and Research (Pilar), 25 November 2002, in Quezon City; and Magayanes.

12 Interviews with Magayanes; Lampon; and Alma Cabal, secretary-general, South Cotabato Division, Akbayan, 22 October 2002, in Marbel, South Cotabato.

13 Interview with Congressman Mario Aguja, 2 December 2003, in Amsterdam.

14 E-mail from Risa Hontiveros-Baraquel, member, National Executive Committee, Akbayan, 5 January 2004; Burgonio 2004:1.

15 The gravity of the problem really hit me when I discovered during my fieldwork that some veteran politicians who were reputed to be progressive and were endorsed by new, leftist parties (including Akbayan) had themselves resorted to vote buying after failing to find ways to counter their opponents' vote buying.

16 Interview with Joel Rocamora, president, Akbayan, 15 January 2003, in Quezon City. It was difficult to obtain exact figures about Akbayan's local candidates in the 1998 and 2001 elections. I discovered that collated reports at the national office contained too many inaccuracies. Moreover, prior to 2003, Akbayan had not made a clear distinction among the three types of local candidates. They sometimes tended to be lumped together as "Akbayan candidates."

17 Interviews with Jose Learto Otig, vice mayor, Banaybanay, Davao Oriental, 10 July 2002, in Banaybanay; Edwin Mayormita, executive director, PADC, 3 August 2002, in Davao City; and Rolando Bangcas, community organizer, PADC, 8 July 2002, in Banaybanay, Davao Oriental.

18 Interviews with Dela Cerna; and Exuperio Lloren, mayor, Jagna, Bohol, 19 and 21 May 2002, in Jagna.

19 In this case, PMP refers to Estrada's Partido ng Masang Pilipino.

20 Interview with Dela Cerna.

21 Interview with Lloren.

22 Interview with Teope.

23 This was former President Fidel Ramos's Lakas ng Sambayanan (Strength of the People)—National Union of Christian Democrats.

24 Interviews with Dela Cerna; and Lloren. Lakas-NUCD did deliver to Dela Cerna and Lloren the promised financial support, especially the crucial "mobilization fund" for the homestretch of the campaign.

25 The Orencias and Dela Cerna switched parties. In 1998, V. Orencia had run under Lakas-NUCD and Dela Cerna under LAMMP-PMP. After the elections, V. Orencia joined LAMMP-PMP, then the administration party, under Estrada. Local politics in Governor Generoso clearly shows that traditional political parties are organizations of convenience whose members come and go whenever it suits them. Since Akbayan regarded all the traditional parties as essentially the same, the choice of which party to run under was a secondary concern. Whichever party could best help Dela Cerna and his municipal slate to win—that was it.

26 Interviews with Mayormita; Ibañez; and Leonila Acaylar-Pabatao, community organizer, PADC, 14 October 2002, in Banaybanay.

27 Interview with Teope.

28 Lloren harped that in terms of economic development in Bohol Province Jagna used to be second only to Tagbilaran but had now been surpassed by several other municipalities.

29 Interview with Bernardo Salas, retired Court of First Instance judge, 16 May 2002, in Jagna, Bohol.

30 Interview with Absalon G. Montesclaros, former chairperson, Barog Katawhan, 5 July 2002, in Governor Generoso.

31 Interviews with Ernesto C. Villanueva, executive assistant for program operations and economic enterprise, Jagna, Bohol, 16–17 May 2002, in Jagna; and Ma. Louella M. Tan, executive assistant for administration, Jagna, Bohol, 16 May 2002, in Jagna.

32 Interviews with Lloren; and Dela Cerna.

33 Interview with Beverly Du-Abadingo, president, Jagna Market Vendors Association, 17 May 2002, in Jagna.

34 Interview with Andres L. Zaragosa, chairperson, Municipal Fisheries and Aquatic Resources Management Council, Governor Generoso, 3 July 2002, in Governor Generoso.

35 Interview with Tan.

36 Interview with Oscar Lugatiman, aide, Commission on Elections, Governor Generoso, 5 July 2002, in Governor Generoso.

37 Interview with Zaragosa.

38 Interviews with Dela Cerna; and Tan.

39 Interview with Soriano.

40 Interviews with Soriano; and Restituto Cacha, vice mayor, Victoria, Laguna, 5 February 2002, in Victoria.

41 Interview with Cacha.

42 Interview with Soriano.

43 Group discussion with nine leaders of Ugnayan-Victoria, 6 February 2002, in Victoria.

44 All three vice-mayoral candidates, curiously enough, had previously been with LAMMP.

45 Interview with Cacha.

46 Group discussion with Ugnayan-Victoria leaders.

47 Interview with Zacate.

48 Interview with Ma. Nelia S. Columbretis, private secretary, Office of the Mayor, Sulat, Eastern Samar, 15 June 2002, in Sulat.

49 Interview with Ma. Milagros Ojeda, former community organizer, Sustainable Local Alternative Technologies (SULAT), 15 July 2002, in Sulat.

50 Since Akbayan did not have a chapter in Sulat, it extended its support mainly through Akbayan members at the Institute for Democratic Participation in Governance (IDPG) based in Tacloban City, and the IDPG network in Leyte-Samar. They helped raise funds and produce campaign materials for Zacate's election campaign.

51 Among the specific features of Zacate's platform were farming system development, capital and marketing support to farmers; crop diversification; sustainable fishing; enforcement of fisheries laws; fisheries conservation; efficient fishery production, utilization and marketing; tourism development; and environmental protection. Zacate (2001:1) advocated popular participation in governance, asserting that "only the members of civil society themselves—households, organized sectors and institutions outside the state—can best articulate and work for their economic, social, political, cultural, and spiritual aspirations."

52 *Lanzadera* is one of the ways in which vote buyers make sure that money paid is translated into votes. In Marvin P. Bionat's description of the *lanzadera* or *cadena* system, the party handler gives "the first mercenary voter an already completed ballot, which he/she submits as his/her own. He/she then takes with him/her the blank ballot he/she was supposed to use. The party handler takes and completes the blank ballot and gives it to the next mercenary voter who is expected to come out with another blank ballot" (1998:105–6).

53 Interviews with Columbretis; Manuel V. Eroda, *barangay* captain, Riverside, Sulat, 14 June 2002, in Sulat; and Lina P. Palines, *barangay* captain, Loyola Heights, Sulat, 15 June 2002, in Sulat.

54 In a petition for writ of certiorari, a losing party asks a higher court to review the decision of a lower court on the grounds that he or she has not received justice in the latter.

55 Interview with Zacate.

56 Interview with Columbretis.

57 Interview with Magayanes, 30 March 2002, in Quezon City; and 5 November 2002, in Daraga.

58 Interviews with Magayanes, 30 March 2002; and Maritess B. Llona, training and organizing officer, Center for Advocacy and Participatory Governance (CAPG), 31 October 2002, in Daraga.

59 Interview with Magayanes, 30 March 2002.

60 Interviews with Magayanes; and Jay A. Carizo, research and advocacy officer, CAPG, 23 March 2002, in Quezon City.

61 Interview with Adelia Macinas, former *barangay* councilor, Inarado, Daraga, 31 October 2002, in Daraga.

62 Interview with Magayanes, 30 March 2002.

63 Interview with Castillo.

64 Interview with Helene Aquino, program coordinator, Pilar, 27 November 2002, in Quezon City.

65 Interview with Castillo.

66 Interview with Maximo D. Erasga, *barangay* captain, Tadlac, Los Baños, Laguna, 8 February 2002, in Calamba, Laguna.

67 With its high income, the *barangay* LGU under Perez's leadership was able to acquire and maintain two fire trucks, two garbage trucks, and an ambulance of its own. From time to time, it lent these vehicles to the municipal LGU, which did not have any.

68 Interview with Castillo.

69 Interview with Castillo.

70 Interview with Caesar P. Perez, mayor, Los Baños, Laguna, 1 April 2002, in Los Baños.

71 Interview with Perez.

72 Interview with Helene Aquino.

73 Interview with Castillo.

74 Interview with Sumog-oy.

75 Interview with Romulo O. Solivio, mayor, Surallah, South Cotabato, 19 October 2002, in Surallah.

76 A *barangay* is divided into several *puroks*.

77 Solivio, "2000–2001 Gawad Galing Pook Program Application," January 2001.

78 The ₱67 million figure is astounding if one considers that Surallah's revenues in 1998 totaled ₱42 million. Of the "pledges" made, however, only 20.44 percent (₱14 million) had been realized as of October 2001 (Iszatt 2004:176–7).

79 Interview with Isidro Suedad, coordinator of the Technical Working Group, municipal government of Surallah, South Cotabato, 18 October 2002, in Lake Sebu, South Cotabato. It is not unusual to find many "unregistered" children in poor *barangays*, as their parents could not afford to pay the birth registration fees.

80 Interview with Jorge J. Bautista, municipal councilor, Surallah, 21 October 2002, in Surallah.

81 Interview with Solivio.

82 Interview with Rolando P. Agrazamendez, executive director, Allah Valley Development Foundation, 21 October 2002, in Surallah.

83 Interview with Pascual de la Cruz, municipal administrator, Surallah, 20 October 2002, in Surallah.

84 Interview with Sumog-oy.

85 Interviews with Solivio; and Suedad.

86 Interviews with Sumog-oy; and Cabal.

87 Interview with Mercado.

88 Interview with Melchor Q. Gagante, mayor, Salcedo, Eastern Samar, 4 June 2002, in Salcedo.

89 Interview with Joselito Abrugar, private secretary to the mayor (2001–4) and former municipal councilor (1992–2001), Salcedo, Eastern Samar, 5 June 2002, in Salcedo.

90 Interview with Donato Padullo, municipal agriculturist, Salcedo, Eastern Samar, 5 June 2002, in Salcedo.

91 Interview with Mercado.

92 Interview with Esteban Regis, Jr., municipal councilor, Salcedo, Eastern Samar, 5 June 2002, in Salcedo. One of the campaign slogans was "MEGA—Moving towards Excellence in Good Administration!"

93 Interview with Mercado.

94 Interview with Ilberto Macale, editor, *Abot-Kamay*, 13 November 2002, in Salcedo.

95 Interview with Mercado.

96 Interview with Mercado.

97 Ten LGU officials were Akbayan members, but they had all run under traditional parties in 2001.

98 Interview with Mercado, 29 October 2003, in Quezon City.

99 The Iranun people live in areas along the border of the provinces of Maguindanao and Lanao del Sur, which are predominantly populated by the Maguindanaoans and the Maranaws.

100 Interview with Abdurahman D. Macabangon, chairperson, Maguindanao Division, Akbayan, 19 July 2002, in Cotabato City.

101 Interview with Delima. The MNLF and the MILF, in fact, do not feel threatened at all by legal electoral parties working and recruiting in their midst. Most Muslim politicians are members of the country's main traditional parties, and they sometimes "recruit" those who support them into these parties. Their recruits often remain nominal party members. The MNLF and the MILF, however, resist the entry of parties or politicians with armed groups—the CPP-NPA and warlords (Christian and Muslim) with private armies—into their areas.

102 This is Gloria Macapagal Arroyo's Kabalikat ng Malayang Pilipino (Partner of the Free Filipino).

103 Interviews with Suharto Ambolodto, executive director, Institute for Strategic Initiatives, 21 July 2002, in Cotabato City; Alexander D. Tomawis, mayor, Barira, Maguindanao, 23 July 2002, in Cotabato City; Suharto I. Ibay, vice mayor, Matanog, Maguindanao, 23 July 2002, in Cotabato City; Cahar P. Ibay, provincial board member, Maguindanao, 23 July 2002, in Cotabato City; Abolais A. Manalao, mayor, Buldon, Maguindanao, and Camar A. Tago, former municipal action officer, Buldon, 30 November 2002, in Manila. The ISI is a research and advocacy NGO that is "dedicated to the formulation, assessment advocacy, administration and development of strategic peace and development interventions in Mindanao" (Institute for Strategic Initiatives and Institute of Politics and Governance 2002:3).

104 Interview with Ambolodto, 30 October 2003, in Makati.

105 Interview with Ambolodto, 30 October 2003, in Makati.

106 Nasser Imam defeated Kahar Macapeges in Matanog's mayoral race in 1998 and 2001. The Macapeges clan had held power in Matanog ever since it was established as a separate municipality in 1975.

107 Interview with Ambolodto, 30 October 2003.

108 In terms of land area (2,444 sq km), Davao City is one of the world's largest cities. Close to 50 percent of this land area, however, is classified as timberland or forest.

109 Interview with Ibañez.

110 Interview with Mayormita. Personnel of PADC often had to travel long distances, partly on bad roads, to get to project sites—a tiring and expensive routine. In July 2003, PADC focused its attention on just one province, Davao Oriental, and shifted its base to Banaybanay (interview with Delima, 26 October 2003, in Davao City).

111 Interview with Delima, 26 October 2003.

112 Interview with Peter Laviña, city councilor, Davao City, 18 August 2002, in Davao City.

113 Interview with Macabangon. By an odd twist, Akbayan's identification (ID) card became some sort of a pass at military checkpoints in the war-affected areas. Soldiers of the AFP demanded some form of identification from those wishing to pass through. Very few local residents had *cedulas* (residence certificates), which required a fee. It happened that Akbayan had issued ID cards to its local members. They were virtually the only ones around with ID cards. When some Akbayan members were able to use their party ID cards to get through the checkpoints, other residents soon wanted to become members of Akbayan too.

114 Local Akbayan leaders complained that Pelonco had not really campaigned hard for Akbayan in 1998 and 2001 and that he wanted his own way and no longer abided by the decisions of the local Akbayan division (interview with Jonathan Cortez, officer in charge, Solidarity for Peace, Empowerment and Equity-Led Development, 23 July 2002, in Cotabato City).

115 Interviews with Ambolodto, 21 July 2002, in Cotabato City; and Cortez.

116 Since 1999, the popdems have ceased to be a distinct political bloc within Akbayan. They now count among the non-bloc members of Akbayan.

117 The foregoing is based on interviews and discussions with members of the Akbayan national council and political education committee.

118 This is distinct from *popular* or mass political education, which is geared for members of POs.

119 Annual membership dues of Akbayan members are as follows: ₱1 per month for unemployed; ₱1 per week for those employed but earning less than the minimum wage; and 1 percent of the basic salary for those employed earning at least the minimum wage.

120 Interviews and discussions with Delima, 31 July 2002; Maritona Labajo, secretary-general, Akbayan, 2 December 2002, in Quezon City; Carmel Abao, member, National Executive Committee, Akbayan, 3 December 2002, in Quezon City; and Rocamora. I also draw on a discussion with members of an ad hoc committee preparing for a conference with Akbayan LGU officials, 28 November 2002.

Conclusion

1 Interview with Carol Añonuevo, 19 June 2004, in Amsterdam.

2 By illiberal democracy, Zakaria (1997:22) means political systems that are democratic (having free, fair, and competitive elections) but do not ensure constitutional liberalism—"the rule of law, a separation of powers, and the protection of basic liberties of speech, assembly, religion and property."

3 It must be pointed out that the concepts of democracy espoused by O'Donnell, Zakaria, and Collier and Levitsky are all of the medium range.

4 The unexpected affinities between populism and neoliberalism are discussed in Roberts 1995; and Weyland 1999.

Interviews

Carmel Abao, member, National Executive Committee, and chairperson, Government Affairs Committee, Akbayan, 3 December 2002, and 4 November 2003, in Quezon City.

Joselito Abrugar, private secretary to the mayor (2001–4), and former municipal councilor (1992–2001), Salcedo, Eastern Samar, 5 June 2002, in Salcedo.

Leonila Acaylar-Pabatao, community organizer, People's Alternative Development Center (PADC), 14 October 2002, in Banaybanay, Davao Oriental.

Rolando P. Agrazamendez, executive director, Allah Valley Development Foundation, 21 October 2002, in Surallah, South Cotabato.

Mario Aguja, congressman, Akbayan, 2 December 2003, in Amsterdam, the Netherlands.

Suharto M. Ambolodto, executive director, Institute for Strategic Initiatives (ISI), 21 July, 2002, in Cotabato City; and 30 October 2003, in Makati.

Carol Añonuevo, former executive director, Center for Women's Resources, 19 June 2004, in Amsterdam, the Netherlands.

Helene Aquino, program coordinator, People's Institute for Local Governance Advocacy and Research (Pilar), 27 November 2002, in Quezon City.

Lecifina Arce, former secretary, Rizal Provincial Committee, Sanlakas, 10 January 2003, in Quezon City.

Bernardo Balagtas, artist and municipal councilor, Angono, 7 April 2002, in Angono.

Rolando Bangcas, community organizer, People's Alternative Development Center (PADC), 8 July 2002, in Banaybanay, Davao Oriental.

Fe Barsaba, municipal councilor, Mercedes, Eastern Samar, 13 November 2002, in Guiuan, Eastern Samar.

Jorge J. Bautista, municipal councilor, Surallah, 21 October 2002, in Surallah.

Helen Bonga, former chairperson, Angono Multisectoral Organizations, 6 January 2003, in Angono.

Victor Gerardo Bulatao, executive director, Empowering Civic Participation in Governance (ECPG), and former member, National Council, Akbayan, 23 January 2002 and 27 August 2002, in Quezon City.

Restituto Cacha, vice mayor, Victoria, Laguna, 5 February 2002, in Victoria.

Gerardo Calderon, mayor, Angono, Rizal, 7 April 2002, in Angono.

Jay A. Carizo, research and advocacy officer, Center for Advocacy and Participatory Governance (CAPG), 23 March 2002, in Quezon City.

Ramon Casiple, executive director, Institute for Political and Electoral Reform (IPER), 2 March 2002, in Quezon City.

Conrad Castillo, chairperson, board of directors, People's Institute for Local Governance Advocacy and Research (Pilar), 25 November 2002, in Quezon City.

Jerry Dela Cerna, mayor, Governor Generoso, Davao Oriental, 3 July 2002, in Governor Generoso.

Ma. Nelia S. Columbretis, private secretary, office of the mayor, Sulat, Eastern Samar, 15 June 2002, in Sulat.

Nilo de la Cruz, head of the peace panel, Rebolusyonaryong Partido ng Manggagawa—Pilipinas (RPM-P), 24 January 2002, in Mandaluyong City.

Roy Delima, chairperson, Mindanao Commission, Akbayan, 31 July 2002, in Digos, Davao del Sur; and 26 October 2003, in Davao City.

Ka Dencio (pseudonym), congressional aide, former ND activist, 22 March 2002, in Makati.

Beverly Du-Abadingo, president, Jagna Market Vendors Association, 17 May 2002, in Jagna.

Matilde Bautista Erasga, candidate for municipal councilor, Los Baños, Laguna, 1 April 2002, in Los Baños.

Maximo D. Erasga, *barangay* captain, Tadlac, Los Baños, Laguna, 8 February 2002, in Calamba, Laguna.

Manuel V. Eroda, *barangay* captain, Riverside, Sulat, 14 June 2002, in Sulat.

Christopher Flores, mayor, Guinobatan, Albay, 30 October 2002, in Quezon City; and 3 November 2002 in Guinobatan.

Wilson Fortaleza, president, Sanlakas, 20 March 2002, in Quezon City.

Melchor Q. Gagante, mayor, Salcedo, Eastern Samar, 4 June 2002, in Salcedo.

Norberto Gonzales, Jr., chairman, Partido Demokratiko-Sosyalista ng Pilipinas (PDSP), 26 June 2002, in Manila.

Michael Ibañez, secretary-general, Davao region, Bisig, 8 August 2002, in Davao City.

Cahar P. Ibay, provincial board member, Maguindanao, 23 July 2002, in Cotabato City.

Suharto I. Ibay, vice mayor, Matanog, Maguindanao, 23 July 2002, in Cotabato City.

Maritona Labajo, secretary-general, Akbayan, 2 December 2002, in Quezon City.

Ma. Louise Lampon, area coordinator, Southeastern Mindanao, Pakisama, 6 August 2002, in Davao City.

Erwin Lara, secretary, House Committee on Suffrage and Electoral Reforms (1994–2001), 3 November 2003, in Quezon City.

Peter Laviña, city councilor, Davao City, 18 August 2002, in Davao City.

Angela Librado, city councilor, Davao City, 17 July 2002, in Davao City.

Maritess B. Llona, training and organizing officer, Center for Advocacy and Participatory Governance (CAPG), 31 October 2002, in Daraga.

Exuperio Lloren, mayor, Jagna, Bohol, 19 and 21 May 2002, in Jagna.

Manjet Manalo Lopez, secretary-general, Sanlakas, 1 July 2002, in Quezon City.

Oscar Lugatiman, aide, Commission on Elections, Governor Generoso, 5 July 2002, in Governor Generoso.

Abdurahman D. Macabangon, chairperson, Maguindanao Division, Akbayan, 19 July 2002, in Cotabato City.

Ilberto Macale, editor, *Abot-Kamay*, 13 November 2002, in Salcedo.

Adelia Macinas, former *barangay* councilor, Inarado, Daraga, 31 October 2002, in Daraga.

Marlene Magayanes, municipal councilor, Daraga, Albay, 30 March 2002, in Quezon City; and 5 November 2002, in Daraga.

Renato Magtubo, congressman, Partido ng Manggagawa, 3 April 2002, in Quezon City.

Abolais A. Manalao, mayor, Buldon, Maguindanao, 30 November 2002, in Manila.

Edwin Mayormita, executive director, People's Alternative Development Center (PADC), 3 August 2002, in Davao City.

Sonny Melencio, chairman, Sosyalistang Partido ng Paggawa (SPP), 5 January 2002; and 25 August 2002, in Quezon City.

Rodel Mercado, executive director, Pneuma, 12 November 2002, in Guiuan, Eastern Samar.

Absalon G. Montesclaros, former chairperson, Barog Katawhan, 5 July 2002, in Governor Generoso.

Horacio Morales, Jr., former agrarian reform secretary, 4 November 2003, in Mandaluyong.

Satur Ocampo, congressman, Bayan Muna, 11 January 2003, in Quezon City.

Ma. Milagros Ojeda, former community organizer, Sustainable Local Alternative Technologies (Sulat), 15 July 2002, in Sulat.

Ka Olive and Ka Nicolas (pseudonyms), spokespersons, Marxista-Leninistang Partido ng Pilipinas (MLPP), 8 April 2002, in Quezon City.

Beth Oñate, member, management staff, office of the mayor, 4 November 2002, in Guinobatan.

Jose Learto Otig, vice mayor, Banaybanay, Davao Oriental, 10 July 2002, in Banaybanay.

Donato Padullo, municipal agriculturist, Salcedo, Eastern Samar, 5 June 2002, in Salcedo.

Lina P. Palines, *barangay* captain, Loyola Heights, Sulat, 15 June 2002, in Sulat.

Patrick Patiño, research associate, Institute for Popular Democracy, 3 April 2002, in Quezon City.

Caesar P. Perez, mayor, Los Baños, Laguna, 1 April 2002, in Los Baños.

Marlon Quesada, executive director, Labor Education and Research Network (LEARN), 8 February 2002, in Los Baños, Laguna.

Rodrigo Realubit, former activist, 3 November 2002, in Guinobatan.

Esteban Regis, Jr., municipal councilor, Salcedo, Eastern Samar, 5 June 2002, in Salcedo.

Ike de los Reyes (pseudonym), chair, Rebolusyonaryong Partido ng Pilipinas—Mindanao (RPM-M), 9 March 2002, in Quezon City; and 8 December 2003, in Amsterdam.

Ricardo Reyes, chairman, Akbayan, and executive director, Partnership for Agrarian Reform and Rural Development Services (PARRDS), 3 November 2003, in Quezon City.

Joel Rocamora, president, Akbayan, and executive director, Institute for Popular Democracy, 17 January 2002; and 15 January 2003, in Quezon City.

Wilber Francis Rontas, action officer, Municipal Disaster Coordinating Council, Guinobatan, 3 November 2002, in Guinobatan

Loretta Ann Rosales, congresswoman, Akbayan, 12 January 2003, in Quezon City.

Bernardo Salas, retired Court of First Instance judge, 16 May 2002, in Jagna, Bohol.

Romulo O. Solivio, mayor, Surallah, South Cotabato, 19 October 2002, in Surallah.

Nick Soriano, community organizer, Center for Agrarian Reform Empowerment and Transformation (Caret), Victoria, Laguna, 5 February 2002, in Victoria; and 29 November 2002, in Quezon City.

Isidro Suedad, coordinator of the Technical Working Group, municipal government of Surallah, South Cotabato, 18 October 2002, in Lake Sebu, South Cotabato.

Benjamin Sumog-oy, executive director, Building Alternative Rural Resource Institutions and Organizing Services (Barrios), and member, Akbayan National Council, 20 November 2002, in Davao City.

Camar A. Tago, former municipal action officer, Buldon, 30 November 2002, in Manila.

Ma. Louella M. Tan, executive assistant for administration, Jagna, Bohol, 16 May 2002, in Jagna.

Martin Tanchuling, executive director of the Philippine Network of Rural Development Institutes (Philnet-RDI), 14 October, 2003, in Amsterdam.

Elaine Teope, member, National Council, Akbayan, 18 March 2002, in Quezon City.

Rodolfo Teope, businessman and former activist, 3 November 2002, in Guinobatan.

Alexander D. Tomawis, mayor, Barira, Maguindanao, 23 July 2002, in Cotabato City.

Fr. Ben Verzosa, assistant parish priest, Banaybanay, Davao Oriental, 10 July 2002, in Banaybanay.

Ernesto C. Villanueva, executive assistant for program operations and economic enterprise, Jagna, Bohol, 16–17 May 2002, in Jagna.

Javier Zacate, mayor, Sulat, Eastern Samar, 16 June 2002, in Sulat.

Andres L. Zaragosa, chairperson, Municipal Fisheries and Aquatic Resources Management Council, Governor Generoso, 3 July 2002, in Governor Generoso.

Bibliography

Abad, Florencio B.

1991 Project 2001: NGO intervention in the electoral process. *Conjuncture* 4(3):11; 4(4):11.

1997 Should the Philippines turn parliamentary? The challenge of democratic consolidation and institutional reform. In *Shift*, edited by Glenda M. Gloria, 48–89. Quezon City: Ateneo Center for Social Policy and Public Affairs.

Abao, Carmel

1997 Dynamics among political blocs in the formation of a political party. In *Philippine Democracy Agenda*. Vol. 3: *Civil Society Making Civil Society*, edited by Miriam Coronel Ferrer, 271–88. Quezon City: Third World Studies Center.

Abelardo, Tet N.

1998 Streams towards the party-list law. *Political Brief* 6(2):6–11.

Abes, Roy

1998 ELF three-year impact evaluation: Experiences and insights. *PLA Notes* 31:62–67.

Abinales, Patricio N.

1988 The Left and other forces: The nature and dynamics of pre-1986 coalition politics. In *Marxism in the Philippines: Second series*, edited by Third World Studies Center, 26–49. Quezon City: Third World Studies Center.

1996a When a revolution devours its children before victory: Operasyon Kampanyang Ahos and the tragedy of Mindanao communism. In *The Revolution Falters: The Left in Philippine Politics after 1986*, edited by Patricio N. Abinales, 154–79. Ithaca: Southeast Asia Program, Cornell University.

2001a Coalition politics in the Philippines. *Current History* 100 (645):154–61.

2001b *Fellow Traveler: Essays on Filipino Communism*. Quezon City: University of the Philippines Press.

Abinales, Patricio N., ed.
1996b *The Revolution Falters: The Left in Philippine Politics after 1986.* Ithaca: Southeast Asia Program, Cornell University.

Abrugar, Joselito, Sr.
2002 Salcedo after one year of Mayor Mega's stewardship. *Abot-Kamay*, July.

Abueva, Jose V.
1970 The Philippines: Tradition and change. *Asian Survey* 10(1): 56–64.

Abueva, Jose V., Rey Magno Teves, Gaudioso C. Sosmena, Jr., Clarita R. Carlos and Michael O. Mastura, eds.
2002 *Towards a Federal Republic of the Philippines with a Parliamentary Government: A Reader*. Marikina: Center for Social Policy and Governance, Kalayaan College.

Adamson, Walter L.
1980 *Hegemony and Revolution: A Study of Antonio Gramsci's Political and Cultural Theory*. Berkeley: University of California Press.

Adriano, Fermin D.
2003a Re-visiting EDSA 2. *Manila Times*, 21 Jan.
2003b Localizing good governance. *Manila Times*, 8 Aug.

Agnote, Dario
1993 Communist rebellion a failure, says Ramos. *Philippine Daily Inquirer*, 27 Dec.

Agpalo, Remigio E.
1969 Pandanggo-sa-ilaw: The politics of Occidental Mindoro. Pamphlet.
1972 *The Political Elite and the People: A Study of Politics in Occidental Mindoro*. Manila: College of Public Administration, University of the Philippines.
1973 The organic-hierarchical paradigm and politics in the Philippines. Pamphlet.

Agra, Alberto
1994 The May 1994 electoral exercise. In *Popular Participation in Electoral Reform and Governance*, edited by the Institute of Politics and Governance, 23–27. Quezon City: Institute of Politics and Governance.

Akbayan

1999 Oppose Erap's cha cha. *Dyaryo Akbayan*, July-Oct.

2004 Primer on the absentee vote. Pamphlet.

Akbayan Executive Committee

2002 Cha cha and the current political conjuncture. Unpublished document, July.

Akbayan National Congress

1998a The Akbayan political platform. Unpublished document, 17–18 Jan.

1998b The Akbayan economic platform. Unpublished document, 17–18 Jan.

1998c The Akbayan cultural platform. Unpublished document, 17–18 Jan.

1998d The Akbayan platform: Special areas of concern. Unpublished document, 17–18 Jan.

1998e Constitution and by-laws. Unpublished document, 17–18 Jan.

2003 Participatory democracy, participatory socialism: The Akbayan narrative. Unpublished document, 30 July.

Akbayan National Council

2002 Guidelines for reconstitution. Unpublished document, 26 Sept.

Akbayan Secretariat

2003 Akbayan leader's murder is treacherous, incomprehensible. Press statement, 28 May.

Alagappa, Muthiah

1995 The Asian spectrum. *Journal of Democracy* 6(1):29–36.

Albano, Jennifer

2001 Crossover: Civil society and government. *Conjuncture* 13(1): 20–22.

Alegre, Alan G., ed.

1996 *Trends and Traditions, Challenges and Choices, a Strategic Study of Philippine NGOs*. Quezon City: Ateneo Center for Social Policy and Public Affairs.

Alejo, Myrna J., Maria Elena P. Rivera, and Noel Inocencio P. Valencia

1996 *[De]scribing Elections: A Study of Elections in the Lifeworld of San Isidro*. Quezon City: Institute for Popular Democracy.

Allen, James S.

1985 *The Radical Left on the Eve of War*. Quezon City: Foundation for Nationalist Studies.

Alternatiba
2003 A call for an alternative against elite rule. Press statement, 20 Nov.

Alves, Maria Helena Moreira
1993 Something old, something new: Brazil's Partido dos Trabalhadores. In *The Latin American Left: From the Fall of Allende to Perestroika*, edited by Barry Carr and Steve Ellner, 225–42. Boulder: Westview Press.

Amnesty International
1992 Philippines: The killing goes on. London: Amnesty International

Anderson, Benedict
1988 Cacique democracy in the Philippines: Origins and dreams. *New Left Review* 169:3–31.
1998a Elections in Southeast Asia. In *The Spectre of Comparisons: Nationalism, Southeast Asia and the World*, edited by Benedict Anderson, 265–84. London: Verso.

Anderson, Benedict, ed.
1998b *The Spectre of Comparisons: Nationalism, Southeast Asia and the World*. London: Verso.

Ando, Hirofumi
1971 Elections in the Philippines: Mass-elite interaction through the electoral process, 1946–1969. Ph.D. diss., University of Michigan.

Antlöv, Hans
2003 Not enough politics! Power, participation, and the new democratic polity in Indonesia. In *Local Power and Politics in Indonesia*, edited by Edward Aspinall and Greg Fealy, 72–86. Singapore: Institute of Southeast Asian Studies.

Aquino, Belinda A.
1987 *The Politics of Plunder: The Philippines under Marcos*. Manila: Great Books Trading and College of Public Administration, University of the Philippines.
2004 Flawed elections. *Philippine Daily Inquirer*, 27 April.

Arato, Andrew
1981 Civil society against the state. *Telos* 47:23–47.

Arguelles, Paco [pseudonym]
1993 *Pagbabalik-Aral* [Review]: Apriorism reaffirmed. *Debate* 7:14–32.
1995 Kahos: A soul searching. *Human Rights Forum* 5(1):105–23.

Arroyo, Gloria Macapagal

2001 Inaugural address of President Gloria Macapagal Arroyo. Edsa Shrine, 20 Jan. http://www.dfa.gov.ph/archive/speech/gma/GMA%20Inauguration.htm

2004 State of the nation address. Presented at the House of Representatives of the Philippine Congress, 26 July.

Asia Watch

1990 The Philippines: Violations of the laws of war by both sides. Pamphlet. New York: Human Rights Watch.

Aspinall, Edward, and Greg Fealy, eds.

2003 *Local Power and Politics in Indonesia*. Singapore: Institute of Southeast Asian Studies.

Atim, C. B.

1989 Students, workers, and democracy in Ghana (1974–88). Unpublished manuscript.

Avendaño, Christine

1993a KMU, other left groups break up. *Philippine Daily Inquirer*, 27 Aug.

1993b Bayan also headed for break up. *Philippine Daily Inquirer*, 28 Aug.

2000 RP world's "largest migrant nation." *Philippine Daily Inquirer*, 30 March.

Balana, Cynthia

2004 Party-list system still vague to voters. *Philippine Daily Inquirer*, two-part series, 2–3 Aug.

Balbin, Leoncio, Jr.

2001 Politics, other angles eyed in ambush of Abra mayor. Inquirer News Service, 28 Dec.

Banlaoi, Rommel C., and Clarita R. Carlos

1996 *Political Parties in the Philippines: From 1900 to the Present*. Makati: Konrad Adenauer Foundation.

Bautista, Cynthia Banzon

1984 Marxism and the peasantry: The Philippine case. In *Marxism in the Philippines: Marx Centennial Lectures*, edited by the Third World Studies Center, 153–82. Quezon City: Third World Studies Center.

2000 Metro Manila's middle classes: Images from a survey. Paper presented at the Philippine Studies Meeting, Amsterdam, the Netherlands, 20 Oct.

2001 The revenge of the elite on the masses. In *Between Fires: Fifteen Perspectives on the Estrada Crisis*, edited by Amando Doronila, 1–42. Pasig: Anvil Publishing.

Bayanihan International Solidarity Conference

2001 *Philippine Civil Society and International Solidarity Partners: Strengthening Local Global Advocacy Initiatives*. Manila: Bayanihan International Solidarity Conference.

Baylosis, Rafael G.

1994 *Ilang Punto Hinggil sa Usaping "Human Rights"* [Some Notes on the Question of "Human Rights"]. Paper presented before a forum of the Gabriela Commission on Political Rights, 18 July.

Bello, Walden

1988 From dictatorship to elite populism: The United States and the Philippine crisis. In *Crisis and Confrontation: Ronald Reagan's Foreign Policy*, edited by Morris H. Morley, 214–50. Totowa, NJ: Rowman and Littlefield.

1992 Interview: The search for alternatives. *Conjuncture* 5(6–7):4–5, 14.

1993 The dual crisis of the Philippine progressive movement. In *Reexamining and Renewing the Philippine Progressive Vision*, edited by John Gershman and Walden Bello, 11–29. Quezon City: Forum for Philippine Alternatives.

2001 The May 1st riot: Birth of Peronism RP style? *Philippine Daily Inquirer* (online), 7 May. www.inq7.net/vwp/2001/may/07/vwp_1-1.htm

Bello, Walden, and John Gershman

1990 Democratization and stabilization in the Philippines. *Critical Sociology* 17(1):35–56.

Bello, Walden, and Marissa de Guzman

2001 Why land reform is no longer possible without revolution. *Philippine Daily Inquirer* (online), 18 June. http://www.inq7.net/vwp/2001/jun/18/text/vwp_2-1-p.htm

Bello, Walden, and Severina Rivera

1977 *Logistics of Repression and Other Essays*. Washington, DC: Friends of the Filipino People.

Bello, Walden, David Kinley, and Elaine Elinson

1982 *Development Debacle: The World Bank in the Philippines*. San Francisco: Institute for Food and Development Policy and the Philippine Solidarity Network.

Bello, Walden, Lidy Nacpil, and Ana Marie Nemenzo
2004 The UP School of Economics report: Overdue, selective, not daring enough. *Business World*, 27 Aug.

Bello, Walden, Herbert Docena, Marissa de Guzman, and Mary Lou Malig
2004 *The Anti-development State: The Political Economy of Permanent Crisis in the Philippines*. Quezon City: Department of Sociology, University of the Philippines, and Focus on the Global South.

Bengco, Regina
2003 One-year amnesty declared for loose guns. *Malaya*, 1 Feb.

Benson, Louis P.
1973 A research note on machine politics as a model for change in a Philippine province. *American Political Science Review* 67(2): 560–66.

Berman, Sheri
1997 Civil society and the collapse of the Weimar Republic. *World Politics* 49(3):401–29.

Bierling, Jacques, and George Lafferty
1998 Pressures for change: Capitalist development and democracy. In *Governance in the Asia-Pacific*, edited by David Goldblatt and Jeremy Mitchell Richard Maidment, 275–300. London: Routledge.

Bionat, Marvin P.
1998 *How to Win (or Lose) in Philippine Elections: The Dynamics of Winning or Losing in Philippine Electoral Contests*. Pasig: Anvil Publishing.

Bobbio, Norberto
1979 Gramsci and the conception of civil society. In *Gramsci and Marxist Theory*, edited by Chantal Mouffe, 21–47. London: Routledge and Kegan Paul.

Bohol Sunday Post
2002 Mayor Lloren home from Brazil. 2 March.

Booth, John, and Patricia Bayer Richard
2001 Civil society and political context in Central America. In *Beyond Tocqueville: Civil Society and the Social Capital Debate in Comparative Perspective*, edited by Bob Edwards, Michael Foley, and Mario Diani, 43–55. Hanover: University Press of New England.

Borras, Saturnino M., Jr.
1998 *The Bibingka Strategy in Land Reform Implementation*. Quezon City: Institute of Popular Democracy.

2001 State-society relations in land reform implementation in the Philippines. *Development and Change* 32(3):531–61.

2004 *Rethinking Redistributive Land Reform: Struggles for Land and Power in the Philippines*. Maastricht: Shaker Publishing.

Boudreau, Vincent

2001 *Grass Roots and Cadre in the Protest Movement*. Manila: Ateneo de Manila University Press.

2004 *Resisting Dictatorship*. Cambridge: Cambridge University Press.

Branigin, William

1993 In Philippines, Communist Party slowly self-destructs. *Washington Post*, 15 Jan.

Brillantes, Alex B., Jr.

1994 Redemocratization and decentralization in the Philippines: The increasing leadership role of NGOs. *International Review of Administrative Sciences* 60(4):575–86.

1996 Decentralization, devolution and democratization: Old concepts, contemporary applications. *Kasarinlan* 12(1):83–88.

Bruns, Gabriele, and Marei John

2002 *Electoral Politics in Southeast and East Asia*. Singapore: Friederich Ebert Stiftung.

Brysk, Alison

2000 Democratizing civil society in Latin America. *Journal of Democracy* 11(3):151–65.

Buenaventura, Rafael B.

2004 Some thoughts on the budget deficit. Paper presented before the Rotary Club of Makati Central, Makati City, 16 April.

Bukluran ng Manggagawang Pilipino

2000 Erap should revamp his head, not just his cabinet. Press statement, 8 Jan.

Bukluran sa Ikauunlad ng Sosyalistang Isip at Gawa

1996a On party building. In *Transforming the Struggle: Bisig and Its Unfolding Narrative*, edited by Bisig, 82–88. Manila: Bisig.

Bukluran sa Ikauunlad ng Sosyalistang Isip at Gawa, ed.

1996b *Transforming the Struggle: Bisig and its Unfolding Narrative*. Manila: Bisig.

Bulatao, Victor Gerardo

1995 Sustainable communities for self-empowerment: Rural development and civil society in the Philippines. Kaisahan

Occasional Paper.

1999 DPG in the context of SIAD: Insights, perspectives and challenges. In *Building Empowered Sustainable Communities through Effective People's Participation in Governance*, edited by Tomasito S. Villarin, 11–30. Quezon City: Kaisahan tungo sa Kaunlaran ng Kanayunan at Repormang Pansakahan, Center for Agrarian Reform Empowerment and Transformation, and the Institute of Politics and Governance.

2000a Governance and modern progressive politics. In *Balangay: An Introductory Course on Barangay Governance*, edited by the Institute of Politics and Governance, 9–33. Quezon City: Institute of Politics and Governance and Friedrich Ebert Stiftung.

2000b Batman @ one: The state of our consortium. In *Balangay: An Introductory Course on Barangay Governance*, edited by the Institute of Politics and Governance, 190–208. Quezon City: Institute of Politics and Governance and Friedrich Ebert Stiftung.

Burgonio, T. J.
2004 Macapagal, Poe, Lacson snub covenant signing. *Philippine Daily Inquirer*, 6 Feb.

Burgonio, T. J., and Anselmo Roque
2002 Election violence latest count: 87 dead, 45 hurt. *Philippine Daily Inquirer*, 17 July.

Cabreza, Vincent
2003 43,000 killed in 34 years of communist rebellion. *Philippine Daily Inquirer*, 29 Jan.

Cala, Cesar
1995 May 8 and beyond. *Conjuncture* 7(2):1, 3, 14.

Cala, Cesar, and Jose Z. Grageda, eds.
1994 *Studies on Coalition Experiences in the Philippines*. Makati: Bookmark.

Calaguas, Bel U.
1989 Socio-economic work: A view to a new social order. *Conjuncture* 2(10):8–9, 11.

Calumpita, Ronnie
2005 DENR finds relocation sites for flash-flood survivors. *Manila Times*, 12 Jan.

Cano Garcia, Maria Gloria
2004 The American construction and portrayal of the caciquil system in the Philippines. Paper presented at the Seventh International

Conference on the Philippines, Leiden, the Netherlands, 17 June.

Canuday, Jowel F.
2002 Bayan Muna worried over declaration of its areas as election "hotspots." *MindaNews*, 7 July.

Caoili, Olivia C.
1991 The Philippine Congress: Executive-legislative relations and the restoration of democracy. *Philippine Political Science Journal* 33:1–24.

Carandang, Ricky
2004 Shrinking middle class. *Newsbreak*, 12 April.

Carbonell-Catilo, Ma. Aurora, Josie H. de Leon, and Eleanor E. Nicolas
1985 *Manipulated Elections*. Manila: Ma. Aurora Carbonell-Catilo.

Carlos, Clarita R.
1998 *History of Electoral Reforms in the Philippines: Pre-Spanish to 1998*. Makati: Konrad Adenauer Foundation.

Carlos, Clarita R., and Rommel C. Banlaoi
1996 *Elections in the Philippines: From Pre-colonial Period to the Present*. Makati: Konrad Adenauer Foundation.

Carothers, Thomas
1999a *Aiding Democracy Abroad: The Learning Curve*. Washington, DC: Carnegie Endowment for International Peace.

1999b Think again: Civil society. *Foreign Policy* 117:18–22.

Carroll, John J.
1997 The development of democracy: The Philippine experience. In *The Development of Democracy in the ASEAN Region*, edited by Leopoldo J. Dejillas and Gunther L. Karcher, 23–33. Makati: Institute for Development Research and Studies, Konrad Adenauer Foundation.

Case, William
1999 The Philippine election in 1998: A question of quality. *Asian Survey* 39(3):468–85.

2002 *Politics in Southeast Asia: Democracy or Less*. Richmond: Curzon.

Casino, Audie
1998 The party-list elections: What's in store for progressives? *Conjuncture*, April.

Casiple, Ramon C.
1996 Fallacies against human rights. *Pingkian* 1(1):9–29.

2003 The party-list path to a broadened Philippine democracy. *Public Policy* 7(1):1–22.

Casper, Gretchen
1995 *Fragile Democracies: Legacies of Authoritarian Rule.* Pittsburgh: University of Pittsburgh Press.

Castillo, Conrad
2004 The rebirth of the Makiling forest dwellers: Environmental governance and empowerment in Bagong Silang. In *Beyond Good Governance: Participatory Democracy in the Philippines,* edited by Marisol Estrella and Nina Iszatt, 117–40. Quezon City: Institute for Popular Democracy.

Center for Environmental Concerns
1996 A primer on Philippine environmental data. Pamphlet, Center for Environmental Concerns, Quezon City.

Center for Legislative Development
2003 Legislative updates. *Legislative Women's Watch* [newsletter], May.

Central Committee, Communist Party of the Philippines
1972 Pang-organisasyong patnubay at balangkas ng mga ulat [Organizational guide and outline for reporting]. Pamphlet.
1976 Our urgent tasks. Pamphlet.
1993 General review of significant events and decisions (1980–91). *Debate* 7:33–95.
2001 No substantial gains for the people in the recently held elections. *Ang Bayan,* May.

Chambers, Robert
1994 Participatory rural appraisal (PRA): Analysis of experience. *World Development* 22(9):1253–68.

Chambers, Simone, and Jeffrey Kopstein
2001 Bad civil society. *Political Theory* 29(6):837–65.

Chutima, Gawin
1994 Thai NGOs and civil society. In *Civil Society in the Asia-Pacific Region,* edited by Isagani R. Serrano, 145–52. Washington, DC: Civicus.

Ciria-Cruz, Rene
1992 Why the Philippine left must take the parliamentary road. *Debate* 2:5–15.

Clarke, Gerard

1998a *The Politics of NGOs in South-East Asia: Participation and Protest in the Philippines*. London: Routledge.

1998b Non-governmental organizations (NGOs) and politics in the developing world. *Political Studies* 46(1):36–52.

Clarke, Gerard, and Marites Sison

2003 Voices from the top of the pile: Elite perceptions of poverty and the poor in the Philippines. *Development and Change* 34(2): 215–42.

Co, Edna

1996 Reinterpreting civil society: The context of the Philippine NGO movement. In *Trends and Traditions, Challenges and Choices*, edited by Alan G. Alegre, 190–205. Quezon City: Ateneo Center for Social Policy and Public Affairs.

Cohen, Carl

1971 *Democracy*. Athens: University of Georgia Press.

Collier, Christopher J.

1997 The politics of insurrection in Davao, Philippines. Ph.D. diss., University of Hawaii.

Collier, David, and Steven Levitsky

1997 Democracy with adjectives: Conceptual innovation in comparative research. *World Politics* 49(3):430–51.

Commission on Elections

2004 In the matter of the registration for the party-list elections of sectoral parties, organizations, coalitions in connection with the May 10, 2004, national elections. Unpublished document, 6 Jan.

Committee Affairs Department, House of Representatives, Congress of the Philippines

2004 Committee favors ₱125 wage increase. *Committee News*, 15 Sept.

Communist Party of the Philippines

1991 The 1991 draft program and constitution of the Communist Party of the Philippines (CPP). Pamphlet.

Concepcion, Jose, Jr., and twenty-two other complainants

2002 Complaint for the impeachment of Commissioner Luzviminda G. Tancangco. Unpublished document, 24 May.

Concerned Communist Party of the Philippines Members

1993 *Krisis ng Sosyalismo, Istratehiya ng Pagkilos, at Internal na Demokrasya: Pag-aaral, Debate, Diskusyon, Paglalagom, Malalimang Muling Pagsusuri, at Pagpapanibagong-Sigla* [Crisis of Socialism,

Strategies of Action and Internal Democracy: Study, Debate, Discussion, Summing-up, Profound Re-examination, and Revitalization]. Within CPP circles, referred to as the Big Red Book. N.p., n.d.

Congress of Re-establishment, Communist Party of the Philippines
1968a Rectify errors and rebuild the party. Pamphlet.
1968b Program for a people's democratic revolution. Pamphlet.

Consortium on Electoral Reforms and Institute for Political and Electoral Reform
1997 Education campaign for clean elections and good governance. Pamphlet.

Constantino, Letizia R.
1991 Reflections on the electoral process. Pamphlet.

Constantino, Renato
1970 *Dissent and Counter-consciousness*. Manila: Erehwon.
1975 *The Philippines: A Past Revisited*. Quezon City: Tala Publishing Services.
1978 *The Philippines: The Continuing Past*. Quezon City: Foundation for Nationalist Studies.
1996 *Fetters on Tomorrow*. Quezon City: Karrel.

Constantino-David, Karina
1997 Intra-civil society relations: An overview. In *Philippine Democracy Agenda*. Vol. 3: *Civil Society Making Civil Society*, edited by Miriam Coronel Ferrer, 21–50. Quezon City: Third World Studies Center.

Contreras, Volt
2004 NPA joins Amnesty Int'l list of rights violators. *Philippine Daily Inquirer*, 29 May.

Cordingley, Peter
2001 Homepage: The cost of corruption. *Asiaweek*, 19 Oct.

Coronel Ferrer, Miriam
1989 A toast to pluralism. *Conjuncture* 2(7):5–6.

Coronel Ferrer, Miriam, ed.
1997 *Philippine Democracy Agenda*. Vol. 3: *Civil Society Making Civil Society*. Quezon City: Third World Studies Center.

Coronel, Sheila S.
1998 The *pare* principle. *i Investigative Reporting Magazine*, Oct.-Dec.

Corpus, Victor N.
1989 *Silent War*. Quezon City: VNC Enterprises.

Cruz, Maricel V.
2003 Solons push bill to increase benefits of retiring private sector employees. *Manila Times*, 23 Nov.

Cullinane, Michael
1988 Playing the game: The rise of Sergio Osmeña, 1898–1907. In *Philippine Colonial Democracy*, edited by Ruby R. Paredes, 70–113. New Haven: Yale University Council on Southeast Asia Studies.

Dacanay, Barbara Mae
2003 Constitutional crisis deepens. *Gulf News*, 6 Nov.

Dahl, Robert
1971 *Polyarchy: Participation and Opposition*. New Haven: Yale University Press.
1989 *Democracy and Its Critics*. New Haven: Yale University Press.
1998 *On Democracy*. New Haven: Yale University Press.

Daily Tribune
2003 Killing the rule of law. Editorial, 7 Nov.

Damazo, Jet
2003 Breaking free. *Newsbreak*, 31 March.

Dancel, Joshua
2002 Floods prevent holding of polls in 472 barangays. *Manila Times*, 15 July.

David, Randolf S.
1978 Development theory: Imperialist legacy. *Diliman Review*, Oct.-Dec.: 41–45.
1980 Philippine underdevelopment and dependency theory. *Philippine Sociological Review* 28(1–4):81–88.
1997 The Philippine party-building experience. In *Papers of a Party in the Making*, edited by Soliman Santos, Jr., 141–50. Quezon City: Institute of Politics and Governance.
2002 The spirit of civil society. *Philippine Daily Inquirer*, 14 July.
2004 Governance by patronage. *Philippine Daily Inquirer*, 14 March.

De Dios, Emmanuel S., Benjamin E. Diokno, Emmanuel F. Esguerra, Raul V. Fabella, Ma. Socorro Gochoco-Bautista, Felipe M. Medalla, Solita C. Monsod, Ernesto M. Pernia, Renato E. Reside, Jr.,

Gerardo P. Sicat, and Edita A. Tan
2004 The deepening crisis: The real score on deficits and the public debt. http://www.econ.upd.edu.ph/respub/dp/pdf/DP2004–09.pdf

De Guzman, Raul P.
1971 Politics in the Philippines. *Philippine Journal of Public Administration* 15(3–4):233–38.

De la Torre, Edicio
1987 Notes on popular democracy and national democracy. Unpublished manuscript.

De Roma, Mervin John C.
2002 Saving the last dance: A dossier of IPD's chacha steps. *Conjuncture* 14(5):4–5.

Democratic Bloc within the CPP
1994 Out of crisis, renewal. *Debate* 9:65–68.

Derbyshire, Charles E.
1963 *The Reign of Greed: A Complete English Version of El Filibusterismo from the Spanish of Jose Rizal.* Manila: Philippine Education Company.

Desai, Vandana, and Rob Imrie
1998 The new managerialism in local governance: North-south dimensions. *Third World Quarterly* 19(4):635–50.

Diamond, Larry, Juan J. Linz, and Seymour Martin Lipset, eds.
1989 *Democracy in Developing Countries.* Vol. 3: *Asia.* Boulder: Lynne Rienner.

Diokno, Maria Serena, ed.
1997 *Philippine Democracy Agenda.* Vol. 1: *Democracy and Citizenship in Filipino Political Culture.* Quezon City: Third World Studies Center.

Doronila, Amando
1985 The transformation of patron-client relations and its political consequences in postwar Philippines. *Journal of Southeast Asian Studies* 16(1):99–116.
1992 *The State, Economic Transformation, and Political Change in the Philippines, 1946–1972.* Singapore: Oxford University Press.
2001a *The Fall of Joseph Estrada: The Inside Story.* Pasig and Makati: Anvil Publications and Philippine Daily Inquirer.
2001b Estrada projects benefited mostly rich, middle class. *Philippine Daily Inquirer,* 12 Aug.

2003 Impeach ruling shows high court's activist role. *Philippine Daily Inquirer*, 17 Nov.

2004 Marcos, Estrada in hall of infamy warning to voters. *Philippine Daily Inquirer*, 29 March.

Dubsky, Roman

1974 The institutionalizing of social conduct and the New Society in the Philippines. *Philippine Journal of Public Administration* 18(2):127–45.

Eaton, Kent

2001 Political obstacles to decentralization: Evidence from Argentina and the Philippines. *Development and Change* 32(1):101–27.

2003 Restoration or transformation? *Trapos* versus NGOs in the democratization of the Philippines. *Journal of Asian Studies* 62(2):469–96.

Editorial Board, *Governance Brief*

1999 The flight of the CONCORD: A primer on the Estrada constitutional reform program. *Governance Brief* 2, special issue.

Editorial Board, *Rebolusyon*

1991 Fulfill the requirements of the current stage. *Rebolusyon*, April-June.

Editorial staff, *Ang Bayan*

1985 Party's style of leadership involves two basic questions. *Ang Bayan*, July.

1987a Bourgeois elections and parliament: Props for counterrevolution. *Ang Bayan*, March.

1987b Sabotage as a revolutionary weapon. *Ang Bayan*, Sept.

1988 Questions concerning analysis of the situation and the party's tactics. In *The Filipino People Will Triumph*, edited by the Editorial staff, *Ang Bayan*, 18–35. Manila: Central Publishing House.

1991 Where to, socialism? *Ang Bayan*, Jan.-Feb.

Editorial Staff, *Praktika*

1986 When a zigzag turn is shorter than a straight route. *Praktika* 1(1):3–22.

Edwards, Bob, and Michael Foley

2001 Civil society and social capital: A primer. In *Beyond Tocqueville: Civil Society and the Social Capital Debate in Comparative Perspective*, edited by Bob Edwards, Michael Foley, and Mario Diani, 1–14. Hanover: University Press of New England.

El Arabiya
2004 De la Cruz freed. TV news report picked up by ABS-CBN News, 20 July.

Ellner, Steve
1993 Introduction: The changing status of the Latin American Left in the recent past. In *The Latin American Left: From the Fall of Allende to Perestroika*, edited by Barry Carr and Steve Ellner, 1–21. Boulder: Westview Press.

Encarnacion, Omar
2000 Tocqueville's missionaries: Civil society advocacy and the promotion of democracy. *World Policy Journal* 17(1):9–18.

Estella, Chit
1993 Showdown: CPP to try 4 leaders of anti-Joma faction. *Malaya*, 14 Dec.

Estrella, Marisol, and Nina Iszatt, eds.
2004 *Beyond Good Governance: Participatory Democracy in the Philippines*. Quezon City: Institute for Popular Democracy.

Executive Committee, Central Committee, Communist Party of the Philippines
1985 Memorandum on the snap presidential election. Mimeographed memorandum, 23 Dec.
2000 Memorandum: Eleksyong [Elections] 2001. Unpublished document, 17 Dec.

Executive Committee, Manila-Rizal Committee, Communist Party of the Philippines
1977 Maghanda sa isang rebolusyonaryong bugso [Prepare for a revolutionary upsurge]. Mimeographed memorandum, May.

Fabe, Vic
1992 On decentralization and the peasantry: Preliminary thoughts. In *Issues in Politics, Governance, and Electoral Reform*, edited by Julio P. Macuja II, 83–85. Quezon City: Center for Social Policy and Public Affairs, Ateneo de Manila University.

Fajardo, Rorie R.
2000 How popular is popular education. *Cyberdyaryo*, 11 April.

Fast, Jonathan
1973 Imperialism and bourgeois dictatorship in the Philippines. *New Left Review* 78:69–96.

Fegan, Brian

1981 Rent capitalism in the Philippines. Pamphlet, Third World Studies Center.

Ferrer, Ricardo D.

1984 On the mode of production in the Philippines: Some old-fashioned questions on Marxism. In *Marxism in the Philippines,* edited by the Third World Studies Center, 187–214. Quezon City: Third World Studies Center.

Ferriols, Des

2002 RP 11th most corrupt among 102 nations—survey. *Philippine Star,* 21 Oct.

Foley, Michael W.

1996 Laying the groundwork: The struggle for civil society in El Salvador. *Latin American Politics and Society* 38(1):67–104.

Foley, Michael W., and Bob Edwards

1996 The paradox of civil society. *Journal of Democracy* 7(3):38–52.

Formilleza, Liezl S.

1994 Countdown on electoral reforms. *Rural Reconstruction Forum.* Oct.-Dec.

Fortaleza, Wilson

1999 Kongreso ng PMP: Pagtatayo ng bagong partido, pagtindig ng manggagawang Pilipino! [Congress of PMP: The establishment of a new party, the rise of the Filipino worker!]. *Tambuli* 3(1):12–18.

Fortaleza, Wilson, Renato Magtubo, and Victor Briz

2002 No to De Venecia's cha-cha. Joint press statement, 5 April.

Fox, Jonathan

1994 The difficult transition from clientelism to citizenship: Lessons from Mexico. *World Politics* 46(2):151–84.

1995 The crucible of local politics. *NACLA Report on the Americas* 29(1):15–19.

1996 How does civil society thicken? The political construction of social capital in rural Mexico. *World Development* 24(6):1089–1103.

Fox, Jonathan, and Jennifer Franco

1994 Obstacles to political democracy: Thinking comparatively. Unpublished manuscript.

Francisco, Oscar D.

1994 The politics of civil society. Unpublished manuscript.

1995 Community organizing in integrated area development. In *SIAD Tool Box: A Collection of Operational Pointers and Instruments for Sustainable Integrated Area Development*, edited by SIAD Organizing Committee, 85–91. Quezon City: SIAD Organizing Committee.

2003 Ituloy at pag-ibayuhin ang pagkakapitbisig para sa repormang panlipunan at kampanya laban sa kahirapan [Continue and advance the cooperation for social reform and the anti-poverty campaign]. Speech delivered at the celebration of Basic Sectors Day, Luneta Park, Manila, 18 Jan.

Franco, Jennifer Conroy
2001 *Elections and Democratization in the Philippines*. New York: Routledge.

Freire, Paulo
1996 *Pedagogy of the Oppressed*. London: Penguin.

Galing, Lorna
2002 Involvement of politicians in barangay polls welcomed. *Ilocos Times*, 4–10 July.

Garcia, Robert Francis
1999a A history of PEPE. In *Of Maps and Leapfrogs: Popular Education and Other Disruptions*, edited by Robert Francis Garcia, 115–19. Quezon City: Popular Education for People's Empowerment.

2001 *To Suffer Thy Comrades*. Pasig: Anvil Publishing.

Garcia, Robert Francis, ed.
1999b *Of Maps and Leapfrogs: Popular Education and Other Disruptions*. Quezon City: Popular Education for People's Empowerment.

Gathering for Peace
2002 Declaration of unity against U.S. military intervention in the Philippines. Press statement, 12 Feb.

George, Terrence
1998 Local governance: People power in the provinces? In *Organizing for Democracy: NGOs, Civil Society, and the Philippine State*, edited by G. Sidney Silliman and Lela Garner Noble, 223–53. Quezon City: Ateneo de Manila University Press.

Gershman, John
1992 The 1992 Philippine elections: An eyewitness report. Unpublished manuscript.

1993 Struggles for democracy and democratic struggle. In *Reexamining and Renewing the Philippine Progressive Vision*, edited by

John Gershman and Walden Bello, 159–76. Quezon City: Forum for Philippine Alternatives.

Gershman, John, and Walden Bello, eds.
1993 *Reexamining and Renewing the Philippine Progressive Vision.* Quezon City: Forum for Philippine Alternatives.

Gerson, Philip
1998 Poverty and economic policy in the Philippines. *Finance and Development* 35(3):46–49.

Gibbon, Peter
1998 Some reflections on "civil society" and political change. In *Democratization in the Third World: Concrete Cases in Comparative and Theoretical Perspective,* edited by Lars Rudebeck and Olle Törnquist with Virgilio Rojas, 23–56. New York: St. Martin's Press.

Gills, Barry, Joel Rocamora, and Richard Wilson, eds.
1993 *Low Intensity Democracy: Political Power in the New World Order.* London: Pluto Press.

Gleeck, Lewis, Jr.
1993 *The Third Philippine Republic, 1946–1972.* Quezon City: New Day Publishers.

Gloria, Glenda
1993 A talk with Manila's foremost rebel. *Manila Chronicle,* 26 July.

Gloria, Glenda M., ed.
1997 *Shift.* Quezon City: Ateneo Center for Social Policy and Public Affairs.

Go, Miriam Grace
2002 From cadre to congressman. *Newsbreak,* 1 April.

Goertzen, Donald
1991 Agents for change. *Far Eastern Economic Review,* 8 Aug.

Goodell, Grace E.
1985 Paternalism, patronage, and potlatch: The dynamics of giving and being given to. *Current Anthropology* 26(2):247–66.

Gramsci, Antonio
1971 *Selections from the Prison Notebooks.* Translated and edited by Quintin Hoare and Geoffrey Nowell Smith. London: Lawrence and Wishart.

Green, Philip
1993 "Democracy" as a contested idea. In *Democracy: Key Concepts in*

Critical Theory, edited by Philip Green, 2–22. Atlantic Highlands, NJ: Humanities Press.

Grossholtz, Jean
1964 *Politics in the Philippines*. Boston and Toronto: Little, Brown.
1974 Philippines 1973: Whither Marcos? *Asian Survey* 14(1):101–12.

Guerrero, Amado [pseudonym of Jose Ma. Sison]
1979a *Philippine Society and Revolution*. International Association of Filipino Patriots.
1979b Specific characteristics of our people's war. In *Philippine Society and Revolution*, by Amado Guerrero, 177–215. United States: International Association of Filipino Patriots.

Gutierrez, Eric U.
1994a *The Ties That Bind*. Pasig: Philippine Center for Investigative Journalism and Institute for Popular Democracy.
1994b Electoral coalitions for the 1992 elections. In *Studies on Coalition Experiences in the Philippines*, edited by Cesar Cala and Jose Z. Grageda, 94–120. Makati: Bookmark.

Gutierrez, Eric U., Ildefonso C. Torrente, and Noli G. Narca
1992 *All in the Family: A Study of Elites and Power Relations in the Philippines*. Quezon City: Institute for Popular Democracy.

Hadiz, Vedi
2003 Power and politics in North Sumatra: The uncompleted *reformasi*. In *Local Power and Politics in Indonesia*, edited by Edward Aspinall and Greg Fealy, 119–31. Singapore: Institute of Southeast Asian Studies.

Hawes, Gary A.
1984 The political economy of transnational corporate investment in Philippine agriculture. Ph.D. diss., University of Hawaii.
1987 *The Philippine State and the Marcos Regime: The Politics of Export*. Ithaca: Cornell University Press.
2000 Local politics in a decentralized system: The structural impact of the 1991 Local Government Code in the Philippines. Unpublished manuscript.

Held, David
1996 *Models of Democracy*. Stanford: Stanford University Press.

Hewison, Kevin, and Garry Rodan
1996 The ebb and flow of civil society and the decline of the Left in Southeast Asia. In *Political Oppositions in Industrialising Asia*, edited by Garry Rodan, 40–71. London: Routledge.

Hewison, Kevin, Richard Robison, and Garry Rodan
1993 *Southeast Asia in the 1990s: Authoritarianism, Democracy, and Capitalism*. Sydney: Allen and Unwin.

Hilhorst, Dorothea
2003 *The Real World of NGOs: Discourses, Diversity, and Development*. London: Zed Books.

Hobday, Charles
1986 *Communist and Marxist Parties of the World*. Essex: Longman House.

Hoeksema, Renze Lyle
1956 Communism in the Philippines: A historical and analytical study of communism and the Communist Party in the Philippines and its relations to communist movements abroad. Ph.D. diss., Harvard University.

Hofileña, Chay Florentino
1997 Tracking the charter amendment debate. In *Shift*, edited by Glenda M. Gloria, 134–69. Quezon City: Ateneo Center for Social Policy and Public Affairs.
2002a Unraveling Bert Gonzales. *Newsbreak*, 24 June.
2002b Playing tough. *Newsbreak*, 16 Sept.

Hollnsteiner, Mary
1963 *The Dynamics of Power in a Philippine Municipality*. Quezon City: University of the Philippines Press.

Howell, Jude, and Jenny Pearce
2001 *Civil Society and Development: A Critical Exploration*. Boulder: Lynne Rienner.

Huber, Evelyne, Dietrich Rueschemeyer, and John D. Stephens
1997 The paradoxes of contemporary democracy: Formal, participatory, and social dimensions. *Comparative Politics* 29(3):323–41.

Huntington, Samuel P.
1968 *Political Order in Changing Societies*. New Haven: Yale University Press.
1991 *The Third Wave: Democratization in the Late Twentieth Century*. Norman: University of Oklahoma Press.

Hutchcroft, Paul D.
1991 Oligarchs and cronies in the Philippine state: The politics of patrimonial plunder. *World Politics* 43(3):414–50.
1993 Predatory oligarchy, patrimonial state: The politics of private domestic commercial banking in the Philippines. Ph.D. diss.,

Yale University.

1998a *Booty Capitalism: The Politics of Banking in the Philippines*. Quezon City: Ateneo de Manila University Press.

1998b Sustaining economic and political reform: The challenges ahead. In *The Philippines: New Directions in Domestic Policy and Foreign Relations*, edited by David Timberman, 23–47. New York and Singapore: Asia Society and Institute of Southeast Asian Studies.

Hutchcroft, Paul D., and Joel Rocamora

2004 Addressing Philippines' democratic deficit. *Philippine Daily Inquirer*, 1 June.

Ileto, Reynaldo C.

2001 Orientalism and the study of Philippine politics. *Philippine Political Science Journal* 45:1–32.

2002 On Sidel's response and bossism in the Philippines. *Philippine Political Science Journal* 46:151–74.

Institute for Political and Electoral Reform

1995a 1995 psychographics study of Filipino voter behavior. Unpublished manuscript.

1995b Coalition Consortium on Electoral Reforms. Pamphlet.

2004 The voter's choice: Myself—a psychographic study of the Filipino voter behavior. Unpublished manuscript.

Institute for Popular Democracy

2003a IPD at the forefront of a grand coalition against Con-Ass. Press release, 13 May.

2003b *Kapihan* for cha-cha. Press release, 13 Nov.

Institute for Strategic Initiatives

2002 Iranun Development Council: Model building in Muslim Mindanao governance. Unpublished manuscript.

Institute for Strategic Initiatives and Institute of Politics and Governance

2002 *Barangay Governance Resource Book*. Davao City: Institute for Strategic Initiatives and Institute of Politics and Governance.

Institute of Politics and Governance

1994 Executive Summary: IPG-FES Conference on "Integrative Participation in Philippine General Politics and Electoral Reforms." In *Popular Participation in Electoral Reform and Governance*, edited by the Institute of Politics and Governance, 9–12. Quezon City: Institute of Politics and Governance.

1997 Report of the NGO-PO Working Group on the LGC Review. In

Working Group, Working Papers: NGO-PO Perspectives for the Local Government Code Review, edited by Soliman Santos, Jr., 15–21. Quezon City: Institute of Politics and Governance.

1999 The necessity of local sectoral representation: The case for people's participation. *Governance Brief* 2(1):1–8.

Institute of Politics and Governance, ed.

1994 *Popular Participation in Electoral Reform and Governance*. Quezon City: Institute of Politics and Governance.

2000 *Balangay: An Introductory Course on Barangay Governance*. Quezon City: Institute of Politics and Governance and Friedrich Ebert Stiftung.

Iszatt, Nina T.

2002 The road to democratization: Partnerships, planning, and participation in Surallah. Kaisahan Occasional Paper.

2004 Innovations in resource mobilization: Surallah does it fiesta-style. In *Beyond Good Governance: Participatory Democracy in the Philippines*, edited by Marisol Estrella and Nina T. Iszatt, 164–88. Quezon City: Institute for Popular Democracy.

Jessop, Bob

1998 The rise of governance and the risks of failure: The case of economic development. *International Social Science Journal* 50(155):29–45.

Jimenez, Cher

2003 Absentee-voting bill still in limbo. *Today*, 10 Jan.

Jimenez-David, Rina

2003 Abanse! Pinay makes it. *Philippine Daily Inquirer*, 6 July.

Jones, Gregg R.

1989 *Red Revolution: Inside the Philippine Guerrilla Movement*. Boulder: Westview Press.

Jose, F. Sionil

1985 The Huks in retrospect: A failed bid for power. *Solidarity* 102:64–103.

Kang, David

2002 *Crony Capitalism: Corruption and Development in South Korea and the Philippines*. Cambridge: Cambridge University Press.

Karaos, Anna Marie

2001 Civil society in the new politics. *Philippine Daily Inquirer*, 4 July.

Kasarinlan
2004 Hostaged? Philippine foreign policy after Angelo dela Cruz: Proceedings of a public forum, 12 Aug. 2004, University of the Philippines. *Kasarinlan* 19(1):113–41.

Kawanaka, Takeshi
1998 The Robredo style: Philippine local politics in transition. *Kasarinlan* 13(3):5–36.

Keane, John
1998 *Civil Society: Old Images, New Visions.* Stanford: Stanford University Press.

Keck, Margaret E.
1992 *The Workers' Party and Democratization in Brazil.* New Haven: Yale University Press.

Kerkvliet, Benedict J. Tria
1972 Peasant rebellion in the Philippines: The origins and growth of the HMB. Ph.D. diss., University of Wisconsin, Madison.
1977 *The Huk Rebellion: A Study of Peasant Revolt in the Philippines.* Berkeley: University of California Press.
1990 *Everyday Politics in the Philippines: Class and Status Relations in a Central Luzon Village.* Berkeley: University of California Press.
1995 Toward a more comprehensive analysis of Philippine politics: Beyond the patron-client, factional framework. *Journal of Southeast Asian Studies* 26(2):401–19.
1996 Contested meanings of elections in the Philippines. In *The Politics of Elections in Southeast Asia,* edited by Robert H. Taylor, 136–63. Cambridge: Cambridge University Press.
2000 Manuela Santa Ana vda. de Maclang and Philippine politics. In *Lives at the Margin: Biography of Filipinos Obscure, Ordinary, and Heroic,* edited by Alfred W. McCoy, 389–421. Madison: Center for Southeast Asia Studies, University of Wisconsin-Madison.

Kerkvliet, Benedict J. Tria, ed.
1974 *Political Change in the Philippines: Studies of Local Politics Preceding Martial Law.* Honolulu: University Press of Hawaii.

Kerkvliet, Benedict J. Tria, and Resil Mojares
1991 *From Marcos to Aquino.* Quezon City and Honolulu: Ateneo de Manila University Press and University of Hawaii Press.

Kilos
1994 The Philippine left: Prospects for resurgence. *Links* 2:83–94.

Kilusang Mamamayan para sa Repormang Elektoral
1997 An appeal for the passage of urgent electoral reforms. Unpublished document, 21 Aug.

Kim, Rahn
2004 Labor movement gains momentum: DLP makes way into Parliament by winning 10 seats. *Korea Times*, 16 April.

Kingsbury, Damien
2001 *South-East Asia: A Political Profile*. Oxford: Oxford University Press.

Konrad Adenauer Foundation
2000 *New Public Management: Public Private Partnership*. Makati: Konrad Adenauer Foundation.

Kopstein, Jeffrey and Stephen Hanson
1998 Paths to uncivil societies and anti-liberal states: A reply to Shenfield. *Post-Soviet Affairs* 14(4):369–75.

Korten, David C.
1990 *Getting to the 21st Century: Voluntary Action and the Global Agenda*. West Hartford, CT: Kumarian Press.

Krinks, Peter, ed.
1987 *The Philippines under Aquino*. Canberra: Australian Development Studies Network.

Kumar, Krishan
1993 Civil society: An inquiry into the usefulness of an historical term. *British Journal of Sociology* 44(3):375–95.

Lacaba, Jose F., ed.
1995 *Boss: Five Case Studies of Local Politics in the Philippines*. Manila: Philippine Center for Investigative Journalism and Institute for Popular Democracy.

Lachica, Eduardo
1971 *The Huks: Philippine Agrarian Society in Revolt*. New York: Praeger Publishers.

Laclau, Ernesto and Chantal Mouffe
1985 *Hegemony and Socialist Strategy: Towards a Radical Democratic Politics*. London: Verso.

1987 Post-Marxism without apologies. *New Left Review* 166:79–106.

Lacuarta, Gerald G.
2000 Fifty percent of trafficked women in SE Asia are Filipinos. *Philippine Daily Inquirer*, 1 July.

Lagman, Filemon

1994 PPW: A new-type revolution of the wrong type. Unpublished manuscript.

Landé, Carl H.

1965 *Leaders, Factions and Parties: The Structure of Philippine Politics*. New Haven: Council on Southeast Asian Studies, Yale University.

1967 The Philippine political party system. *Journal of Southeast Asian History* 8(1):19–39.

1968 Parties and politics in the Philippines. *Asian Survey* 8(9):725–47.

1973 Networks and groups in Southeast Asia: Some observations on the group theory of politics. *American Political Science Review* 67(1):103–27.

1981 Philippine prospects after martial law. *Foreign Affairs* 59(5): 1147–68.

2001 The return of "people power" in the Philippines. *Journal of Democracy* 12(2):88–102.

2002 Political clientelism, developmentalism, and postcolonial theory: A reply to Ileto. *Philippine Political Science Journal* 46:119–28.

Laothamatas, Anek

1997 *Democratization in Southeast and East Asia*. Singapore: Institute of Southeast Asian Studies.

Lawyers Committee for Human Rights

1988 Vigilantes in the Philippines: A threat to democratic rule. New York: Lawyers Committee for Human Rights.

1990 *Out of control: Militia abuses in the Philippines*. New York: Lawyers Committee for Human Rights.

Lava, Jesus B.

2002 *Memoirs of a Communist*. Pasig: Anvil Publishing.

Leagues of Provinces, Cities, and Municipalities in the Philippines and the NGO-PO Working Group on the LGC Review

1997 Joint statement of the leagues and the NGO-PO Working Alliance: Toward a strategic alliance. In *Working Group, Working Papers: NGO-PO Perspectives for the Local Government Code Review*, edited by Soliman Santos, Jr., 151–53. Quezon City: Institute of Politics and Governance.

Leftwich, Adrian

1993 Governance, democracy, and development in the Third World. *Third World Quarterly* 14(3):605–24.

Levi, Margaret

1996 Social and unsocial capital: A review essay of Robert Putnam's *Making Democracy Work. Politics and Society* 24(1):45–55.

Lichauco, Alejandro

1973 The Lichauco paper: Imperialism in the Philippines. *Monthly Review* 25(3):1–111.

Linantud, John L.

1998 Whither guns, goons, and gold? The decline of factional election violence in the Philippines. *Contemporary Southeast Asia* 20(3):298–318.

Linz, Juan J.

1990 Transitions to democracy. *Washington Quarterly* 13(3):143–64.

Linz, Juan J., and Alfred Stepan

1996 Toward consolidated democracies. *Journal of Democracy* 7(2):14–33.

Liwanag, Armando [pseudonym]

1992a Reaffirm our basic principles and rectify the errors. Pamphlet, Central Publishing House, Communist Party of the Philippines.

1992b Stand for socialism against modern revisionism. Pamphlet, National Democratic Front International Office, Utrecht, the Netherlands.

2001 Hail the rising revolutionary forces and the upsurge of the mass movement. *Ang Bayan*, 26 Dec.

2002 Prepare against further U.S. military intervention, intensify and advance the people's war! *Ang Bayan*, 29 March.

Llamas, Ronald

1996 Renewing the struggle: Obstacles and opportunities for progressive intervention. In *Transforming the Struggle: Bisig and its Unfolding Narrative*, edited by Bukluran sa Ikauunlad ng Sosyalistang Isip at Gawa, 60–76. Manila: Bisig.

Local Government Development Foundation

2000 *Local Political and Administrative Reforms*. Pasay: Logodef.

2001 *Dissemination of Best Practices in Local Governance*. Pasay: Logodef.

Lopa, Margarita A.

1995 *Singing the Same Song: Reflections of Two Generations of NGO Workers in the Philippines*. Manila: Asian NGO Coalition for Agrarian Reform and Rural Development and Philippine Partnership for the Development of Human Resources in Rural Areas.

Loredo, Roy
1999 A history of popular education (or how we are evolving from being transmission belts). In *Of Maps and Leapfrogs: Popular Education and Other Disruptions*, edited by Robert Francis Garcia, 77–94. Quezon City: Popular Education for People's Empowerment.

Lynch, Frank
1959 Social class in a Bikol town. Ph.D. diss., University of Chicago.

Macale, Ilberto
2001 Salcedo has new mayor. *Abot-Kamay*, July.

Macaraig, Mynardo
2004 Afghanistan learns from Philippine elections. *Philippine Daily Inquirer*, 18 May.

Machado, Kit Gordon
1971 Changing aspects of factionalism in Philippine local politics. *Asian Survey* 11(12):1182–99.

1972 Leadership and organization in Philippine local politics. Ph.D. diss., University of Washington, Seattle.

1974a Changing patterns of leadership recruitment and the emergence of the professional politician in Philippine local politics. In *Political Change in the Philippines: Studies of Local Politics Preceding Martial Law*, edited by Benedict J. Tria Kerkvliet, 77–129. Honolulu: University Press of Hawaii.

1974b From traditional faction to machine: Changing patterns of political leadership in the rural Philippines. *Journal of Asian Studies* 33(4):523–47.

Macuja, Julio P., II, ed.
1992 *Issues in Politics, Governance, and Electoral Reform*. Quezon City: Center for Social Policy and Public Affairs, Ateneo de Manila University.

Magadia, Jose
1999 Contemporary civil society in the Philippines. In *Southeast Asian Affairs 1999*, edited by Institute of Southeast Asian Studies, 253–68. Singapore: Institute of Southeast Asian Studies.

2003 *State-Society Dynamics: Policy Making in a Restored Democracy*. Quezon City: Ateneo de Manila University Press.

Magallona, Merlin M.
1982 A contribution to the study of feudalism and capitalism in the Philippines. In *Feudalism and Capitalism in the Philippines: Trends and Implications*, edited by Temario C. Rivera, Merlin M.

Magallona, Rigoberto D. Tiglao, Ernesto M. Valencia, and Alex R. Magno, 14–44. Quezon City: Foundation for Nationalist Studies.

Magdoff, Harry
1969 *The Age of Imperialism: The Economics of U.S. Foreign Policy*. New York: Monthly Review Press

Magno, Alex R.
1982 Authoritarianism and underdevelopment: Notes on the political order of a dependent-capitalist Filipino mode. In *Feudalism and Capitalism in the Philippines: Trends and Implications*, edited by Temario C. Rivera, Merlin M. Magallona, Rigoberto D. Tiglao, Ernesto M. Valencia, and Alex R. Magno, 87–105. Quezon City: Foundation for Nationalist Studies.

Magno, Francisco A.
1989 State, patronage, and local elites. *Kasarinlan* 4(3):10–18.

Magtubo, Renato B.
1998 First privileged speech, House of Representatives, Philippine Congress.
2000 Reform or revolution. Privileged speech, House of Representatives, Philippine Congress, 8 May.

Mainwaring, Scott
1999 *Rethinking Party Systems in the Third Wave of Democratization: The Case of Brazil*. Stanford: Stanford University Press.

Mainwaring, Scott, and Timothy R. Scully
1995 *Building Democratic Institutions: Party Systems in Latin America*. Stanford: Stanford University Press.

Mainwaring, Scott, Guillermo O'Donnell, and J. Samuel Valenzuela, eds.
1992 *Issues in Democratic Consolidation: The New South American Democracies in Comparative Perspective*. Notre Dame, IN: University of Notre Dame Press.

Maisrikrod, Surin
1997 The making of Thai democracy: A study of political alliances among the state, the capitalists, and the middle class. In *Democratization in Southeast and East Asia*, edited by Anek Laothamatas, 141–66. Singapore: Institute of Southeast Asian Studies.

Maitem, Jeoffrey
2002 Matanog mayor's house set on fire, cops say political rivalry to blame. *Manila Times*, 30 Nov.

Manapat, Ricardo

1991 *Some Are Smarter Than Others: The History of Marcos's Crony Capitalism.* New York: Aletheia Publications.

Mangahas, Mahar

2001 Tracking public sentiment on corruption. Press release, Social Weather Stations, 3 Aug.

Manila Times

2002 Former MILF stronghold gets a new name. 3 July.

2003 Eighteen murdered daily in 2002, highest in 9 years—police. 17 Feb.

Marfil, Martin

2004 Comelec Chairman Abalos won't quit. *Philippine Daily Inquirer,* 8 Feb.

Marfil, Martin, and Jerry Esplanada

2000 Congressmen allegedly got ₱500,000 each. *Philippine Daily Inquirer,* 17 April.

Marks, Thomas Andrew

1991 Making revolution: The insurgency of the Communist Party of Thailand (CPT) in structural perspective. Ph.D. diss., University of Hawaii.

Martinez, Rommel

2001 Promoting local initiatives for public-private partnership in Los Baños, Laguna. In *Civic Engagement for Development: Case Examples from Indonesia, Philippines, Thailand, Vietnam,* edited by the World Bank, 15–18. Bangkok: World Bank.

May, Ron

1998 State, society, and governance: Reflections on a Philippines-Papua New Guinea comparison. In *Weak and Strong States in Asia-Pacific Societies,* edited by Peter Dauvergne, 60–76. Canberra: Allen and Unwin.

2002 Elections in the Philippines, May 2001. *Electoral Studies* 21(4): 673–80.

McAdam, Doug, Sidney Tarrow, and Charles Tilly

2001 *Dynamics of Contention.* Cambridge: Cambridge University Press.

McCoy, Alfred W.

1988 Quezon's Commonwealth: The emergence of Philippine authoritarianism. In *Philippine Colonial Democracy,* edited by Ruby R. Paredes, 114–60. New Haven: Southeast Asia Council, Yale University.

1993a "An anarchy of families": The historiography of state and family in the Philippines. In *An Anarchy of Families: State and Family in the Philippines,* edited by Alfred W. McCoy, 1–32. Madison: Center for Southeast Asian Studies, University of Wisconsin.

McCoy, Alfred W., ed.
1993b *An Anarchy of Families: State and Family in the Philippines.* Madison: Center for Southeast Asian Studies, University of Wisconsin.

McCoy, Alfred W., and Ed. C. de Jesus
1982 *Philippine Social History: Global Trade and Local Transformations.* Quezon City and Sydney: Ateneo de Manila University Press and George Allen and Unwin.

Melegrito, Ma. Lourdes F., and Diana J. Mendoza
1999 NGOs, politics, and governance. In *Politics and Governance: Theory and Practice in the Philippine Context,* edited by Diana J. Mendoza and Lydia N. Yu-Jose, 229–64. Quezon City: Office of Research and Publications, Ateneo de Manila University Press.

Melencio, Sonny
1994 Leninism versus Stalinism: Current debate in the Communist Party of the Philippines. *Links* 1:29–42.

1995 Filipinos protest over plight of overseas workers. *Green Left Weekly,* 29 March.

Melencio, Sonny, and Reihana Mohideen
2002 Lessons and prospects for the Philippine Left. *Links* 20:69–83.

Mendoza, Diana
1995 Dependence or self-reliance? The Philippine NGO experience. *Philippine Political Science Journal* 39:143–72.

Mindanao Cross
2002 Still a battle ground. Editorial, 24 Aug.

Miranda, Felipe B.
1991 Leadership and political stabilization in a post-Aquino Philippines. *Philippine Political Science Journal* 33:142–222.

1993 The logic of coalition politics. *Manila Chronicle,* 14 Jan.

Miranda, Felipe B., ed.
1997 *Democratization: Philippine Perspectives.* Quezon City: University of the Philippines Press.

Mogato, Manny
2003 To fund a revolution. *Newsbreak,* 31 March.

Mohan, Giles, and Kristian Stokke

2000 Participatory development and empowerment: The dangers of localism. *Third World Quarterly* 21(2):247–68.

Mohanty, Manoranjan, and Partha Nath Mukherji, with Olle Törnquist, eds.

1998 *People's Rights: Social Movements and the State in the Third World*. New Delhi and Thousand Oaks, CA: Sage Publications.

Monsod, Christian S.

1997 Furthering democratization and development through elections. In Education campaign for clean elections and good governance, 22–33. Pamphlet, Consortium on Electoral Reforms and Institute for Political and Electoral Reform, Quezon City.

Montemayor, Carla, Edicio de la Torre, and Cesar Cala

1995 Civil society rising: Why Philippines 2000 is not the only story around. *Political Brief*, Nov.-Dec.

Montiel, Tina

1997 Cultural directions of a new party. In *Papers of a Party in the Making*, edited by Soliman Santos, Jr., 111–123. Quezon City: Institute of Politics and Governance.

Moore, Barrington, Jr.

1969 *Social Origins of Dictatorship and Democracy: Lord and Peasant in the Making of the Modern World*. Harmondsworth: Penguin Books.

Morales, Horacio, Jr.

1990 *A Call for People's Development*. Quezon City: National Council of Churches of the Philippines.

1993 Preface. In *On Civil Society*, by Isagani R. Serrano, vii–xi. Quezon City: Philippine Rural Reconstruction Movement.

Mouffe, Chantal

1979a Hegemony and ideology in Gramsci. In *Gramsci and Marxist Theory*, edited by Chantal Mouffe, 168–204. London: Routledge and Kegan Paul.

1988 Hegemony and new political subjects: Toward a new concept of democracy. In *Marxism and the Interpretation of Culture*, edited by Cary Nelson and Lawrence Grossberg, 89–104. Urbana and Chicago: University of Illinois Press.

1993 *The Return of the Political*. London: Verso.

1996 Radical democracy or liberal democracy. In *Radical Democracy: Identity, Citizenship, and the State*, edited by David Trend, 19–26. New York and London: Routledge.

Mouffe, Chantal, ed.
1979b *Gramsci and Marxist Theory*. London: Routledge and Kegan Paul.

Muego, Benjamin N.
1975 The "New Society" of the Philippines: A case study of a developmental movement regime. Ph.D. diss., Southern Illinois University, Carbondale.

Muslim, Macapado A., and Rufa Cagoco-Guiam
1999 Mindanao: Land of Promise. *Accord* 6:10–19.

Myers, David J.
1996 Review of Scott Mainwaring and Timothy R. Scully's *Building Democratic Institutions: Party Systems in Latin America. Journal of Politics* 58(3):924–26.

National Democratic Front of Metro Manila-Rizal
1991 Politico-military struggle in the main urban center. *Debate,* pilot issue (March):65–71.

National Federation of Labor Unions, National Federation of Labor, and United Workers of the Philippines
1993 Joint statement on disaffiliation from KMU. Unpublished manuscript, 29 Sept.

National Peasant Secretariat, Comunist Party of the Philippines
1978 Community organization: Reform or revolution? A critique of the CO approach. Mimeo.

National Statistical Coordination Board
2003 *2003 Philippine Statistical Yearbook*. Manila: National Economic and Development Authority.

National Statistics Office
2002 2000 Family Income and Expenditures Survey (FIES) Final Results.

National United Front Commission, Communist Party of the Philippines
1982 Comprehensive orientation and tasks in our united front work. Unpublished document.

National Youth and Student Department, Communist Party of the Philippines
1986 Against the snap election boycott. *Praktika* 1(1):23–37.

Nazareno, Rocky
2002 RP has dirtiest environment in SEA—survey. *Philippine Daily Inquirer,* 2 March.

Nelson, Cary, and Lawrence Grossberg

1988 *Marxism and the Interpretation of Culture.* Urbana and Chicago: University of Illinois Press.

Nemenzo, Francisco, Jr.

1984a Rectification process in the Philippine communist movement. In *Armed Communist Movements in Southeast Asia,* edited by Lim Joo-Jock and Vani S., 71–101. New York: St. Martin's Press.

1984b The millenarian-populist aspects of Filipino Marxism. In *Marxism in the Philippines: Marx Centennial Lectures,* edited by Third World Studies Center, 1–40. Quezon City: Third World Studies Center.

1984c An irrepressible revolution: The decline and resurgence of the Philippine communist movement. Work in progress seminar, Research School of Pacific Studies, Australian National University, 13 Nov.

1985 The Left and the traditional opposition. In *The Philippines after Marcos,* edited by R. J. May and Francisco Nemenzo, 45–69. London and Sydney: Croom Helm.

1988 From autocracy to elite democracy. In *Dictatorship and Revolution: Roots of People's Power,* edited by Aurora Javate-de Dios, Petronilo Bn. Daroy, and Lorna Kalaw-Tirol, 221–68. Metro Manila: Conspectus Foundation.

1996a Questioning Marx, critiquing Marxism: Reflections on the ideological crisis of the Left. In *Transforming the Struggle: Bisig and Its Unfolding Narrative,* edited by Bukluran sa Ikauunlad ng Sosyalistang Isip at Gawa, 35–59. Manila: Bisig.

1996b Reinventing socialism. In *Transforming the Struggle: Bisig and Its Unfolding Narrative,* edited by Bukluran sa Ikauunlad ng Sosyalistang Isip at Gawa, 143–53. Manila: Bisig.

Nowak, Thomas C.

1974 Class and clientelist systems in the Philippines. Ph.D. diss., Cornell University.

Nowak, Thomas C., and Kay A. Snyder

1970 Urbanization and clientelist systems in the Philippines. *Philippine Journal of Public Administration* 14(3):259–75.

1974a Economic concentration and political change in the Philippines. In *Political Change in the Philippines: Studies of Local Politics Preceding Martial Law,* edited by Benedict J. Tria Kerkvliet, 153–241. Honolulu: University Press of Hawaii.

1974b Clientelist politics in the Philippines: Integration or instability? *American Political Science Review* 68(3):1147–70.

Nuguid, Nati, and Manuel L. Quezon III
2003 Champions of a lost cause. *Philippines Free Press*, 18 Jan.

O'Donnell, Guillermo
1992 Transitions, continuities, and paradoxes. In *Issues in Democratic Consolidation: The New South American Democracies in Comparative Perspective*, edited by Scott Mainwaring, Guillermo O'Donnell, and J. Samuel Valenzuela, 17–56. Notre Dame, IN: University of Notre Dame Press.

1994 Delegative democracy. *Journal of Democracy* 5(1):55–69.

Office of the Press Secretary
1999 Q & A on the CONCORD. http://www.concord.ops.gov.ph

Opiniano, Jeremaiah
2001 OFWs push hard for absentee voting bill. *Cyberdyaryo*, 25 Aug.

Oversight Committee, Philippine Congress
1992 *Rules and Regulations Implementing the Local Government Code of 1991*. Manila: Department of Interior and Local Government.

Pablo, Carlito
2002 Gloria said to be gearing for 2004. *Philippine Daily Inquirer*, 22 April.

2004 Constitutional convention polls pushed by Speaker. *Philippine Daily Inquirer*, 7 Jan.

Pablo, Carlito, and Delfin T. Mallari, Jr.
2002 Palace negotiator seeks CPP peace terms. *Philippine Daily Inquirer*, 12 Aug.

Padayon
1999 Concord or discord? Padayon statement on the cha-cha. Press statement, 17 Sept.

Paredes, Ruby R.
1998a Introduction: The paradox of Philippine colonial democracy. In *Philippine Colonial Democracy*, edited by Ruby R. Paredes, 1–12. New Haven: Council on Southeast Asian Studies, Yale University

Paredes, Ruby R., ed.
1988b *Philippine Colonial Democracy*. New Haven: Council on Southeast Asian Studies, Yale University.

Parreño, Earl G.
1993 The shift to parliamentary system: Changing the terrain for

PO/NGO intervention. Paper presented at a consultation on parliamentary and electoral work, 24 Oct., Quezon City.

Partido Demokratiko Sosyalista ng Pilipinas
1982 Basic documents of the Partido Demokratiko Sosyalista ng Pilipinas. Pamphlet, 1 May.

Partido Komunista ng Pilipinas
1996 *Communism in the Philippines: The P.K.P., Book 1*, Metro Manila: Partido Komunista ng Pilipinas.

Partido ng Bayan
1986 Program of action. Mimeo.
1993 Grassroots electoral politics: An evaluation of the electoral performance of PnB and allied organizations in the 1987 and 1992 elections. Pamphlet.

Partido ng Manggagawang Pilipino
1999 Mga Dokumento ng Kongreso ng Pagtatatag [Documents of the Founding Congress]. Pamphlet.
2002 Programa ng Partido ng Manggagawang Pilipino (Pinagsanib) [Program of the Filipino Workers' Party (Merged)]. Unpublished document.

Party Organizations in the Visayas
1993 Declaration of Autonomy. *Debate* 8:60–72.

Pascual, Federico D., Jr.
2003 Postscript. *Philippine Star*, 23 Feb.

Patiño, Patrick I.
1999 Has traditional politics polluted new politics? *Work in Progress*, Occasional Papers, no. 10, Institute for Popular Democracy, Quezon City.

Perez, Caesar P., Patricio S. Faylon, Leozardo C. Pantua, and Vivian B. Valdez
2002 Managing town-community solid waste: Malinis at maayos na kapaligiran, malusog at matinong pamayanan [Clean and orderly surroundings, a healthy and sound community]. Paper presented at the 2002 PACS Seminar Series of the Philippine Association of Career Scientists, 11 April, Quezon City.

Perlez, Jane
2002 Educated Filipinos pack up. *International Herald Tribune*, 9 April.

Pertierra, Raul
1995a *Philippine Localities and Global Perspectives: Essays on Society and Culture*. Quezon City: Ateneo de Manila University Press.

1995b Political consciousness versus cultural identity. In *Philippine Localities and Global Perspectives: Essays on Society and Culture,* by Raul Pertierra, 15–38. Quezon City: Ateneo de Manila University Press.

Petras, James

1999 Globalization: A critical analysis. *Journal of Contemporary Asia* 29(1):3–37.

Philippine Daily Inquirer

1992 CPP split confirmed, peace talks perilled. 10 Dec.

1994 Bare people's court judges, "renegades" dare Sison bloc. 27 April.

1995 US report declares NPA split, defeated. 24 May.

2004 "Parties." Editorial, 13 Jan.

Pimentel, Aquilino, Jr.

1994 The Local Government Code: An overview. In *Popular Participation in Electoral Reform and Governance,* edited by Institute of Politics and Governance, 93–104. Quezon City: Institute of Politics and Governance.

Politburo, Communist Party of the Philippines

1986 Resolution on the party's tactic regarding the snap election. Mimeo.

Political Forces Study Group

1989 A preliminary study on democratic socialism in the Philippines. Mimeo.

Pomeroy, William J.

1970 *American Neo-colonialism: Its Emergence in the Philippines and Asia.* New York: International Publishers.

1992 *The Philippines: Colonialism, Collaboration, and Resistance!* New York: International Publishers.

1993 Negotiation as a form of struggle: The PKP experience. *Debate* 6: 61–76.

PO-NGO Conference

1994 Proceedings. Quezon City, 6 March.

Powell, John Duncan

1970 Peasant society and clientelist politics. *American Political Science Review* 64(2):411–25.

Putnam, Robert D.

1993 *Making Democracy Work: Civic Traditions in Modern Italy.* Princeton: Princeton University Press.

1995 Bowling alone: America's declining social capital. *Journal of Democracy* 6(1):65–78.

2000 *Bowling Alone: The Collapse and Revival of American Community.* New York: Simon and Schuster.

Putzel, James

1995a Democratization and clan politics: The 1992 Philippine elections. *South East Asia Research* 3(1):18–45.

1995b "Managing" the main force: The Communist Party and the peasantry in the Philippines. *Journal of Peasant Studies* 22(4):645–71.

1997 Accounting for the "dark side" of social capital: Reading Robert Putnam on democracy. *Journal of International Development* 9(7):939–49.

1998 NGOs and rural poverty. In *Organizing for Democracy: NGOs, Civil Society, and the Philippine State,* edited by G. Sidney Silliman and Lela Garner Noble, 77–112. Quezon City: Ateneo de Manila University Press.

1999 Survival of an imperfect democracy in the Philippines. *Democratization* 6(1):198–223.

Quimpo, Nathan Gilbert

1993 The debate in the CPP-NDF and its implications on the peace process. Paper presented at a Philippine solidarity conference sponsored by the Philippinenburo, Frankfurt, Germany, 13 March.

2000 Colonial name, colonial mentality, and ethnocentrism. *Public Policy* 4(1):1–49.

2001a Options in the pursuit of a just, comprehensive, and stable peace in the southern Philippines. *Asian Survey* 41(2):271–289.

2001b The revolutionary left: Back to center stage? *Philippine Daily Inquirer*. Two-part article, 23–24 June.

2002 Barangay, SK elections: A season of vote-buying and "kidnappings." *Today*. Three-part article, 3–5 July.

2003 Red leaders afraid Kintanar knew too much. *Philippine Daily Inquirer*, 28 January.

Ramirez, Patricio

2002a A rejection of the all-out war policy. Press statement, 23 Dec.

2002b GMA's ouster through an uprising is a possibility; rejection of rival's rise to power is a necessity. Press statement, 29 Dec.

Rebolusyonaryong Partido ng Manggagawa—Pilipinas

1998 Mga Batayang Dokumento ng RPM-P [Basic Documents of RPM-P]. Pamphlet.

2000 "Civil Society": Critique and anatomy. *Revolutionary Workers Journal*, Jan.

Reid, Ben

2000 *Philippine Left: Political Crisis and Social Change*. Manila: Journal of Contemporary Asia Publishers.

2004 EDSA II, the Arroyo government, and the "democratic left" in the Philippines. *Links* 25:29–40.

Representatives of political parties

2002 United declaration of the First Philippine Political Parties Conference (3–5 May 2002). *Today*, 13 May.

Republic of the Philippines

1995 Winning the future: The social reform agenda. Pamphlet.

Reuter

1994 Communist rebels agree to resume talks. *Philippine Daily Inquirer*, 14 June.

Reyes, Ricardo B.

1998 A new left project: A proposal. *Alternatives* 23(1):93–108.

2001 People power comes into the new millenium. *Political Brief*, March.

2003 Let's have truth, not publicity work. *Philippine Daily Inquirer*, 9 Feb.

Rivera, Temario C.

1982a On the contradictions of rural development. *Diliman Review* 30(5):49–54.

1982b Rethinking the Philippine social formation: Some problematic concepts and issues. In *Feudalism and Capitalism in the Philippines: Trends and Implications*, edited by Temario C. Rivera, Merlin M. Magallona, Rigoberto D. Tiglao, Ernesto M. Valencia, and Alex R. Magno, 1–13. Quezon City: Foundation for Nationalist Studies.

1992 Adapt or perish. *Solidaridad* 14(3):48–50.

1994 *Landlords and Capitalists: Class, Family and State in Philippine Manufacturing*. Quezon City: University of the Philippines Press and the Center for Integrative and Development Studies.

2002 Transition pathways and democratic consolidation in the post-Marcos Philippines. *Contemporary Southeast Asia* 24(3):466–83.

Rivera, Temario C., Merlin M. Magallona, Rigoberto D. Tiglao, Ernesto M. Valencia, and Alex R. Magno, eds.

1982 *Feudalism and Capitalism in the Philippines: Trends and Implications*. Quezon City: Foundation for Nationalist Studies.

Roberts, Kenneth

1995 Neoliberalism and the transformation of populism in Latin America. *World Politics* 48(1):82–116.

1998 *Deepening Democracy? The Modern Left and Social Movements in Chile and Peru*. Stanford: Stanford University Press.

Robison, Richard, Kevin Hewison, and Garry Rodan

1993 Political power in industrialising capitalist societies: Theoretical approaches. In *Southeast Asia in the 1990s: Authoritarianism, Democracy, and Capitalism*, edited by Kevin Hewison, Richard Robison, and Garry Rodan, 9–38. Sydney: Allen and Unwin.

Rocamora, Joel

1992 The NDF program and the CPP program for a people's democratic revolution: Umbilical cord or lifeline? *Debate* 5:3–38.

1993 The three little pigs and the big bad wolf. *Conjuncture* 6(2):5, 10.

1994a *Breaking Through: The Struggle within the Communist Party of the Philippines*. Pasig: Anvil Publishing.

1994b The new political terrain of NGO development work. *Debate* 10:47–65.

1997a Aksyon: Progressive intervention in electoral politics. *Aksyon*, Aug.

1997b The original concept paper for a progressive electoral party. In *Papers of a Party in the Making*, edited by Soliman Santos, Jr., 19–24. Quezon City: Institute of Politics and Governance.

1997c The constitutional amendment debate: Reforming political institutions, reshaping political culture. In *Shift*, edited by Glenda M. Gloria, 90–133. Quezon City: Ateneo Center for Social Policy and Public Affairs.

1998 Philippine political parties: Continuity and change. Paper prepared for the National Democratic Institute, Washington, DC, 27 Feb.

2000a The Left in the Philippines: Learning from the people, learning from each other. Paper presented in Colombo, Sri Lanka, 25 March.

2000b Formal democracy and its alternatives in the Philippines: Parties, elections, and social movements. Unpublished manuscript.

2001 Akbayan and the politics of reform. *Political Brief,* May.

2002 Between state and civil society: Can good people survive in bad government? Unpublished manuscript.

2003a Are we up to the challenge of constitutional reform? Press statement, 13 Feb.

2003b President's report. Paper presented at the Akbayan Second Regular Congress, 30–31 July.

2004 Empowerment and governance. In *Beyond Good Governance: Participatory Democracy in the Philippines,* edited by Marisol Estrella and Nina Iszatt, 330–49. Quezon City: Institute for Popular Democracy.

Rodan, Garry

1996a Theorising political opposition in East and Southeast Asia. In *Political Oppositions in Industrialising Asia,* edited by Garry Rodan, 1–39. London: Routledge.

1997 Civil society and other political possibilities in Southeast Asia. *Journal of Contemporary Asia* 27(2):156–78.

Rodan, Garry, ed.

1996b *Political Oppositions in Industrialising Asia.* London and New York: Routledge.

Rojas, Virgilio

1992 The mode of production controversy in the Philippines: Anatomy of a lingering theoretical stalemate. *Debate* 4:3–43.

Romero, Paolo, and Sheila Crisostomo

2001 Bloodiest elections in 15 years—AFP. *Philippine Star,* 24 May.

Rood, Steven

1991 Non-government organizations and the 1992 Philippine elections. *Philippine Political Science Journal* 33:97–119.

1998 Decentralization, democracy, and development. In *The Philippines: New Directions in Domestic Policy and Foreign Relations,* edited by David G. Timberman, 111–36. New York and Singapore: Asia Society and Institute of Southeast Asian Studies.

Rosales, Loretta Ann P.

1999 House Bill No. 7243: An act providing for a system of overseas voting for qualified Filipinos abroad and appropriating funds therefore.

2003a Illegitimate court acted as accuser/judge/executioner. *Philippine Daily Inquirer,* 10 Feb.

2003b Report of Rep. Loretta Ann P. Rosales to the Akbayan Second

National Regular Congress. Unpublished manuscript.
2004 The NPA as the new mafia. *Newsbreak*, 1 March.

Rosenberg, David A.
1984 Communism in the Philippines. *Problems of Communism* 33(5): 24–46.

Rosenberg, David A., ed.
1979 *Marcos and Martial Law in the Philippines*. Ithaca: Cornell University Press.

Rousset, Pierre
2003 After Kintanar, the killings continue: The post-1992 CPP assassination policy in the Philippines. 4 July, http://www.okde.org/divers/cpp_asspol_030703.htm

Rudebeck, Lars and Olle Törnquist, with Virgilio Rojas, eds.
1998 *Democratization in the Third World: Concrete Cases in Comparative and Theoretical Perspective*. New York: St. Martin's Press.

Rueschemeyer, Dietrich, Evelyne Huber Stephens, and John D. Stephens
1992 *Capitalist Development and Democracy*. Chicago: University of Chicago Press.

Rutten, Rosanne
1994 Courting the workers' vote in a hacienda region: Rhetoric and response in the 1992 Philippine election. *Pilipinas* 22:1–34.
1996 Popular support for the revolutionary movement CPP-NPA: Experiences in a hacienda in Negros Occidental, 1978–1995. In *The Revolution Falters: The Left in Philippine Politics after 1986*, edited by Patricio N. Abinales, 110–53. Ithaca: Southeast Asia Program, Cornell University.

Salonga, Jovito
2001 *A Struggle of Journey and Hope*. Manila: Anvil Publishing.

Santa Ana, Men
1992 A turf for local struggle. *Conjuncture* 5(2):3, 9.

Santayana, Gregorio [pseudonym of Jose Lava]
1950 Milestones in the history of the Communist Party of the Philippines (PKP). Unpublished manuscript.

Santos, Soliman, Jr.
1997a Introduction: Romancing the Local Government Code. In *Working Group, Working Papers: NGO-PO Perspectives for the Local Government Code Review*, edited by Soliman Santos, Jr., 9–12. Quezon City: Institute of Politics and Governance.

1997b Commentary: Last chance for LSR. Unpublished manuscript.

2003 The human rights implication of the Left purge. Paper delivered at a forum sponsored by the Netherlands Embassy, 15 Feb. 2003, San Agustin Museum, Intramuros, Manila.

Santos, Soliman, Jr., ed.

1997c *Working Group, Working Papers: NGO-PO Perspectives for the Local Government Code Review*. Quezon City: Institute of Politics and Governance.

1997d *Papers of a Party in the Making*. Quezon City: Institute of Politics and Governance.

Sarenas, Patricia

1999 Advancing gender concerns in the Estrada administration. Paper presented at a public forum on the Philippines, 23 April, Utrecht, the Netherlands.

Sarmiento, Juan V., Jr.

2003 Victims of Communist Party purge seek justice, closure. *Philippine Daily Inquirer*, five-part series, 26–30 Dec.

Saulo, Alfredo

1990 *Communism in the Philippines: An Introduction*. Quezon City: Ateneo de Manila University Press.

Schaffer, Frederic Charles

2001 Clean elections and the "great unwashed": Class divide and electoral reform in the Philippines. Paper delivered at the 2001 Annual Meeting of the American Political Science Association, San Francisco, 30 Aug.–2 Sept.

2003 Assessing the effectiveness of anti-vote-buying public education ads in the Philippines: Preliminary report. Unpublished manuscript.

Schedler, Andreas

1998 What is democratic consolidation? *Journal of Democracy* 9(2):91–107.

Schmidt, Steffen W., Laura Guasti, Carl H. Landé, and James C. Scott, eds.

1977 *Friends, Followers, and Factions: A Reader in Political Clientelism*. Berkeley and Los Angeles: University of California Press.

Schönwälder, Gerd

1998 Local politics and the Peruvian Left: The case of El Agustino. *Latin American Research Review* 33(2):73–102.

Schumpeter, Joseph

1943 *Capitalism, Socialism, and Democracy*. London: Unwin University

Books.

Scott, James C.

1969 Corruption, machine politics, and political change. *American Political Science Review* 63(4):1142–58.

1972a Patron-client politics and political change in Southeast Asia. *American Political Science Review* 66(1):91–113.

1972b The erosion of patron-client bonds and social change in rural Southeast Asia. *Journal of Asian Studies* 32(1):5–37.

1977 Political clientelism: A bibliographical essay. In *Friends, Followers, and Factions: A Reader in Political Clientelism*, edited by Steffen W. Schmidt, Laura Guasti, Carl H. Lande and James C. Scott, 483–505. Berkeley and Los Angeles: University of California Press.

1979 Revolution in the revolution: Peasants and commissars. *Theory and Society* 7:97–134.

1985 *Weapons of the Weak*. New Haven: Yale University Press.

Serfino, Dennis C.

2003 61% rate themselves "mahirap" [poor]. *Manila Standard*, 17 Jan.

Serrano, Isagani R.

1992a Sustainable development in Eastern Europe. *Debate* 2:16–22.

1992b NGOs and politics. *Conjuncture* 6(1):13–14.

1993 Civil society and democracy in the Philippines. In *On Civil Society*, edited by Isagani R. Serrano, 43–58. Quezon City: Philippine Rural Reconstruction Movement.

1994 *Civil Society in the Asia-Pacific Region*. Washington, DC: Civicus.

Shalom, Stephen Rosskamm

1981 *The United States and the Philippines: A Study of Neocolonialism*. Philadelphia: Institute for the Study of Human Issues.

Shantz, Arthur Alan

1972 Political parties: The changing foundations of Philippine democracy. Ph.D. diss., University of Michigan.

SIAD Organizing Committee, ed.

1995 *SIAD Tool Box: A Collection of Operational Pointers and Instruments for Sustainable Integrated Area Development*. Quezon City: SIAD Organizing Committee.

Sidel, John T.

1989 Beyond patron-client relations: Warlordism and local politics in the Philippines. *Kasarinlan* 4(3):19–30.

1995 Coercion, capital, and the post-colonial state: Bossism in the postwar Philippines. Ph.D. diss., Cornell University.

1999 *Capital, Coercion, and Crime: Bossism in the Philippines.* Stanford: Stanford University Press.

2002 Response to Ileto; or, why I am not an orientalist. *Philippine Political Science Journal* 46:129–38.

Silliman, G. Sidney, and Lela Garner Noble

1998a Citizen movements and Philippine democracy. In *Organizing for Democracy: NGOs, Civil Society, and the Philippine State,* edited by G. Sidney Silliman and Lela Garner Noble, 280–310. Quezon City: Ateneo de Manila University Press.

Silliman, G. Sidney, and Lela Garner Noble, eds.

1998b *Organizing for Democracy: NGOs, Civil Society, and the Philippine State.* Quezon City: Ateneo de Manila University Press.

Simbulan, Dante C.

1965 A study of the socio-economic elite in Philippine politics and government, 1946–1963. Ph.D. diss., Australian National University, Canberra.

1970 National decolonization movement demands university Filipinization. *Guidon,* 2 Sept.

Simon, Roger

1982 *Gramsci's Political Thought: An Introduction.* London: Lawrence and Wishart.

Sison, Jose Ma.

1985 Keynote address to the first regular congress of the Nationalist Alliance for Justice, Freedom and Democracy—National Capital Region. Mimeo, 15 Dec.

1995 Strengthen the alliance for human rights in the national-democratic movement. Message to the founding congress of Karapatan, 17 Aug.

2003 Experience of the Communist Party of the Philippines in the anti-imperialist and anti-war fronts. Paper presented at the Brussels Communist Seminar, Brussels, 4 May.

Sison, Jose Ma., with Rainer Werning

1989 *The Philippine Revolution: The Leader's View.* New York: Crane Russak.

Sison, Marites N.
2001 Voting remains a dream for overseas Filipinos. *Asia Times Online*, 13 Sept.

Slovo, Joe
1989 Has socialism failed? *South Africa Labour Bulletin* 14(6):11–28.

Sørensen, Georg
1993 *Democracy and Democratization*. Boulder: Westview Press.

Soriano, Clark
1992 Problems and prospects for local governance. *Conjuncture* 5(2):15–16.

Sosyalistang Partido ng Paggawa
2001 Pag-aalsang EDSA at ating linya ng martsa [The EDSA uprising and our line of march], *Proletaryo*, Aug.

Spaeth, Anthony
2001 Ousting presidents by revolution has become a bad national habit. *Time*, 29 Jan.

Sprague, Jonathan, and Antonio Lopez
2000 Act II for Estrada. *Asiaweek*, 21 Jan.

Standing Group, Visayas Commission
1993 Party unity and leadership processes. In *Krisis ng Sosyalismo*, by Concerned CPP Members, 41–49. N.p., n.d.

Stanmeyer, Anastasia, and Antonio Lopez
1999 Final showdown ahead? Estrada and the communists gird for battle. *Asiaweek*, 13 Aug.

Stauffer, Robert B.
1973 The Marcos coup in the Philippines. *Monthly Review* 24(11):19–27.
1977a Philippine corporatism: A note on the "New Society." *Asian Survey* 17(4):393–407.
1977b Philippine authoritarianism: Framework for peripheral "development." *Pacific Affairs* 50(3):365–86.
1979 The political economy of refeudalization. In *Marcos and Martial Law in the Philippines*, edited by David A. Rosenberg, 180–218. Ithaca: Cornell University Press.
1990 Philippine democracy: Contradictions of Third World redemocratization. *Kasarinlan* 6(1):7–22.

Stoker, Gerry
1998 Governance as theory: Five propositions. *International Social Science Journal* 50(155):17–28.

Suh, Sangwon, and Antonio Lopez
1997 Showdown in Manila. *Asiaweek*, 3 Oct.

Sumaylo, Kissy Haynes
2004 Mainstreaming gender in local governance. In *Beyond Good Governance: Participatory Democracy in the Philippines*, edited by Marisol Estrella and Nina Iszatt, 211–32. Quezon City: Institute for Popular Democracy.

Sycip, Washington
2001 Impoverished democracy. *Asiaweek*, 2 Feb.

Syjuco, Augusto
2002 Absentee voting for qualified Filipinos abroad. Paper presented at a forum on electoral reforms at the University of the Philippines, 7 March.

Tamir, Yael
1998 Revisiting the civic sphere. In *Freedom of Association*, edited by Amy Gutmann, 214–38. Princeton: Princeton University Press.

Tan, Antonio S.
1985 The ideology of Pedro Abad Santos' Socialist Party. *Solidarity* 102:28–38.

Tarrow, Sidney
1998 *Power in Movement: Social Movements and Contentious Politics*. Cambridge: Cambridge University Press.

Taylor, Robert H.
1996 *The Politics of Elections in Southeast Asia*. Cambridge: Cambridge University Press.

Tesoro, Jose Manuel, and Antonio Lopez
1996 A nightmare finally ends: Balabagan returns as a symbol of injustice. *Asiaweek*, 16 Aug.

Texier, Jacques
1979 Gramsci, theoretician of the superstructures. In *Gramsci and Marxist Theory*, edited by Chantal Mouffe, 48–79. London: Routledge and Kegan Paul.

Third World Studies Center, ed.
1984 *Marxism in the Philippines: Marx Centennial Lectures*. Quezon City: Third World Studies Center.
1988 *Marxism in the Philippines: Second Series*. Quezon City: Third World Studies Center.

Thompson, Herb
2001 Corruption, poverty, and the loss of biological treasure in the

Philippines. *Antepodium Electronic Journal*, May.

Thompson, Mark R.

1995 *The Anti-Marcos Struggle: Personalistic Rule and Democratic Transition in the Philippines*. New Haven: Yale University Press.

1996 Off the endangered list: Philippine democratization in comparative perspective. *Comparative Politics* 28(2):179–205.

1997 The worldwide wave of democratization and the experience of ASEAN. In *The Development of Democracy in the ASEAN Region*, edited by Leopoldo J. Dejillas and Gunther L. Karcher, 23–33. Makati: Institute for Development Research and Studies, Konrad Adenauer Foundation.

2004 *Democratic Revolutions: Asia and Eastern Europe*. London: Routledge.

Tiglao, Rigoberto D.

1979 Non-progress in the periphery. *Diliman Review*, April-June.

1982 Tenancy in an underdeveloped capitalism. In *Feudalism and Capitalism in the Philippines: Trends and Implications*, edited by Temario C. Rivera, Merlin M. Magallona, Rigoberto D. Tiglao, Ernesto M. Valencia, and Alex R. Magno, 45–59. Quezon City: Foundation for Nationalist Studies.

Tigno, Jorge V.

1993 Democratization through non-governmental and people's organizations. *Kasarinlan* 8(3):58–73.

1997 People empowerment: Looking into NGOs, POs, and selected organizations. In *Democratization: Philippine Perspectives*, edited by Felipe B. Miranda, 115–34. Quezon City: University of the Philippines Press.

Timberman, David G.

1991 *A Changeless Land: Continuity and Change in Philippine Politics*. New York and Singapore: M.E. Sharpe and Institute of Southeast Asian Studies.

Timonera, Bobby

1993a Metro reds break with Joma. *Philippine Daily Inquirer*, 16 July.

1993b Leftist peasant group breaks up. *Philippine Daily Inquirer*, 5 Sept.

1993c RP reds in Europe secede from Joma. *Philippine Daily Inquirer*, 19 Dec.

Today

2001 The devil again. Editorial, 6 Feb.

Tolosa, Benjamin T., Jr.

1990 The underpinnings of Pandayan's democratic socialist ideology. *Conjuncture* 3(7):8–9, 14.

Törnquist, Olle

1990 Democracy and the Philippine Left. *Kasarinlan* 6(1):23–50.

1991 Communists and democracy in the Philippines. *Economic and Political Weekly*, 6–13 July.

1993 Democratic "empowerment" and democratisation of politics: Radical popular movements and the May 1992 Philippine elections. *Third World Quarterly* 14(3):485–515.

1998a Making democratization work: From civil society and social capital to political inclusion and politicization—theoretical reflections on concrete cases in Indonesia, Kerala, and the Philippines. In *Democratization in the Third World: Concrete Cases in Comparative and Theoretical Perspective*, edited by Lars Rudebeck and Olle Törnquist with Virgilio Rojas, 107–43. New York: St. Martin's Press.

1998b Popular movements and politics of democratisation: The Philippine experience in comparative perspective. In *People's Rights: Social Movements and the State in the Third World*, edited by Manoranjan Mohanty, and Partha Nath Mukherji with Olle Törnquist, 189–221. New Delhi and Thousand Oaks, CA: Sage Publications.

1999 *Politics and Development: A Critical Introduction*. London, Thousand Oaks,CA, and New Delhi: Sage Publications.

2002 *Popular Development and Democracy: Case Studies with Rural Dimensions in the Philippines, Indonesia, and Kerala*. Oslo: University of Oslo.

Tubeza, Philip C.

2004 High Court ruling leaves May elections in a mess. *Philippine Daily Inquirer*, 14 Jan.

Tubongbanwa, Sergio [pseudonym]

1992 "Stalinist distortions" and their implications for the Philippine Left. *Debate* 2:23–42.

Tupaz, Omar [pseudonym of Nathan Gilbert Quimpo]

1991 Toward a revolutionary strategy of the 90s. *Debate* 1:6–40.

1992 'Proper channelling' and democratic centralism. Debate 5:39–52.

Turner, Mark

1984 National level elites in the Philippines, 1945–84: A framework for analysis. Occasional Papers, Centre for South-East Asian Studies, University of Hull.

1999a Philippines: From centralism to localism. In *Central-Local Relations in Asia-Pacific: Convergence or Divergence?* edited by Mark Turner, 97–122. Basingstoke and London: Macmillan.

Turner, Mark, ed.

1999b *Central-Local Relations in Asia-Pacific: Convergence or Divergence?* Basingstoke and London: Macmillan.

Ungpakorn, Ji Giles, ed.

2003 *Radicalising Thailand: New Political Perspectives*. Bangkok: Institute of Asian Studies, Chulalongkorn University.

Valte, Maricris

1992 Bisig expands the avenues for socialist struggles. *Conjuncture* 5(9):5, 14.

Van de Loo, Bastiaan

2004 The election and presidency of Joseph Ejercito Estrada: A case study of Philippine politics. M.A. thesis, University of Leiden.

Vandenbroeck, Arnold

1995 Effective SIAD program implementation in a provincial setting. In *SIAD Tool Box: A Collection of Operational Pointers and Instruments for Sustainable Integrated Area Development*, edited by the SIAD Organizing Committee, 187–91. Quezon City: SIAD Organizing Committee.

1998 Dynamics, patterns, and trends in an integrated area development program: Seven years in retrospect. Unpublished manuscript.

Villacorta, Wilfredo V.

1994 The curse of the weak state: Leadership imperatives for the Ramos government. *Contemporary Southeast Asia* 16(1):67–92.

Villarin, Tomasito S.

1996 *People Empowerment: A Guide to NGO-PO Partnership with Local Governments*. Quezon City: Kaisahan tungo sa Kaunlaran ng Kanayunan at Repormang Pansakahan.

1997 Towards further strengthening devolution, democratization, and development. In *Working Group, Working Papers: NGO-PO Perspectives for the Local Government Code Review*, edited by Soliman Santos, Jr., 121–26. Quezon City: Institute of Politics and Governance.

2000 Democratic participation in governance in multiple lanes of engagement between the state, social movements, and civil society. Kaisahan Occasional Papers.

2001 State of the Barangay-Bayan Governance Consortium. Paper presented at a national conference of the Barangay-Bayan Governance Consortium, 19 Oct., Quezon City.

2003 Why the Barangay? *Governance Brief*, special edition.

2004 Finding meaning in local governance through popular participation at the barangay-bayan. In *Beyond Good Governance: Participatory Democracy in the Philippines*, edited by Marisol Estrella and Nina Iszatt, 1–39. Quezon City: Institute for Popular Democracy.

Villarin, Tomasito S., ed.

1999 *Building Empowered Sustainable Communities through Effective People's Participation in Governance*. Quezon City: Kaisahan tungo sa Kaunlaran ng Kanayunan at Repormang Pansakahan, Center for Agrarian Reform Empowerment and Transformation, and Institute of Politics and Governance.

Vizmanos, Danilo P.

1987 The Magnificent 7 of Partido ng Bayan. *Midweek*, 1 April.

Volk, Steven

1997 "Democracy" versus "democracy." *NACLA Report on the Americas* 30(4):6–12.

Wallace, Peter

2004 The Wallace report: Where to, the Philippines? (or does the Philippines have a chance?). http://www.dataphil.com/special%20reports/does%20the%20phils.pdf.

Weekley, Kathleen

1996 From vanguard to rearguard: The theoretical roots of the crisis of the Communist Party of the Philippines. In *The Revolution Falters: The Left in Philippine Politics after 1986*, edited by Patricio N. Abinales, 28–59. Ithaca: Southeast Asia Program, Cornell University.

2001 *The Communist Party of the Philippines 1968–1993: A Story of Its Theory and Practice*. Quezon City: University of the Philippines Press.

West Mindanao Regional White Area Leading Cadres Conference

1993 Uphold Marxist-Leninist principles! Advance the national democratic revolution! *Debate* 8:73–82.

Weyland, Kurt

1999 Neoliberal populism in Latin America and Eastern Europe. *Comparative Politics* 31(4):379–401.

Wolters, Willem

1975 Class relationships and political processes in Central Luzon, Philippines. Ph.D. diss. University of Amsterdam.

1983 *Politics, Patronage, and Class Conflict in Central Luzon*. The Hague: Institute of Social Studies.

World Bank

1999 *Entering the 21st Century: World Development Report, 1999/2000*. Oxford: Oxford University Press.

2000 Combating Corruption in the Philippines. Paper prepared by the Philippine Country Management Unit, East Asia and Pacific Region, May 3.

Wui, Marlon A., and Ma. Glenda S. Lopez

1997 *Philippine Democracy Agenda*. Vol. 2: *State-Civil Society Relations in Policy-Making*. Quezon City: Third World Studies Center.

Wurfel, David

1988 *Filipino Politics: Development and Decay*. Ithaca: Cornell University Press.

1990 Transition to political democracy in the Philippines, 1978–88. In *Democratic Transition and Consolidation in Southern Europe, Latin America, and Southeast Asia*, edited by Diane Ethier, 110–35. Basingstoke: Macmillan.

1997 The party-list elections: Sectoral or national? Success or failure? *Kasarinlan* 13(2):19–30.

Yorac, Haydee, and Alberto Agra

1994 Our electoral reform agenda. In *Popular Participation in Electoral Reform and Governance*, edited by Institute of Politics and Governance, 69–74. Quezon City: Institute of Politics and Governance.

Zacate, Javier Evardone

2001 An alternative agenda: The Sulat municipal development proposal. Unpublished document.

Zakaria, Fareed

1997 The rise of illiberal democracy. *Foreign Affairs* 76(6):22–43.

INDEX

Design and typography,
layout and production
by **H.G. Salome** of

METAGLYFIX

Vermont USA
www.metaglyfix.com

Made in the USA
Las Vegas, NV
18 January 2021

16128000R00245